Jos. P. Holbrook

Worship in Song

A selection of hymns and tunes for the service of the sanctuary

Jos. P. Holbrook

Worship in Song
A selection of hymns and tunes for the service of the sanctuary

ISBN/EAN: 9783337038311

Printed in Europe, USA, Canada, Australia, Japan

Cover: Foto ©Lupo / pixelio.de

More available books at **www.hansebooks.com**

A SELECTION OF HYMNS AND TUNES

FOR THE

Service of the Sanctuary.

BY

JOS. P. HOLBROOK, Mus. Doc.

MUSICAL EDITOR OF "SONGS OF THE CHURCH," "SONGS FOR THE SANCTUARY," "BAPTIST PRAISE BOOK," "METHODIST HYMNAL;" AUTHOR OF "QUARTET AND CHORUS CHOIR," AND "PART SONGS FOR CHURCH AND HOME."

COPYRIGHTED, 1880, BY J. P. HOLBROOK.

PUBLISHED BY

A. S. BARNES & COMPANY,

NEW YORK

CLASSIFIED SUBJECTS.

I. WORSHIP. See First Lines on the page following this Index.
Invocations--Calls to Worship.
Sabbath and Sanctuary.
Evening Songs.
Close of Worship.

II. GOD. First Lines on page 48.
Eternal Being.
Majesty and Might.
Omnipresence and Omniscience.
Providential Rule and Care.
Love and Grace.

III. CHRIST. First Lines on pages 76, 77.
Incarnation and Advent.
His Life our Example.
Teaching, Miracles, Transfiguration, Triumphal Entry.
Sufferings and Death.
The Lord's Supper (Memorial), and Hymns of the Cross.
Resurrection and Ascension.
Enthronement.
Songs of Adoration and Love.

IV. THE HOLY SPIRIT. First Lines on page 154.

V. THE SCRIPTURES. First Lines on page 162.

VI. THE CHURCH. First Lines on page 168.
Foundation.
Baptism in the Name.
Confession of the Faith.
Ministry.

VII. "THE SPIRIT AND BRIDE SAY, COME." See page 180
Reasoning and Invitation.
Expostulation and Warning.

VIII. THE CHRISTIAN. First Lines on pages 192, 193.
Penitence--Self-Surrender.
Gladness--Gratitude. Faith--Trust.
Aspiration. Assurance. Consecration.
Duty--Toil.
Spiritual Conflict.
Burdens and Sorrows.
Pilgrim Songs.

IX. THE LAST THINGS. First Lines on page 296.
Death: Hymns of Monition, Hope, and Expectation.
The Judgment.
Heaven: The Eternal City, Sabbath, and Home.

X. THE CHRISTIAN AND CHURCH. First Lines p. 332.
Unity and Fellowship.
Prayer and Revival.
Charities--Helpfulness.
Missions: Prayers, Appeals, and Assurances of Triumph.

XI. OCCASIONAL. First Lines on page 366.
Children's Songs.
National and Thanksgiving.
The Year: Opening and Close.
Those at Sea.

XII. SELECTIONS. First Lines on page 382.
For Opening or Close of Service.
For Intermediate Use.
Responses, Baptism, Offering.

DOXOLOGIES ON PAGE 431.
OLD TUNES FOR USE AS SUBSTITUTES, ON PAGE 432.
ALPHABETICAL INDEX OF TUNES; PAGES 433.
ALPHABETICAL INDEX OF HYMNS; PAGES 437.

EXPLANATORY.—The title of this volume expresses its purpose. Relevancy to the hour, the place, and the actual circumstances of worship, has been the controlling aim of its compilers.

The selected hymns are thoughtful, scriptural, and lyrical—expressions of true sentiment or feeling in the various moods of a worshipping spirit. Careful study has been given to all compositions of acknowledged excellence with reference to the thought or feeling they contain, their lyrical character, and various forms; and thus the choice of each hymn and of its form has been determined. Suitableness to the hour and service has abbreviated some of the hymns, although care has been taken not to mar the unity or usefulness of any. In the moderate number of hymns, a just proportion under each subject has been sought.

The Classification of *Twelve Main Subjects* is based upon a natural and logical order. All the headings in its *subdivisions* are drawn directly from the subject-matter of the hymns. Connected closely with the above synopsis is a new feature which answers all the ends of a detailed index of topics, and will soon make the entire body of hymns familiar and easy of reference. It is the setting, upon every page which begins a Main Subject, of the *First Lines of Hymns under the subdivisions of that Subject*. All the hymns of each Subject are thus placed beneath the eye and within near reach of the hand.

The *selected* tunes, like the hymns, taken from the best sources, the classical and tested, old and new, are believed to have a solid excellence and permanent value, with the elements of usefulness and popularity. In all the Tune-music, as in the liberal selections from the later German and Anglican sources, the author and compiler has aimed: 1st, To present such compositions as embody a clearly-defined melody united with an effective harmony, and such music as can be *sung*. 2d, To give careful heed that every musical production shall be suitably matched with its corresponding expression in devotional sentiment. To this vital matter of adaptation of words and music, the closest study has in every instance been given. A familiar tune will be found in connection with almost every new one, while many hymns and tunes upon the same page-opening may be interchanged.

WORSHIP.

First Lines of Hymns.

INVOCATIONS—CALLS TO WORSHIP.

HYMNS
1 Praise God, from whom all blessings flow!
2 From all that dwell below the skies,
3 Before Jehovah's awful throne,
4 All people that on earth do dwell
5 Father of heaven, whose love profound
6 O holy, holy, holy Lord,
7 Lord God of hosts, by all adored,
8 Bless, O my soul, the living God;
9 Sing to the Lord a joyful song;
10 Holy, holy, holy, Lord God Almighty!
11 Holy, holy, holy Lord.
12 Come, thou desire of all thy saints!
13 Lord, when we bend before thy throne.
14 Praise, my soul, the King of heaven.
15 Glory be to God the Father!
16 Songs anew of honor framing,
17 Come, my soul, thy suit prepare.
18 Lord, we come before thee now,
19 Jesus! name of wondrous love!
20 Heavenly Father, to whose eye
21 Joyful be the hours to-day;
22 For the beauty of the earth,
23 Praise the Lord, his glories show,
24 Songs of praise the angels sang.
25 O worship the King, all-glorious
26 Ye servants of God, your Master
27 Come, we that love the Lord.
28 Awake, and sing the song
29 Lord, with glowing heart I'd praise
30 Stand up and bless the Lord.
31 We love the place, O God.
32 Glory to God on high!
33 Come, thou almighty King.

SABBATH AND SANCTUARY.

34 Welcome, sweet day of rest.
35 This is the day of light :
36 Awake, ye saints, awake.
37 Lord of the worlds above.
38 Welcome, delightful morn,
39 Now to thy sacred house
40 Safely through another week
41 God of mercy, God of grace.
42 Pleasant are thy courts above.
43 Let us with a joyful mind
44 Another six days work is done,
45 Sweet is the work, my God, my King.
46 Great God, attend while Zion sings

HYMNS.
47 How pleasant, how divinely fair,
48 With joy we hail the sacred day
49 The Lord of glory is my light,
50 This is the day the Lord hath made ;
51 My soul, how lovely is the place
52 Thou, Lord, who daily feed'st thy sheep,
53 Sweet the time, exceeding sweet,
54 Saviour, whom I fain would love,
55 This day at thy creating word.
56 Great God, this sacred day of thine,
57 O day of rest and gladness.
58 The day of resurrection,
59 Now, when the dusky shades
60 Still, still with thee

EVENING SONGS.

61 Saviour, breathe an evening blessing,
62 Gently, Lord, O gently lead us
63 Praises to him whose love has given,
64 My God, my King, thy various praise
65 Thine earthly Sabbaths, Lord, we love,
66 Again as evening's shadow falls,
67 Not only doth the voiceful day
68 Our day of praise is done;
69 Sweet is the work, O Lord,
70 Softly now the light of day
71 Ere another Sabbath's close,
72 Softly fades the twilight ray
73 Sun of my soul, thou Saviour dear,
74 Lord, when this holy morning broke
75 Father, adored in worlds above.
76 Glory to thee, my God, this night,
77 Thus far the Lord has led me on.
78 The day is gently sinking to a close,
79 Hail, tranquil hour of closing day !
80 Thou Lord of life, whose tender care,

CLOSE OF WORSHIP.

81 Now God be with us, for the night
82 Now the day is over,
83 The day is past and over,
84 As Christ upon the cross
85 God, that madest earth and heaven.
86 Through the day thy love has spared us.
87 The Lord be with us as we bend,
88 Guide me, O thou great Jehovah,
89 Lord, dismiss us with thy blessing,
90 May the grace of Christ the Saviour,
91 Saviour! again to thy dear name
92 Sweet Saviour! bless us ere we go;

OLD HUNDRED. L. M.

G. FRANC.

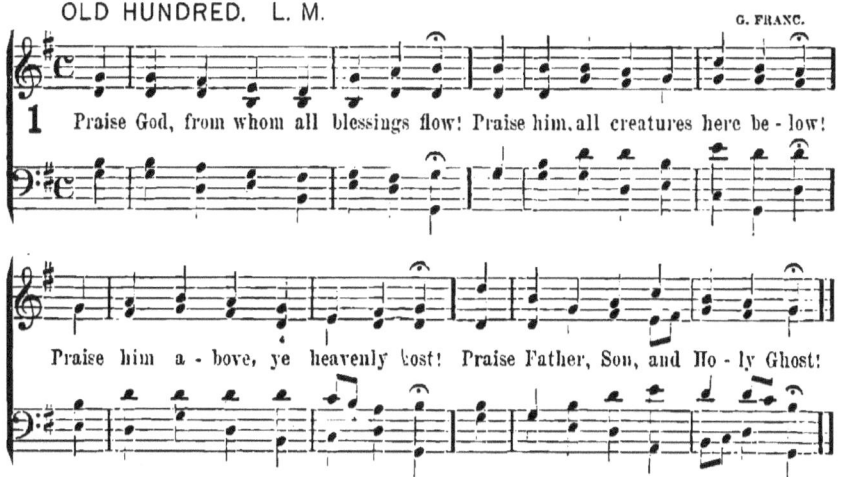

1 Praise God, from whom all blessings flow! Praise him, all creatures here be-low! Praise him a-bove, ye heavenly host! Praise Father, Son, and Ho-ly Ghost!

2   *I. Watts.*
From all that dwell below the skies,
  Let the Creator's praise arise;
Let the Redeemer's name be sung,
  Through every land, by every tongue.

2 Eternal are thy mercies, Lord;
Eternal truth attends thy word;
Thy praise shall sound from shore to shore,
  Till suns shall rise and set no more.

3   *I. Watts.*
Before Jehovah's awful throne,
  Ye nations, bow with sacred joy;
Know that the Lord is God alone;
  He can create, and he destroy.

2 We are his people, we his care,
  Our souls and all our mortal frame:
What lasting honors shall we rear,
  Almighty Maker, to thy name?

3 We'll crowd thy gates with thankful songs,
  High as the heavens our voices raise;
And earth, with her ten thousand tongues,
  Shall fill thy courts with sounding praise.

4 Wide as the world is thy command,
  Vast as eternity thy love;
Firm as a rock thy truth shall stand,
  When rolling years shall cease to move.

4   *W. Kethe.*
All people that on earth do dwell,
  Sing to the Lord with cheerful voice;
Him serve with fear, his praise forth tell,
  Come ye before him and rejoice.

2 The Lord, ye know, is God indeed,
  Without our aid he did us make;
We are his flock, he doth us feed,
  And for his sheep he doth us take.

3 O enter then his gates with praise;
  Approach with joy his courts unto;
Praise, laud, and bless his name always,
  For it is seemly so to do.

4 Because the Lord our God is good,
  His mercy is forever sure;
His truth at all times firmly stood,
  And shall from age to age endure.

WORSHIP.

GILEAD. L. M.
MERUL.

1. Father of heaven, whose love profound
A ransom for our souls hath found,
Before thy throne we sinners bend:
To us thy pardoning love extend.

5   *J. Cooper.*

FATHER of heaven, whose love profound
A ransom for our souls hath found,
Before thy throne we sinners bend:
To us thy pardoning love extend.

2 Almighty Son, incarnate Word,
Our Prophet, Priest, Redeemer, Lord,
Before thy throne we sinners bend:
To us thy saving grace extend.

3 Eternal Spirit, by whose breath
The soul is raised from sin and death,
Before thy throne we sinners bend:
To us thy quickening power extend.

4 Jehovah,—Father, Spirit, Son,—
Mysterious Godhead, Three in One,
Before thy throne we sinners bend:
Grace, pardon, life, to us extend.

6   *J. W. Eastburn.*

O HOLY, holy, holy Lord,
Bright in thy deeds and in thy name,
Forever be thy name adored,
Thy glories let the world proclaim.

2 O Jesus, Lamb once crucified
To take our load of sin away,
Thine be the hymn that rolls its tide
Along the realms of upper day.

3 O Holy Spirit from above,
In streams of light and glory given,
Thou source of ecstasy and love,
Thy praises ring through earth and heaven.

4 O God triune, to thee we owe
Our every thought, our every song;
And ever may thy praises flow
From saint and seraph's burning tongue.

SAMSON. L. M.
HANDEL.

1. O holy, holy, holy Lord! Bright in thy deeds and in thy name
Forever be thy name adored, Thy glories let the world proclaim!

Invocations—Calls to Worship.

LOWRY. L. M.   GEO. F. ROOT.

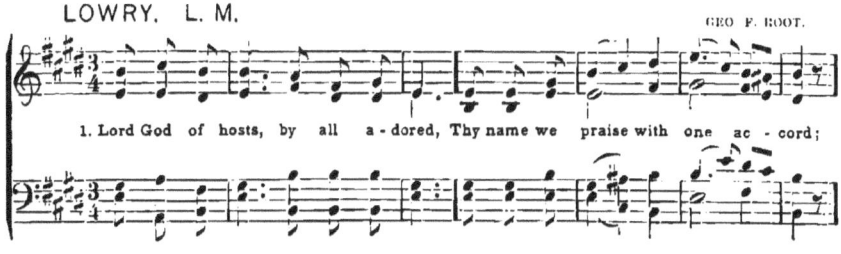

1. Lord God of hosts, by all a-dored, Thy name we praise with one ac-cord;

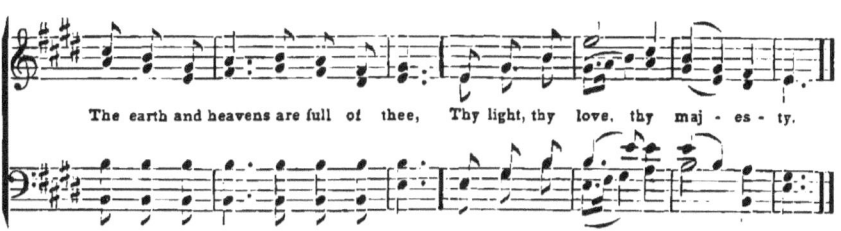

The earth and heavens are full of thee, Thy light, thy love, thy maj-es-ty.

7

Lord God of hosts, by all adored,
Thy name we praise with one accord;
The earth and heavens are full of thee,
Thy light, thy love, thy majesty.

2 Loud hallelujahs to thy name
Angels and seraphim proclaim;
Eternal praise to thee is given
By all the powers and thrones in heaven.

3 The holy church in every place
Throughout the world exalts thy praise;
Both heaven and earth do worship thee,
Thou Father of eternity!

4 Glory to thee, O God most high!
Father, we praise thy majesty!
The Son, the Spirit, we adore!
One Godhead, blest for evermore.

8   *I. Watts.*

Bless, O my soul, the living God;
Call home thy thoughts that rove abroad:
Let all the powers within me join
In work and worship so divine.

2 Bless, O my soul, the God of grace:
His favors claim thy highest praise;
Why should the wonders he hath wrought
Be lost in silence and forgot?

3 'T is he, my soul, that sent his Son
To die for crimes which thou hast done;
He owns the ransom, and forgives
The hourly follies of our lives.

4 Let every land his power confess;
Let all the earth adore his grace:
My heart and tongue with rapture join,
In work and worship so divine.

9   *J. S. B. Monsell.*

Sing to the Lord a joyful song;
  Lift up your hearts, your voices raise;
To us his gracious gifts belong,
  To him our songs of love and praise.

2 For life and love, for rest and food,
  For daily help and nightly care,
Sing to the Lord, for he is good,
  And praise his name, for it is fair.

3 For strength to those who on him wait,
  His truth to prove, his will to do,
Praise ye our God, for he is great,
  Trust in his name, for it is true.

4 Sing to the Lord of heaven and earth,
  Whom angels serve and saints adore,
The Father, Son, and Holy Ghost,
  To whom be praise for evermore.

WORSHIP.

NICÆA. P. M.   J. B. DYKES.

10
     R. Heber

Holy, holy, holy, Lord God Almighty!
Early in the morning our song shall rise to thee;
Holy, holy, holy! Merciful and Mighty!
God in Three Persons, Blessèd Trinity!

2 Holy, holy, holy! all the saints adore thee,
Casting down their golden crowns around the glassy sea;
Cherubim and seraphim falling down before thee,
Which wert, and art, and evermore shalt be.

3 Holy, holy, holy! though the darkness hide thee,
Though the eye of sinful man thy glory may not see,
Only thou art holy, there is none beside thee,
Perfect in power, in love, and purity.

4 Holy, holy, holy! Lord God Almighty!
All thy works shall praise thy name, in earth, and sky, and sea;
Holy, holy, holy! merciful and mighty!
God in Three Persons, Blessèd Trinity!

11
   7s.   *B. Williams.*

Holy, holy, holy Lord,
Be thy glorious name adored:
Lord, thy mercies never fail;
Hail, celestial goodness, hail!

2 While on earth ordained to stay,
Guide our footsteps in thy way,
Till we come to dwell with thee,
Till we all thy glory see.

3 Then with angel-harps again
We will wake a nobler strain;
There, in joyful songs of praise,
Our triumphant voices raise.

Invocations—Calls to Worship.

BEMERTON. C. M. H. W. GREATOREX.

12 *Anne Steele.*

Come, thou desire of all thy saints!
Our humble strains attend,
While with our praises and complaints,
Low at thy feet we bend.

2 Come, Lord, thy love alone can raise
In us the heavenly flame;
Then shall our lips resound thy praise,
Our hearts adore thy name.

3 Dear Saviour, let thy glory shine,
And fill thy dwellings here,
Till life, and love, and joy divine
A heaven on earth appear.

4 Then shall our hearts enraptured say,
Come, great Redeemer, come,
And bring the bright, the glorious day,
That calls thy children home.

13 *J. D. Carlyle.*

Lord, when we bend before thy throne,
And our confessions pour,
Teach us to feel the sins we own,
And hate what we deplore.

2 Our broken spirits, pitying, see;
And penitence impart;
Then let a kindling glance from thee,
Beam hope upon the heart.

3 When we disclose our wants in prayer,
May we our wills resign;
And not a thought our bosom share,
Which is not wholly thine.

4 Let faith each meek petition fill,
And waft it to the skies;
And teach our hearts 'tis goodness still
That grants it, or denies.

CARPENTER. 7s. J. P. HOLBROOK.

WORSHIP.

STOWE. 8s, 7s, 4s.   J. P. HOLBROOK.

14
H. F. Lyte.

Praise, my soul, the King of heaven,
To his feet thy tribute bring;
Ransomed, healed, restored, forgiven,
Evermore his praises sing;
   Alleluia! Alleluia!
Praise the everlasting King.

2 Praise him for his grace and favor
To our fathers in distress;
Praise him still the same as ever,
Slow to chide and swift to bless;
   Alleluia! Alleluia!
Glorious in his faithfulness.

3 Father-like, he tends and spares us,
Well our feeble frame he knows;
In his hands he gently bears us,
Rescues us from all our foes;
   Alleluia! Alleluia!
Widely yet his mercy flows.

4 Angels in the height, adore him;
Ye behold him face to face;
Saints, triumphant bow before him,
Gathered in from every race;
   Alleluia! Alleluia!
Praise with us the God of grace.

Dox. 1. Praise and honor to the Father,
Praise and honor to the Son,
Praise and honor to the Spirit,
Ever Three and ever One,
   One in might, and one in glory,
While eternal ages run.

8s, 7s, 4s.

Dox. 2. Great Jehovah! we adore thee,
God, the Father, God, the Son,
God, the Spirit, joined in glory
On the same eternal throne;
   Endless praises
To Jehovah, Three in One.

Invocations—Calls to Worship. 7

GLADNESS. 8s, 7s, 4s.   H. SMART.

1. Glo-ry be to God, the Fa-ther! Glo-ry be to God, the Son!
Glo-ry be to God, the Spir-it!— Great Je-ho-vah, three in one!
Glo-ry in the high-est, glo-ry, While e-ter-nal a-ges run!

15 *H. Bonar.*

GLORY be to God the Father!
  Glory be to God the Son!
Glory be to God the Spirit!—
  Great Jehovah, three in one!
Glory, in the highest, glory,
  While eternal ages run!

2 Glory be to him who loved us,
  Washed us from each spot and stain;
Glory be to him who bought us,
  Made us kings with him to reign;
Glory, everlasting glory,
  To the Lamb that once was slain!

3 Glory to the King of angels!
  Glory to the church's King!
Glory to the King of nations!
  Heaven and earth your praises bring;
Glory, everlasting glory,
  To the King of glory bring!

4 Glory, blessing, praise eternal!
  Thus the choir of angels sings;
Honor, riches, power, dominion!
  Thus its praise creation brings:
Glory, everlasting glory,
  Glory to the King of kings!

16 *W. Goode.*

SONGS anew of honor framing,
  Sing ye to the Lord alone,
All his wondrous works proclaiming;—
  Jesus wondrous works hath done;
    Glorious victory
  His right hand and arm have won.

2 Shout aloud and hail the Saviour;
  Jesus, Lord of all proclaim;
As ye triumph in his favor,
  All ye saints, declare his fame;
    Loud rejoicing,
  Shout the honors of his name.

WORSHIP.

SEYMOUR. 7s.
WEBER.

17 J. Newton.

Come, my soul, thy suit prepare,
Jesus loves to answer prayer;
He himself has bid thee pray,
Therefore will not say thee nay.

2 Lord, I come to thee for rest,
Take possession of my breast;
There thy blood-bought right maintain,
And without a rival reign.

3 While I am a pilgrim here,
Let thy love my spirit cheer;
As my guide, my guard, my friend,
Lead me to my journey's end.

4 Show me what I have to do,
Every hour my strength renew;
Let me live a life of faith,
Let me die thy people's death.

FISK. 7s.

18 W. Hammond.

Lord, we come before thee now;
At thy feet we humbly bow;
O do not our suit disdain,
Shall we seek thee, Lord, in vain?

2 Lord, on thee our souls depend;
In compassion now descend;
Fill our hearts with thy rich grace,
Tune our lips to sing thy praise.

3 In thine own appointed way,
Now we seek thee, here we stay:
Lord, we know not how to go,
Till a blessing thou bestow.

4 Send some message from thy word,
That may joy and peace afford;
Let thy Spirit now impart
Full salvation to each heart.

Invocations—Calls to Worship.

WALSHAM. 7s. R. REDHEAD.

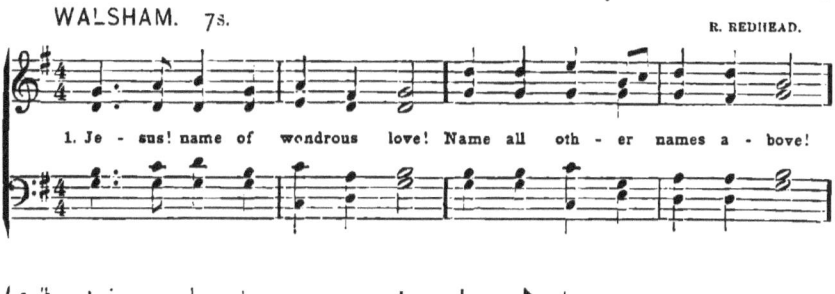

1. Jesus! name of wondrous love! Name all other names above! Unto which must every knee Bow in deep humility.

19
W. W. How.

Jesus! name of wondrous love!
Name all other names above!
Unto which must every knee
Bow in deep humility.

2 Jesus! name of priceless worth
To the fallen sons of earth,
For the promise that it gave,—
"Jesus shall his people save."

3 Jesus! only name that's given
Under all the mighty heaven,
Whereby man, to sin enslaved,
Bursts his fetters, and is saved.

4 Jesus! name of wondrous love!
Human name of God above!
Pleading only this we flee,
Helpless, O our God, to thee.

20
J. Condor.

Heavenly Father, to whose eye
Future things unfolded lie,
Through the desert where I stray,
Let thy counsels guide my way.

2 Lord, uphold me day by day,
Shed thy light upon my way;
Guide me through perplexing snares,
Care for me in all my cares.

3 Lord, my times are in thy hand;
All my sanguine hopes have planned
To thy wisdom I resign,
And would mould my will to thine.

4 Let me neither faint nor fear,
Feeling still that thou art near;
In the course my Saviour trod,
Tending still to thee, my God!

21
T. Kelly.

Joyful be the hours to-day;
  Joyful let the season be;
Let us sing, for well we may:
  Jesus! we will sing of thee.

2 Joyful are we now to own,
  Rapture thrills us as we trace
All the deeds thy love hath done,
  All the riches of thy grace.

3 'Tis thy grace alone can save;
  Every blessing comes from thee—
All we have and hope to have,
  All we are and hope to be.

4 Thine the name to sinners dear!
  Thine the Name all names before!
Blessèd here and everywhere;
  Blessèd now and evermore!

WORSHIP.

ONIDO. 7s, D.   PLEYEL.

22   *F. S. Pierpoint.*
For the beauty of the earth,
  For the glory of the skies,
For the love which from our birth
  Over and around us lies;
Lord of all to thee we raise,
This our grateful psalm of praise.

2 For the wonder of each hour
  Of the day and of the night,
Hill and vale, and tree and flower,
  Sun and moon, and stars of light,
Lord of all, to thee we raise
This our grateful psalm of praise.

3 For the joy of human love,
  Brother, sister, parent, child,
Friends on earth, and friends above,
  Pleasures pure and undefiled,
Lord of all, to thee we raise
This our grateful psalm of praise.

4 For thy church that evermore
  Lifteth holy hands above,

Offering up on every shore
  Her pure sacrifice of love,
Lord of all, to thee we raise
This our grateful psalm of praise.

23   *H. F. Lyte.*
Praise the Lord, his glories show,
  Saints within his courts below,
Angels round his throne above,
  All that see and share his love!

2 Earth to heaven and heaven to earth,
  Tell his wonders, sing his worth;
Age to age and shore to shore,
  Praise him, praise him evermore!

3 Praise the Lord, his mercies trace;
  Praise his providence and grace—
All that he for man hath done,
  All he sends us through his Son.

4 Strings and voices, hands and hearts,
  In the concert bear your parts;
All that breathe, your Lord adore;
  Praise him, praise him evermore!

Invocations—Calls to Worship.

MENDELSSOHN. 7s.

Songs of praise the angels sang, Heaven with hallelujahs rang, When Jehovah's work begun, When he spake and it was done. 2. Songs of praise awoke the morn, When the Prince of Peace was born; Songs of praise arose, when he Captive led captivity; Songs of praise arose, when he Captive led captivity.

24
J. Montgomery.

Songs of praise the angels sang,
Heaven with hallelujahs rang,
When Jehovah's work begun,
When he spake and it was done.

2 Songs of praise awoke the morn,
When the Prince of Peace was born;
Songs of praise arose, when he
Captive led captivity.

3 Heaven and earth must pass away—
Songs of praise shall crown that day;
God will make new heavens and earth—
Songs of praise shall hail their birth.

4 And shall man alone be dumb
Till that glorious kingdom come?
No; the Church delights to raise
Psalms and hymns and songs of praise.

5 Saints below, with heart and voice,
Still in songs of praise rejoice;
Learning here, by faith and love,
Songs of praise to sing above.

6 Borne upon their latest breath
Songs of praise shall conquer death;
Then amid eternal joy,
Songs of praise their powers employ.

WORSHIP.

LYONS. 10s, 11s. HAYDN.

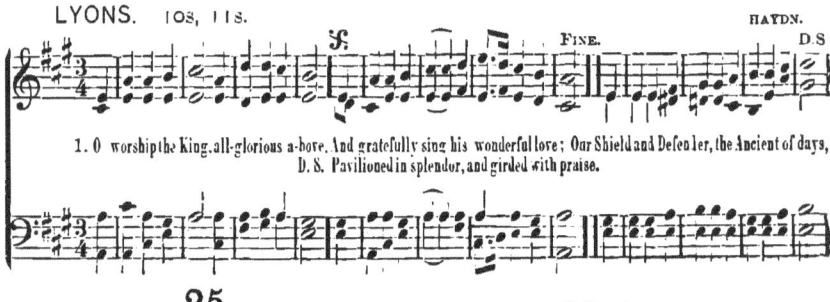

1. O worship the King, all-glorious above, And gratefully sing his wonderful love; Our Shield and Defender, the Ancient of days,
D. S. Pavilioned in splendor, and girded with praise.

25
R. Grant.

O WORSHIP the King, all-glorious above,
And gratefully sing his wonderful love;
Our Shield and Defender, the Ancient of days,
Pavilioned in splendor, and girded with praise.

2 O tell of his might, and sing of his grace,
Whose robe is the light, whose canopy space;
His chariots of wrath the deep thunder-clouds form,
And dark is his path on the wings of the storm.

3 Thy bountiful care what tongue can recite?
It breathes in the air, it shines in the light,
It streams from the hills, it descends to the plain,
And sweetly distills in the dew and the rain.

4 Frail children of dust, and feeble as frail,
In thee do we trust, nor find thee to fail;
Thy mercies how tender, how firm to the end,
Our Maker, Defender, Redeemer and Friend.

26
C. Wesley.

YE servants of God, your Master proclaim,
And publish abroad his wonderful Name;
The name all-victorious of Jesus extol;
His kingdom is glorious, and rules over all.

2 God ruleth on high, almighty to save;
And still he is nigh, his presence we have;
The great congregation his triumph shall sing,
Ascribing salvation to Jesus our King.

3 "Salvation to God who sits on the throne,"
Let all cry aloud, and honor the Son;
The praises of Jesus the angels proclaim,
Fall down on their faces, and worship the Lamb.

4 Then let us adore, and give him his right,
All glory and power, and wisdom and might;
All honor and blessing, with angels above,
And thanks never ceasing, and infinite love.

Invocations—Calls to Worship.

LEIGHTON. S. M.   GREATOREX.

1. Come, we that love the Lord, And let our joys be known; Join in a song of sweet accord, And thus surround the throne.

27   *I. Watts.*

Come, we that love the Lord,
  And let our joys be known;
Join in a song of sweet accord,
  And thus surround the throne.

2 Let those refuse to sing
  That never knew our God;
But children of the heavenly King
  May speak their joys abroad.

3 The men of grace have found
  Glory begun below;

Celestial fruits on earthly ground
  From faith and hope may grow.

4 The hill of Zion yields
  A thousand sacred sweets
Before we reach the heavenly fields,
  Or walk the golden streets.

5 Then let our songs abound,
  And every tear be dry;
We're marching thro' Immanuel's ground
  To fairer worlds on high.

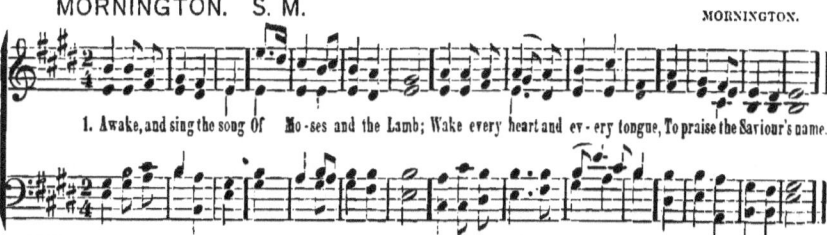

MORNINGTON. S. M.   MORNINGTON.

1. Awake, and sing the song Of Mo-ses and the Lamb; Wake every heart and ev-ery tongue, To praise the Saviour's name.

28   *Madan—Hammond.*

Awake, and sing the song
  Of Moses and the Lamb;
Wake every heart and every tongue,
  To praise the Saviour's name.

2 Sing of his dying love;
  Sing of his rising power;
Sing how he intercedes above
  For those whose sins he bore.

3 Sing on your heavenly way,
  Ye ransomed sinners, sing;

Sing on, rejoicing every day
  In Christ th' eternal King.

4 Soon shall ye hear him say,
  "Ye blessed children, come;"
Soon will he call you hence away,
  And take his wanderers home.

5 There shall our raptured tongue
  His endless praise proclaim,
And sweeter voices swell the song
  Of Moses and the Lamb.

WORSHIP.

CARLTON. 8s, 7s. QUARTET & CHORUS CHOIR.

1. Lord, with glowing heart I'd praise thee For the bliss thy love bestows; For the pardoning grace that saves me, And the peace that from it flows: Help, O God, my weak endeavor; This dull soul to rapture raise; Thou must light the flame, or never Can my love be warmed to praise.

29
F. S. Key.

Lord, with glowing heart I'd praise thee
 For the bliss thy love bestows;
For the pardoning grace that saves me,
 And the peace that from it flows:
Help, O God, my weak endeavor;
 This dull soul to rapture raise;
Thou must light the flame, or never
 Can my love be warmed to praise.

2 Praise, my soul, the God that sought thee,
 Wretched wanderer, far astray;
Found thee lost, and kindly brought thee
 From the paths of death away;
Praise with love's devoutest feeling,
 Him who saw thy guilt-born fear,
And, the light of hope revealing,
 Bade the blood-stained cross appear.

3 Lord, this bosom's ardent feeling
 Vainly would my lips express:
Low before thy footstool kneeling,
 Deign thy suppliant's prayer to bless;
Let thy grace, my soul's chief treasure,
 Love's pure flame within me raise;
And since words can never measure,
 Let my life show forth thy praise.

ST. CHAD. 8s, 7s, D. R. REDHEAD.

1. { Lord, with glowing heart I'd praise thee For the bliss thy love bestows; }
   { For the pardoning grace that saves me, (Omit)......................... } And the peace that from it flows:
D.C. Thou must light the flame, or never (Omit)......................... Can my love be warmed to praise.

Invocations—Calls to Worship.

ST. CHAD. CONCLUDED.

Help, O God, my weak en-deav-or; This dull soul to rap-ture raise:

PRAISE. 6s.
J. BARNBY.

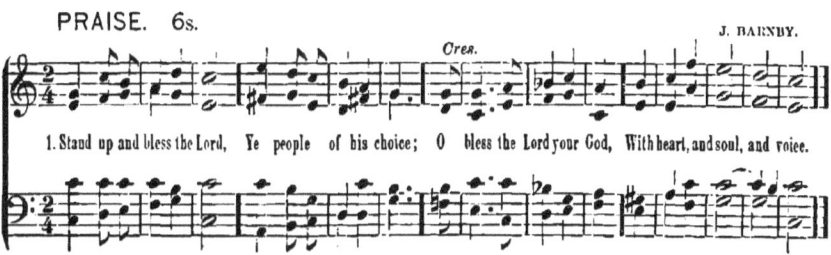

1. Stand up and bless the Lord, Ye people of his choice; O bless the Lord your God, With heart, and soul, and voice.

---

30 J. Montgomery.

STAND up and bless the Lord,
  Ye people of his choice;
O bless the Lord your God,
  With heart, and soul, and voice.

2 Though high above all praise,
  Above all blessing high,
Who would not fear his name,
  And laud and magnify?

3 O, for the living flame
  From his own altar brought,
Our lips and souls to fire,
  And wing to heaven our thought!

4 God is our strength and song,
  And his salvation ours;
Then be his love proclaimed
  With all our ransomed powers.

5 Stand up and bless the Lord;
  The Lord your God adore;
O bless his glorious name,
  Henceforth, for evermore!

31 W. Bullock.

WE love the place, O God,
  Wherein thine honor dwells;
The joy of thine abode
  All earthly joy excels.

2 It is the house of prayer,
  Wherein thy servants meet;
And thou, O Lord, art there
  Thy chosen flock to greet.

3 We love the word of life,
  The word that tells of peace,
Of comfort in the strife,
  Of joys that never cease.

4 We love to sing below
  For mercies freely given;
But O, we long to know
  The triumph-song of heaven.

5 Lord Jesus, give us grace
  On earth to love thee more,
In heaven to see thy face,
  And with thy saints adore.

WORSHIP.

BRUNSWICK. 6s, 4s.

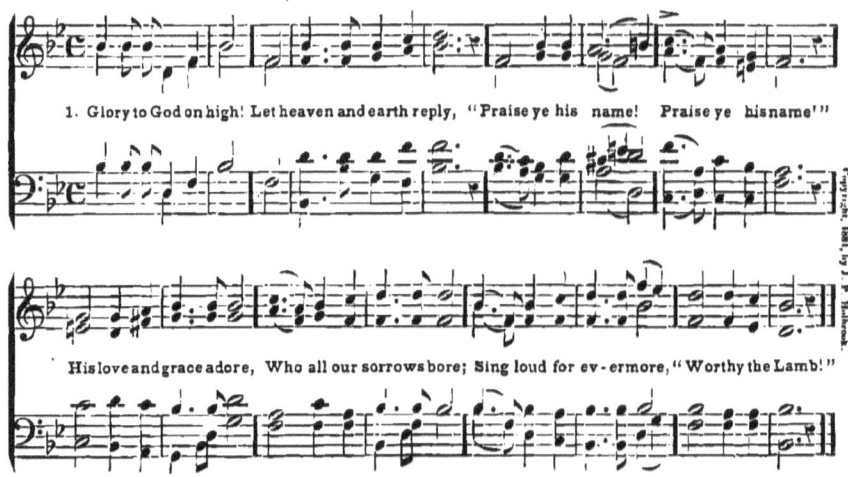

1. Glory to God on high! Let heaven and earth reply, "Praise ye his name! Praise ye his name!"
His love and grace adore, Who all our sorrows bore; Sing loud for ev-ermore, "Worthy the Lamb!"

32   J. Allen.

GLORY to God on high!
Let heaven and earth reply,
  "Praise ye his name!"
His love and grace adore,
Who all our sorrows bore;
Sing loud for evermore,
  "Worthy the Lamb!"

2 While they around the throne
Cheerfully join in one,
  Praising his name,—
Ye, who have felt his blood
Sealing your peace with God,
Sound his dear name abroad,
  "Worthy the Lamb!"

3 Join, all ye ransomed race,
Our Lord and God to bless:
  Praise ye his name!
In him we will rejoice,
And make a joyful noise,
Shouting with heart and voice,
  "Worthy the Lamb!"

4 Soon must we change our place,
Yet will we never cease
  Praising his name:
To him our songs we bring;
Hail him our gracious King;
And through all ages sing,
  "Worthy the Lamb!"

33   C. Wesley.

COME, thou almighty King,
Help us thy name to sing,
  Help us to praise!
Father all glorious,
O'er all victorious,
Come and reign over us,
  Ancient of Days!

2 Come, thou incarnate Word,
Gird on thy mighty sword;
  Our prayer attend:
Come, and thy people bless,
And give thy word success:
Spirit of holiness,
  On us descend.

3 Come, holy Comforter,
Thy sacred witness bear
  In this glad hour:
Thou, who almighty art,
Now rule in every heart,
And ne'er from us depart,
  Spirit of power.

4 To thee, great One in Three.
The highest praises be,
  Hence evermore!
Thy sovereign majesty
May we in glory see,
And to eternity
  Love and adore.

Sabbath and Sanctuary. 17

THATCHER. S. M. — HANDEL.

1. Welcome, sweet day of rest, That saw the Lord arise; Welcome to this reviving breast, And these rejoicing eyes.

34 *I. Watts.*

Welcome, sweet day of rest,
That saw the Lord arise;
Welcome to this reviving breast,
And these rejoicing eyes.

2 The King himself comes near,
And feasts his saints to-day;
Here we may sit, and see him here,
And love, and praise, and pray.

3 One day amidst the place
Where my dear God hath been,
Is sweeter than ten thousand days
Of pleasurable sin.

4 My willing soul would stay
In such a frame as this,
And sit and sing herself away
To everlasting bliss.

35 *J. Ellerton.*

This is the day of light:
Let there be light to-day;
O Day-spring, rise upon our night,
And chase its gloom away.

2 This is the day of rest:
Our failing strength renew;
On weary brain and troubled breast
Shed thou thy freshening dew.

3 This is the day of prayer:
Let earth to heaven draw near;
Lift up our hearts to seek thee there;
Come down to meet us here.

4 This is the first of days:
Send forth thy quickening breath,
And wake dead souls to love and praise,
O Vanquisher of death!

ITALIAN HYMN. 6s, 4s. — GIARDINI.

1. Come, thou almighty King, Help us thy name to sing, Help us to praise! Father all glorious, O'er all victorious, Come and reign over us, Ancient of Days!

WORSHIP.

FRANKLIN. H. M.   J. P. HOLBROOK.

36   *T. Cotterill.*

Awake, ye saints, awake,
  And hail this sacred day;
In loftiest songs of praise
  Your joyful homage pay:
Come, bless the day that God hath blest,
The type of heaven's eternal rest.

2 On this auspicious morn
  The Lord of life arose;
He burst the bars of death,
  And vanquished all our foes;
And now he pleads our cause above,
And reaps the fruit of all his love.

3 All hail, triumphant Lord!
  Heaven with hosannas rings,
And earth in humbler strains,
  Thy praise responsive sings:
Worthy the Lamb, that once was slain,
Through endless years to live and reign!

37   *I. Watts.*

Lord of the worlds above,
  How pleasant and how fair
The dwellings of thy love,
  Thine earthly temples are!
To thine abode my heart aspires,
With warm desires to see my God.

2 O happy souls, that pray
  Where God appoints to hear!
O happy men that pay
  Their constant service there!
They praise thee still; and happy they
That love the way to Zion's hill.

3 They go from strength to strength,
  Through this dark vale of tears,
Till each arrives at length,
  Till each in heaven appears:
O glorious seat, when God our King
Shall thither bring our willing feet!

Sabbath and Sanctuary.

MALAN. H. M.

38
Hayward.

Welcome, delightful morn,
  Thou day of sacred rest:
I hail thy kind return;
  Lord, make these moments blest;
From the low train of mortal toys,
I soar to reach immortal joys.

2 Now may the King descend,
  And fill his throne of grace:
Thy sceptre, Lord, extend,
  While saints address thy face;
Let sinners feel thy quickening word,
And learn to know and fear the Lord.

3 Descend, celestial Dove,
  With all thy quickening powers,
Disclose a Saviour's love,
  And bless these sacred hours;
Then shall my soul new life obtain,
Nor Sabbaths be enjoyed in vain.

39
T. Dwight.

Now to thy sacred house
  I come with willing feet,
Where saints, with morning vows,
  In full assembly meet:
Thy power divine shall there be shown,
And from thy throne thy mercy shine.

2 Oh, send thy light abroad!
  Thy truth with heavenly ray
Shall lead my soul to God,
  And guide my doubtful way:
I'll hear thy word with faith sincere,
And learn to fear and praise the Lord.

3 Now in thy holy hill,
  Before thine altar, Lord,
My harp and song shall sound
  The glories of thy word:
Henceforth to thee, O God of grace,
A hymn of praise my life shall be.

WORSHIP.

SABBATH. 7s. 6l.   L. MASON.

1. Safely through another week, God has brought us on our way; Let us now a blessing seek, Waiting in his courts to-day: Day of all the week the best, Emblem of eternal rest, Day of all the week the best, Emblem of eternal rest.

40   J. Newton.

Safely through another week,
  God has brought us on our way;
Let us now a blessing seek,
  Waiting in his courts to-day:
Day of all the week the best,
Emblem of eternal rest.

2 While we pray for pardoning grace,
  Through the dear Redeemer's name,
Show thy reconciléd face,
  Take away our sin and shame;
From our worldly cares set free,
May we rest this day in thee.

3 Here we come thy name to praise;
  May we feel thy presence near:
May thy glory meet our eyes,
  While we in thy house appear:
Here afford us, Lord, a taste
Of our everlasting feast.

41   H. F. Lyte.

God of mercy, God of grace,
  Show the brightness of thy face;
Shine upon us, Saviour, shine,
  Fill thy church with light divine;
And thy saving health extend
Unto earth's remotest end.

2 Let the people praise thee, Lord,
  Be by all that live adored:
Let the nations shout and sing,
  Glory to their Saviour-King;
At thy feet their tributes pay,
And thy holy will obey.

3 Let the people praise thee, Lord,
  Earth shall then her fruits afford:
God to man his blessing give,
  Man to God devoted live;
All below and all above,
One in joy and light and love.

Sabbath and Sanctuary. 21

42   *H. F. Lyte.*

PLEASANT are thy courts above,
In the land of light and love;
Pleasant are thy courts below,
In this land of sin and woe.
O, my spirit longs and faints
For the converse of thy saints,
For the brightness of thy face,
For thy fullness, God of grace!

2 Happy souls! their praises flow,
Even in this vale of woe;
Waters in the desert rise,
Manna feeds them from the skies;
On they go from strength to strength,
Till they reach thy throne at length;
At thy feet adoring fall,
Who hast led them safe through all.

3 Lord, be mine this prize to win;
Guide me through this world of sin;
Keep me by thy saving grace;
Give me at thy side a place;

Sun and Shield alike thou art,
Guide and guard my erring heart;
Grace and glory flow from thee,
Shed, O shed them, Lord, on me!

43   *Milton.*

LET us with a joyful mind
Praise the Lord, for he is kind,
For his mercies shall endure,
Ever faithful, ever sure.
He by wisdom did create
Heaven's expanse and all its state;
And by his commanding might,
Filled the new-made world with light.

2 All his creatures God doth feed,
His full hand supplies their need;
He hath, with a piteous eye,
Looked upon our misery;
Let us then with gladsome mind,
Praise the Lord, for he is kind:
For his mercies shall endure,
Ever faithful, ever sure.

22 WORSHIP.

EELLS. L. M. D.   QUARTET & CHORUS CHOIR.

44   *J. Stennett.*

Another six days' work is done,
Another Sabbath is begun;
Return, my soul, enjoy thy rest,
Improve the day thy God hath blest.

2 O that our thoughts and thanks may rise,
As grateful incense to the skies;
And draw from heaven that sweet repose,
Which none but he that feels it knows.

3 This heavenly calm within the breast
Is the dear pledge of glorious rest,
Which for the Church of God remains,
The end of cares, the end of pains.

4 In holy duties let the day,
In holy pleasures, pass away;
How sweet a Sabbath thus to spend,
In hope of one that ne'er shall end.

45   *I. Watts.*

Sweet is the work, my God, my King,
To praise thy name, give thanks and sing,
To show thy love by morning light,
And talk of all thy truth at night.

2 My heart shall triumph in my Lord,
And bless his works and bless his word;
Thy works of grace how bright they shine!
How deep thy counsels! how divine!

3 Lord, I shall share a glorious part,
When grace hath well refined my heart,
And fresh supplies of joy are shed,
Like holy oil to cheer my head.

4 Then shall I see, and hear, and know
All I desired or wished below;
And every power find sweet employ
In that eternal world of joy.

Sabbath and Sanctuary. 23

HURSLEY. L. M. ARR. BY W. H MONK.

1. Great God, attend while Zion sings The joy that from thy presence springs: To spend one day with thee on earth, Exceeds a thousand days of mirth.

46   *I. Watts.*

GREAT God, attend while Zion sings
The joy that from thy presence springs:
To spend one day with thee on earth,
Exceeds a thousand days of mirth.

2 God is our sun, he makes our day;
God is our shield, he guards our way
From all assaults of hell and sin,
From foes without and foes within.

3 All needful grace will God bestow,
And crown that grace with glory too;
He gives us all things, and withholds
No real good from upright souls.

4 O God, our King, whose sovereign sway
The glorious host of heaven obey,
Display thy grace, exert thy power,
Till all on earth thy name adore!

ROSE HILL. L. M   J. E. SWEETSER.

1. How pleasant, how divinely fair, O Lord of hosts, thy dwellings are! With long desire, my spirit faints, To meet th'assemblies of thy saints.

47   *I. Watts.*

HOW PLEASANT, how divinely fair,
O Lord of hosts, thy dwellings are!
With long desire my spirit faints,
To meet th'assemblies of thy saints.

2 Blest are the souls who find a place
Within the temple of thy grace;
There they behold thy gentler rays,
And seek thy face, and learn thy praise.

3 Blest are the men whose hearts are set
To find the way to Zion's gate:
God is their strength, and through the road
They lean upon their helper, God.

4 Cheerful they walk with growing strength,
Till all shall meet in heaven at length;
Till all before thy face appear,
And join in nobler worship there.

WORSHIP.

NEWBOLD. C. M.   GEO. KINGSLEY.

1. With joy we hail the sacred day Which God hath called his own; With joy the sum-mons we o-bey To worship at his throne, To worship at his throne.

48

WITH joy we hail the sacred day
Which God hath called his own;
With joy the summons we obey
To worship at his throne.

2 Spirit of grace! O deign to dwell
Within thy church below;
Make her in holiness excel,
With pure devotion glow.

3 Let peace within her walls be found;
Let all her sons unite,
To spread with grateful zeal around
Her clear and shining light.

4 Great God, we hail the sacred day
Which thou hast called thine own;
With joy the summons we obey
To worship at thy throne.

49
I. Watts.

THE Lord of glory is my light,
And my salvation, too;
God is my strength,—nor will I fear
What all my foes can do.

2 One privilege my heart desires,
O grant me an abode
Among the churches of thy saints,
The temples of my God.

3 There shall I offer my requests,
And see thy beauty still;
Shall hear thy messages of love,
And there inquire thy will.

4 When troubles rise and storms appear
There may his children hide;
God has a strong pavillion, where
He makes my soul abide.

HUMMEL. C. M.   C. ZEUNER.

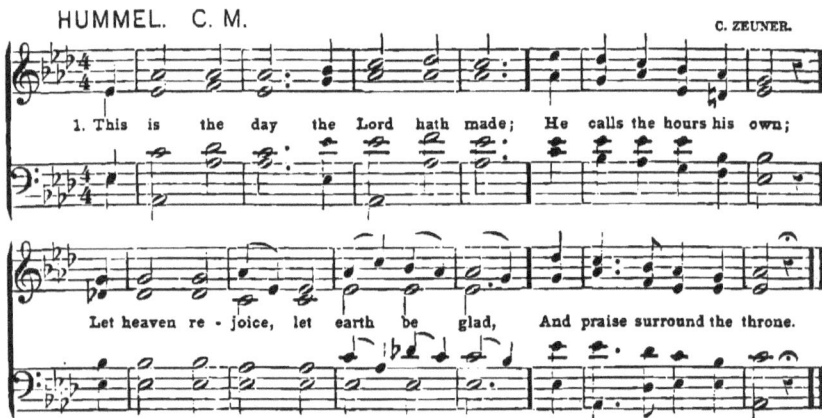

1. This is the day the Lord hath made; He calls the hours his own; Let heaven re-joice, let earth be glad, And praise surround the throne.

Sabbath and Sanctuary. 25

50 *I. Watts.*

This is the day the Lord hath made;
He calls the hours his own;
Let heaven rejoice, let earth be glad,
And praise surround the throne.

2 To-day he rose and left the dead,
And Satan's empire fell;
To-day the saints his triumph spread,
And all his wonders tell.

3 Hosanna to the anointed King,
To David's holy Son;
Help us, O Lord! descend and bring
Salvation from thy throne.

4 Blest be the Lord who comes to men
With messages of grace;
Who comes in God his Father's name,
To save our sinful race.

5 Hosanna in the highest strains
The church on earth can raise;
The highest heavens, in which he reigns,
Shall give him nobler praise.

CHURCH. C. M.   J. P. HOLBROOK.

1. My soul, how lovely is the place, To which thy God resorts 'Tis heaven to see his smiling face, Though in his earthly courts.

51 *I. Watts.*

My soul, how lovely is the place
To which thy God resorts!
'Tis heaven to see his smiling face,
Though in his earthly courts.

2 There the great Monarch of the skies
His saving power displays;
And light breaks in upon our eyes,
With kind and quickening rays.

3 With his rich gifts the heavenly Dove
Descends and fills the place;
While Christ reveals his wondrous love,
And sheds abroad his grace.

4 There, mighty God, thy words declare
The secrets of thy will;
And still we seek thy mercy there,
And sing thy praises still.

52 *J. Mason.*

Thou, Lord, who daily feed'st thy sheep,
Mak'st them a weekly feast;
Thy flocks meet in their several folds
Upon this day of rest.

2 Welcome and dear unto my soul
Are these sweet feasts of love;
But what a sabbath shall I keep
When I shall rest above!

3 I bless thy wise and wondrous love,
Which binds us to be free;
Which makes us leave our earthly snares,
That we may come to thee.

4 I come, I wait, I hear, I pray,
Thy footsteps, Lord, I trace;
I sing to think this is the way
Unto my Saviour's face!

WORSHIP.

LOWELL. 7s. QUARTET & CHORUS CHOIR.

1. Sweet the time, ex-ceed-ing sweet, When the saints to-geth-er meet, When the Sav-iour is the theme, When they join to sing of him.

2. Sing we then e-ter-nal love, Such as did the Fa-ther move: He be-held the world un-done, Loved the world, and gave his Son.

53 *G. Burder.*

Sweet the time, exceeding sweet,
When the saints together meet,
When the Saviour is the theme,
When they join to sing of him.

2 Sing we then eternal love,
Such as did the Father move;
He beheld the world undone,
Loved the world, and gave his Son.

3 Sing the Son's amazing love,
How he left the realms above,
Took our nature and our place,
Lived and died to save our race.

4 Sing we, too, the Spirit's love;
With our wretched hearts he strove,
Took the things of Christ, and showed
How to reach his blest abode.

54 *A. M. Toplady.*

Saviour, whom I fain would love,
Jesus, crucified for me,
Fix my roving heart above,
Draw me nearer unto thee.

2 Thee to praise and thee to know
Make the joy of saints below;
Thee to see and thee to love
Make the bliss of saints above.

3 Lord, it is not life to live,
If thy presence thou deny:
Lord, if thou thy presence give,
'Tis no longer death to die.

4 Source and Giver of repose,
From thee all my comfort flows:
Peace and happiness are thine;
Mine they are if thou art mine.

Sabbath and Sanctuary.

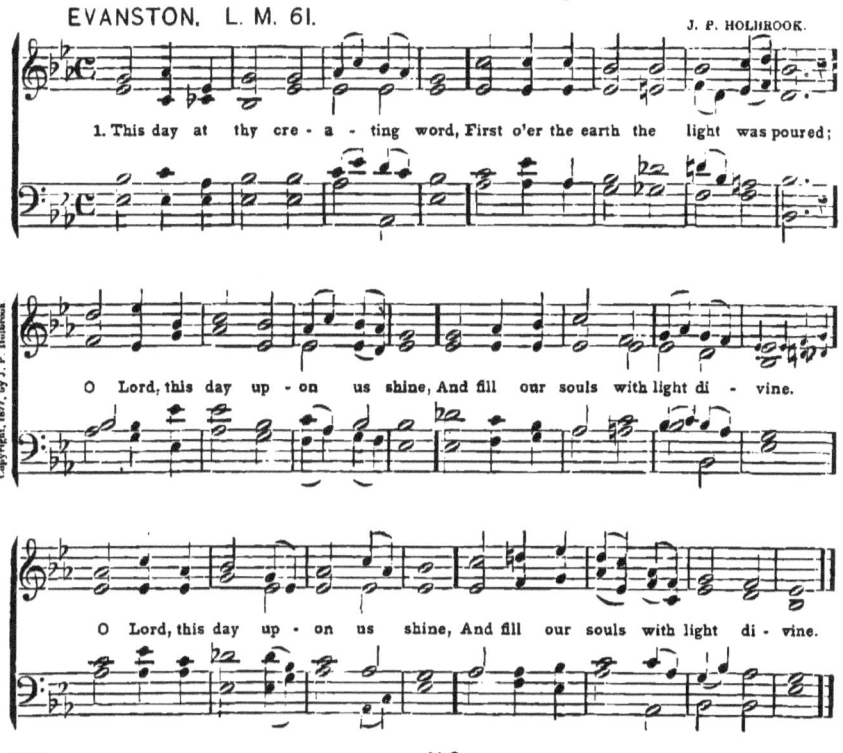

55   W. W. How.

This day at thy creating word,
First o'er the earth the light was poured;
O Lord, this day upon us shine,
And fill our souls with light divine.

2 This day the Lord for sinners slain,
In might victorious rose again;
O Jesus, may we raised be
From death of sin to life in thee.

3 This day the Holy Spirit came
With fiery tongues of cloven flame:
O Spirit, fill our hearts this day,
With grace to hear and grace to pray.

4 O day of light, and life, and grace!
From earthly toils sweet resting place;
Thy hallowed hours, blest gift of love,
Give we again to God above.

56   A. Steele.

Great God, this sacred day of thine,
Demands the soul's collected powers:
With joy we now to thee resign
These solemn, consecrated hours:
O may our souls adoring own
The grace that calls us to thy throne!

2 All-seeing God! thy piercing eye
Can every secret thought explore;
May worldly cares our bosoms fly,
And where thou art intrude no more:
O may thy grace our spirits move,
And fix our minds on things above!

3 Thy Spirit's powerful aid impart,
And bid thy word, with life divine,
Engage the ear and warm the heart:
Then shall the day indeed be thine;
Then shall our souls adoring own
The grace that calls us to thy throne!

WORSHIP.

57 *C. Wordsworth.*

O DAY of rest and gladness,
  O day of joy and light,
O balm of care and sadness,
  Most beautiful, most bright:
On thee, the high and lowly,
  Through ages joined in tune,
Sing Holy, Holy, Holy,
  To the Great God Triune.

2 On thee, at the creation,
  The light first had its birth;
On thee, for our salvation,
  Christ rose from depths of earth;
On thee, our Lord, victorious,
  The Spirit sent from heaven;
And thus on thee, most glorious,
  A triple light was given.

3 To-day on weary nations
  The heavenly manna falls;
To holy convocations
  The silver trumpet calls,
Where gospel light is glowing
  With pure and radiant beams,
And living water flowing
  With soul-refreshing streams.

4 New graces ever gaining
  From this our day of rest,
We reach the rest remaining
  To spirits of the blest;
To Holy Ghost be praises,
  To Father, and to Son;
The Church her voice upraises
  To Thee, blest Three in One.

Sabbath and Sanctuary. 29

58 *J. M. Neale, tr.*

THE day of resurrection,
　Earth, tell it out abroad:
The Passover of gladness,
　The Passover of God.
From death to life eternal,
　From earth unto the sky,
Our Christ hath brought us over,
　With hymns of victory.

2 Our hearts be pure from evil,
　That we may see aright
The Lord in rays eternal
　Of resurrection light;
And listening to his accents,
　May hear, so calm and plain,
His own "All hail!" and hearing,
　May raise the victor-strain.

3 Now let the heavens be joyful;
　Let earth her song begin:
Let the round world keep triumph,
　And all that is therein;
Invisible and visible,
　Their notes let all things blend;
For Christ the Lord hath risen,
　Our Joy that hath no end.

Dox.—To thee be praise for ever
　Thou glorious King of kings!
Thy wondrous love and favor
　Each ransomed spirit sings:
We'll celebrate thy glory
　With all thy saints above,
And shout the joyful story
　Of thy redeeming love.

WORSHIP.

STAINER. 11s, 10s. J. STAINER.

1. Now, when the dusk-y shades of night retreating Be-fore the sun's red banner swiftly flee;
Now, when the ter-rors of the dark are fleeting, O Lord, we lift our thankful hearts to thee.

59

Now, when the dusky shades of night retreating
Before the sun's red banner swiftly flee;
Now, when the terrors of the dark are fleeting,
O Lord, we lift our thankful hearts to thee.

2 Look from the height of heaven, and send to cheer us
Thy light and truth, and guide us onward still;
Still let thy mercy, as of old, be near us,
And lead us safely to thy holy hill.

3 So, when that morn of endless light is waking
And shades of evil from its splendors flee,
Safe may we rise, this earth's dark vale forsaking,
Through all the long bright day to dwell with thee.

BERLIN. 11s, 10s. MENDELSSOHN.

1. Still, still with thee—when purple morning breaketh, When the bird waketh, and the shadows flee;
Fairer than morning, lovelier than the daylight, Dawns the sweet consciousness, I am with thee!

60
H. B. Stowe.

Still, still with thee—when purple morning breaketh,
When the bird waketh, and the shadows flee;
Fairer than morning, lovelier than the daylight,
Dawns the sweet consciousness, I am with thee!

2 Still, still with thee! as to each new-born morning
A fresh and solemn splendor still is given,
So does this blessed consciousness awaking,
Breathe, each day, nearness unto thee and heaven.

3 When sinks the soul, subdued by toil to slumber
Its closing eye looks up to thee in prayer,
Sweet the repose beneath thy wings o'ershading
But sweeter still, to wake and find thee there.

4 So shall it be at last, in that bright morning,
When the soul waketh, and life's shadows flee;
O in that hour, fairer than daylight dawning,
Shall rise the glorious thought—I am with thee.

Evening Songs.

61 *J. Edmeston.*

Saviour, breathe an evening blessing,
　Ere repose our spirits seal;
Sin and want we come confessing,
　Thou canst save, and thou canst heal.

2 Though destruction walk around us,
　Though the arrow past us fly,
Angel-guards from thee surround us,
　We are safe if thou art nigh.

3 Though the night be dark and dreary,
　Darkness cannot hide from thee;
Thou art he who, never weary,
　Watchest where thy people be.

4 Should swift death this night o'ertake us,
　And our couch become our tomb,
May the morn in heaven awake us,
　Clad in light and deathless bloom

62 *T. Hastings.*

Gently, Lord, O gently lead us
　Through this lonely vale of tears;
Through the changes thou'st decreed us,
　Till our last great change appears.

2 When temptation's darts assail us,
　When in devious paths we stray,
Let thy goodness never fail us,
　Lead us in thy perfect way.

3 In the hour of pain and anguish,
　In the hour when death draws near,
Suffer not our hearts to languish,
　Suffer not our souls to fear.

4 And when mortal life is ended,
　Bid us on thy bosom rest,
Till by angel-bands attended,
　We awake among the blest.

WORSHIP.

JANES. L. M. — MOZART.

63
H. Bonar.

Praises to him whose love has given,
In Christ his Son, the life of heaven;
Who for our darkness gives us light,
And turns to day our deepest night.

2 Praises to him in grace who came
To bear our woe and sin and shame;
Who lived to die, who died to rise,
The God-accepted sacrifice.

3 Praises to him who sheds abroad
Within our hearts the love of God—
The Spirit of all truth and peace,
The source of joy and holiness.

4 To Father, Son, and Spirit, now
The hands we lift, the knee we bow;
To God Jehovah thus we raise
The ransomed sinner's song of praise!

LOWRY. L. M. — GEO. F. ROOT.

64
I Watts.

My God, my King, thy various praise
Shall fill the remnant of my days:
Thy grace employ my humble tongue
Till death and glory raise the song.

2 The wings of every hour shall bear
Some thankful tribute to thine ear;
And every setting sun shall see
New works of duty done for thee.

3 Thy works with sovereign glory shine,
And speak thy majesty divine:
Let Zion in her courts proclaim
The sound and honor of thy name.

4 But who can speak thy wondrous deeds?
Thy greatness all our thoughts exceeds:
Vast and unsearchable thy ways;
Vast and immortal be thy praise.

Evening Songs.

DAWSON. L. M. — J. P. HOLBROOK.

1. Thine earth-ly Sabbaths, Lord, we love,— But there's a no-bler rest a-bove: To that our long-ing souls as-pire, With cheer-ful hope and strong de-sire.

65 *P. Doddridge.*

Thine earthly Sabbaths, Lord, we love,—
But there's a nobler rest above :
To that our longing souls aspire,
With cheerful hope and strong desire.

2 No more fatigue, no more distress,
Nor sin nor death shall reach the place;
No sighs shall mingle with the songs
Which warble from immortal tongues.

3 No rude alarms of raging foes;
No cares to break the long repose;
No midnight shade, no clouded sun;
But sacred, high, eternal noon!

4 O long-expected day, begin,
Dawn on these realms of woe and sin;
Fain would we leave this weary road,
And sleep in death to rest with God.

66 *S. Longfellow.*

Again as evening's shadow falls,
We gather in these sacred walls;
And vesper hymn and vesper prayer
Rise mingling on the holy air.

2 May struggling hearts that seek release
Here find the rest of God's own peace;
And strengthened here by hymn and
  prayer,
Cast off their burden and their care.

3 O God, our Light, to thee we bow;
Within all shadows standest thou;
Give deeper calm than night can bring;
Give sweeter songs than lips can sing.

4 Life's tumult we must meet again,
We cannot in thy courts remain;
But in the spirit's secret cell,
May hymn and prayer for ever dwell.

67 *W. H. Burleigh.*

Nor only doth the voiceful day
  Thy loving kindness, Lord, proclaim—
But night, with its sublime array
  Of worlds, doth magnify thy name!

2 O Holy Father! 'mid the calm
  And stillness of this evening hour,
We, too, would lift our solemn psalm
  To praise thy goodness, and thy power!

3 For over us, as over all,
  Thy tender mercies still extend,
Nor vainly shall the contrite call
  On thee, our Father and our Friend!

4 In grief, console—in gladness, bless---
  In darkness, guide—in sickness, cheer--
Till, in the Saviour's righteousness,
  Before thy throne our souls appear!

WORSHIP.

68 *J. Ellerton.*

Our day of praise is done;
  The evening shadows fall;
Yet pass not from us with the sun,
  True Light that lightenest all.

2 Too faint our anthems here;
  Too soon of praise we tire;
But, O the strains, how full and clear,
  Of the eternal choir.

3 Yet, Lord, to thy dear will
  If thou attune the heart,

We in thine angels' music still
  May bear our lower part.

4 'Tis thine each soul to calm,
  Each wayward thought reclaim,
And make our daily life a psalm
  Of glory to thy name.

5 A little while, and then
  Shall come the glorious end;
And songs of angels and of men
  In perfect praise shall blend.

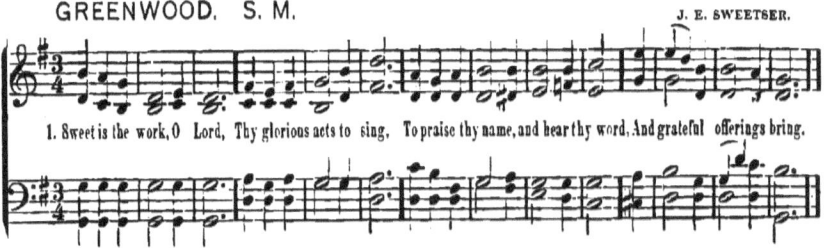

69 *H. Auber.*

Sweet is the work, O Lord,
  Thy glorious acts to sing,
To praise thy name, and hear thy word,
  And grateful offerings bring.

2 Sweet, at the dawning light,
  Thy boundless love to tell;
And when approach the shades of night,
  Still on the theme to dwell.

3 Sweet, on this day of rest,
  To join in heart and voice
With those who love and serve thee best,
  And in thy name rejoice.

4 To songs of praise and joy
  Be every Sabbath given,
That such may be our blest employ
  Eternally in heaven.

Evening Songs. 35

SEYMOUR. 7s. WEBER.

1. Soft-ly now the light of day Fades up-on my sight a-way;
Free from care, from la-bor free, Lord, I would com-mune with thee.

70 *G. W. Doane.*

Softly now the light of day
Fades upon my sight away;
Free from care, from labor free,
Lord, I would commune with thee.

2 Thou, whose all-pervading eye
Naught escapes without, within,
Pardon each infirmity,
Open fault and secret sin.

3 Soon for me the light of day
Shall forever pass away;
Then from sin and sorrow free,
Take me, Lord, to dwell with thee.

4 Thou who, sinless, yet hast known
All of man's infirmity;
Then from thine eternal throne,
Jesus, look with pitying eye.

71

Ere another Sabbath's close,
Ere again we seek repose,
Lord, our song ascends to thee;
At thy feet we bow the knee.

2 For the mercies of the day,
For this rest upon our way,
Thanks to thee alone be given,
Lord of earth and King of Heaven.

3 Whilst this thorny path we tread,
May thy love our footsteps lead:
When our journey here is past,
May we rest with thee at last.

4 Let these earthly Sabbaths prove
Foretastes of our joys above;
While their steps thy pilgrims bend
To the rest which knows no end.

72 *S. F. Smith.*

Softly fades the twilight ray
Of the holy Sabbath day;
Gently as life's setting sun
When the Christian's course is run.

2 Night her solemn mantle spreads
O'er the earth, as daylight fades;
All things tell of calm repose
At the holy Sabbath's close.

3 Still the Spirit lingers near
Where the evening worshipper
Seeks communion with the skies,
Pressing onward to the prize.

4 Saviour, may our Sabbaths be
Days of peace and joy in thee,
Till in heaven our souls repose,
Where the Sabbath ne'er shall close.

36 WORSHIP.

HURSLEY. L. M.   ARR. BY W. H. MONK.

73
J. Keble.

Sun of my soul, thou Saviour dear,
It is not night if thou be near;
O may no earth-born cloud arise
To hide thee from thy servant's eyes.

2 When the soft dews of kindly sleep,
My wearied eyelids gently steep,
Be my last thought, how sweet to rest
For ever on my Saviour's breast.

3 Abide with me from morn till eve,
For without thee I cannot live;
Abide with me when night is nigh,
For without thee I dare not die.

4 If some poor wandering child of thine
Have spurned to-day the voice divine,
Now, Lord the gracious work begin;
Let him no more lie down in sin.

5 Watch by the sick; enrich the poor
With blessings from thy boundless store;
Be every mourner's sleep to-night,
Like infant's slumbers, pure and light!

6 Come near and bless us when we wake,
Ere through the world our way we take;
Till, in the ocean of thy love,
We lose ourselves in heaven above.

74
J. Montgomery.

Lord, when this holy morning broke
O'er island, continent, and deep,
Thy far-spread family awoke,
Sabbath all round the world to keep.

2 And not a prayer, a tear, a sigh,
Hath failed this day some suit to gain,
To those in trouble thou wert nigh:
Not one hath sought thy face in vain.

3 Yet one prayer more, and be it one
In which both heaven and earth accord:
Fulfill thy promise to thy Son;
Let all that breathe call Jesus Lord.

75

Father, adored in worlds above,
Thy glorious name be hallowed still;
Thy kingdom come in truth and love;
And earth, like heaven, obey thy will.

2 Lord, make our daily wants thy care;
Forgive the sins which we forsake;
In thy compassion let us share,
As fellow-men of ours partake.

3 Evils beset us every hour;
Thy kind protection we implore;
Thine is the kingdom, thine the power,
The glory thine for evermore.

Evening Songs.

TALLIS EVENING HYMN. L. M.
T. TALLIS.

1. Glo-ry to thee, my God, this night, For all the blessings of the light; Keep me, O keep me, King of kings, Beneath thine own almighty wings.

76   *T. Ken.*

Glory to thee, my God, this night,
For all the blessings of the light;
Keep me, O keep me, King of kings,
Beneath thine own almighty wings.

2 Forgive me, Lord, for thy dear Son,
The ill that I this day have done;
That with the world, myself, and thee,
I, ere I sleep, at peace may be.

3 Teach me to live, that I may dread
The grave as little as my bed;
To die, that this vile body may
Rise glorious at the awful day.

4 O may my soul on thee repose,
And may sweet sleep my eyelids close;
Sleep that shall me more vigorous make,
To serve my God when I awake.

5 Praise God, from whom all blessings flow;
Praise him, all creatures here below;
Praise him above, ye heavenly host;
Praise Father, Son, and Holy Ghost.

HEBRON. L. M.
LOWELL MASON.

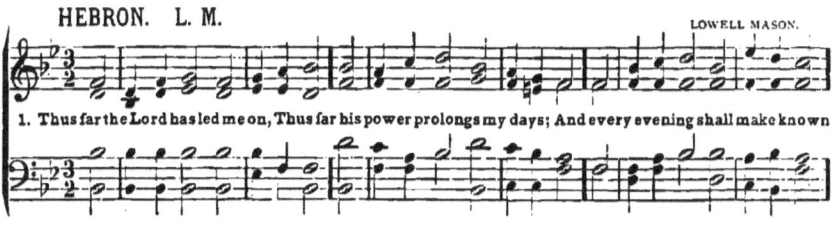

1. Thus far the Lord has led me on, Thus far his power prolongs my days; And every evening shall make known Some fresh me-mo-rial of his grace.

77   *I. Watts.*

Thus far the Lord has led me on,
Thus far his power prolongs my days;
And every evening shall make known
Some fresh memorial of his grace.

2 Much of my time has run to waste,
And I perhaps am near my home;
But he forgives my follies past,
And gives me strength for days to come.

3 I lay my body down to sleep;
Peace is the pillow for my head,
While well-appointed angels keep
Their watchful stations round my bed.

4 Faith in his name forbids my fear;
O may thy presence ne'er depart;
And, in the morning, make me hear
The love and kindness of thy heart.

5 Thus, when the night of death shall come,
My flesh shall rest beneath the ground;
And wait thy voice to rouse my tomb,
With sweet salvation in the sound.

WORSHIP.

CARMEL. 10s. H. SMART.

78 C. Wordsworth.

THE day is gently sinking to a close,
Fainter and yet more faint the sunlight glows;
O Brightness of thy Father's glory, thou
Eternal Light of light, be with us now;
Where thou art present, darkness cannot be,
Midnight is glorious noon, O Lord, with thee.

2 Our changeful lives are ebbing to an end,
Onward to darkness and to death we tend;
O Conqueror of the grave, be thou our Guide,
Be thou our light in death's dark eventide;
Then in our mortal hour will be no gloom,
No sting in death, no terror in the tomb.

Evening Songs.

3 Thou, who in darkness walking didst appear
Upon the waves, and thy disciples cheer,
Come, Lord, in lonesome days, when storms assail,
And earthly hopes and human succors fail:
When all is dark, may we behold thee nigh,
And hear thy voice, "Fear not, for it is I."

4 The weary world is mouldering to decay,
Its glories wane, its pageants fade away;
In that last sunset, when the stars shall fall,
May we arise, awakened by thy call,
With thee, O Lord, for ever to abide
In that blest day which has no eventide.

BEMERTON. C. M.   H. W. GREATOREX.

1. Hail, tran-quil hour of clos-ing day! Be-gone, dis-turb-ing care!
And look, my soul, from earth a-way To him who hear-eth prayer.

79
L. Bacon.

Hail, tranquil hour of closing day!
Begone, disturbing care!
And look, my soul, from earth away
To him who heareth prayer.

2 How sweet the tear of penitence,
Before his throne of grace,
While to the contrite spirit's sense,
He shows his smiling face.

3 How sweet, through long-remembered years,
His mercies to recall,
And pressed with wants, and griefs, and fears,
To trust his love for all.

4 How sweet to look, in thoughtful hope,
Beyond this fading sky,
And hear him call his children up
To his fair home on high.

5 Calmly the day forsakes our heaven
To dawn beyond the west;
So let my soul in life's last even,
Retire to glorious rest.

80

Thou Lord of life, whose tender care,
Hast led us on till now!
We in this quiet hour of prayer
Before thy presence bow.

2 Thou, blessed God! hast been our Guide,
Through life our Guard and Friend;
O still, on life's uncertain tide,
Preserve us to the end!

3 To thee our grateful praise we bring
For mercies day by day;
Lord, teach our hearts thy love to sing,
Lord teach us how to pray.

WORSHIP.

NIGHTFALL. 11s, 5s.
J. BARNBY

1. Now God be with us, for the night is closing, The light and darkness are of his dis- pos - ing; And 'neath his shadow here to rest we yield us, For he will shield us.

81
C. Winkworth, tr.

Now God be with us, for the night is closing,
The light and darkness are of his disposing;
And 'neath his shadow here to rest we yield us,
    For he will shield us.

2 Let evil thoughts and spirits flee before us;
Till morning cometh, watch, O Father! o'er us;
In soul and body thou from harm defend us,
    Thine angels send us.

3 Let holy thoughts be ours when sleep o'ertakes us;
Our earliest thoughts be thine when morning wakes us;
All sick and mourners we to thee commend them,
    Do thou befriend them.

4 We have no refuge, none on earth to aid us,
But thee, O Father! who thine own hast made us;
Keep us in life; forgive our sins; deliver
    Us now and ever.

NOW THE DAY IS OVER. 6s, 5s.
J. BARNBY.

1. Now the day is o - ver, Night is drawing nigh, Shadows of the evening Steal across the sky.

82
S. Baring-Gould.

Now the day is over,
  Night is drawing nigh,
Shadows of the evening
  Steal across the sky.

2 Jesus, give the weary
  Calm and sweet repose,
With thy tenderest blessing
  May our eyelids close.

3 Grant to little children
  Visions bright of thee,
Guard the sailors, tossing
  On the deep blue sea.

4 Comfort every sufferer
  Watching late in pain,
Those who plan some evil
  From their sins restrain.

5 When the morning wakens,
  Then may I arise
Pure and fresh and sinless
  In thy holy eyes.

6 Glory to the Father,
  Glory to the Son,
And to thee, blest Spirit,
  Whilst all ages run.

Close of Worship. 41

ST. ANATOLIUS. 7s, 6s, 8s. A. H. BROWN.

83 *J. M. Neale*, tr.

The day is past and over;
All thanks, O Lord! to thee;
We pray thee now that sinless
The hours of dark may be;
O Jesus! keep us in thy sight,
And guard us through the coming night.

2 The day is past and over;
We raise our hymn to thee;
And ask that free from peril
The hours of dark may be;
O Jesus! keep us in thy sight,
And guard us through the coming night.

3 Be thou our souls' preserver,
O God! for thou dost know
How many are the perils
Through which we have to go;
O loving Jesus! hear our call,
And guard and save us from them all.

CASWALL 6s, 4s, IRR. H. SMART.

84 *E. Caswall*, tr.

As Christ upon the cross
His Head inclined,
And to his Father's hands
His parting soul resigned;

2 So now herself my soul
Would wholly give
Into his sacred charge,
In whom all spirits live.

3 Thus would I live; yet now
Not I, but he
In all his power and love
Henceforth alive in me.

4 One sacred Trinity!
One Lord Divine!
May I be ever his,
And he forever mine.

WORSHIP.

CHILDREY. 8s, 4s, IRR.   E. MOSS.

1. God, that mad-est earth and heaven, Darkness and light; Who the day for toil hast giv-en, For rest the night: May thine an-gel-guards de-fend us, Slumber sweet thy mer-cy send us, Holy dreams and hopes attend us, This live-long night.

85
R. Heber.

God, that madest earth and heaven,
  Darkness and light;
Who the day for toil hast given,
  For rest the night:
May thine angel-guards defend us,
Slumber sweet thy mercy send us,
Holy dreams and hopes attend us,
  This live-long night.

2 Guard us waking, guard us sleeping,
  And when we die,
May we in thy mighty keeping
  All peaceful lie;
When the last dread call shall wake us,
Do not thou our God forsake us,
But to reign in glory take us
  With thee on high.

STONELEIGH 8s, 7s, IRR.   C. S. JEKYLL.

1. Through the day thy love has spared us, Night once more invites to rest; Thro' the silent watches guard us,

Close of Worship.

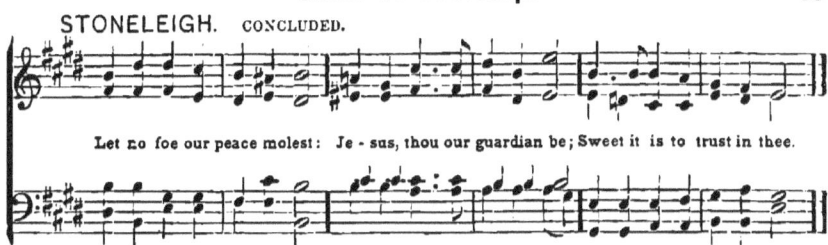

STONELEIGH. CONCLUDED.

Let no foe our peace molest: Jesus, thou our guardian be; Sweet it is to trust in thee.

86 *T. Kelly.*

Through the day thy love has spared us,
Night once more invites to rest;
Through the silent watches guard us,
Let no foe our peace molest:
Jesus, thou our guardian be;
Sweet it is to trust in thee.

2 Pilgrims here on earth, and strangers,
Dwelling in the midst of foes,
Us and ours preserve from dangers;
In thine arms may we repose;
And, when life's short day is past,
Rest with thee in heaven at last.

EVAN. C. M.   W. H. HAVERGAL.

1. The Lord be with us as we bend, His bless-ing to re-ceive;
His gift of peace up-on us send, Be-fore his courts we leave.

87

The Lord be with us as we bend,
His blessing to receive;
His gift of peace upon us send,
Before his courts we leave.

2 The Lord be with us as we walk
Along our homeward road;
In silent thought or friendly talk,
Our hearts be still with God.

3 The Lord be with us till the night
Shall close the day of rest;
Be he of every heart the light,
Of every home the guest!

4 And when our nightly prayers we say,
His watch he still shall keep,
Crown with his grace his own blest day,
And guard his people's sleep.

44 WORSHIP.

SEGUR. 8s, 7s, 4s. J. F. HOLBROOK.

1. Guide me, O thou great Jehovah, Pilgrim through this barren land; I am weak, but thou art mighty; Hold me with thy powerful hand. Bread of heaven! Bread of heaven! Feed me till I want no more.

88 *Williams.*

GUIDE me, O thou great Jehovah,
 Pilgrim through this barren land;
I am weak, but thou art mighty;
 Hold me with thy powerful hand:
  Bread of heaven!
 Feed me till I want no more.

2 Open thou the crystal fountain,
 Whence the healing streams do flow;
Let the fiery, cloudy pillar
 Lead me all my journey through:
  Strong Deliverer!
 Be thou still my strength and shield.

3 When I tread the verge of Jordan,
 Bid my anxious fears subside;
Death of death! and hell's Destruction!
 Land me safe on Canaan's side:
  Songs of praises
 I will ever give to thee.

89 *W. Shirley.*

LORD, dismiss us with thy blessing,
 Fill our hearts with joy and peace;
Let us each, thy love possessing,
 Triumph in redeeming grace;
  Oh! refresh us,
 Traveling through this wilderness.

2 Thanks we give, and adoration,
 For thy gospel's joyful sound:
May the fruits of thy salvation
 In our hearts and lives abound;
  May thy presence
 With us evermore be found.

3 So, whene'er the signal's given,
 Us from earth to call away,
Borne on angels' wings to heaven,
 Glad the summons to obey,
  We shall ever
 Reign with Christ in endless day.

Close of Worship. 45

NELSON. 8s, 7s, 4s. — J. P. HOLBROOK.

1. Guide me, O thou great Jehovah, Pilgrim through this barren land;
I am weak, but thou art mighty; Hold me with thy powerful hand;
Bread of heaven! Bread of heaven! Feed me till I want no more.

SICILIAN HYMN. 8s, 7s.

1. May the grace of Christ the Saviour, And the Father's boundless love, With the Holy Spirit's favor, Rest upon us from above.

90
J. Newton.

May the grace of Christ the Saviour,
And the Father's boundless love,
With the Holy Spirit's favor,
Rest upon us from above.

2 Thus may we abide in union
With each other and the Lord,
And possess, in sweet communion,
Joys which earth cannot afford.

WORSHIP.

BENEDICTION. 10s. E. J. HOPKINS.

1. Saviour! again to thy dear name we raise With one accord our parting hymn of praise; A - gain we bless thee ere our worship cease, And, ere de-part-ing, wait thy word of peace. Amen.

91
J. Ellerton.

SAVIOUR! again to thy dear name we raise
With one accord our parting hymn of praise;
Again we bless thee ere our worship cease,
And, ere departing, wait thy word of peace.

2 Grant us thy peace upon our homeward way;
With thee began, with thee shall end, the day;
Guard thou the lips from sin, the hearts from shame,
That in this house have called upon thy name.

3 Grant us thy peace, Lord! through the coming night,
Turn thou for us its darkness into light;
From harm and danger keep thy children free,
For dark and light are both alike to thee.

4 Grant us thy peace throughout our earthly life,
Our balm in sorrow and our stay in strife;
Then when thy voice shall bid our conflict cease,
Call us, O Lord! to thine eternal peace.

PAX DEI. 10s. J. B. DYKES.

1. Saviour! a - gain to thy dear name we raise With one accord our parting hymn of praise; A - gain we bless thee ere our worship cease, And, ere departing, wait thy word of peace. Amen.

Close of Worship.

VALETE. L. M. 6l. A. S. SULLIVAN.

92 F. W. Faber.

Sweet Saviour! bless us ere we go;
 Thy word into our minds instill,
And make our lukewarm hearts to glow
 With lowly love and fervent will;
Thro' life's long day and death's dark night,
 O gentle Jesus! be our Light.

2 The day is done, the hours have run,
 And thou hast taken count of all—
The scanty triumphs grace hath won,
 The broken vow, the frequent fall;
Thro' life's long day and death's dark night,
 O gentle Jesus! be our Light.

3 Grant us, dear Lord! from evil ways
 True absolution and release,
And bless us more than in past days
 With purity and inward peace;
Thro' life's long day and death's dark night,
 O gentle Jesus! be our Light.

4 Do more than pardon, give us joy,
 Sweet fear and sober liberty,
And loving hearts without alloy
 That only long to be like thee;
Thro' life's long day and death's dark night,
 O gentle Jesus! be our Light.

5 All toil is blest, for thou hast toiled,
 And care is light, for thou hast cared;
Let not our works with self be soiled,
 Nor we in evil ways ensnared;
Thro' life's long day and death's dark night,
 O gentle Jesus! be our Light.

6 For all we love, the poor, the sad,
 The sinful, unto thee we call;
Oh, let thy mercy make us glad;
 Thou art our Jesus and our All;
Thro' life's long day and death's dark night,
 O gentle Jesus! be our Light.

GOD.

First Lines of Hymns.

ETERNAL BEING.
HYMNS.
93 Full of glory, full of wonders,
94 O Source Divine, and Life of all,
95 God the Lord a King remaineth,
96 Thou had'st no youth, great God,
97 Our God, our help in ages past,
98 Great God, how infinite art thou,
99 Mighty God, the First, the Last,
100 O God, the Rock of Ages,

MAJESTY AND MIGHT.
101 Praise to thee, thou great Creator.
102 Praise the Lord, ye heavens adore him,
103 Lord, thy glory fills the heaven,
104 Blest be thou, O God of Israel,
105 Praise the Lord, who reigns above,
106 Meet and right it is to sing,
107 The Lord Jehovah reigns, And royal
108 My heart and voice I raise,
109 Jehovah reigns! his throne is high,
110 Jehovah reigns! he dwells in light,
111 Holy, holy, holy Lord,
112 Lord of earth! thy forming hand,
113 The Lord our God is clothed with might.
114 God is the name my soul adores,
115 Great is the Lord, what tongue can frame,
116 Lord of all being! throned afar,

OMNIPRESENCE AND OMNISCIENCE.
117 Through every age, eternal God,
118 Lord, thou hast searched and seen me
119 In all my vast concerns with thee,
120 Jehovah, God, thy gracious power.

PROVIDENTIAL RULE AND CARE.
HYMNS.
121 Wait, O my soul, thy Maker's will,
122 The Lord is just; this is his throne,
123 O Father, humbly we repose,
124 High in the heavens, eternal God,
125 God is the refuge of his saints,
126 Keep silence, all created things,
127 God moves in a mysterious way,
128 I cannot walk in darkness long,
129 O thou, in all thy might so far,
130 My God, my Father, blissful name,
131 There is a safe and secret place,
132 O bless the Lord, my soul, His grace
133 My soul, repeat his praise,
134 O bless the Lord, my soul, Let all
135 Upward I lift mine eyes,
136 While thee I seek, protecting Power,
137 When all thy mercies, O my God,
138 Through all the changing scenes of life,
139 God, my supporter and my hope,
140 My God, how wonderful thou art,
141 No change of time shall ever shock,
142 Call Jehovah thy salvation,

LOVE AND GRACE.
143 God is love; that anthem olden,
144 God's free mercy streameth,
145 God, my King, thy might confessing,
146 God is love; his mercy brightens,
147 Eternal Light! Eternal Light!

BEETHOVEN. L. M. ARR. G. KINGSLEY.

1. O Source di - vine, and Life of all. Thou Fount of be - ing's wondrous sea!
Thy depth would ev - ery heart ap - pall, That saw not Love su - preme in thee.

Eternal Being. 49

GLENTWORTH. 8s, 5s, Irr.   J. P. HOLBROOK.

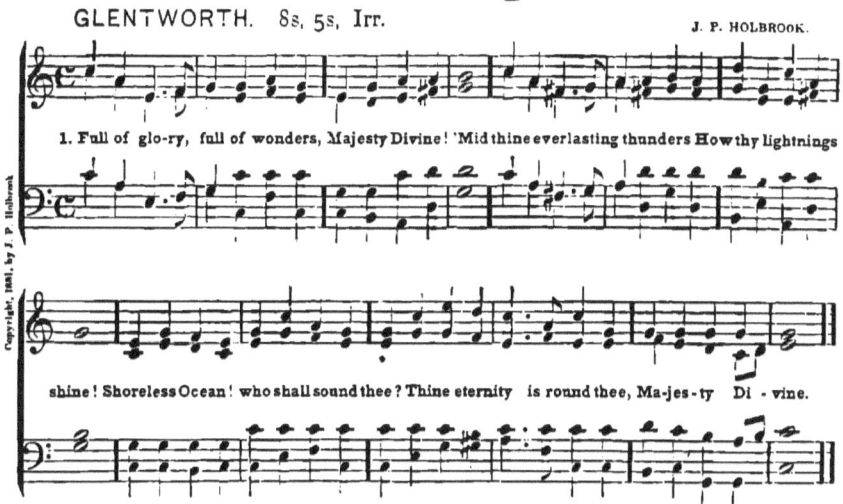

1. Full of glo-ry, full of wonders, Majesty Divine! 'Mid thine everlasting thunders How thy lightnings shine! Shoreless Ocean! who shall sound thee? Thine eternity is round thee, Ma-jes-ty Di - vine.

93
F. W. Faber.

FULL of glory, full of wonders,
  Majesty Divine!
'Mid thine everlasting thunders
  How thy lightnings shine!
Shoreless Ocean! who shall sound thee?
Thine eternity is round thee,
  Majesty Divine.

2 Timeless, spaceless, single, lonely,
  Yet sublimely Three,
Thou art grandly, always, only,
  God in Unity.
Lone in grandeur and in glory,
Who shall tell thy wondrous story,
  Awful Trinity?

3 Speechlessly, without beginning,
  Sun that never rose!
Vast, adorable, and winning,
  Day that hath no close!
Bliss from thine own glory tasting,
Everlasting, everlasting,
  Life that never grows!

4 'Mid thine uncreated morning
  Like a trembling star,
I behold creation's dawning
  Glimmering from afar;
Nothing giving, nothing taking—
Nothing changing, nothing breaking,
  Waiting at time's bar!

5 Splendors upon splendors beaming
  Change and intertwine;
Glories over glories streaming,
  All transparent shine!
Blessings, praises, adorations
Greet thee from the trembling nations,
  Majesty Divine!

94
BEETHOVEN. L. M.   *J. Sterling.*

O SOURCE Divine, and Life of all,
  Thou Fount of being's wondrous sea!
Thy depth would every heart appall,
  That saw not Love supreme in thee.

2 We shrink before thy vast abyss,
  Where worlds on worlds unnumbered
    brood;
We know thee truly but in this,—
  That thou bestowest all our good.

3 And so 'mid boundless time and space,
  O grant us still in thee to dwell,
And through the ceaseless web to trace
  Thy presence working all things well!

4 Bestow on every joyous thrill
  A deeper tone of reverent awe;
Make pure thy children's erring will,
  And teach their hearts to love thy law.

50 GOD.

GLADNESS. 8s, 7s, 4s.   H. SMART.

1. God the Lord a King remaineth, Robed in his own glorious light! On th' eternal throne he reigneth! He hath girded him with might! Hallelujah! Hallelujah! God is King in depth and height!

95

God the Lord a King remaineth,
  Robed in his own glorious light!
On th' eternal throne he reigneth!
  He hath girded him with might!
    Hallelujah!
  God is King in depth and height!

2 In her everlasting station
  Earth is poised to swerve no more;
Thou hast laid thy throne's foundation,
  From all time where thought can soar.
    Hallelujah!
  Lord, thou art for evermore.

3 Lord, the water-floods have lifted,
  Ocean-floods have lift their roar;
Now they pause where they have drifted,
  Now they burst upon the shore.
    Hallelujah!
  For the oceans sounding store!

4 With all tones of waters blending,
  Glorious is the breaking deep!
Glorious, beauteous, without ending,
  God who reigns on heaven's high steep!
    Hallelujah!
  Songs of ocean never sleep!

5 Lord, the words thy lips are telling,
  Are the perfect verity;
Of thine high eternal dwelling
  Holiness shall inmate be!
    Hallelujah!
  Pure is all that lives with thee!

Dox.—Great Jehovah, we adore thee,
  God the Father, God the Son,
God the Spirit, joined in glory
  On the same eternal throne;
    Endless praises
  To Jehovah, Three in One.

Eternal Being.

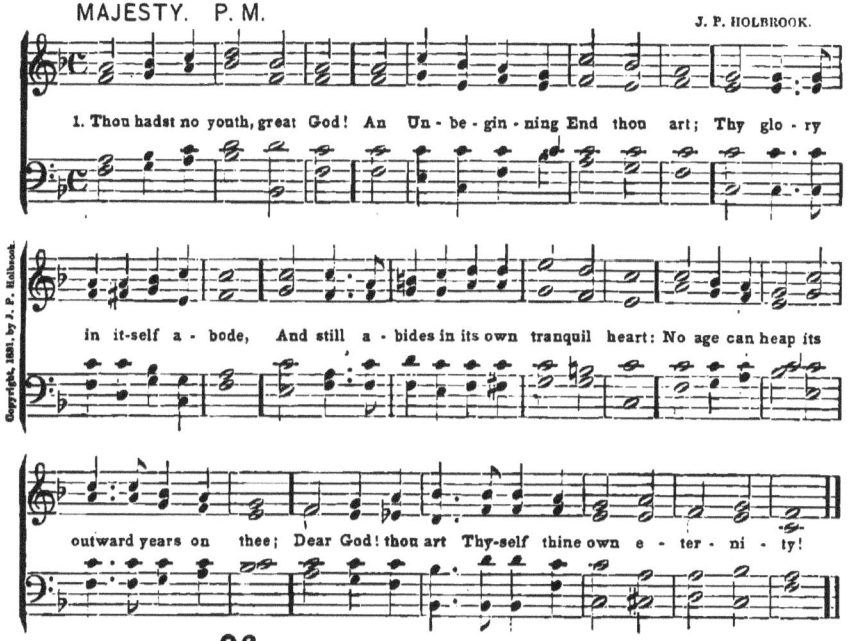

96 F. W. Faber.

THOU hadst no youth, great God!
 An Unbeginning End thou art;
Thy glory in itself abode,
 And still abides in its own tranquil heart!
No age can heap its outward years on thee;
 Dear God! thou art Thyself thine own eternity!

2 Without an end or bound
 Thy life lies all outspread in light;
Our lives feel Thy life all around,
 Making our weakness strong, our darkness bright;
For weakest hearts can lift their thoughts to Thee;
 It makes us strong to think of thine eternity!

3 Oh, thou art very great
 To set thyself so far above!
But we partake of thine estate,
 Established in thy strength and in thy love;
That love hath made eternal room for me
 In the sweet vastness of its own eternity!

4 Farewell, vain joys of earth!
 Farewell, all love that is not His!
Dear God! be thou my only mirth,
 Thy majesty my trust, and rest, and bliss!
Oh, in the bosom of eternity
 Thou dost not weary of Thyself, nor we of Thee!

GOD.

LLANDAFF. C. M.
E. MOSS.

1. Our God, our help in a-ges past, Our hope for years to come;

Our shel-ter from the storm-y blast, And our e-ter-nal home:

97 *I. Watts.*

Our God, our help in ages past,
  Our hope for years to come;
Our shelter from the stormy blast,
  And our eternal home:

2 Under the shadow of thy throne
  Thy saints have dwelt secure;
Sufficient is thine arm alone,
  And our defence is sure.

3 Before the hills in order stood,
  Or earth received her frame,

From everlasting thou art God,
  To endless years the same.

4 Time, like an ever-rolling stream,
  Bears all its sons away;
They fly, forgotten, as a dream
  Dies at the opening day.

5 Our God, our help in ages past,
  Our hope for years to come,
Be thou our guard while troubles last,
  And our eternal home.

DUNDEE. C. M.
SCOTCH PSALTER.

1. Great God, how in-fi-nite art thou, What worthless worms are we: Let the whole race of creatures bow, And pay their praise to thee.

98 *I. Watts.*

Great God, how infinite art thou,
  What worthless worms are we:
Let the whole race of creatures bow,
  And pay their praise to thee.

2 Thy throne eternal ages stood,
  Ere seas or stars were made;
Thou art the ever-living God,
  Were all the nations dead.

3 Eternity with all its years,
  Stands present in thy view;

To thee there's nothing old appears,
  Great God, there's nothing new.

4 Our lives through various scenes are drawn,
  And vexed with trifling cares;
While thine eternal thought moves on
  Thine undisturbed affairs.

5 Great God, how infinite art thou,
  What worthless worms are we;
Let the whole race of creatures bow,
  And pay their praise to thee.

Eternal Being. 53

E. C. Gaskell.

99
MIGHTY God, the First, the Last,
  What are ages in thy sight
But as yesterday when past,
  Or a watch within the night?

2 All that being ever knew,
  Down, far down, ere time had birth
Stands as clear within thy view
  As the present things of earth.

3 All that being e'er shall know,
  On, still on, through farthest years,
All eternity can show,
  Bright before thee now appears.

4 Whatsoe'er our lot may be,
  Calmly in this thought we'll rest,—
Could we see as thou dost see,
  We should choose it as the best.

100   *E. Bickersteth.*
O GOD, the Rock of Ages,
  Who evermore hast been,
What time the tempest rages,
  Our dwelling-place serene:
Before thy first creations,
  O Lord, the same as now,
To endless generations,
  The Everlasting thou!

2 Our years are like the shadows
  O'er sunny hills that fly,
Or grasses in the meadows
  That blossom but to die:
A sleep, a dream, a story,
  By strangers quickly told,
An unremaining glory
  Of things that soon are old.

3 O thou, who canst not slumber,
  Whose light grows never pale,
Teach us aright to number
  Our years before they fail.
On us thy mercy lighten,
  On us thy goodness rest;
And let thy Spirit brighten
  The hearts thyself hast blessed.

GOD.

SALTZBURG. 8s, 7s.   ARR. GEO. KINGSLEY.

101
J. Fawcett.

Praise to thee, thou great Creator!
Praise to thee from every tongue:
Join, my soul, with every creature,
Join the universal song.

2 Father, Source of all compassion
Pure, unbounded grace is thine;
Hail the God of our salvation!
Praise him for his love divine.

3 For ten thousand blessings given,
For the hope of future joy,
Sound his praise through earth and heaven,
Sound Jehovah's praise on high.

4 Joyfully on earth adore him,
Till in heaven our song we raise;
There, enraptured, fall before him,
Lost in wonder, love, and praise.

CARTHAGE. 8s, 7s.   A. T. LWOFF.

102

Praise the Lord! ye heavens, adore him,
Praise him, angels in the height;
Sun and moon, rejoice before him;
Praise him, all ye stars of light!

2 Praise the Lord—for he hath spoken;
Worlds his mighty voice obeyed;
Laws which never shall be broken,
For their guidance he hath made.

3 Praise the Lord—for he is glorious;
Never shall his promise fail;
God hath made his saints victorious,
Sin and death shall not prevail.

4 Praise the God of our salvation,
Hosts on high his power proclaim:
Heaven and earth, and all creation,
Laud and magnify his name.

Majesty. 55

103
R. Mant.

Lord, thy glory fills the heaven;
Earth is with its fullness stored;
Unto thee be glory given,
Holy, holy, holy Lord!
Heaven is still with anthems ringing;
Earth takes up the angels' cry,
Holy, holy, holy, singing,
Lord of hosts, thou Lord most high.

2 Ever thus in God's high praises,
Brethren, let our tongues unite,
While our thoughts his greatness raises,
And our love his gifts excite:
With his seraph train before him,
With his holy church below,
Thus unite we to adore him,
Bid we thus our anthem flow.

3 Lord, thy glory fills the heaven;
Earth is with its fullness stored;
Unto thee be glory given,
Holy, holy, holy Lord!
Thus thy glorious name confessing,
We adopt the angels' cry,
Holy, holy, holy, blessing
Thee, the Lord our God most high!

104

Blest be thou, O God of Israel!
Thou, our Father and our Lord!
Majesty is thine for ever;
Ever be thy name adored.
Thine, O Lord, are power and greatness;
Glory, victory, are thine own;
All is thine in earth and heaven,
Over all thy boundless throne.

2 Riches come of thee, and honor:
Power and might to thee belong;
Thine it is to make us prosper,
Only thine to make us strong.
Lord, our God, for these thy bounties,
Hymns of gratitude we raise;
To thy name for ever glorious,
Ever we address our praise.

Dox. Praise the God of all creation;
Praise the Father's boundless love:
Praise the Lamb, our expiation,
Priest and King enthroned above:
Praise the Fountain of salvation,
Him by whom our spirits live:
Undivided adoration
To the one Jehovah give.

56 GOD.

RUSSELL PLACE. 7s, 6s.   W. S. BENNETT.

105

Praise the Lord, who reigns above,
  And keeps his courts below;
Praise the holy God of love,
  And all his greatness show:
Praise him for his noble deeds;
  Praise him for his matchless power;
Him, from whom all good proceeds,
  Let earth and heaven adore.

2 Publish, spread to all around
  The great Jehovah's name;
Let the trumpet's martial sound
  The Lord of Hosts proclaim!
Praise him every tuneful string!
  All the reach of heavenly art,
All the powers of music bring,—
  The music of the heart.

3 Him, in whom they move and live,
  Let every creature sing;
Glory to their Maker give,
  And homage to their King:
Hallowed be his name beneath;
  As in heaven, on earth adored;
Praise the Lord in every breath;
  Let all things praise the Lord.

106   *C. Wesley.*

Meet and right it is to sing,
  In every time and place;
Glory to our heavenly King,
  The God of truth and grace.
Join we then with sweet accord,
  All in one thanksgiving join!
Holy, holy, holy Lord,
  Eternal praise be thine!

2 Thee, the first born sons of light,
  In choral symphonies,
Praise by day, day without night,
  And never, never cease;
Angels and archangels, all
  Praise the mystic Three in One;
Sing, and stop, and gaze, and fall,
  O'erwhelmed before thy throne!

3 Father, God, thy love we praise,
  Which gave thy Son to die;
Jesus, full of truth and grace,
  Alike we glorify;
Spirit, Comforter divine,
  Praise by all to thee be given,
Till we in full chorus join,
  And earth is turned to heaven.

Majesty. 57

FISKE. S. P. M.
J. P. HOLBROOK.

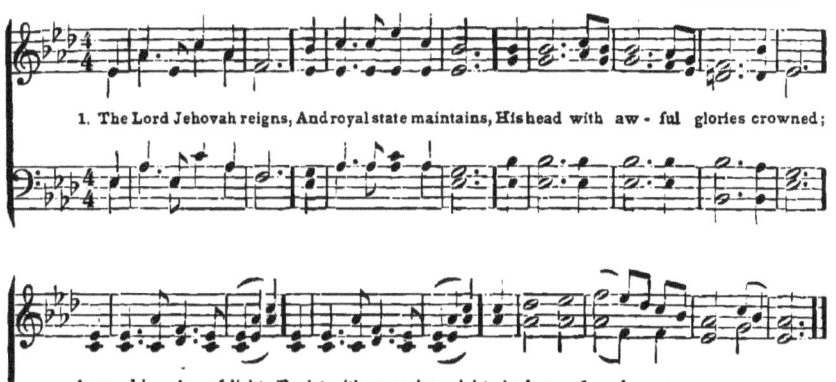

107
I. Watts.

THE Lord Jehovah reigns,
And royal state maintains,
His head with awful glories crowned;
Arrayed in robes of light,
Begirt with sovereign might,
And rays of majesty around.

2 Upheld by thy commands,
The world securely stands,
And skies and stars obey thy word:
Thy throne was fixed on high
Before the starry sky:
Eternal is thy kingdom, Lord!

3 Let floods and nations rage,
And all their powers engage;
Let swelling tides assault the sky:
The terrors of thy frown
Shall beat their madness down:
Thy throne for ever stands on high.

4 Thy promises are true;
Thy grace is ever new;
There fixed, thy church shall ne'er remove:
Thy saints, with holy fear,
Shall in thy courts appear,
And sing thine everlasting love.

108
B. Rhodes.

My heart and voice I raise,
To spread Messiah's praise;
Messiah's praise let all repeat;
The universal Lord,
By whose almighty word
Creation rose in form complete.

2 With mercy's mildest grace,
He governs all our race
In wisdom, righteousness, and love:
Who to Messiah fly
Shall find redemption nigh,
And all his great salvation prove.

3 Hail, Saviour, Prince of peace!
Thy kingdom shall increase,
Till all the world thy glory see;
And righteousness abound,
As the great deep profound,
And fill the earth with purity.

4 Reign, true Messiah, reign!
Thy kingdom shall remain
When stars and suns no more shall shine;
Mysterious Deity,
Who ne'er began to be,
To sound thine endless praise be mine!

58 ATTLEFIELD. L. M.
Allegro Moderato.   SCHUBERT.

109   *I. Watts.*

JEHOVAH reigns! his throne is high,
His robes are light and majesty;
His glory shines with beams so bright,
No mortal can sustain the sight.

2 His terrors keep the world in awe;
His justice guards his holy law;
His love reveals a smiling face,
His truth and promise seal the grace.

3 Through all his works his wisdom shines,
And baffles Satan's deep designs;
His power is sovereign to fulfill
The noblest counsels of his will.

4 And will this glorious Lord descend
To be my Father and my Friend?
Then let my songs with angels join;
Heaven is secure, if God be mine.

ARNHEIM. L. M.   S. HOLYOKE.

110   *I. Watts.*

JEHOVAH reigns! He dwells in light,
Girded with majesty and might;
The world, created by his hands,
Still on its firm foundation stands.

2 But ere this spacious world was made,
Or had its first foundation laid,
Thy throne eternal ages stood,
Thyself the ever-living God.

3 Like floods the angry nations rise,
And aim their rage against the skies:
Vain floods, that aim their rage so high!
At thy rebuke the billows die.

4 Forever shall thy throne endure;
Thy promise stand forever sure;
And everlasting holiness
Becomes the dwelling of thy grace.

Lord of Heaven and Earth. 59

ONIDO. 7s, D.   PLEYEL.

1. Ho-ly, ho-ly, holy Lord God of Hosts! when heaven and earth, Out of darkness at thy word Is-sued in-to glor-ious birth, All thy works be-fore thee stood, And thine eye be-held them good; While they sang with sweet accord, Ho-ly, ho-ly, ho-ly Lord!

111 *J. Montgomery.*

HOLY, holy, holy Lord
  God of Hosts! when heaven and earth,
Out of darkness, at thy word
  Issued into glorious birth,
All thy works before thee stood,
And thine eye beheld them good;
While they sang with sweet accord,
Holy, holy, holy Lord!

2 Holy, holy, holy! thee,
  One Jehovah evermore,
Father, Son, and Spirit! we,
  Dust and ashes, would adore:
Lightly by the world esteemed,
From that world by thee redeemed,
Sing we here with glad accord,
Holy, holy, holy Lord!

3 Holy, holy, holy! all
  Heaven's triumphant choir shall sing,
While the ransomed nations fall
  At the footstool of their King:
Then shall saints and seraphim,
Harps and voices, swell one hymn,
Blending in sublime accord,
Holy, holy, holy Lord!

112 *R. Grant.*

LORD of earth! thy forming hand
  Well this beauteous frame hath planned,—
Woods that wave, and hills that tower,
  Ocean rolling in his power:
Yet, amid this scene so fair,
Should I cease thy smile to share,
What were all its joys to me?
Whom have I on earth but thee?

2 Lord of heaven! beyond our sight
  Shines a world of purer light;
There, in love's unclouded reign,
  Parted hands shall meet again:
Oh, that world is passing fair!
Yet, if thou wert absent there,
What were all its joys to me?
Whom have I in heaven but thee?

3 Lord of earth and heaven! my breast
  Seeks in thee its only rest;
I was lost; thy accents mild
  Homeward lured thy wandering child.
Oh! should once thy smile divine,
Cease upon my soul to shine,
What were earth or heaven to me?
Whom have I in each but thee?

GOD.

SIDON. C. M. — HAYDN.
Allegro moto con fuoco.

1. The Lord our God is clothed with might, The winds o-bey his will; He speaks, and in his heavenly height The roll-ing sun stands still: Re-bel, ye waves, and o'er the land With threatening as-pect roar; The Lord uplifts his aw-ful hand, And chains you to the shore.

113 *H. K. White.*

The Lord our God is clothed with might;
The winds obey his will;
He speaks, and in his heavenly height
The rolling sun stands still.

2 Rebel, ye waves, and o'er the land
With threatening aspect roar;
The Lord uplifts his awful hand,
And chains you to the shore.

3 Howl, winds of night; your force combine;
Without his high behest,

Ye shall not, in the mountain pine,
Disturb the sparrow's nest.

4 His voice sublime is heard afar;
In distant peals it dies;
He yokes the whirlwind to his car,
And sweeps the howling skies.

5 Ye nations, bend; in reverence bend;
Ye monarchs, wait his nod,
And bid the choral song ascend
To celebrate our God.

DUNDEE C. M. Verse 5. — SCOTCH PSALTER.

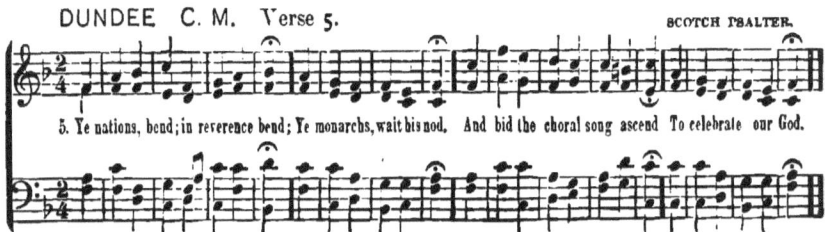

5. Ye nations, bend; in reverence bend; Ye monarchs, wait his nod, And bid the choral song ascend To celebrate our God.

Might.

LOUVAN. L. M.   V. C. TAYLOR.

1. God is the name my soul a-dores, Th'al-might-y Three, th'e-ter-nal One:

Na-ture and grace, with all their powers, Con-fess the In-fin-ite Un-known.

114   *I. Watts.*

God is the name my soul adores,
Th' almighty Three, th'eternal One;
Nature and grace, with all their powers,
Confess the Infinite Unknown.

2 Thy voice produced the seas and spheres,
Bade the waves roar, and planets shine;
But nothing like thyself appears
Through all these spacious works of thine.

3 Still restless nature dies and grows;
From change to change the creatures run;
Thy being no succession knows,
And all thy vast designs are one.

4 Who can behold thy blazing light?
Who can approach consuming flame?
None but thy wisdom knows thy might,
None but thy word can speak thy name.

115

Great is the Lord! what tongue can frame,
An honor equal to his name?
How awful are his glorious ways!
The Lord is dreadful in his praise!

2 Vast are thy works, almighty Lord!
All nature rests upon thy word;
And clouds, and storms, and fire obey
Thy wise and all-controlling sway.

3 Thy glory, fearless of decline,
Thy glory, Lord, shall ever shine;
Thy praise shall still our breath employ
Till we shall rise to endless joy.

116   *O. W. Holmes.*

Lord of all being! throned afar,
Thy glory flames from sun and star;
Centre and soul of every sphere,
Yet to each loving heart how near!

2 Sun of our life! thy quickening ray
Sheds on our path the glow of day;
Star of our hope! thy softened light
Cheers the long watches of the night.

3 Our midnight is thy smile withdrawn;
Our noontide is thy gracious dawn;
Our rainbow arch thy mercy's sign;
All save the clouds of sin are thine.

4 Lord of all life! below, above,
Whose light is truth, whose warmth is love,
Before thy ever-blazing throne
We ask no lustre of our own.

5 Grant us thy truth to make us free,
And kindling hearts that burn for thee,
Till all thy living altars claim
One holy light, one heavenly flame.

GOD.

117 *I. Watts.*

Through every age, eternal God,
Thou art our rest, our safe abode;
High was thy throne ere heaven was made,
Or earth thy humble footstool laid.

2 Long hadst thou reigned ere time began,
Or dust was fashioned into man;
And long thy kingdom shall endure,
When earth and time shall be no more.

3 But man, weak man, is born to die,
Made up of guilt and vanity:
Thy dreadful sentence, Lord, was just—
"Return, ye sinners, to your dust."

4 Death, like an overflowing stream,
Sweeps us away: our life's a dream—
An empty tale—a morning flower,
Cut down and withered in an hour!

5 Teach us, O Lord, how frail is man;
And kindly lengthen out our span,
Till, by thy grace, we all may be
Prepared to die, and dwell with thee.

118 *I. Watts.*

Lord, thou hast searched and seen me through:
Thine eye commands, with piercing view,
My rising and my resting hours,
My heart and flesh with all their powers.

2 My thoughts, before they are my own,
Are to my God distinctly known;
He knows the words I mean to speak,
Ere from my opening lips they break.

3 Within thy circling power I stand;
On every side I find thy hand:
Awake, asleep, at home, abroad,
I am surrounded still with God.

4 Amazing knowledge, vast and great!
What large extent! what lofty height!
My soul, with all the powers I boast,
Is in the boundless prospect lost.

5 Oh! may these thoughts possess my breast,
Where'er I rove, where'er I rest,
Nor let my weaker passions dare
Consent to sin, for God is there.

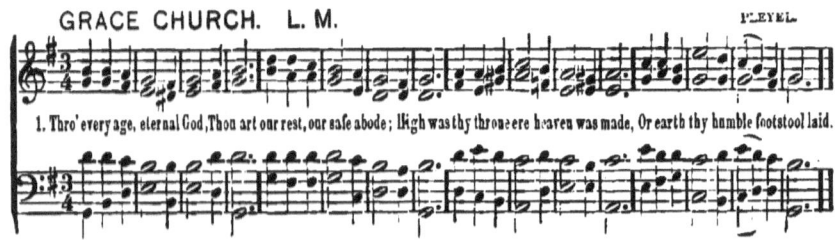

Omniscient—Omnipresent. 63

BELMONT. C. M. — S. WEBBE.

1. In all my vast con-cerns with thee, In vain my soul would try
To shun thy presence, Lord, or flee The no-tice of thine eye.

119   *I. Watts.*

In all my vast concerns with thee,
In vain my soul would try
To shun thy presence, Lord, or flee
The notice of thine eye.

2 Thine all-surrounding sight surveys
My rising and my rest;
My public walks, my private ways,
The secrets of my breast.

3 My thoughts lie open to the Lord,
Before they're formed within;
And, ere my lips pronounce the word,
He knows the sense I mean.

4 Oh, wondrous knowledge, deep and high!
Where can a creature hide!
Within thy circling arms I lie,
Enclosed on every side.

5 So let thy grace surround me still,
And like a bulwark prove,
To guard my soul from every ill,
Secured by sovereign love.

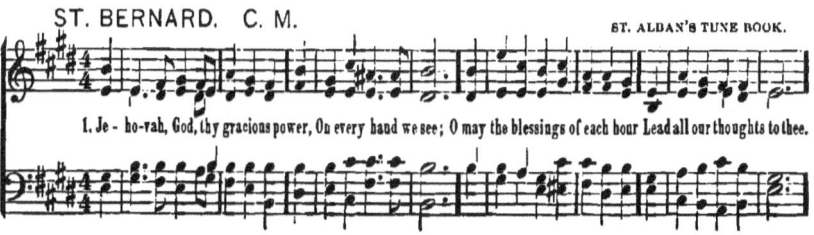

ST. BERNARD. C. M. — ST. ALBAN'S TUNE BOOK.

1. Je-ho-vah, God, thy gracious power, On every hand we see; O may the blessings of each hour Lead all our thoughts to thee.

120   *J. Thomson.*

Jehovah, God, thy gracious power
On every hand we see;
O may the blessings of each hour
Lead all our thoughts to thee.

2 If on the wings of morn we speed
To earth's remotest bound,
Thy hand will there our footsteps lead,
Thy love our path surround.

3 Thy power is in the ocean deeps,
And reaches to the skies;
Thine eye of mercy never sleeps,
Thy goodness never dies.

4 From morn till noon, till latest eve,
Thy hand, O God, we see;
And all the blessings we receive,
Proceed alone from thee.

5 In all the varying scenes of time,
On thee our hopes depend;
Through every age, in every clime,
Our Father, and our Friend.

GOD.

DAWSON. L M — J. P. HOLBROOK.

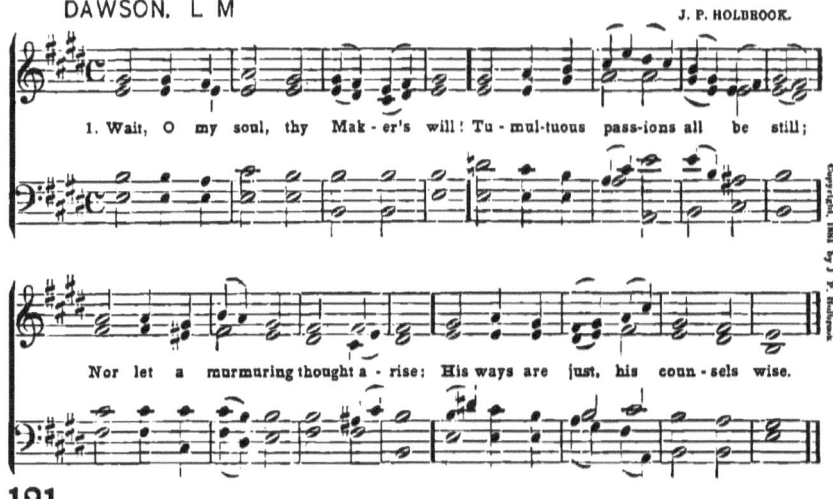

1. Wait, O my soul, thy Maker's will! Tumultuous passions all be still; Nor let a murmuring thought arise: His ways are just, his counsels wise.

121
B. Beddome.

Wait, O my soul, thy Maker's will!
Tumultuous passions, all be still;
Nor let a murmuring thought arise:
His ways are just, his counsels wise.

2 He in the thickest darkness dwells,
Performs his work, the cause conceals;
And, though his footsteps are unknown,
Judgment and truth support his throne.

3 In heaven, and earth, and air, and seas,
He executes his firm decrees;
And by his saints it stands confessed,
That what he does is ever best.

4 Wait, then, my soul, submissive wait,
With reverence bow before his seat;
And, 'mid the terrors of his rod,
Trust in a wise and gracious God.

122
Hymns of the Spirit.

The Lord is just; this is his throne:
The world his righteousness shall own;
Yea, all the world with awe shall see
He reigns and rules in equity.

2 His perfect law the world surrounds,
And sets to every wrong his bounds;
Through ways oft hid from human sight,
Makes sure the triumph of the right.

3 Let none who suffer wrong despair;
The God of justice hears their prayer:
Let none dare break his statutes pure;
God's justice, though it wait, is sure.

4 Just is our God, for ever just;
Upon this rock I fix my trust:
This faith shall every fear remove;
His justice is his perfect love.

123
W. Gaskell.

O Father, humbly we repose
Our souls on thee, who dwell'st above;
And bless thee for the peace which flows
From faith in thine encircling love.

2 Though every earthly trust may break,
Infinite might belongs to thee;
Though every earthly friend forsake,
Unchangeable thou still wilt be.

3 Though clouds may gather darkly round,
They cannot veil us from thy sight;
Though vain all human aid be found,
Thou every grief canst turn to light.

4 All things thy wise designs fulfil,
In earth beneath and heaven above;
And good breaks out from every ill,
Through faith in thine encircling love.

Providence.

ALL SAINTS. L. M. W. KNAPP.

1. High in the heavens, eternal God! Thy goodness in full glory shines; Thy truth shall break through every cloud That veils and darkens thy designs.

124
I. Watts.

High in the heavens, eternal God!
Thy goodness in full glory shines;
Thy truth shall break through every cloud
That veils and darkens thy designs.

2 Forever firm thy justice stands,
As mountains their foundations keep:
Wise are the wonders of thy hands;
Thy judgments are a mighty deep.

3 My God, how excellent thy grace!
Whence all our hope and comfort springs;
The sons of Adam, in distress,
Fly to the shadow of thy wings.

4 Life, like a fountain rich and free,
Springs from the presence of my Lord;
And in thy light our souls shall see
The glories promised in thy word.

DUKE STREET. L. M. J. HATTON.

1. God is the refuge of his saints, When storms of sharp distress invade: Ere we can offer our complaints, Behold him present with his aid.

125
I. Watts.

God is the refuge of his saints,
When storms of sharp distress invade;
Ere we can offer our complaints,
Behold him present with his aid.

2 There is a stream whose gentle flow
Supplies the city of our God,
Life, love, and joy, still gliding through,
And watering our divine abode.

3 That sacred stream, thine holy word,
Our grief allays, our fear controls;
Sweet peace thy promises afford,
And give new strength to fainting souls.

4 Zion enjoys her Monarch's love,
Secure against a threatening hour;
Nor can her firm foundation move,
Built on his truth, and armed with power.

66 GOD.

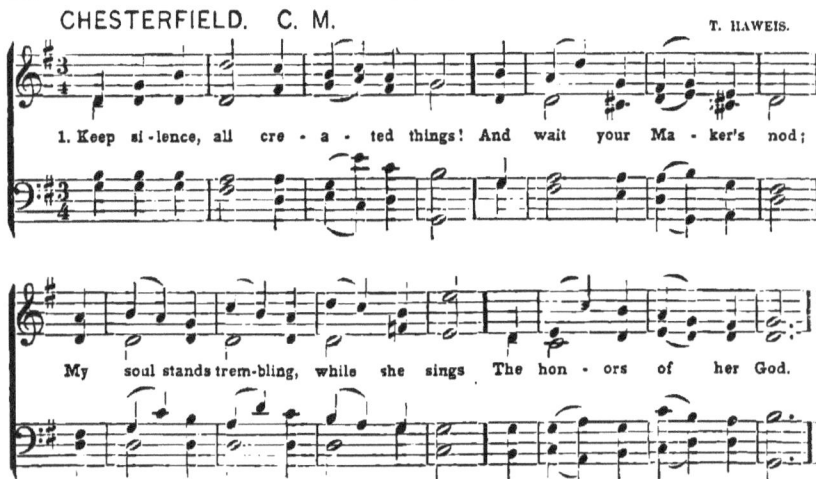

CHESTERFIELD. C. M.   T. HAWEIS.

1. Keep si-lence, all cre-a-ted things! And wait your Ma-ker's nod; My soul stands trem-bling, while she sings The hon-ors of her God.

126   *I. Watts.*

KEEP silence, all created things!
   And wait your Maker's nod;
My soul stands trembling, while she sings
   The honors of her God.

2 Life, death, and hell, and worlds unknown,
   Hang on his firm decree:
He sits on no precarious throne,
   Nor borrows leave to be.

3 His providence unfolds the book,
   And makes his counsels shine;
Each opening leaf, and every stroke,
   Fulfils some deep design.

4 My God! I would not long to see
   My fate with curious eyes,—
What gloomy lines are writ for me,
   Or what bright scenes may rise:

5 In thy fair book of life and grace,
   May I but find my name,
Recorded in some humble place,
   Beneath my Lord, the Lamb.

127   *W. Cowper.*

GOD moves in a mysterious way
   His wonders to perform;
He plants his footsteps in the sea,
   And rides upon the storm.

2 Deep in unfathomable mines
   Of never-failing skill,
He treasures up his bright designs,
   And works his sovereign will.

3 Judge not the Lord by feeble sense,
   But trust him for his grace;
Behind a frowning providence
   He hides a smiling face.

4 His purposes will ripen fast,
   Unfolding every hour;
The bud may have a bitter taste,
   But sweet will be the flower.

5 Blind unbelief is sure to err,
   And scan his work in vain;
God is his own interpreter,
   And he will make it plain.

128   *O. A. Mason.*

I CANNOT walk in darkness long,
   My God is by my side!
I cannot stumble or go wrong
   While following such a Guide.

2 He is my stay and my defence,
   How shall I fail or fall?
My Keeper is Omnipotence;
   My Ruler ruleth all.

3 The powers below and powers above
   Are subject to his care;
I cannot wander from his love,
   Whose love is everywhere.

Providence.

BEMERTON. C. M.   H. W. GREATOREX.

1. O thou, in all thy might so far, In all thy love so near,—

Beyond the range of sun and star, And yet beside us here:—

129
F. L. Hosmer.

O THOU, in all thy might so far,
  In all thy love so near,—
Beyond the range of sun and star,
  And yet beside us here:—

2 What heart can comprehend thy name,
  Or, searching, find thee out?
Who art within, a quickening Flame,
  A Presence round about.

3 Yet though I know thee but in part
  I ask not, Lord, for more:
Enough for me to know thou art,
  To love thee and adore!

4 And dearer than all things I know,
  Is childlike faith to me,
That makes the darkest way I go
  An open path to thee.

130
A. Steele.

My God, my Father, blissful name!
  O, may I call thee mine?
May I with sweet assurance claim
  A portion so divine?

2 Whate'er thy providence denies
  I calmly would resign;
For thou art good, and just, and wise:
  O, bend my will to thine!

3 Whate'er thy sacred will ordains,
  O, give me strength to bear!
And let me know my Father reigns,
  And trust his tender care.

4 Thy sovereign ways are all unknown
  To my weak, erring sight;
Yet let my soul adoring own
  That all thy ways are right.

131
H. F. Lyte.

THERE is a safe and secret place
  Beneath the wings divine,
Reserved for all the heirs of grace:
  O, be that refuge mine!

2 The least and feeblest there may bide,
  Uninjured and unawed;
While thousands fall on every side,
  He rests secure in God.

3 He feeds in pastures large and fair,
  Of love and truth divine;
O child of God, O glory's heir!
  How rich a lot is thine!

4 A hand almighty to defend,
  An ear for every call,
An honored life, a peaceful end,
  And heaven to crown it all!

GOD.

132   *J. Montgomery.*

Oh, bless the Lord, my soul!
  His grace to thee proclaim;
And all that is within me join
  To bless his holy name.

2 Oh, bless the Lord, my soul!
  His mercies bear in mind;
Forget not all his benefits:
  The Lord to thee is kind.

3 He will not always chide:
  He will with patience wait:
His wrath is ever slow to rise,
  And ready to abate.

4 He pardons all thy sins,
  Prolongs thy feeble breath;
He healeth thy infirmities,
  And ransoms thee from death.

133   *I. Watts.*

My soul, repeat his praise
  Whose mercies are so great;
Whose anger is so slow to rise,
  So ready to abate.

2 His power subdues our sins,
  And his forgiving love,
Far as the east is from the west,
  Doth all our guilt remove.

3 Our days are as the grass,
  Or like the morning flower;
If one sharp blast sweep o'er the field
  It withers in an hour.

4 But thy compassions, Lord,
  To endless years endure;
And children's children ever find
  The word of promise sure.

Providence.

HAYDN. S. M. HAYDN.

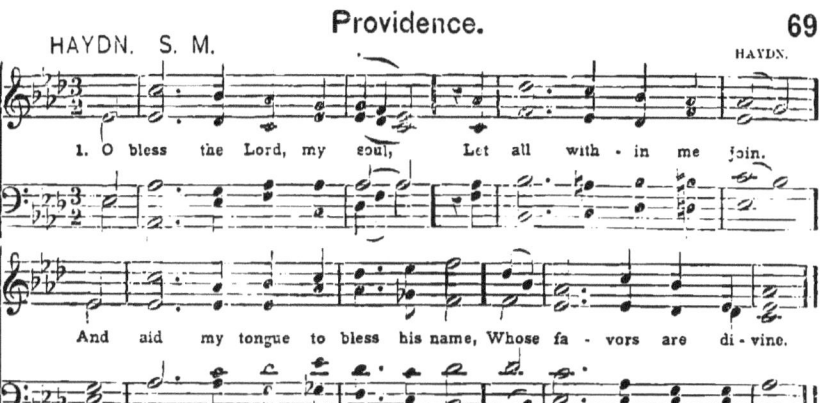

1. O bless the Lord, my soul, Let all with-in me join. And aid my tongue to bless his name, Whose fa-vors are di-vine.

134

O bless the Lord, my soul,
 Let all within me join,
And aid my tongue to bless his name,
 Whose favors are divine.

2 O bless the Lord, my soul,
 Nor let his mercies lie
Forgotten in unthankfulness,
 And without praises die.

3 'Tis he forgives thy sins,
 'Tis he relieves thy pain,
'Tis he that heals thy sicknesses,
 And makes thee young again.

4 He crowns thy life with love,
 When ransomed from the grave;
He that redeemed my soul from hell,
 Hath sovereign power to save.

FRANKLIN. H. M. J. P. HOLBROOK.

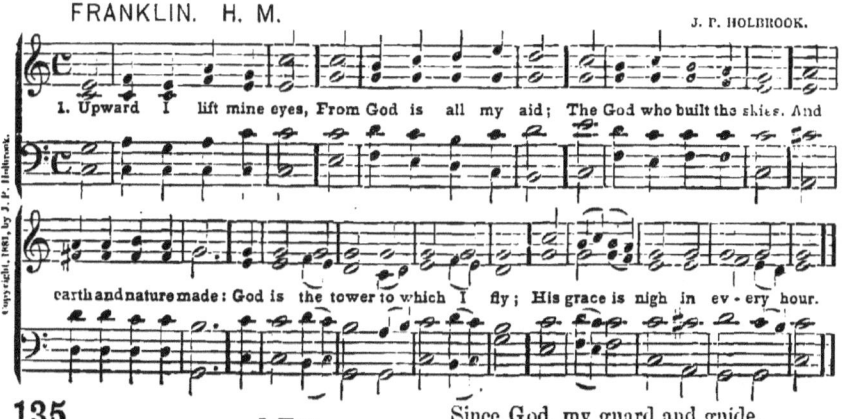

1. Upward I lift mine eyes, From God is all my aid; The God who built the skies. And earth and nature made: God is the tower to which I fly; His grace is nigh in ev-ery hour.

135 *I. Watts.*

Upward I lift mine eyes,
 From God is all my aid;
The God who built the skies,
 And earth and nature made:
God is the tower | His grace is nigh
To which I fly; | In every hour.

2 My feet shall never slide,
 And fall in fatal snares,
Since God, my guard and guide,
 Defends me from my fears;
Those wakeful eyes, | Shall Israel keep
That never sleep, | When dangers rise.

3 Hast thou not given thy word
 To save my soul from death?
And I can trust my Lord
 To keep my mortal breath:
I'll go and come, | Till from on high
Nor fear to die, | Thou call me home.

GOD.

ST. LEONARD. C. M. D.   H. HILES.

136   *H. M. Williams.*

While thee I seek, protecting Power!
Be my vain wishes stilled;
And may this consecrated hour
With better hopes be filled!
2 Thy love the power of thought bestowed;
To thee my thoughts would soar:
Thy mercy o'er my life has flowed;
That mercy I adore.
3 In each event of life, how clear
Thy ruling hand I see!
Each blessing to my soul more dear,
Because conferred by thee.
4 In every joy that crowns my days,
In every pain I bear,
My heart shall find delight in praise,
Or seek relief in prayer.
5 When gladness wings my favored hour,
Thy love my thoughts shall fill;
Resigned, when storms of sorrow lower,
My soul shall meet thy will.
6 My lifted eye, without a tear,
The gathering storm shall see;
My steadfast heart shall know no fear;
That heart shall rest on thee.

137   *J. Addison.*

When all thy mercies, O my God,
My rising soul surveys,
Transported with the view, I'm lost
In wonder, love, and praise.
2 O how shall words with equal warmth
The gratitude declare
That glows within my ravish'd heart?
But thou canst read it there.
3 Unnumbered comforts to my soul
Thy tender care bestowed,
Before my infant heart conceived
From whom those comforts flowed.
4 Ten thousand thousand precious gifts
My daily thanks employ;
Nor is the least a cheerful heart
That tastes those gifts with joy.
5 Through every period of my life
Thy goodness I'll pursue;
And after death, in distant worlds,
The glorious theme renew.
6 Through all eternity to thee
A joyful song I'll raise;
But O, eternity's too short
To utter all thy praise.

Providence.

TRUMAN. C. M. D. — J. P. HOLBROOK.

1. While thee I seek, pro-tect-ing Power! Be my vain wish-es stilled; And may this con-se-cra-ted hour With bet-ter hopes be filled! Thy love the power of thought be-stowed; To thee my thoughts would soar: Thy mercy o'er my life has flowed; That mercy I a-dore.

138 *Tate-Brady.*

Through all the changing scenes of life,
In trouble and in joy,
The praises of my God shall still
My heart and tongue employ.

2 The hosts of God encamp around
The dwellings of the just;
Deliverance he affords to all
Who on his succor trust

3 O make but trial of his love:
Experience will decide
How blest are they, and only they,
Who in his truth confide.

4 Fear him, ye saints, and you will then
Have nothing else to fear;
Make you his service your delight,
Your wants shall be his care.

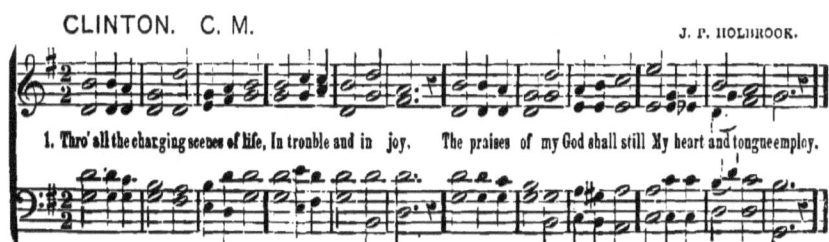

CLINTON. C. M. — J. P. HOLBROOK.

1. Thro' all the changing scenes of life, In trouble and in joy. The praises of my God shall still My heart and tongue employ.

72   GOD.

MARIAN. C. M.   J. P. HOLBROOK.

1. God, my sup-port-er and my hope, My help for ev-er near,

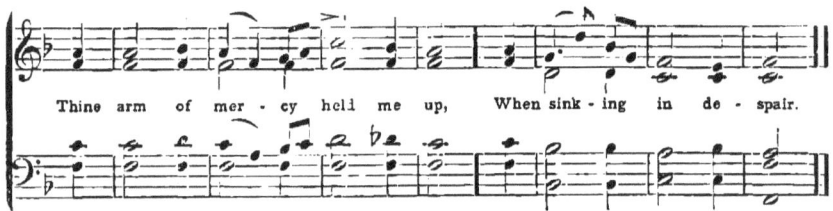

Thine arm of mer-cy held me up, When sink-ing in de-spair.

139   *I. Watts.*

God, my supporter and my hope,
  My help for ever near,
Thine arm of mercy held me up,
  When sinking in despair.

2 Thy counsels, Lord, shall guide my feet
  Through this dark wilderness;
Thy hand conduct me near thy seat,
  To dwell before thy face.

3 What if the springs of life were broke,
  And flesh and heart should faint?
God is my soul's eternal rock,
  The strength of every saint.

4 Then, to draw near to thee, my God,
  Shall be my sweet employ;
My tongue shall sound thy works abroad,
  And tell the world my joy.

140   *F. W. Faber.*

My God, how wonderful thou art,
  Thy majesty how bright!
How glorious is thy mercy seat,
  In depths of burning light!

2 Yet I may love thee too, O Lord,
  Almighty as thou art;
For thou hast stooped to ask of me
  The love of my poor heart.

3 No earthly father loves like thee,
  No mother half so mild
Bears and forbears, as thou hast done
  With me, thy sinful child.

4 My God, how wonderful thou art,
  Thou everlasting Friend!
On thee I stay my trusting heart,
  Till faith in vision end.

141   *Tate-Brady.*

No CHANGE of time shall ever shock
  My trust, O Lord, in thee;
For thou hast always been my Rock,
  A sure defense to me.

2 Thou my deliverer art, O God;
  My trust is in thy power:
Thou art my shield from foes abroad,
  My safeguard, and my tower.

3 To thee will I address my prayer,
  To whom all praise I owe;
So shall I, by thy watchful care,
  Be saved from every foe.

4 Then let Jehovah be adored,
  On whom my hopes depend;
For who, except the mighty Lord,
  His people can defend?

Providence.

HOPE. 8s, 7s.   BEETHOVEN.

142   *J. Montgomery.*

CALL Jehovah thy salvation,
  Rest beneath th' Almighty's shade,
In his secret habitation
  Dwell, and never be dismayed.

2 There no tumult can alarm thee,
  Thou shalt dread no hidden snare;
Guile nor violence can harm thee,
  In eternal safeguard there.

3 From the sword, at noonday wasting,
  From the noisome pestilence,
In the depth of midnight, blasting,
  God shall be thy sure defence.

4 God shall charge his angel legions
  Watch and ward o'er thee to keep;
Though thou walk through hostile regions,
  Though in desert wilds thou sleep.

5 Since, with pure and firm affection,
  Thou on God hast set thy love,
With the wings of his protection
  He will shield thee from above.

6 Thou shalt call on him in trouble,
  He will hearken, he will save;
Here for grief reward thee double,
  Crown with life beyond the grave.

WESTMINSTER. 8s, 7s.   J. P. HOLBROOK.

GOD.

143

God is love; that anthem olden,
  Sing the glorious orbs of light,
In their language glad and golden
  Telling to us day and night
    Their great story,
God is love, and God is might!

2 And the teeming earth rejoices
  In that message from above,
With ten thousand thousand voices,
  Telling back from hill and grove,
    Her glad story,
God is might, and God is love!

3 Through these anthems of creation,
  Struggling up with gentle strife,
Christian songs of Christ's salvation,
  To the world with blessings rife,
    Tell their story,
God is love, and God is life!

4 Up to him let each affection,
  Daily rise and round him move;
Our whole lives one resurrection,
  To the life of life above;
    Our glad story,
God is life, and God is love!

GREEK HYMN. CONCLUDED.

Broad, and deep, and glorious, As the heavens above, Shines in might victorious, His e-ter-nal love.

144
God's free mercy streameth
Over all the world,
And his banner gleameth
Every where unfurled,
Broad and deep and glorious
As the heavens above,
Shines in might victorious
His eternal Love.

2 Lord, upon our blindness
Thy pure radiance pour;
For thy loving kindness
Make us love thee more.

And when clouds are drifting
Dark across our sky,
Then, the veil uplifting,
Father, be thou nigh.

3 We will never doubt thee
Though thou veil thy light,
Life is dark without thee
Death with thee is bright.
Light of light! shine o'er us,
On our pilgrim way,
Go thou still before us
To the endless day.

RATHBUN. 8s, 7s.
I. CONKEY.

1. God, my King, thy might confessing, Ev-er will I bless thy name; Day by day thy throne ad-dressing, Still will I thy praise proclaim.

145
R. Mant.
God, my King, thy might confessing,
Ever will I bless thy name;
Day by day thy throne addressing,
Still will I thy praise proclaim.

2 Honor great our God befitteth;
Who his majesty can reach?
Age to age his works transmitteth,
Age to age his power shall teach.

3 Full of kindness and compassion,
Slow to anger, vast in love,
God is good to all creation;
All his works his goodness prove.

4 All thy works, O Lord, shall bless thee,
Thee shall all thy saints adore;
King supreme shall they confess thee
And proclaim thy sovereign power.

146
J. Bowring.
God is love; his mercy brightens
All the path in which we rove;
Bliss he wakes, and woe he lightens:
God is wisdom, God is love.

2 Chance and change are busy ever;
Man decays, and ages move;
But his mercy waneth never:
God is wisdom, God is love.

3 E'en the hour that darkest seemeth
Will his changeless goodness prove;
From the mist his brightness streameth:
God is wisdom, God is love.

4 He with earthly cares entwineth
Hope and comfort from above;
Everywhere his glory shineth:
God is wisdom, God is love.

CHRIST.

NEWCASTLE. C. M.
H. L. MORLEY.

147
T. Binney.

ETERNAL Light! Eternal Light!
How pure the soul must be,
When, placed within thy searching sight
It shrinks not, but with calm delight
Can live and look on thee.

2 O how shall I, whose native sphere
Is dark, whose mind is dim,
Before the Ineffable appear,
And on my naked spirit bear
That uncreated beam.

3 There is a way for man to rise
To that sublime abode;
An offering and a sacrifice,
A Holy Spirit's energies,
An Advocate with God.

4 These, these prepare us for the light
Of majesty above:
The sons of ignorance and night
Can stand in the Eternal Light,
Through the Eternal Love.

CHRIST.
First Lines of Hymns.

INCARNATION AND ADVENT.

HYMNS.
148 Of the Father's love begotten,
149 Jesus is God! the glorious bands
150 Whither goest thou, O Saviour?
151 Ere the blue heavens were stretched
152 Go, worship at Immanuel's feet;
153 When marshalled on the nightly plain
154 All praise to thee, eternal Lord!
155 The Word is made incarnate,
156 Jesus, the Christ of God!
157 God from on high hath heard!
158 As with gladness men of old
159 Joy to the world, the Lord is come:
160 Hark, the glad sound, the Saviour comes,
161 Hosanna! raise the pealing hymn
162 To us a child of hope is born,
163 While shepherds watched their flocks
164 It came upon the midnight clear,
165 Hark, hark, the notes of joy

HYMNS.
166 Lo, God, our God, has come!
167 Hark, the herald angels sing,
168 Brightest and best of the sons
169 Hark, what mean those holy voices,
170 Come, thou long-expected Jesus,

HIS LIFE OUR EXAMPLE.

171 O Lord, we would the path retrace
172 Servant, at once, and Lord of all
173 The loving Friend to all who bowed
174 Lord, as to thy dear cross we flee,
175 What grace, O Lord, and beauty shone
176 A pilgrim through this lonely world
177 How wondrous was the burning zeal
178 Christ is his own best evidence
179 O who like thee, so calm, so bright,
180 My dear Redeemer and my Lord.
181 There's not a hope with comfort fraught,
182 Awhile in spirit, Lord, to thee,

CHRIST.
First Lines of Hymns. CONCLUDED.

HYMNS.
183 How sweetly flowed (*Teaching.*)
184 O Lord of health ⎫
185 Thine arm, O Lord ⎬ *Miracles.*
186 Fierce raged the tempest ⎪
187 Behold, the blind ⎭
188 O wondrous type, (*Transfiguration.*)
189 Hail, Israel's King! ⎫ *Triumphal Entry.*
190 Ride on, ride on ⎭

SUFFERINGS AND DEATH.
191 'Tis midnight, and on Olive's brow
192 "'Tis finished!"—so the Saviour cried,
193 Go to dark Gethsemane
194 Jesus, Lamb of God, for me
195 What laws, my blessed Saviour,
196 Eternal King! in power and love
197 There's a wideness in God's mercy

THE LORD'S SUPPER.
198 Come, let us sing the song of songs,
199 Draw near, O holy Dove, draw near,
200 When I survey the wondrous cross
201 O the sweet wonders of that cross
202 Lord Jesus, when we stand afar
203 Before thy cross, my dying Lord
204 At thy command, our dearest Lord,
205 Upon thy grace we banquet here,
206 We come, O only Saviour,
207 Here, O my Lord, I see thee
208 By Christ redeemed, in Christ restored,
209 Salvation's Giver, Christ, God's only Son,
210 Hark, the voice of love and mercy
211 Bread of the world, in mercy
212 Rock of Ages, cleft for me!
213 "   "   "   "   "   "
214 Son of God, to thee I cry:
215 Lamb of God, whose bleeding love
216 O sacred Head, now wounded,
217 There is a fountain filled with blood
218 To Calvary, Lord, in spirit now,
219 O Jesus, sweet the tears I shed,
220 Sweet the moments, rich in blessing.
221 My faith looks up to thee,
222 Not all the blood of beasts,
223 I hear the words of love,
224 Blessed Saviour, thee I love,
225 Chief of sinners though I be,
226 "Till he come," O let the words
227 Alas, and did my Saviour bleed,
228 How sweet and awful is the place.
229 Thou art coming, at thy table

RESURRECTION AND ASCENSION.
230 Welcome, happy morning, age to age
231 Lift your glad voices in triumph
232 Christ the Lord is risen to-day,

HYMNS.
233 Christ the Lord is risen again,
234 Our Lord is risen from the dead,
235 Hallelujah! Hallelujah!
236 Christ, above all glory seated
237 Thou art gone up on high
238 Th'eternal gates lift up their heads

ENTHRONEMENT.
239 Jesus, hail! enthroned in glory,
240 Crown his head with endless blessing,
241 See the Conqueror mounts in triumph
242 Mighty God, while angels bless thee,
243 Praise Him! Praise the conquering King!
244 Look, ye saints! the sight is glorious,
245 Hark, ten thousand harps and voices
246 Crown him with many crowns,
247 Come, let us join our cheerful songs
248 The head that once was crowned
249 Christ, with eternal glory crowned,
250 All hail the power of Jesus' name,
251 My Saviour, my Almighty Friend,

SONGS OF ADORATION AND LOVE.
252 O could I speak the matchless worth,
253 O Love Divine, how sweet thou art,
254 Now to the Lord a noble song!
255 Now for a song of lofty praise
256 Complete in thee, no work of mine,
257 Jesus, engrave it on my heart,
258 Fountain of grace, rich, full and free,
259 He lives! the great Redeemer lives!
260 Jesus! thy blood and righteousness
261 There is none other name than thine,
262 In the cross of Christ I glory,
263 Come, thou Fount of every blessing,
264 Awake, my soul, to joyful lays,
265 Around the Saviour's lofty throne,
266 To thee, my Shepherd and my Lord,
267 Come, let us join in songs of praise,
268 With joy we meditate the grace
269 Majestic sweetness sits enthroned
270 Father, how wide thy glory shines,
271 To our Redeemer's glorious name,
272 O for a thousand tongues to sing
273 How sweet the name of Jesus sounds
274 O Jesus, when I think of thee,
275 Salvation! O the joyful sound!
276 Plunged in a gulf of dark despair
277 In vain we seek for peace with God
278 Christ is my Prophet, Priest and King
279 Thou art the Way; to thee alone
280 Lord Jesus, are we one with thee?
281 O One with God the Father,
282 The atoning work is done,
283 Join all the glorious names
284 Rejoice, the Lord is King!

78 CHRIST.

CLEMENS 8s, 7s, 7s.   H. SMART.

148
J. M. Neale, Tr.

OF the Father's love begotten,
  Ere the worlds began to be,
He, the Alpha and Omega,
  He the Source, the Ending He,
Of the things that are, that have been,
  And that future years shall see,
    Evermore and evermore!

2 He is come, whom seers in old time
  Chanted of, while ages ran;
Whom the voices of the prophets
  Promised since the world began;
Long foretold, at length appearing,
  Praise him, every child of man,
    Evermore and evermore!

3 Praise him, O ye heaven of heavens!
  Praise him, angels in the height!
All dominions bow before him,
  And exalt his boundless might;
Let no tongue of man be silent,
  Let each heart and voice unite,
    Evermore and evermore!

4 Christ, to thee, with God the Father,
  And, O Holy Ghost, to thee,
Hymn and chant and high thanksgiving,
  And unwearied praises be,
Honor, glory, might, dominion,
  And eternal victory,
    Evermore and evermore!

Incarnation and Advent.

149
F. W. Faber.

JESUS is God! the glorious bands
Of golden angels sing
Songs of adoring praise to him,
Their Maker and their King.

2 He was true God in Bethlehem's crib;
On Calvary's cross true God;
He who in heaven eternal reigned,
In time on earth abode.

3 Jesus is God! if on the earth
This blessed faith decays,
More tender must our love become,
More plentiful our praise.

4 Oh, had I but an angel's voice,
I would proclaim aloud,—
Jesus, the good, the beautiful,
Is everlasting God!

150

"Whither goest thou, O Saviour,
  Without royal diadem,
With thy regal hand unsceptred?"
  "Bethlehem."

2 "Whither goest thou, O Saviour,
  Lord of Life and Lord of Death,
Light of men in darkness shining?"
  "Nazareth."

3 "Whither goest thou, O Saviour?
  We would rise and follow thee,
Glory of thy people Israel."
  "Calvary."

4 "Whither goest thou, O Saviour,
  From the grave returned to be
Resurrection, Life, and Glory?"
  "Bethany."

151
L. Watts.

Ere the blue heavens were stretched abroad,
From everlasting was the Word:
With God he was; the Word was God,
And must divinely be adored.

2 By his own power were all things made;
By him supported, all things stand:
He is the whole creation's head,
And angels fly at his command.

3 Mortals with joy behold his face,
Th'eternal Father's only Son;
How full of truth, how full of grace,
When thro' his eyes the Godhead shone!

4 Archangels leave their high abode
To learn new mysteries here, and tell
The love of our descending God,
The glories of Immanuel.

152
L. Watts.

Go, worship at Immanuel's feet;
See in his face what wonders meet:
Earth is too narrow to express
His worth, his glory, or his grace.

2 Bright image of the Father's face,
Shining with undiminished rays;
Th'eternal God's eternal Son,
The heir and partner of his throne.

3 Nor earth, nor sea, nor sun, nor stars,
Nor heaven, his full resemblance bears;
His beauties we can never trace,
Till we behold him face to face.

4 O let me climb those higher skies,
Where storms and darkness never rise:
There he displays his power abroad,
And shines, and reigns, th'incarnate God!

Incarnation and Advent.

MISSIONARY CHANT. L. M. — CH. ZEUNER.

1. When marshalled on the night-ly plain, The glittering host be-stud the sky; One star a-lone of all the train Can fix the sin-ner's wandering eye.

153
H. K. White.

When marshalled on the nightly plain,
 The glittering host bestud the sky;
One star alone of all the train
 Can fix the sinner's wandering eye.

2 Hark! hark! to God the chorus breaks,
 From every host, from every gem;
But one alone the Saviour speaks,
 It is the Star of Bethlehem.

3 Once on the raging seas I rode,
 The storm was loud, the night was dark,
The ocean yawned, and rudely blowed
 The wind that tossed my foundering bark.

4 Deep horror then my vitals froze;
 Death-struck, I ceased the tide to stem;
When suddenly a star arose,
 It was the Star of Bethlehem.

5 It was my guide, my light, my all,
 It bade my dark forebodings cease;
And, through the storm and danger's thrall,
 It led me to the port of peace.

6 Now safely moored, my perils o'er,
 I'll sing, first in night's diadem,
Forever and for evermore,
 The Star, the Star of Bethlehem.

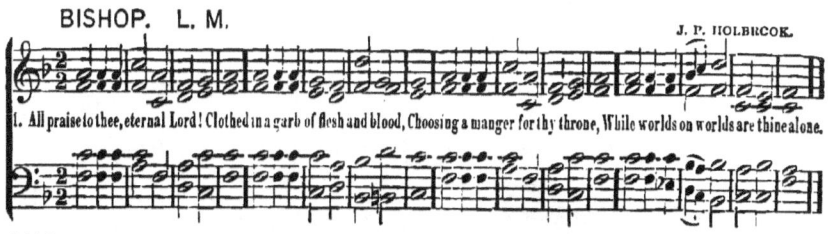

BISHOP. L. M. — J. P. HOLBROOK.

1. All praise to thee, eternal Lord! Clothed in a garb of flesh and blood, Choosing a manger for thy throne, While worlds on worlds are thine alone.

154
Luther.

All praise to thee, eternal Lord!
Clothed in a garb of flesh and blood,
Choosing a manger for thy throne,
While worlds on worlds are thine alone.

2 A little child, thou art our guest,
That little ones in thee may rest;
Forlorn and lowly is thy birth,
That we may rise to heaven from earth.

3 Thou comest in the darksome night
To make us children of the light,—
To make us, in the realms divine,
Like thine own angels round thee shine.

4 All this for us thy love hath done,
By this to thee our love is won;
For this we tune our cheerful lays,
And shout our thanks in ceaseless praise.

CHRIST.

LANCASHIRE. 7s, 6s.   H. SMART.

155
J. M. Neale, Tr.

The Word is made incarnate,
  And yet remains on high;
And cherubim sing anthems
  To shepherds, from the sky.
And we with them triumphant,
  Repeat the hymn again:
"To God on high be glory,
  And peace on earth to men!"

2 Since all he came to ransom,
  By all be he adored,
The Infant born in Bethlehem,
  The Saviour and the Lord!
And idol forms shall perish,
  And error shall decay;
And Christ shall wield his sceptre,
  Our Lord and God for aye.

FERGUSON. S. M.   G. KINGSLEY.

156
H. Bonar.

Jesus, the Christ of God!
  The Father's blessed Son!
The Father's bosom thine abode,
  The Father's love thine own.
2 God, and yet man, thou art;
  True God, true man art thou;
Of man, and of man's earth, a part,
  One with us thou art now.

3 To thee, the Christ of God,
  Thy saints exulting sing;
The bearer of our heavy load,
  Our own anointed King.
4 Rest of the weary, thou!
  To thee our rest we come;
In thee to find our dwelling now,
  Our everlasting home.

Incarnation and Advent.

157
God from on high hath heard!
Let sighs and sorrows cease;
The skies unfold, and lo!
Descends the gift of peace!

2 Hark! on the midnight air,
Celestial voices swell;
The hosts of heaven proclaim
"God comes on earth to dwell!"

3 Haste with the shepherds; see
The mystery of grace:
A manger-bed, a child,
Is all the eye can trace.

4 But Faith can pierce the cloud
Which shrouds his glory now;
And hails him God, and Lord,
To whom all creatures bow.

158
W. C. Dix.

As with gladness men of old
Did the guiding star behold;
As with joy they hailed its light,
Leading onward, beaming bright;
So, most gracious Lord, may we
Evermore be led to thee.

2 As with joyful steps they sped
To that lowly manger-bed;
There to bend the knee before
Him whom heaven and earth adore;
So may we with willing feet
Ever seek the mercy-seat.

3 As they offered gifts most rare
At that manger rude and bare;
So may we with holy joy,
Pure and free from sin's alloy,
All our costliest treasures bring,
Christ! to thee, our heavenly King.

4 Holy Jesus, every day
Keep us in the narrow way;
And, when earthly things are past,
Bring our ransomed souls at last
Where they need no star to guide,
Where no clouds thy glory hide.

CHRIST.

ANTIOCH. C. M.
HANDEL. ARR. BY L. MASON.

159   *I. Watts.*

Joy to the world, the Lord is come:
Let earth receive her King;
Let every heart prepare him room,
And heaven and nature sing.

2 Joy to the earth, the Saviour reigns:
Let men their songs employ;
While fields and floods, rocks, hills, and
Repeat the sounding joy. [plains,

3 No more let sins and sorrows grow,
Nor thorns infest the ground:
He comes to make his blessings flow
Far as the curse is found.

4 He rules the world with truth and grace,
And makes the nations prove
The glories of his righteousness,
And wonders of his love.

NEWBOLD. C. M.
G. KINGSLEY.

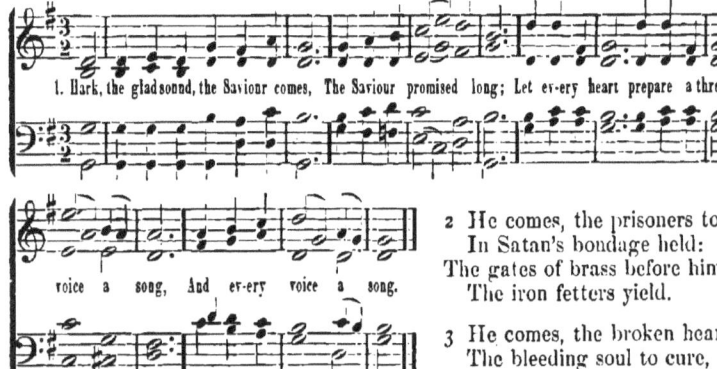

160   *P. Doddridge.*

Hark, the glad sound, the Saviour comes,
The Saviour promised long;
Let every heart prepare a throne,
And every voice a song.

2 He comes, the prisoners to release
In Satan's bondage held:
The gates of brass before him burst,
The iron fetters yield.

3 He comes, the broken heart to bind,
The bleeding soul to cure,
And with the treasures of his grace
Enrich the humble poor.

4 Our glad hosannas, Prince of Peace,
Thy welcome shall proclaim,
And heaven's eternal arches ring
With thy beloved name.

Incarnation and Advent. 85

CHRISTMAS. C. M. — HANDEL.

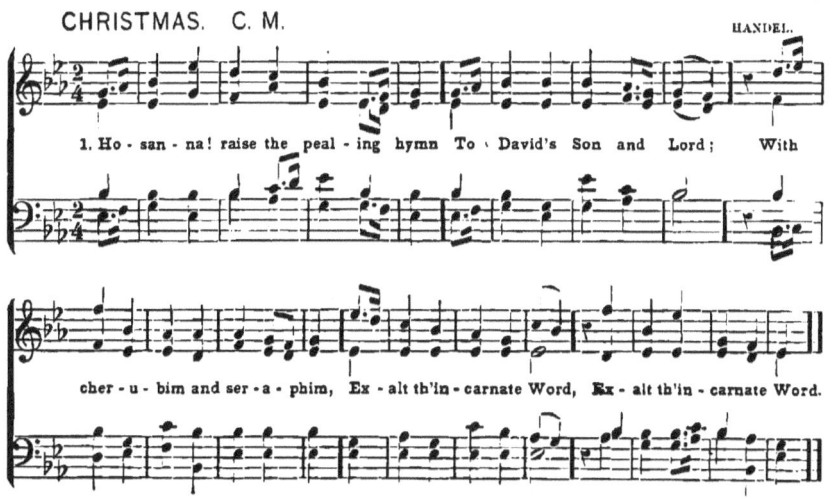

161 *W. H. Havergal.*

Hosanna! raise the pealing hymn
To David's Son and Lord;
With cherubim and seraphim,
Exalt th' incarnate Word.

2 Hosanna! Sovereign, Prophet, Priest!
How vast thy gifts, how free!
Thy blood, our life; thy word, our feast;
Thy name, our only plea.

3 Hosanna, Master, here we bring
Our offerings to thy throne,
Not gold, nor myrrh, nor mortal thing,
But hearts to be thine own.

162 *J. Morrison.*

To us a Child of hope is born,
To us a Son is given;
Him shall the tribes of earth obey,
Him all the hosts of heaven.

2 His name shall be the Prince of Peace,
For evermore adored;
The Wonderful, the Counselor,
The great and mighty Lord!

3 His power, increasing, still shall spread;
His reign no end shall know:
Justice shall guard his throne above,
And peace abound below.

163 *Tate-Brady.*

While shepherds watched their flocks by
night,
All seated on the ground,
The angel of the Lord came down,
And glory shone around.

2 "Fear not," said he,—for mighty dread
Had seized their troubled mind,—
"Glad tidings of great joy I bring,
To you and all mankind.

3 "To you, in David's town this day,
Is born of David's line,
The Saviour, who is Christ, the Lord,
And this shall be the sign;—

4 "The heavenly babe you there shall find
To human view displayed,
And meanly wrapped in swathing bands,
And in a manger laid."

5 Thus spake the seraph—and forthwith
Appeared a shining throng
Of angels praising God, who thus
Addressed their joyful song:—

6 "All glory be to God on high,
And to the earth be peace;
Good-will henceforth from heaven to men
Begin, and never cease!"

86 CHRIST.

BEECHER. C. M.   QUARTET & CHORUS CHOIR.
J. P. HOLBROOK.

164
E. H. Sears.

It came upon the midnight clear,
  That glorious song of old,
From angels bending near the earth,
  To touch their harps of gold:
"Peace on the earth, good will to men
  From heaven's all gracious King."
The world in solemn stillness lay
  To hear the angels sing.

2 Still through the cloven skies they come,
  With peaceful wings unfurled;
And still their heavenly music floats
  O'er all the weary world:
Above its sad and lowly plains
  They bend on hovering wing,
And ever o'er its Babel sounds
  The blessed angels sing.

3 O ye, beneath life's crushing load
  Whose forms are bending low,
Who toil along the climbing way,
  With painful steps and slow,—
Look up; for glad and golden hours
  Come swiftly on the wing:
O rest beside the weary road,
  And hear the angels sing.

4 For lo, the days are hastening on
  By prophet bards foretold,
When with the ever circling years
  Comes round the age of gold:
When Peace shall over all the earth
  Its ancient splendors fling,
And the whole world give back the song
  Which now the angels sing.

Incarnation and Advent. 87

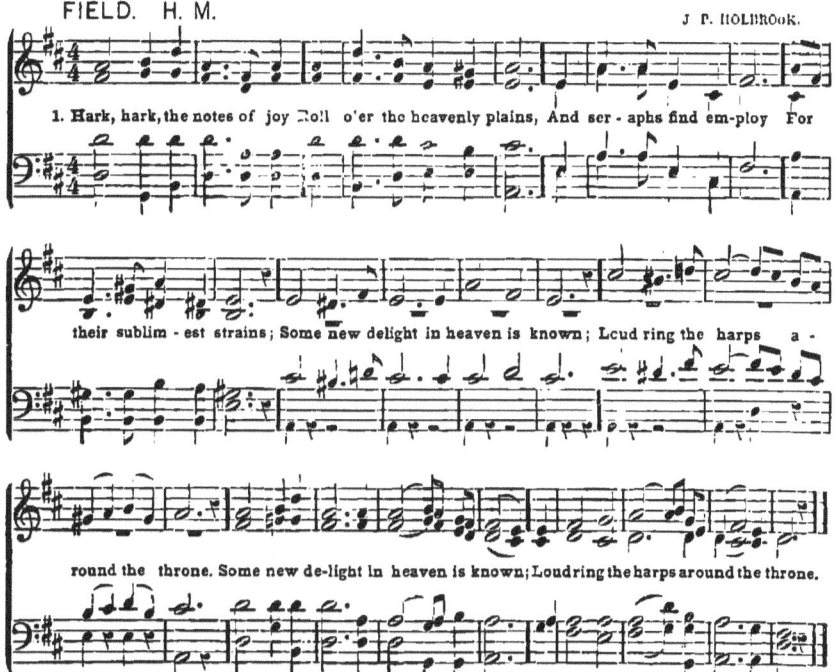

165 *A. Reed.*

Hark, hark, the notes of joy
  Roll o'er the heavenly plains,
And seraphs find employ
  For their sublimest strains;
Some new delight in heaven is known;
Loud ring the harps around the throne.

2 Hark, hark, the sounds draw nigh,
  The joyful hosts descend;
Jesus forsakes the sky,
  To earth his footsteps bend;
He comes to bless our fallen race,
He comes with messages of grace.

3 Bear, bear the tidings round;
  Let every mortal know
What love in God is found;
  What pity he can show:
Ye winds that blow, ye waves that roll,
Bear the glad news from pole to pole.

4 Strike, strike the harps again,
  To great Immanuel's name;
Arise ye sons of men,
  And all his grace proclaim:
Angels and men, wake every string,
'Tis God the Saviour's praise we sing.

166 *H. Bonar.*

Lo, God, our God, has come!
  To us a child is born,
  To us a Son is given;
Bless, bless the blessed morn,
O happy, lowly, lofty birth,
Now God, our God, has come to earth.

2 Rejoice, our God has come,
  In love and lowliness;
The Son of God has come,
  The sons of men to bless:
God with us now descends to dwell,
God in our flesh, Immanuel.

3 Praise ye the Word made flesh!
  True God, true man is he:
Praise ye the Christ of God!
  To whom all glory be:
Praise ye the Lamb that once was slain,
Praise ye the King that comes to reign.

88 CHRIST.

MENDELSSOHN, 7s.

Organ pedal.

167
C. Wesley.

Hark! the herald angels sing
Glory to the new-born King;
Peace on earth, and mercy mild,
God and sinners reconciled!
Joyful, all ye nations, rise,
Join the triumph of the skies;
With th' angelic host proclaim,
Christ is born in Bethlehem!

2 Christ, by highest heaven adored;
Christ the everlasting Lord;
Late in time behold him come,
Offspring of the virgin's womb:
Veil'd in flesh the Godhead see;
Hail, Incarnate Deity,
Pleased as man with men to dwell!
Jesus, our Immanuel!

3 Hail! the heaven-born Prince of peace!
Hail! the Sun of righteousness!
Light and life to all he brings,
Risen with healing in his wings.
Mild he lays his glory by,
Born that man no more may die:
Born to raise the sons of earth,
Born to give them second birth.

Incarnation and Advent.   89

MOZART. 7s.

1. Hark! the her-ald an-gels sing, "Glo-ry to the new-born King! Peace on earth, and mercy mild; God and sin-ners re-conciled, God and sin-ners re-con-ciled."

HANOVER. 11s, 10s.

1. Brightest and best of the sons of the morning, Dawn on our dark-ness and lend us thine aid; Star of the east, the ho-ri-zon a-dorn-ing, Guide where our in-fant Re-deem-er is laid.

168 R. Heber.

BRIGHTEST and best of the sons of the morning, [aid;
Dawn on our darkness and lend us thine
Star of the east, the horizon adorning,
Guide where our infant Redeemer is laid.

2 Cold on his cradle the dew-drops are
shining, [stall;
Low lies his head with the beasts of the
Angels adore him in slumber reclining,
Maker, and Monarch, and Saviour of all.

3 Say, shall we yield him in costly devotion,
Odors of Edom, and offerings divine,
Gems of the mountain, and pearls of the ocean,
Myrrh from the forest, or gold from the mine?

4 Vainly we offer each ample oblation;
Vainly with gifts would his favor secure;
Richer by far is the heart's adoration;
Dearer to God are the prayers of the poor.

CHRIST.

90. SALTZBURG. 8s, 7s.
ARR. G. KINGSLEY.

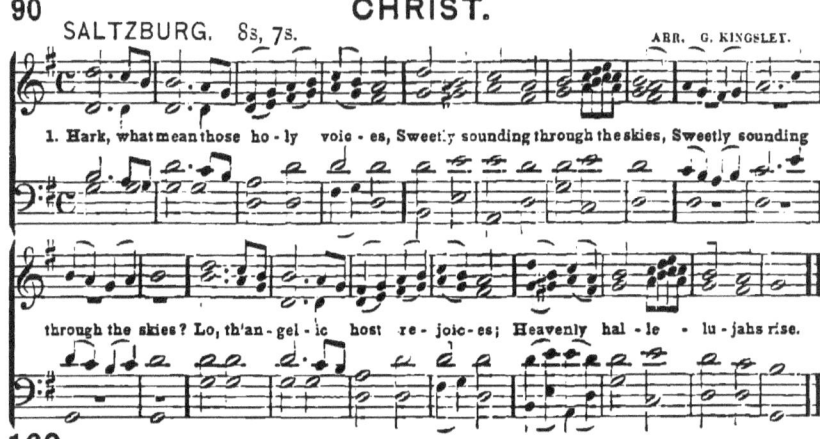

169
J. Cawood.

HARK, what mean those holy voices,
Sweetly sounding through the skies?
Lo, the angelic host rejoices;
Heavenly hallelujahs rise.

2 Hear them tell the wondrous story,
Hear them chant in hymns of joy,
"Glory in the highest! glory!
Glory be to God most high!

3 "Peace on earth; good will from heaven,
Reaching far as man is found."
"Souls redeemed, and sins forgiven,"
Loud our golden harps shall sound.

4 Christ is born, the great Anointed;
Heaven and earth his praises sing;
O, receive whom God appointed,
For your Prophet, Priest, and King.

RATHBUN. 8s, 7s.
I. CONKEY.

170
C. Wesley.

COME, thou long-expected Jesus,
Born to set thy people free:
From our fears and sins release us,
Let us find our rest in thee.

2 Israel's Strength and Consolation,
Hope of all the earth thou art;
Dear Desire of every nation,
Joy of every longing heart.

3 Born thy people to deliver,
Born a Child, and yet a King,
Born to reign in us forever,
Now thy gracious kingdom bring.

4 By thine own eternal Spirit,
Rule in all our hearts alone;
By thine all-sufficient merit,
Raise us to thy glorious throne.

His Life our Example.

BELMONT. C. M. — S. WEBBE.

1. O Lord, we would the path re-trace Which thou on earth hast trod; To man thy wondrous love and grace, Thy faith-ful-ness to God.

171 *J. G. Deck.*

O Lord, we would the path retrace
Which thou on earth hast trod;
To man thy wondrous love and grace,
Thy faithfulness to God.

2 Thy love, by man so sorely tried,
Proved stronger than the grave;
The very spear that pierced thy side
Drew forth the blood to save.

3 Faithful amid unfaithfulness,
'Mid darkness only light,
Thou did'st thy Father's name confess,
And in his will delight.

4 Unmoved by Satan's subtle wiles,
Or suffering, shame, and loss,
Thy path, uncheered by earthly smiles,
Led only to the cross.

5 Give us thy meek, thy lowly mind:
We would obedient be;
And all our rest and pleasure find
In fellowship with thee.

172 *C. Wesley.*

Servant, at once, and Lord of all
While dwelling here below,
Thou did'st not scorn our earthly toil,
And weariness to know.

2 Thy bright example I pursue,
To thee in all things rise,
Let all I think, or speak, or do,
Be one great sacrifice.

3 Careless through outward cares I go,
From all distraction free;
My hands are but engaged below,
My heart is still with thee.

4 O when wilt thou, my life, appear?
Then gladly will I cry,
"'Tis done, the work thou gav'st me here,
'Tis finished, Lord," and die!

173 *S. Longfellow.*

The loving Friend to all who bowed
Beneath life's weary load,
From lips baptized in fervent prayer
His consolations flowed.

2 The faithful Witness to the truth,
His just rebuke was hurled
Out from a heart that burned to break
The fetters of the world.

3 No hollow rite, no lifeless creed,
His piercing glance could bear;
But longing hearts which sought him found
That God and heaven were there.

CHRIST.

PALMER. C. M.
J. P. HOLBROOK.

174
J. H. Gurney.

Lord, as to thy dear cross we flee,
 And pray to be forgiven,
So let thy life our pattern be,
 And form our souls for heaven.

2 Help us, through good report and ill,
 Our daily cross to bear;
Like thee, to do our Father's will,
 Our brother's griefs to share.

3 Let grace our selfishness expel,
 Our earthliness refine;
And kindness in our bosoms dwell
 As free and true as thine.

4 Kept peaceful in the midst of strife,
 Forgiving and forgiven,
O may we lead the pilgrim's life,
 And follow thee to heaven!

SIMPSON. C. M.
L. SPOHR.

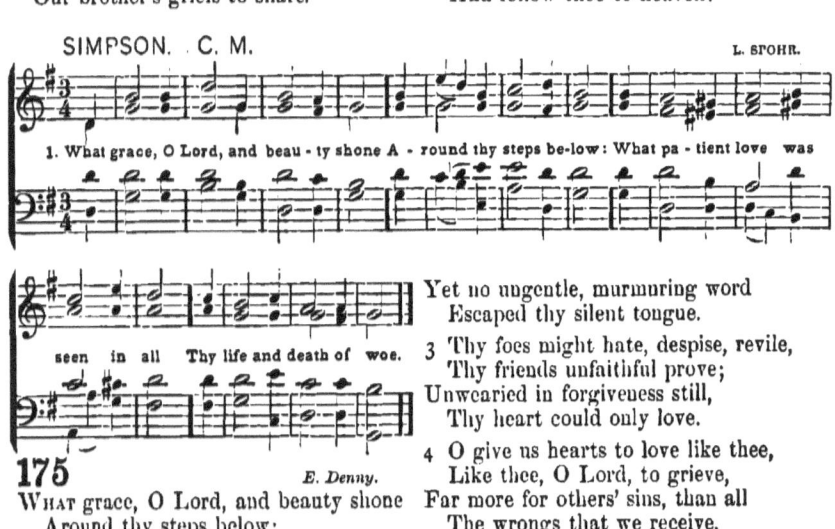

175
E. Denny.

What grace, O Lord, and beauty shone
 Around thy steps below:
What patient love was seen in all
 Thy life and death of woe.

2 Forever on thy burdened heart
 A weight of sorrow hung;
Yet no ungentle, murmuring word
 Escaped thy silent tongue.

3 Thy foes might hate, despise, revile,
 Thy friends unfaithful prove;
Unwearied in forgiveness still,
 Thy heart could only love.

4 O give us hearts to love like thee,
 Like thee, O Lord, to grieve,
Far more for others' sins, than all
 The wrongs that we receive.

5 One with thyself, may every eye
 In us, thy brethren, see
That gentleness and grace that springs
 From union, Lord with thee.

His Life our Example.   93

BURLINGTON. C. M.   J. F. BURROWES.

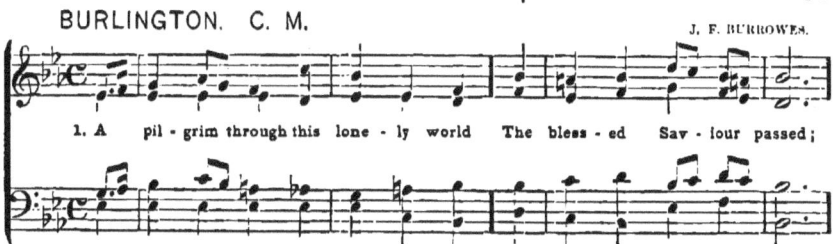

176   *E. Denny.*
A PILGRIM through this lonely world,
  The blessèd Saviour passed;
A mourner all his life was he,
  A dying Lamb at last.

2 That tender heart that felt for all,
    For all its life-blood gave;
  It found on earth no resting place,
    Save only in the grave.

3 Such was our Lord; and shall we fear
    The cross with all its scorn?
  Or love a faithless, evil world,
    That wreathed his brow with thorn?

4 No, facing all its frowns or smiles,
    Like him, obedient still,
  We homeward press, through storm or calm,
    To Zion's blessed hill.

177
How wondrous was the burning zeal
  Which filled the Master's breast,
When, all his sufferings full in view,
  To Salem's towers he pressed!

2 Dear Lord! no tongue can duly tell
    Thy love's prevailing might;
  No thought can comprehend its length,
    And breadth, and depth, and height!

3 Yet grant that we may follow thee
    Through all thine hours of scorn;
  And learn with thee to watch and pray,
    With thee to weep and mourn.

4 And still, O blessèd Jesus Christ!
    The more thy cross we see,
  The more may each exclaim with joy,
    The Saviour died for me!

178   *J. G. Whittier.*
CHRIST is his own best evidence
  His witness is within;
In joy of inward peace, or sense
  Of sorrow over sin.

2 And warm, sweet, tender, even yet
    A present help is he;
  And faith has yet its Olivet,
    And love its Galilee.

3 Through him the first fond prayers are
    Our lips of childhood frame;   [said,
  The last low whispers of our dead
    Are burdened with his name.

4 O Lord and Master of us all,
    Whate'er our name or sign,
  We own thy sway, we hear thy call,
    We test our lives by thine!

CHRIST.

ODEON. L. M.
Andante.
ARR. MENDELSOHN.

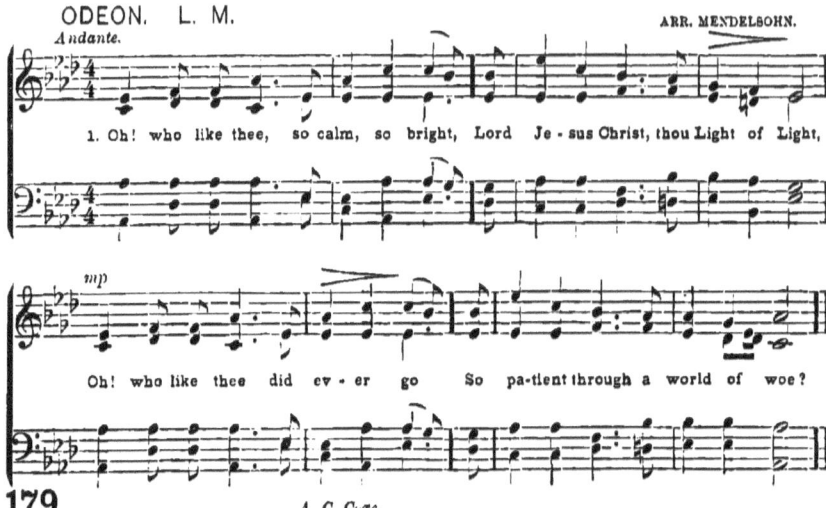

179
A. C. Coxe.

O who like thee, so calm, so bright,
Lord Jesus Christ, thou Light of Light,
O who like thee did ever go
So patient through a world of woe?

2 O who like thee so humbly bore
The scorn, the scoffs of men, before;
So meek, so lowly—yet so high,
So glorious in humility?

3 Through all thy life-long weary years,
A man of sorrows and of tears,
The cross, where all our sins were laid
Upon thy bending shoulders weighed;

4 And death, that sets the prisoner free,
Was pang and scoff and scorn to thee;
Yet love through all thy torture glowed,
And mercy with thy life-blood flowed.

5 O wondrous Lord, our souls would be
Still more and more conformed to thee;
And learn of thee, the lowly One,
And like thee, all our journey run.

6 Be with us as we onward go;
Illumine all our way of woe;
And grant us ever on the road
To trace the footsteps of our God.

ST. ALBAN. L. M.
ST. ALBAN'S BOOK.

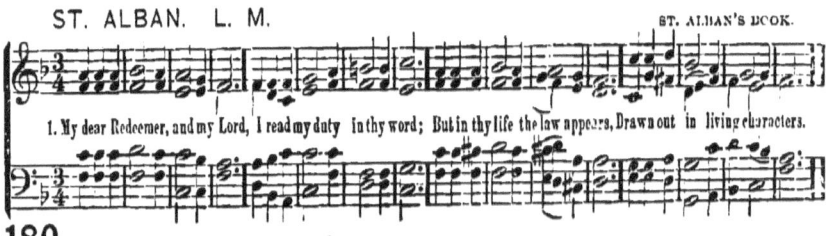

180
I. Watts.

My dear Redeemer and my Lord,
I read my duty in thy word;
But in thy life the law appears,
Drawn out in living characters.

2 Such was thy truth, and such thy zeal,
Such deference to thy Father's will,
Such love, and meekness so divine,
I would transcribe and make them mine.

3 Cold mountains and the midnight air
Witnessed the fervor of thy prayer;
The desert thy temptations knew,
Thy conflict and thy victory too.

4 Be thou my pattern; make me bear
More of thy gracious image here;
Then God, the Judge, shall own my name
Among the followers of the Lamb.

Example—Teaching—Miracles.

SEASONS. L. M.   PLEYEL.

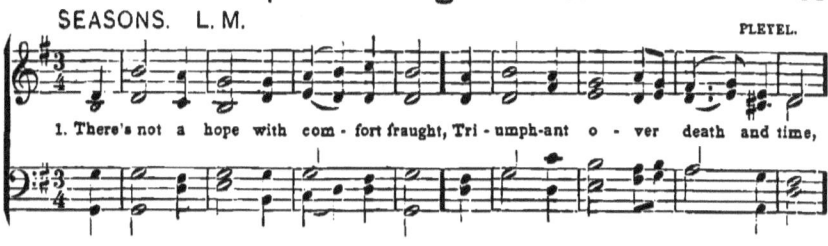

1. There's not a hope with com-fort fraught, Tri-umph-ant o-ver death and time,

But Je-sus min-gles in the thought, Fore-run-ner of our course sublime.

181   *E. Taylor.*

There's not a hope with comfort fraught,
  Triumphant over death and time,
But Jesus mingles in the thought,
  Forerunner of our course sublime.

2 His image meets me in the hour
  Of joy, and brightens every smile;
I see him, when the tempests lower,
  Each terror soothe, each grief beguile.

3 I see him in the daily round
  Of social duty, calm and meek;
With him I tread the hallowed ground,
  Communion with my God to seek.

4 I see his pitying, gentle eye,
  When lonely want appeals for aid;
I hear him in the frequent sigh,
  That mourns the waste which sin has made.

5 I meet him at the lonely tomb;
  I weep where Jesus wept before;
And there, above the grave's dark gloom,
  I see him rise, and weep no more.

182   *J. F. Thrupp.*

Awhile in spirit, Lord, to thee
  Into the desert would we flee;
Awhile upon the barren steep
  Thy fast with thee in spirit keep;

2 Awhile from thy temptation learn
  The daily snares of sin to spurn;
And in our hearts to feel and own
  Man liveth not by bread alone.

3 And when at thy command we pray,
  Give us our bread from day to day,
May we with thee, O Christ, be fed,
  Thou Word of God, thou living Bread.

4 Incarnate Lord, we come to thee,
  Thou knowest our infirmity;
Be thou our helper in the strife,
  Be thou our true, our inward Life.

183   *J. Bowring.*

How sweetly flowed the gospel's sound
  From lips of gentleness and grace,
When listening thousands gathered round,
  And joy and reverence filled the place.

2 From heaven he came, of heaven he spoke,
  To heaven he led his followers' way;
Dark clouds of gloomy night he broke,
  Unveiling an immortal day.

3 "Come, wanderers, to my Father's home,
  Come, all ye weary ones, and rest:"
Yes, sacred Teacher, we will come,
  Obey thee, love thee, and be blest.

CHRIST.

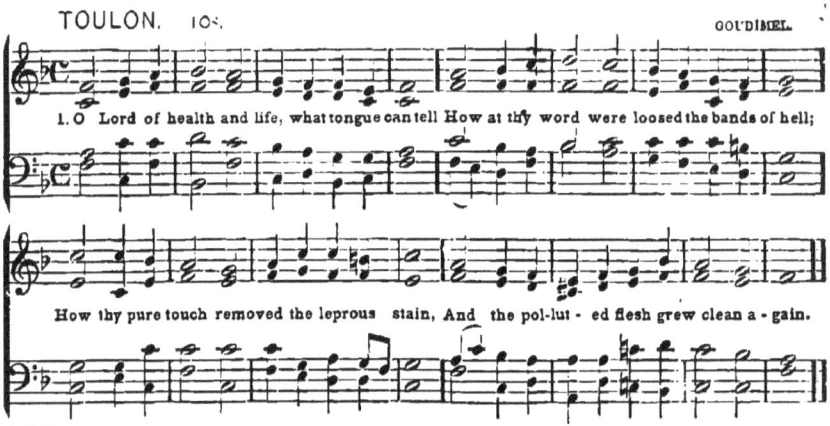

TOULON. 10s.   GOUDIMEL.

1. O Lord of health and life, what tongue can tell How at thy word were loosed the bands of hell; How thy pure touch removed the leprous stain, And the pol-lut-ed flesh grew clean a-gain.

184

1 O Lord of health and life, what tongue can tell
How at thy word were loosed the bands of hell;
How thy pure touch removed the leprous stain,
And the polluted flesh grew clean again?

2 O wash our hearts, restore the contrite soul,
Stretch forth thy healing hand and make us whole;
O bend our stubborn knees to kneel to thee;
Speak but the word, and we once more are free.

3 Yea, Lord, we claim the promise of thy love,
Thy love which can all guilt, all pain remove;
Nigh to our souls thy great salvation bring,
Then sickness hath no pang, and death no sting.

4 We hail this pledge in all thy deeds of grace;
As once disease and sorrow fled thy face,
So, when that face again unveiled we see,
Sickness and tears and death no more shall be.

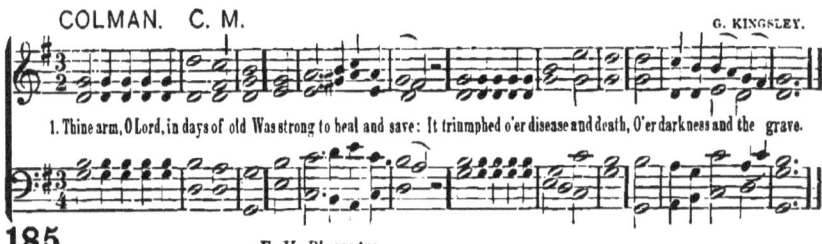

COLMAN. C. M.   G. KINGSLEY.

1. Thine arm, O Lord, in days of old Was strong to heal and save: It triumphed o'er disease and death, O'er darkness and the grave.

185
E. H. Plumptre.

1 Thine arm, O Lord, in days of old
Was strong to heal and save;
It triumphed o'er disease and death,
O'er darkness and the grave.

2 To thee they went, the blind, the dumb,
The palsied and the lame,
The leper with his tainted life,
The sick with fevered frame.

3 And lo, thy touch brought life and health,
Gave speech and strength and sight;
And youth renewed and frenzy calmed
Owned thee, the Lord of Light.

4 Be thou our great Deliverer still,
Thou Lord of life and death;
Restore and quicken, soothe and bless,
With thine almighty breath.

GALILEE. 8s, 3.

186
G. Thring.

Fierce raged the tempest o'er the deep,
Watch did thine anxious servants keep,
But thou wast wrapped in guileless sleep,
  Calm and still.

2 "Save, Lord, we perish," was their cry,
"O save us in our agony!"
Thy word above the storm rose high,
  "Peace, be still."

3 The wild winds hushed; the angry deep
Sank, like a little child, to sleep;
The sullen billows ceased to leap,
  At thy will.

4 So, when our life is clouded o'er,
And storm-winds drift us from the shore,
Say, lest we sink to rise no more,
  "Peace, be still."

ALL SAINTS. L. M.
WILLIAM KNAPP.

187
I. Watts.

Behold, the blind their sight receive;
Behold, the dead awake and live;
The dumb speak wonders, and the lame
Leap like the hart, and bless his name.

2 Thus doth the eternal Spirit own
And seal the mission of the Son;
The Father vindicates his cause,
While he hangs bleeding on the cross.

3 He dies, the heavens in mourning stood;
He rises, the triumphant God;
Behold the Lord ascending high,
No more to bleed, no more to die.

4 Hence, and for ever, from my heart,
I bid my doubts and fears depart;
And to those hands my soul resign,
Which bear credentials so divine.

CHRIST.

98. ST. EDMUNDS. L. M. — HAYDN.

1. O wondrous type, O vision fair, Of glory that the Church shall share,

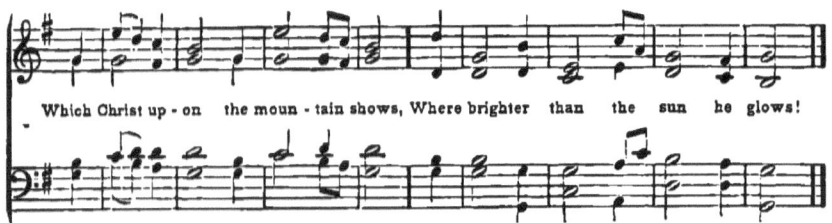

Which Christ up-on the moun-tain shows, Where brighter than the sun he glows!

188 Transfiguration. *J. M. Neale, Tr.*

O WONDROUS type, O vision fair,
Of glory that the Church shall share,
Which Christ upon the mountain shows,
Where brighter than the sun he glows!

2 With shining face and bright array,
Christ deigns to manifest to-day
What glory shall be theirs above,
Who joy in God with perfect love.

3 And faithful hearts are raised on high
By this great vision's mystery;
For which in joyful strains we raise
The voice of prayer, the hymn of praise.

4 O Father, with the Eternal Son,
And Holy Spirit, ever One,
Vouchsafe to bring us by thy grace
To see thy glory face to face.

189 Triumphal Entry. *C. Tr.*

HAIL, Israel's King! Hail, David's Son!
Hail, thou that in Jehovah's name
Didst come thy people to redeem,
And comest now thy crown to claim!

2 Then, in thy way to Salem's courts,
They met thee with triumphal palms;
Now, for thy glad return we watch
With longing prayers and vows and
 psalms

3 Then, from the shouts of fickle joy
Thou passedst to thy cross, thy grave;
Now, from the dawn of endless day
We welcome him that comes to save.

4 To thee, Redeemer, Saviour, King,
To thee be glory, honor, praise!
At thine approach, with joy inspired,
Thy children loud hosannas raise.

190 Triumphal Entry. *H. H. Milman.*

RIDE on, ride on in majesty!
Hark, all the tribes Hosanna cry;
O Saviour meek, pursue thy road
With palms and scattered garments
 strowed.

2 Ride on, ride on in majesty!
In lowly pomp, ride on to die;
O Christ, thy triumphs now begin
O'er captive death and conquered sin.

3 Ride on, ride on in majesty!
Thy last and fiercest strife is nigh:
The Father on his sapphire Throne
Expects his own anointed Son.

4 Ride on, ride on in majesty!
In lowly pomp, ride on to die:
Bow thy meek head to mortal pain,
Then take, O God, thy power, and reign.

The Garden—the Cross. 99

SOLITUDE. L. M. — V. C. TAYLOR.

191
W. B. Tappan.

'Tis midnight; and on Olive's brow
The star is dimmed that lately shone:
'Tis midnight; in the garden now,
The suffering Saviour prays alone.

2 'Tis midnight; and from all removed,
The Saviour wrestles lone with fears;
Ev'n that disciple whom he loved
Heeds not his Master's grief and tears.

3 'Tis midnight; and for others' guilt
The Man of Sorrows weeps in blood;
Yet he that hath in anguish knelt
Is not forsaken by his God.

4 'Tis midnight; and from ether-plains
Is borne the song that angels know;
Unheard by mortals are the strains
That sweetly soothe the Saviour's woe

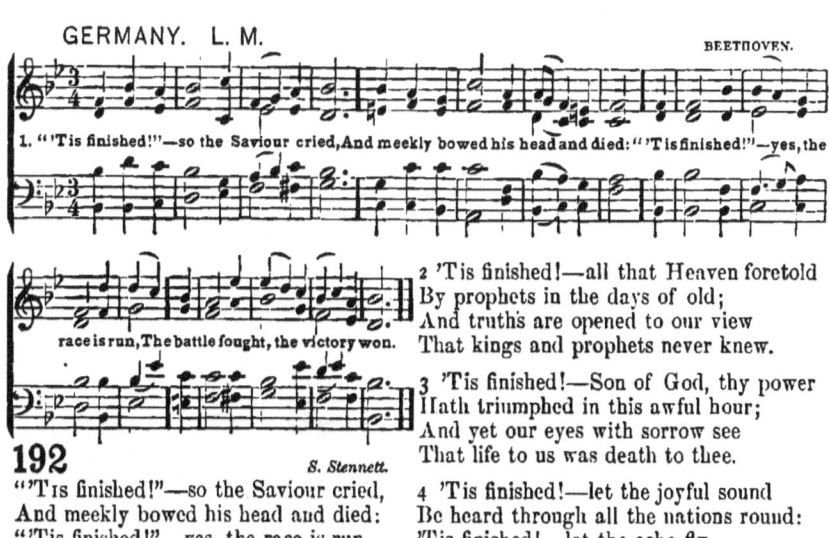

GERMANY. L. M. — BEETHOVEN.

192
S. Stennett.

"'Tis finished!"—so the Saviour cried,
And meekly bowed his head and died:
"'Tis finished!"—yes, the race is run,
The battle fought, the victory won.

2 'Tis finished!—all that Heaven foretold
By prophets in the days of old;
And truths are opened to our view
That kings and prophets never knew.

3 'Tis finished!—Son of God, thy power
Hath triumphed in this awful hour;
And yet our eyes with sorrow see
That life to us was death to thee.

4 'Tis finished!—let the joyful sound
Be heard through all the nations round:
'Tis finished!—let the echo fly
Thro' heaven and hell, thro' earth and sky

CHRIST.

CULBERTSON. 7s, 6l.

1. Go to dark Gethse-ma-ne, Ye that feel the tempter's power; Your Redeemer's conflict see, Watch with him one bitter hour: Turn not from his griefs away, Learn of Jesus Christ to pray.

193
J. Montgomery.

Go to dark Gethsemane,
  Ye that feel the tempter's power;
Your Redeemer's conflict see,
  Watch with him one bitter hour:
Turn not from his griefs away,
Learn of Jesus Christ to pray.

2 Follow to the judgment-hall,
  View the Lord of life arraigned;
O the wormwood and the gall!
  O the pangs his soul sustained!
Shun not suffering, shame, or loss;
Learn of Him to bear the cross.

3 Calvary's mournful mountain climb;
  There, adoring at his feet,
Mark the miracle of time,
  God's own sacrifice complete:
"It is finished," hear the cry;
Learn of Jesus Christ to die.

4 Early hasten to the tomb,
  Where they laid his breathless clay:
All is solitude and gloom;
  Who hath taken him away?
Christ is risen; he meets our eyes;
Saviour, teach us so to rise.

GETHSEMANE. 7s, 6l.   R. REDHEAD.

1. Go to dark Geth-se-ma-ne, Ye that feel the tempter's power; Your Redeemer's conflict see, Watch with him one bit-ter hour: Turn not from his griefs a-way, Learn of Jesus Christ to pray.

His Sufferings and Death. 101

CUTLER. 7s. 6l. (A.)

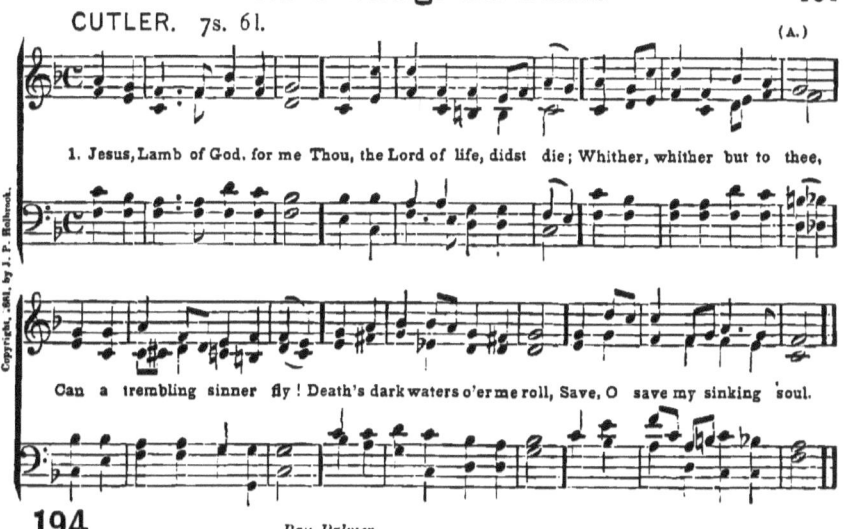

1. Jesus, Lamb of God, for me Thou, the Lord of life, didst die; Whither, whither but to thee, Can a trembling sinner fly! Death's dark waters o'er me roll, Save, O save my sinking soul.

194
Ray Palmer.

Jesus, Lamb of God, for me
 Thou, the Lord of life, didst die;
Whither, whither but to thee,
 Can a trembling sinner fly?
Death's dark waters o'er me roll,
Save, O save my sinking soul!

2 Never bowed a martyred head,
 Weighed with equal sorrow down;
Never blood so rich was shed,
 Never king wore such a crown;
To thy cross and sacrifice
Faith now lifts her tearful eyes.

3 All my soul, by love subdued,
 Melts in deep contrition there;
By thy mighty grace renewed,
 New-born hope forbids despair:
Lord, thou canst my guilt forgive,
Thou hast bid me look and live.

4 While with broken heart I kneel,
 Sinks the inward storm to rest;
Life, immortal life I feel
 Kindled in my throbbing breast;
Thine, forever thine, I am,
Glory to the bleeding Lamb!

ROSEFIELD. 7s. 6l. C. H. A. MALAN.

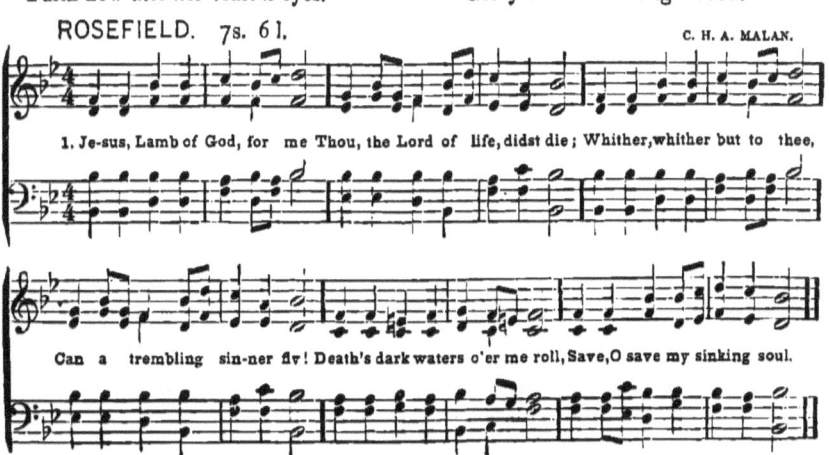

1. Je-sus, Lamb of God, for me Thou, the Lord of life, didst die; Whither, whither but to thee, Can a trembling sin-ner fly! Death's dark waters o'er me roll, Save, O save my sinking soul.

CHRIST.

GOODRICH. 11s, 5s.

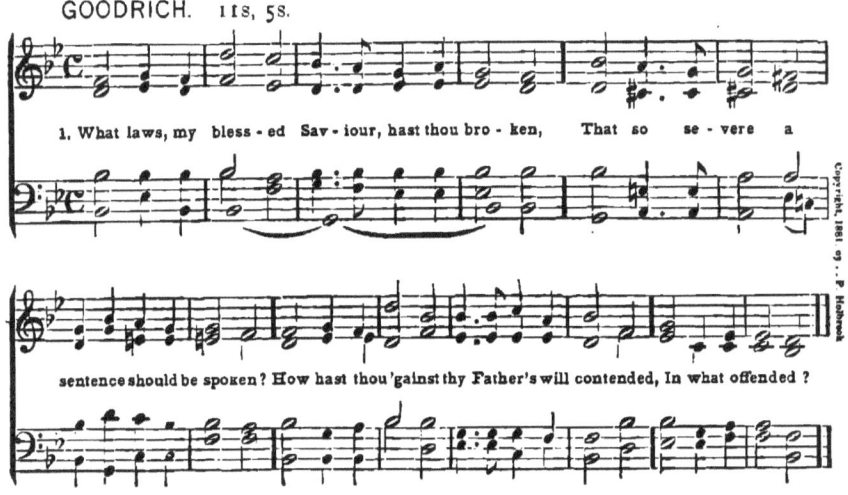

195
F. E. Cox, tr.

WHAT laws, my blessèd Saviour, hast thou broken,
That so severe a sentence should be spoken?
How hast thou 'gainst thy Father's will contended,
    In what offended?

2 With scourges, blows, and spitting, they reviled thee:
They crowned thy brow with thorns, while King they styled thee;
When, faint with pains, thy tortured body suffered,
    Then gall they offered.

3 Say! wherefore thus by woes wast thou surrounded?
Ah! Lord, for my transgressions thou wast wounded,
God took the guilt from me, who should have paid it;
    On thee he laid it.

4 How strange and marvellous was this correction!
Falls the good Shepherd in his sheep's protection;
The servants' debt behold the Master paying,
    For them obeying.

5 The righteous dies, who walked with God truehearted:
The sinner lives, who has from God departed;
By man came death, yet man its fetters breaketh;
    God it o'ertaketh.

6 But O the depth of love beyond comparing,
That brought thee down from heaven our burden bearing!
I taste all peace and joy that life can offer,
    Whilst thou must suffer!

His Sufferings and Death.

196 11s, 5s. *F. E. Cox, tr.*

Eternal King! in power and love excelling,
Fain would my heart and mouth thy praise be telling;
But how can man's weak powers at all come nigh thee,
 How magnify thee?

2 Yet this shall please thee, if devoutly trying
To keep thy laws, mine own wrong will denying,
I watch my heart, lest sin again ensnare it
 And from thee tear it.

3 But since I have not strength to flee temptation,
To crucify each sinful inclination,
O let thy Spirit, grace and strength provide me,
 And gently guide me.

4 Then shall I see thy grace, and duly prize it,
For thee renounce the world, for thee despise it;
Then of my life thy laws shall be the measure,
 Thy will my pleasure.

DULCETTA. 8s, 7s. BEETHOVEN.

1. There's a wide-ness in God's mer-cy, Like the wide-ness of the sea;
There's a kind-ness in his jus-tice, Which is more than lib-er-ty.

197 *F. W. Faber.*

There's a wideness in God's mercy,
 Like the wideness of the sea;
There's a kindness in his justice,
 Which is more than liberty.

2 There is plentiful redemption
 In the blood that has been shed;
There is joy for all the members
 In the sorrows of the Head.

3 There is welcome for the sinner,
 And more graces for the good;
There is mercy with the Saviour;
 There is healing in his blood.

4 For the love of God is broader
 Than the measure of man's mind;
And the heart of the Eternal
 Is most wonderfully kind.

5 Was there ever kindest shepherd
 Half so gentle, half so sweet
As the Saviour, who would have us
 Come and gather round his feet?

6 If our love were but more simple,
 We should take him at his word;
And our lives would be all sunshine
 In the sweetness of our Lord.

CHRIST.

DUKE STREET. L. M. — J. HATTON.

1. Come, let us sing the song of songs, The saints in heaven began the strain,
The homage which to Christ belongs: "Worthy the Lamb, for he was slain!"

198
J. Montgomery.

Come, let us sing the song of songs,
 The saints in heaven began the strain,
The homage which to Christ belongs:
 "Worthy the Lamb, for he was slain!"

2 Slain to redeem us by his blood,
 To cleanse from every sinful stain,
And make us kings and priests to God:
 "Worthy the Lamb, for he was slain!"

3 To him enthroned by filial right,
 All power in heaven and earth proclaim,
Honor, and majesty, and might:
 "Worthy the Lamb, for he was slain!"

4 Long as we live, and when we die,
 And while in heaven with him we reign,
This song our song of songs shall be:
 "Worthy the Lamb, for he was slain!"

FEDERAL STREET. L. M. — H. K. OLIVER.

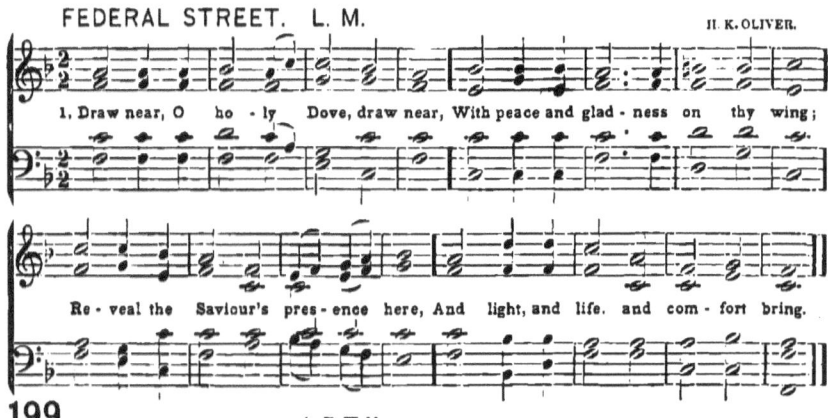

1. Draw near, O holy Dove, draw near, With peace and gladness on thy wing;
Reveal the Saviour's presence here, And light, and life, and comfort bring.

199
A. R. Wolfe.

Draw near, O holy Dove, draw near,
 With peace and gladness on thy wing;
Reveal the Saviour's presence here,
 And light, and life, and comfort bring.

2 "Eat, O my friends, drink, O beloved!"
 We hear the Master's voice exclaim:
Our hearts with new desire are moved,
 And kindled with a heavenly flame.

3 No room for doubt, no room for dread,
 Nor tears, nor groans, nor anxious sighs;
We do not mourn a Saviour dead,
 But hail him living in the skies.

4 While this we do, remembering thee,
 Dear Saviour, let our graces prove
We have thy blessèd company,
 Thy banner over us is love.

The Lord's Supper. 105

CALVARY. L. M. J. P. HOLBROOK.

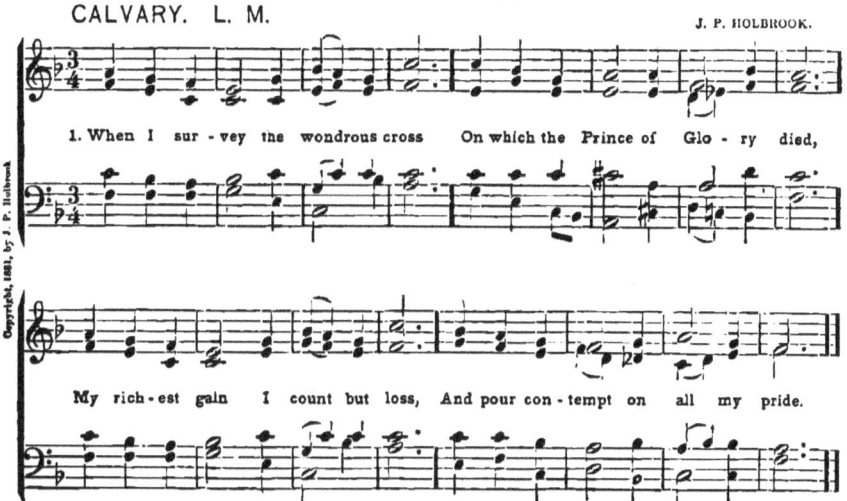

1. When I survey the wondrous cross On which the Prince of Glory died, My richest gain I count but loss, And pour contempt on all my pride.

200   *I. Watts.*

When I survey the wondrous cross
  On which the Prince of Glory died,
My richest gain I count but loss,
  And pour contempt on all my pride.

2 Forbid it, Lord, that I should boast,
  Save in the death of Christ my God;
All the vain things that charm me most—
  I sacrifice them to his blood.

3 See, from his head, his hands, his feet,
  Sorrow and love flow mingled down!
Did e'er such love and sorrow meet,
  Or thorns compose so rich a crown?

4 Were the whole realm of nature mine,
  That were an offering far too small:
Love so amazing, so divine,
  Demands my soul, my life, my all!

201   *I. Watts.*

O the sweet wonders of that cross
  Where my Redeemer loved and died:
Her noblest life my spirit draws
  From his dear wounds, and bleeding side.

2 I would forever speak his name
  In sounds to mortal ears unknown;
With angels join to praise the Lamb,
  And worship at his Father's throne.

202   *W. W. How.*

Lord Jesus, when we stand afar
  And gaze upon thy holy cross,
In love of thee and scorn of self,
  O may we count the world as loss.

2 When we behold thy bleeding wounds,
  And the rough way that thou hast trod,
Make us to hate the load of sin
  That lay so heavy on our God.

3 O holy Lord, uplifted high
  With outstretched arms, in mortal woe,
Embracing in thy wondrous love
  The sinful world that lies below.

4 Give us an ever-living faith
  To gaze beyond the things we see;
And in the mystery of thy death,
  Draw us and all men unto thee.

203   *W. H Bathurst.*

Before thy cross, my dying Lord,
  I cast my soul, and trust thy love,
Oh, here thy saving power afford,
  And seal my pardon from above!

2 Washed in thy blood, I shall be pure;
  Cheered by thy smile, shall feel no shame;
Saved by thy love, I stand secure,
  And triumph in a Saviour's name!

CHRIST.

ODEON. L. M. — ARR. MENDELSSOHN.

204   *I. Watts.*

At thy command, our dearest Lord,
  Here we attend thy dying feast;
Thy blood, like wine, adorns thy board,
  And thine own flesh feeds every guest.

2 Our faith adores thy bleeding love,
  And trusts for life in One that died;
We hope for heavenly crowns above,
  From a Redeemer crucified.

3 Let the vain world pronounce it shame,
  And fling their scandals on thy cause;
We come to boast our Saviour's name,
  And make our triumphs in his cross.

4 With joy we tell the scoffing age,
  He that was dead has left his tomb;
He lives above their utmost rage,
  And we are waiting till he come.

205   *T. H. Gill.*

Upon thy grace we banquet here;
  We know thee true, we feel thee near;
The balm of thy dear blood we bless;
  We wear thy robe of righteousness.

2 But greater shall the wonder grow,
  And mightier shall the joy o'erflow;
Upon thee, Lord, we yet shall gaze,
  And look our love in sweet amaze.

3 O make me meet for joy like this!
  O grant me grace to bear the bliss!
Now set my heart on thee below,
  No other lord or love to know.

4 Then shall I set mine eyes on thee;
  The King in all his beauty see;
And gazing on for evermore,
  Glow with the beauty I adore.

INGHAM. L. M. — L. MASON.

The Lord's Supper.

VOX JESU. 7s, 6s. — J. P. HOLBROOK.

1. We come, O only Saviour, On thee, the Lamb, to feed; Thy flesh is bread from heaven, Thy blood is drink indeed. 2. Thou standest at the altar, Thou offerest every prayer; In faith's unclouded vision, We see thee ever there.

206

We come, O only Saviour,
On thee, the Lamb, to feed;
Thy flesh is bread from heaven,
Thy blood is drink indeed.

2 Thou standest at the altar,
Thou offerest every prayer;
In faith's unclouded vision,
We see thee ever there.

3 Out of thy hand the incense
Ascends before the throne,
Where thou art interceding,
Lord Jesus, for thine own.

4 And through thy blood accepted
With thee we keep the feast;
Thou art thyself the Victim,
Thou art thyself the Priest.

KEALL. 7s, 6s. — E. & KEALL.

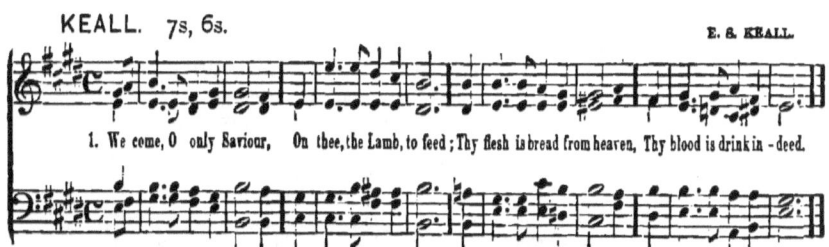

1. We come, O only Saviour, On thee, the Lamb, to feed; Thy flesh is bread from heaven, Thy blood is drink indeed.

CHRIST.

LANGRAN. 10s.   J. LANGRAN.

207
             H. BONAR.

Here, O my Lord, I see thee face to face;
   Here would I touch and handle things unseen;
Here grasp with firmer hand the eternal grace,
   And all my weariness upon thee lean.

2 Here would I feed upon the bread of God;
   Here drink with thee the royal wine of heaven;
Here would I lay aside each earthly load,
   Here taste afresh the calm of sin forgiven.

3 I have no help but thine; nor do I need
   Another arm save thine to lean upon:
It is enough, my Lord, enough, indeed;
   My strength is in thy might,—thy might alone.

4 Mine is the sin, but thine the righteousness;
   Mine is the guilt, but thine the cleansing blood;
Here is my robe, my refuge and my peace,—
   Thy blood, thy righteousness, O Lord my God.

5 Feast after feast thus comes and passes by;
   Yet, passing, points to the glad Feast above,
Giving sweet foretaste of the festal joy,
   The Lamb's great Bridal Feast of bliss and love.

The Lord's Supper.

SACRAMENT. 8s, 4s — J. P. HOLBROOK.

208
G. Rawson.

By Christ redeemed, in Christ restored,
We keep the memory adored,
And show the death of our dear Lord,
    Until he come.

2 His body, slain upon the tree,
His life-blood, shed for us, we see;
Thus faith shall read the mystery,
    Until he come.

3 And thus his dark betrayal-night
With his last advent we unite,
And keep the world's great Hope in sight
    Until he come.

4 O blessed hope! with this elate
Let not our hearts be desolate,
But strong in faith, in patience wait
    Until he come.

CŒNA DOMINI. 10s. — s.

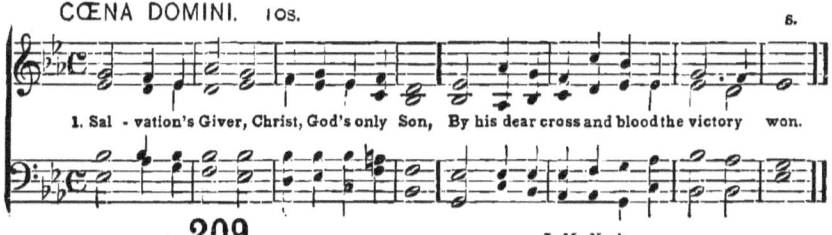

209
J. M. Neale.

Salvation's Giver, Christ, God's only Son,
By his dear cross and blood the victory won.

2 Offered was he for greatest and for least,
Himself the Victim and himself the Priest.

3 Victims were offered by the law of old,
Which in a type this heavenly mystery told.

4 He, Ransomer from death, and Light from shade,
Now gives his holy grace his saints to aid.

5 Approach we then with faithful hearts sincere,
And taste the pledges of salvation here.

6 O First and Last to whom all creatures bow,
Our God and Saviour, be thou with us now.

CHRIST.

210 *J. Evans.*

Hark, the voice of love and mercy
  Sounds aloud from Calvary;
See, it rends the rocks asunder,
  Shakes the earth, and veils the sky:
    "It is finished!"
  Hear the dying Saviour cry.

2 "It is finished!" O what pleasure
  Do these wondrous words afford!
Heavenly blessings without measure
  Flow to us from Christ, the Lord:
    "It is finished!"
  Saints, the dying words record.

3 Finished all the types and shadows
  Of the ceremonial law;
Finished all that God had promised;
  Death and hell no more shall awe:
    "It is finished!"
  Saints, from hence your comfort draw.

4 Tune your harps anew, ye seraphs,
  Join the triumph to proclaim!
All on earth and all in heaven,
  Join to praise Immanuel's name:
    Hallelujah!
  Glory to the bleeding Lamb.

The Lord's Supper.

ZION. 8s, 7s, 4s.   T. HASTINGS.

1. Hark, the voice of love and mer - cy Sounds a - loud from Cal - va - ry;
   See, it rends the rocks a - sun - der, Shakes the earth, and veils the sky: "It is finished!" Hear the dying Sav - iour cry. "It is finished!" Hear the dy - ing Saviour cry.

BEDELL. 9s, 8s.   E. S. KEALL.

1. Bread of the world, in mer - cy bro - ken! Wine of the soul, in mer - cy shed! By whom the words of life were spok - en, And in whose death our sins are dead.

211   *R. Heber.*

BREAD of the world, in mercy broken!
Wine of the soul, in mercy shed!
By whom the words of life were spoken,
And in whose death our sins are dead.

2 Look on the heart by sorrow broken,
Look on the tears by sinners shed,
And be thy feast to us the token
That by thy grace our souls are fed.

CHRIST.

112 ROSAN 7s. 6l. J. P. HOLBROOK.

1. Rock of A-ges, cleft for me! Let me hide my-self in thee;
Let the wa-ter and the blood, From thy riv-en side that flowed,
Be of sin the dou-ble cure; Cleanse me from its guilt and power,
Rock of A-ges, cleft for me, Let me hide my-self in thee.

212
A. M. Toplady.

Rock of Ages, cleft for me!
Let me hide myself in thee;
Let the water and the blood,
From thy riven side that flowed,
Be of sin the double cure;
Cleanse me from its guilt and power.

2 Not the labor of my hands
Can fulfil thy law's demands;
Could my zeal no respite know,
Could my tears forever flow,
All for sin could not atone;
Thou must save, and thou alone.

3 Nothing in my hand I bring;
Simply to thy cross I cling;
Naked, come to thee for dress,
Helpless look to thee for grace;
Foul, I to the fountain fly,
Wash me, Saviour, or I die!

4 While I draw this fleeting breath,
When my eyelids close in death,
When I soar to worlds unknown,
See thee on thy judgment-throne,
Rock of Ages, cleft for me,
Let me hide myself in thee.

The Lord's Supper.   113

DYKES. 7s. 6 l.   J. B. DYKES.

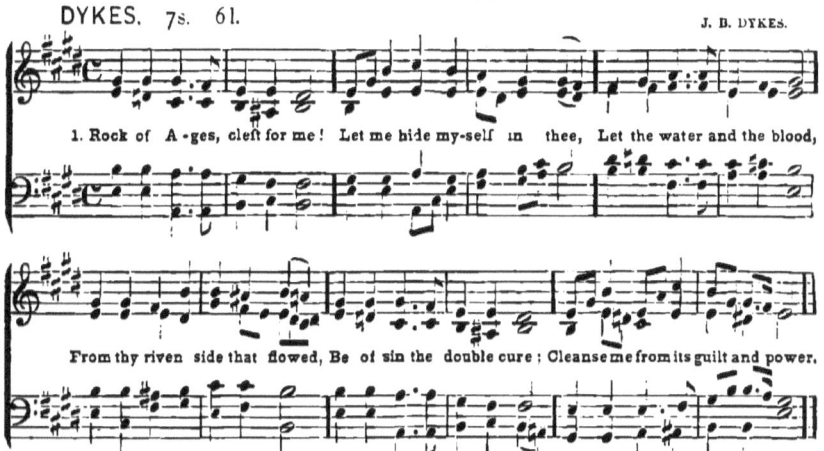

1. Rock of Ages, cleft for me! Let me hide myself in thee, Let the water and the blood, From thy riven side that flowed, Be of sin the double cure; Cleanse me from its guilt and power.

213   *A. M. Toplady.*

Rock of Ages, cleft for me !
Let me hide myself in thee;
Let the water and the blood,
From thy riven side that flowed,
Be of sin the double cure;
Cleanse me from its guilt and power.

2 Could my zeal no respite know,
Could my tears forever flow,
All for sin could not atone,
Thou must save, and thou alone.
Nothing in my hand I bring;
Simply to thy cross I cling.

3 While I draw this fleeting breath,
When my eyelids close in death,
When I soar to worlds unknown,
See thee on thy judgment throne,
Rock of Ages, cleft for me!
Let me hide myself in thee.

214   *R. Mant.*

Son of God, to thee I cry:
By the holy mystery
Of thy dwelling here on earth,
By thy pure and holy birth,
Lord, thy presence let me see,
Manifest thyself to me.

2 Lamb of God, to thee I cry;
By thy bitter agony,
By thy pangs to us unknown,
By thy Spirit's parting groan,
Lord, thy presence let me see,
Manifest thyself to me.

3 Prince of Life, to thee I cry:
By thy glorious majesty,
By thy triumph o'er the grave,
Meek to suffer, strong to save,
Lord, thy presence let me see,
Manifest thyself to me.

4 Lord of glory, God most high,
Man exalted to the sky
With thy love my bosom fill,
Prompt me to perform thy will;
Then thy glory I shall see,
Thou wilt bring me home to thee.

TOPLADY. 7s. 6 l.   T. HASTINGS.

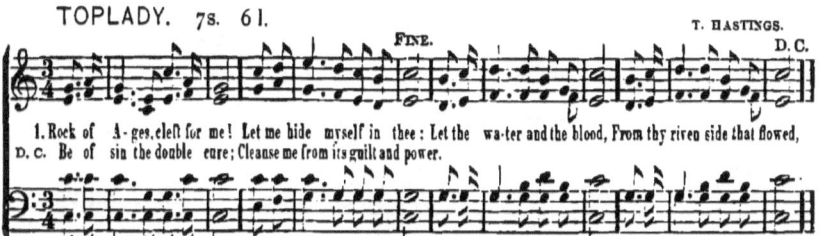

1. Rock of Ages, cleft for me! Let me hide myself in thee: Let the water and the blood, From thy riven side that flowed,
D. C. Be of sin the double cure; Cleanse me from its guilt and power.

CHRIST.

PERRINA. 7s, 6s. (Trochaic.) J. P. HOLBROOK.

1. Lamb of God, whose bleeding love We now re-call to mind, Send the an-swer from above, And let us mer-cy find; Think on us who think on thee; Ev-ery bur-dened soul re-lease; O re-mem-ber Cal-va-ry, And bid us go in peace.

215
C. Wesley.

Lamb of God, whose bleeding love
 We now recall to mind,
Send the answer from above,
 And let us mercy find;
Think on us who think on thee;
Every burdened soul release;
O remember Calvary,
 And bid us go in peace.

2 By thine agonizing pain
 And bloody sweat, we pray,
By thy dying love to man,
 Take all our sins away;
Burst our bonds and set us free,
From all sin do thou release;
O remember Calvary,
 And bid us go in peace.

3 Let thy blood, by faith applied,
 The sinner's pardon seal;
Speak us freely justified,
 And all our sickness heal;
By thy passion on the tree,
Let our griefs and troubles cease;
O remember Calvary,
 And bid us go in peace.

PASSION CHORALE. 7s, 6s. H. L. HASSLER.

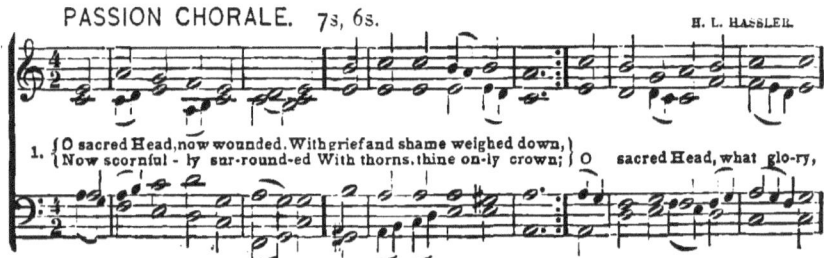

1. { O sacred Head, now wounded, With grief and shame weighed down, }
   { Now scornful-ly sur-round-ed With thorns, thine on-ly crown; } O sacred Head, what glo-ry,

The Lord's Supper.

216 *J. W. Alexander, tr.*

O sacred Head, now wounded,
 With grief and shame weighed down,
Now scornfully surrounded
 With thorns, thine only crown;
O sacred Head, what glory,
 What bliss, till now was thine!
Yet, though despised and gory,
 I joy to call thee mine.

2 What thou, my Lord, hast suffered
 Was all for sinners' gain;
Mine, mine was the transgression,
 But thine the deadly pain;
Lo, here I fall, my Saviour!
 'Tis I deserve thy place;
Look on me with thy favor,
 Vouchsafe to me thy grace.

3 The joy can ne'er be spoken,
 Above all joys beside,
When in thy body broken
 I thus with safety hide:
My Lord of Life, desiring
 Thy glory now to see,
Beside thy cross expiring,
 I'd breathe my soul to thee.

4 Be near me when I'm dying:
 O show thy cross to me;
And for my succor flying,
 Come, Lord, and set me free!
These eyes, new faith receiving,
 From Jesus shall not move;
For he who dies believing,
 Dies safely, through thy love.

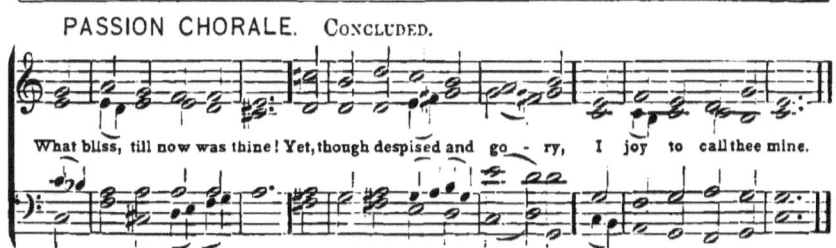

CHRIST.

BURLINGTON. C. M.
J. F. BURROWES.

1. There is a fount-ain filled with blood Drawn from Im-man-uel's veins;
And sin-ners, plunged be-neath that flood, Lose all their guilt-y stains.

217 *W. Cowper.*

There is a fountain filled with blood
Drawn from Immanuel's veins;
And sinners, plunged beneath that flood,
Lose all their guilty stains.

2 Dear dying Lamb, thy precious blood
Shall never lose its power,
Till all the ransomed church of God
Be saved, to sin no more.

3 E'er since, by faith, I saw the stream
Thy flowing wounds supply,
Redeeming love has been my theme,
And shall be till I die.

4 Then in a nobler, sweeter song,
I'll sing thy power to save,
When this poor lisping, stammering tongue
Lies silent in the grave.

218 *E. Denny.*

To Calvary, Lord, in spirit now,
Our weary souls repair,
To dwell upon thy dying love,
And taste its sweetness there.

2 Sweet resting-place of every heart
That feels the plague of sin,
Yet knows that deep mysterious joy,
The peace of God within.

3 Dear suffering Lamb, thy bleeding
With cords of love divine,   [wounds,
Have drawn our willing hearts to thee,
And linked our life with thine.

4 Thy sympathies and hopes are ours:
Dear Lord, we wait to see
Creation, all—below, above,
Redeemed and blest by thee.

COWPER. C. M.
L. MASON.

1. There is a fount-ain filled with blood Drawn from Im-man-uel's veins; And sinners, plunged beneath that flood, Lose all their guilt-y stains, Lose all their guilt-y stains.

The Lord's Supper.

219
Ray Palmer.

O Jesus, sweet the tears I shed,
　While at thy cross I kneel,
Gaze at thy wounded, fainting head,
　And all thy sorrows feel.

2 'Twas for the sinful thou didst die,
　And I a sinner stand:
What love speaks from thy dying eye,
　And from each pierced hand.

3 I know this cleansing blood of thine
　Was shed, dear Lord, for me:
For me, for all, O grace divine!
　Who look by faith on thee.

4 O Christ of God, O spotless Lamb,
　By love my soul is drawn;
Henceforth, for ever, thine I am;
　Here life and peace are born.

220
J. Allen.

Sweet the moments, rich in blessing,
　Which before the cross I spend;
Life, and health, and peace possessing,
　From the sinner's dying Friend.

2 Here it is I find my heaven,
　While upon the cross I gaze;
Love I much? I've much forgiven;
　I'm a miracle of grace.

3 Love and grief my heart dividing,
　With my tears his feet I'll bathe;
Constant still, in faith abiding,
　Life deriving from his death.

4 Lord, in ceaseless contemplation
　Fix my thankful heart on thee,
Till I taste thy full salvation
　And thine unveiled glory see.

CHRIST.

BARNES. 6s, 4s.
J. P. HOLBROOK.

221
Ray Palmer.

My faith looks up to thee,
Thou Lamb of Calvary,
  Saviour Divine:
Now hear me while I pray,
Take all my guilt away,
O let me from this day
  Be wholly thine.

2 May thy rich grace impart
Strength to my fainting heart,
  My zeal inspire;
As thou hast died for me,
O may my love to thee
Pure, warm, and changeless be,
  A living fire.

3 While life's dark maze I tread,
And griefs around me spread,
  Be thou my Guide;
Bid darkness turn to day,
Wipe sorrow's tears away,
Nor let me ever stray
  From thee aside.

4 When ends life's transient dream,
When death's cold, sullen stream
  Shall o'er me roll;
Blest Saviour, then, in love,
Fear and distrust remove;
O bear me safe above,
  A ransomed soul.

ST. AMBROSE. 6s, 4s.
J. B. DYKES.

The Lord's Supper. 119

AUGUSTA. S. M. — J. P. HOLBROOK.

1. Not all the blood of beasts, On Jewish altars slain, Could give the guilty conscience peace, Or wash away the stain.

222   *I. Watts.*

Not all the blood of beasts,
On Jewish altars slain,
Could give the guilty conscience peace,
Or wash away the stain.

2 But Christ, the heavenly Lamb,
Takes all our sins away—
A sacrifice of nobler name,
And richer blood than they.

3 My faith would lay her hand
On that dear head of thine,
While like a penitent I stand,
And there confess my sin.

4 Believing, we rejoice
To see the curse remove;
We bless the Lamb with cheerful voice,
And sing his bleeding love.

223   *H. Bonar.*

I hear the words of love,
I gaze upon the blood,
I see the mighty Sacrifice,
And I have peace with God.

2 My love is ofttimes low,
My joy still ebbs and flows;
But peace with him remains the same,
No change Jehovah knows.

3 I change, he changes not,
The Christ can never die;
His love, not mine, the resting place;
His truth, not mine, the tie.

4 I know he liveth now,
At God's right hand above;
I know the throne on which he sits,
I know his truth and love!

OLIVET. 6s, 4s. — L. MASON.

1. My faith looks up to thee, Thou Lamb of Cal-va-ry, Sav-iour di-vine! Now hear me while I pray, Take all my guilt a-way, O, let me from this day Be whol-ly thine!

CHRIST.

DUFFIELD. 7s. 6 l. W. WEDERMANN.

1. Bless-ed Sav-iour, thee I love, All my oth-er joys a-bove:
D. C. Ev-er let my glo-ry be, On-ly, on-ly, on-ly thee.

All my hopes in thee a-bide, Thou my hope, and naught be-side;

224
G. Duffield.

BLESSED Saviour, thee I love,
All my other joys above;
All my hopes in thee abide,
Thou my hope, and naught beside;
Ever let my glory be,
Only, only, only thee.

2 Once again beside the cross,
All my gain I count but loss;
Earthly pleasures fade away;
Clouds they are that hide my day:
Hence, vain shadows, let me see
Jesus, crucified for me.

3 From beneath that thorny crown
Trickle drops of cleansing down;
Pardon from thy piercéd hand
Now I take, while here I stand;
Only then I live to thee,
When thy wounded side I see.

4 Blesséd Saviour, thine am I,
Thine to live, and thine to die;
Height or depth, or earthly power,
Ne'er shall hide my Saviour more:
Ever shall my glory be,
Only, only, only thee.

225
W. McComb.

CHIEF of sinners though I be,
Jesus shed his blood for me;
Died, that I might live on high;
Lived, that I might never die;
As the branch is to the vine,
I am his and he is mine.

2 O the height of Jesus' love!
Higher than the heavens above,
Deeper than the depths of sea,
Lasting as eternity;
Love that found me, wondrous thought!
Found me when I sought him not!

3 Chief of sinners though I be,
Christ is all in all to me;
All my wants to him are known,
All my sorrows are his own;
Safe with him from earthly strife,
He sustains the hidden life.

4 O my Saviour! help afford,
By thy Spirit and thy Word!
When my wayward heart would stray,
Keep me in the narrow way;
Grace in time of need supply,
While I live, and when I die.

The Lord's Supper. 121

HALLE. 7s. 6l.   ARR. THOS. HASTINGS.

226 *E. Bickersteth.*

"Till he come."—Oh! let the words
Linger on the trembling chords;
Let the little while between
In their golden light be seen;
Let us think how heaven and home
Lie beyond that "Till he come."

2 When the weary ones we love
Enter on their rest above,
Seems the earth so poor and vast,
All our life-joy overcast?
Hush, be every mourner dumb;
It is only—till he come.

3 Clouds and conflicts round us press;
Would we have one sorrow less?
All the sharpness of the cross,
All that tells the world is loss,
Death and darkness and the tomb
Only whisper, "Till he come."

4 See, the feast of love is spread!
Drink the wine and break the bread;
Sweet memorials—till the Lord
Call us round his heavenly board;
Some from earth, from glory some,
Severed only—till he come.

MADRID 7s. 6l.   SPANISH MELODY

CHRIST.

MARTYRDOM. C. M.   H. WILSON.

1. A-las, and did my Sav-iour bleed? And did my Sovereign die? Would he de-vote that sa-cred head For such a worm as I?

227   *I. Watts.*

Alas, and did my Saviour bleed?
  And did my Sovereign die?
Would he devote that sacred head
  For such a worm as I?

2 Was it for crimes that I had done
  He groaned upon the tree?
Amazing pity! grace unknown!
  And love beyond degree!

3 Well might the sun in darkness hide,
  And shut his glories in,
When Christ, the mighty Maker, died
  For man the creature's sin.

4 Thus might I hide my blushing face,
  While his dear cross appears;
Dissolve my heart in thankfulness,
  And melt mine eyes to tears.

5 But drops of grief can ne'er repay
  The debt of love I owe:
Here, Lord, I give myself away;
  'Tis all that I can do.

DUNDEE. C. M   SCOTTISH.

1. How sweet and aw-ful is the place, With Christ within the doors: While ev-er-last-ing love displays The choicest of her s'ores!

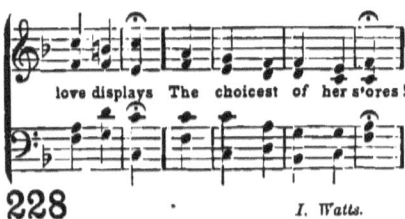

228   *I. Watts.*

How sweet and awful is the place,
  With Christ within the doors;
While everlasting love displays
  The choicest of her stores!

2 While all our hearts and all our songs
  Join to admire the feast,
Each of us cries, with thankful tongue,
  "Lord, why was I a guest?

3 "Why was I made to hear thy voice,
  And enter while there's room,
When thousands make a wretched choice,
  And rather starve than come?

4 'Twas the same love that spread the
  That sweetly drew us in; [feast,
Else we had still refused to taste,
  And perished in our sin.

5 Pity the nations, O our God!
  Constrain the earth to come;
Send thy victorious word abroad,
  And bring the strangers home.

The Lord's Supper. 123

THOU ART COMING. P. M

J. P. HOLBROOK.

Copyright, 1881, by J. P. Holbrook.

1. Thou art coming; at thy table We are witnesses for this; While remembering hearts thou meetest In communion clearest, sweetest, Earnest of our coming bliss, Showing not thy death alone, And thy love exceeding great, But thy coming and thy throne, All for which we long and wait.

229 F. R. Havergal.

Thou art coming; at thy table
 We are witnesses for this;
While remembering hearts thou meetest
 In communion clearest, sweetest,
Earnest of our coming bliss,
Showing not thy death alone,
 And thy love exceeding great,
But thy coming and thy throne,
 All for which we long and wait.

2 Thou art coming; we are waiting
 With a hope that cannot fail,
Asking not the day or hour,
 Resting on thy word of power,
Anchored safe within the vail.

Time appointed may be long,
 But the vision must be sure;
Certainty shall make us strong,
 Joyful patience can endure.

3 O the joy to see thee reigning,
 Thee, our own beloved Lord!
Every tongue thy name confessing,
 Worship, honor, glory, blessing,
Brought to thee with one accord;
Thee, our Master and our Friend,
 Vindicated and enthroned,
Unto earth's remotest end
 Glorified, adored and owned.

CHRIST.

124. WELCOME, HAPPY MORNING!
A. Sullivan.

230
J. Ellerton.

"Welcome, happy morning!" age to age shall say;
Hell to-day is vanquish'd; Heaven is won to-day!
Lo! the Dead is living, God for evermore!
Him their true Creator, all his works adore!
"Welcome, happy morning!" age to age shall say.

2 Maker and Redeemer, Life and Health of all,
Thou from heaven beholding human nature's fall,
Of the Father's Godhead, true and only Son,
Manhood to deliver, Manhood didst put on:
Hell to-day is vanquished; heaven is won to-day!

3 Thou of Life the Author, death didst undergo,
Tread the path of darkness, saving strength to show;
Come, then, True and Faithful, now fulfil thy word;
'Tis thine own third morning! come, O risen Lord!
"Welcome, happy morning!" age to age shall say.

4 Loose the souls long prisoned, bound with Satan's chain,
All that now is fallen raise to life again;
Show thy face in brightness, bid the nations see,
Bring again our daylight: day returns with thee!
Hell to-day is vanquished; heaven is won to-day!

Resurrection. 125

TRIUMPH. 10s, 11s, 12s. A. H. BROWN.

1. Lift your glad voices in triumph on high, For Jesus hath ris-en, and man shall not die.

Vain were the terrors that gathered around him, And short the domin-ion of death and the grave;

He burst from the fetters of darkness that bound him, Resplendent in glo-ry to live and to save.

Loud was the chorus of angels on high, "For Je-sus hath ris-en, and men shall not die."

231 H. Ware, Jr.

Lift your glad voices in triumph on high,
For Jesus hath risen, and man shall not die.
Vain were the terrors that gathered around him,
  And short the dominion of death and the grave;
He burst from the fetters of darkness that bound him,
  Resplendent in glory to live and to save.
Loud was the chorus of angels on high,
" For Jesus hath risen, and man shall not die."

2 Glory to God, in full anthems of joy!
The being he gave us, death cannot destroy;
Sad were the life we must part with to-morrow,
  If tears were our birthright, and death were our end!
But Jesus hath cheered the dark valley of sorrow,
  And bade us, immortal, to heaven ascend.
Lift your glad voices in triumph on high,
For Jesus hath risen, and man shall not die.

126 CHRIST.

HASTINGS. 7s.   CONCONE.

1. Christ the Lord is risen to-day, Sons of men and angels say; Raise your joys and triumphs high, Sing, ye heavens, and earth, reply. 2. Love's redeeming work is done, Fought the fight, the battle won: Lo! our sun's eclipse is o'er; Lo! he sets in blood no more.

232   *C. Wesley.*
Christ the Lord is risen to-day,
Sons of men and angels say;
Raise your joys and triumphs high,
Sing, ye heavens, and earth, reply.

2 Love's redeeming work is done,
Fought the fight, the battle won:
Lo! our sun's eclipse is o'er;
Lo! he sets in blood no more.

3 Vain the stone, the watch, the seal—
Christ hath burst the gates of hell:
Death in vain forbids his rise,
Christ hath opened paradise.

4 Lives again our glorious King:
Where, O death, is now thy sting?
Once he died our souls to save:
Where thy victory, O grave?

5 Soar we now where Christ has led,
Following our exalted head;
Made like him, like him we rise;
Ours the cross, the grave, the skies.

6 Hail the Lord of earth and heaven!
Praise to thee by both be given;
Thee we greet triumphant now:
Hail! the Resurrection Thou!

233   *C. Winkworth, tr.*
Christ the Lord is risen again,
Christ hath broken every chain;
Hark, angelic voices cry,
Singing evermore on high.

2 He who bore all pain and loss
Comfortless upon the cross,
Lives in glory now on high,
Pleads for us and hears our cry.

3 He who slumbered in the grave
Is exalted now to save;
Now through Christendom it rings
That the Lamb is King of kings.

4 Now he bids us tell abroad
How the lost may be restored,
How the penitent forgiven,
How we too may enter heaven.

Resurrection and Ascension. 127

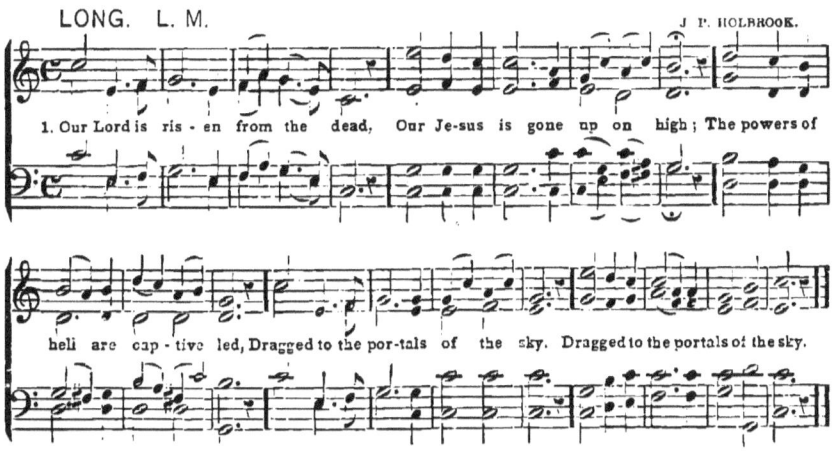

LONG. L. M. — J. P. HOLBROOK.

1. Our Lord is ris-en from the dead, Our Jesus is gone up on high; The powers of hell are cap-tive led, Dragged to the por-tals of the sky. Dragged to the portals of the sky.

234
C. Wesley.

Our Lord is risen from the dead,
 Our Jesus is gone up on high;
 The powers of hell are captive led,
 Dragged to the portals of the sky.

2 There his triumphal chariot waits,
 And angels chant the solemn lay:
 Lift up your heads, ye heavenly gates!
 Ye everlasting doors! give way.

3 Loose all your bars of massy light,
 And wide unfold the ethereal scene:
 He claims these mansions as his right;
 Receive the King of glory in.

4 Who is the King of glory—who?
 The Lord who all our foes o'ercame;
 Who sin, and death, and hell o'erthrew;
 And Jesus is the conqueror's name.

5 Lo! his triumphal chariot waits,
 And angels chant the solemn lay:
 Lift up your heads, ye heavenly gates!
 Ye everlasting doors! give way.

6 Who is the King of glory—who?
 The Lord of boundless power possessed;
 The King of saints and angels too,
 God over all, forever blessed.

MOZART. 7s. — MOZART.

1. Christ the Lord is risen a-gain, Christ hath brok-en ev-ery chain; Hark, an-gel-ic voic-es cry, Singing ev-er-more on high, Sing-ing ev-er-more on high.

CHRIST.

128 CARTHAGE. 8s, 7s. ARR. G. F. ROOT.

1. Christ, a-bove all glo-ry seat-ed! King tri-umph-ant, strong to save! Dy-ing, thou hast death de-feat-ed, Bur-ied, thou hast spoiled the grave.

235

Christ, above all glory seated!
 King triumphant, strong to save!
Dying, thou hast death defeated,
 Buried, thou hast spoiled the grave.

2 Thou art gone, where now is given,
 What no mortal might could gain;
On the eternal throne of heaven,
 In thy Father's power to reign.

3 We, O Lord, with hearts adoring,
 Follow thee above the sky;
Hear our prayers thy grace imploring,
 Lift our souls to thee on high.

4 So when thou again in glory
 On the clouds of heaven shalt shine,
We thy flock shall stand before thee,
 Owned for evermore as thine.

236 *C. Wordsworth.*

Hallelujah! hallelujah!
 Hearts to heaven and voices raise;
Sing to God a hymn of gladness,
 Sing to God a hymn of praise.

2 He, who on the cross a Victim
 For the world's salvation bled,
Jesus Christ, the King of glory,
 Now is risen from the dead.

3 Christ is risen, we are risen;
 Shed upon us heavenly grace,
Rain, and dew, and gleams of glory
 From the brightness of thy face.

4 Christ is risen, Christ the First-fruits
 Of the holy harvest field,
Which will all its full abundance
 At his second coming yield.

RATHBUN. 8s, 7s. I. CONKEY.

1. Hal-le-lu-jah! hal-le-lu-jah! Hearts to heaven and voic-es raise; Sing to God a hymn of glad-ness, Sing to God a hymn of praise.

Resurrection and Ascension.

ASCENSION. S. M. D. — H. J. GAUNTLETT.

Voices in unison. ... *In harmony.*

1. Thou art gone up on high To mansions in the skies; And round thy throne unceasingly The songs of praise arise. 2. But we are lingering here With sin and care oppressed: Lord, send thy promised Comforter, And lead us to thy rest.

237   *E. Toke.*

Thou art gone up on high
To mansions in the skies;
And round thy throne unceasingly
The songs of praise arise.

2 But we are lingering here
With sin and care oppressed:
Lord, send thy promised Comforter,
And lead us to thy rest!

3 Thou art gone up on high:
But thou didst first come down,
Through earth's most bitter agony
To pass unto thy crown.

4 And girt with griefs and fears
Our onward course must be;
But only let that path of tears
Lead us at last to thee.

5 Thou art gone up on high:
But thou shalt come again
With all the bright ones of the sky
Attendant in thy train.

6 O by thy saving power
So make us live and die,
That we may stand in that dread hour,
At thy right hand on high.

RIALTO. S. M. — G. F. ROOT.

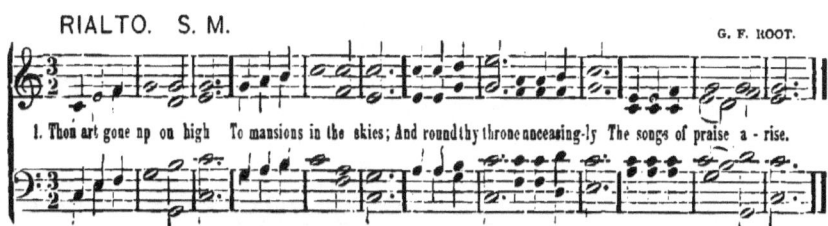

1. Thou art gone up on high To mansions in the skies; And round thy throne unceasingly The songs of praise arise.

CHRIST.

ALEXANDER. C. M. J. P. HOLBROOK.

1. Th' e-ter-nal gates lift up their heads, The doors are o-pened wide;
The King of glo-ry is gone up Un-to his Fa-ther's side.
That we may be where now thou art, And look up-on thy face.

2. Thou art gone in be-fore us, Lord, Thou hast pre-pared a place,

4. Lift up our thoughts, lift up our songs, And let thy grace be given,
That, while we lin-ger yet be-low, Our hearts may be in heaven;
Dwell in us now, that we may dwell For ev-er-more in thee.

5. That, where thou art at God's right hand, Our hope, our love may be:

Ascension.

ALEXANDER. CONCLUDED.

C. F. Alexander.

238

Tʜ' eternal gates lift up their heads,
　The doors are opened wide;
　The King of glory is gone up
　　Unto his Father's side.

2 Thou art gone in before us, Lord,
　Thou hast prepared a place,
That we may be where now thou art,
　And look upon thy face.

3 And ever on thine earthly path
　A gleam of glory lies;

A light still breaks behind the cloud
　That vails thee from our eyes.

4 Lift up our thoughts, lift up our songs,
　And let thy grace be given,
That while we linger yet below,
　Our hearts may be in heaven;—

5 That where thou art at God's right hand,
　Our hope, our love may be:
Dwell in us now, that we may dwell
　For evermore in thee.

CHRIST.

SALZBURG. 8s, 7s.   ARR. G. KINGSLEY.

239
J. Bakewell.

JESUS, hail! enthroned in glory,
  There forever to abide;
All the heavenly hosts adore thee,
  Seated at thy Father's side.

2 There for sinners thou art pleading,
  There thou dost our place prepare;
Ever for us interceding,
  Till in glory we appear.

3 Worship, honor, power, and blessing,
  Thou art worthy to receive;
Loudest praises, without ceasing,
  Meet it is for us to give.

4 Help, ye bright angelic spirits!
  Bring your sweetest, noblest lays:
Help to sing our Saviour's merits;
  Help to chant Immanuel's praise.

240
W. Goode.

CROWN his head with endless blessing,
  Who, in God the Father's name,
With compassions never ceasing,
  Comes salvation to proclaim.

2 Lo! Jehovah, we adore thee;
  Thee, our Saviour; thee, our God!
From his throne his beams of glory
  Shine through all the world abroad.

3 Jesus, thee our Saviour hailing,
  Thee, our God, in praise we own;
Highest honors, never failing,
  Rise eternal round thy throne.

4 Now, ye saints, his power confessing,
  In your grateful strains adore;
For his mercy, never ceasing,
  Flows, and flows for evermore.

WILMOT. 8s, 7s.   WEBER.

Enthronement. 133

STOUGHTON. 8s, 7s.   J. P. HOLBROOK.

1. See, the Conqueror mounts in tri-umph! See the King in roy-al state,

D.S.—And the por-tals high are lift-ed To re-ceive their heaven-ly King.

Rid-ing on the clouds, his cha-riot, To his heavenly pal-ace gate!

Hark, the choirs of an-gel voic-es Joy-ful al-le-lu-ias sing,

241
C. Wordsworth.

SEE, the Conqueror mounts in triumph!
  See the King in royal state,
Riding on the clouds, his chariot,
  To his heavenly palace gate!
Hark! the choirs of angel voices
  Joyful alleluias sing,
And the portals high are lifted
  To receive their heavenly King.

2 See him, who is gone before us,
  Heavenly mansions to prepare;
See him, who is ever pleading
  For us with prevailing prayer;
See him, who with sound of trumpet
  And with his angelic train,
Summoning the world to judgment,
  On the clouds will come again.

3 Thou hast raised our human nature,
  On the clouds to God's right hand;
There we sit in heavenly places,
  There with thee in glory stand;
Jesus reigns, adored by angels;
  Man with God is on the throne;
Mighty Lord! in thine ascension,
  We by faith behold our own.

242
R. Robinson.

MIGHTY God, while angels bless thee,
  May a mortal sing thy name?
Lord of men, as well as angels,
  Thou art every creature's theme.
Lord of every land and nation,
  Ancient of eternal days,
Sounded through the wide creation,
  Be thy just and lawful praise.

2 For the grandeur of thy nature,
  Grand, beyond a seraph's thought;
For the wonders of creation,
  Works with skill and kindness wrought;
For thy providence, that governs
  Through thine empire's wide domain,
Wings an angel, guides a sparrow;
  Blessèd be thy gentle reign.

3 For thy rich, thy free redemption,
  Bright, though veiled in darkness long,
Thought is poor, and poor expression;
  Who can sing that wondrous song?
Brightness of the Father's glory!
  Shall thy praise unuttered lie?
Break, my tongue, such guilty silence,
  Sing the Lord who came to die!

Enthronement. 135

CHRISTUS VICTOR. CONCLUDED.

243 *Ray Palmer.*

PRAISE him! Praise the conquering King!
  Christ our Lord is Lord of all;
Nations, joyful tribute bring!
Princes, low before him fall!
See unfurled his royal banner!
  On he cometh to subdue;
Earth's long wail becomes Hosanna!
  Lo! he maketh all things new.
    Hallelujah!
  Reign, O Christ, thou just and true!

2 Praise him! Praise the Prince of Peace!
  Angels, wake your strain again;
Chant his triumphs, ne'er to cease
Till our God shall dwell with men.
Christ hath heard the ages sighing;
  Christ hath pitied mortal grief.
At his coming tears are drying,
  Millions hail the glad relief.
    Hallelujah!
  Hell, thy reign shall now be brief.

3 Praise him! Praise the Lord of Life!
  Him that liveth and was dead;
Past the cross and dying strife,
  Vanquished Death he captive led,
Ever-living, Life-bestowing,

In Thee all the holy live;
Fount exhaustless, overflowing,
  Health and gladness thou dost give;
    Hallelujah!
  Earth and heaven from thee receive.

4 Praise him! Praise the Lamb enthroned!
  Radiant at his Father's side;
Him who by his blood atoned,
  Him who names the church his Bride!
Thou, O Lamb of God, forever,
  Where eternal noontide glows,
Thine own flock wilt feed, and never
  Cease to guard their sweet repose.
    Hallelujah!
  Thou hast crushed their mighty foes.

5 Praise him! Praise Incarnate Love!
  Ranks seraphic, legions bright,
Souls redeemed, who, fixed above,
  Glow in his eternal light;
All on earth who upward gazing,
  See his beauty and adore,
One far-sounding chorus raising,
  Speak that name for evermore.
    Hallelujah!
  Crown him! Once the cross he bore.

136 CHRIST.

STOWE. 8s, 7s, 4s.   J. P. HOLBROOK.

1. Look, ye saints, the sight is glorious, See "the Man of Sorrows" now; From the fight re-turned vic-to-rious, Ev-ery knee to him shall bow; Crown him, crown him, crown him, crown him: Crowns be-come the Vic-tor's brow.

244
T. Kelly.

Look, ye saints, the sight is glorious,
　See "The Man of Sorrows" now;
From the fight returned victorious,
　Every knee to him shall bow;
　　Crown him, crown him;
Crowns become the Victor's brow.

2 Crown the Saviour, angels, crown him:
　Rich the trophies Jesus brings:
In the seat of power enthrone him,
　While the vault of heaven rings:
　　Crown him, crown him:
Crown the Saviour "King of kings."

3 Sinners in derision crowned him,
　Mocking thus the Saviour's claim;
Saints and angels crowd around him,
　Own his title, praise his name:
　　Crown him, crown him;
Spread abroad the Victor's fame.

4 Hark, those bursts of acclamation!
　Hark, those loud triumphant chords!
Jesus takes the highest station:

O what joy the sight affords!
　　Crown him, crown him;
"King of kings, and Lord of lords."

245
T. Kelly.

Hark, ten thousand harps and voices
　Sound the note of praise above!
Jesus reigns, and heaven rejoices;
　Jesus reigns, the God of love;
See, he sits on yonder throne;
Jesus rules the world alone.

2 King of glory, reign forever!
　Thine an everlasting crown;
Nothing from thy love shall sever
　Those whom thou hast made thine own;
Happy objects of thy grace,
Destined to behold thy face.

3 Saviour, hasten thine appearing;
　Bring, O bring the glorious day,
When the awful summons hearing,
　Heaven and earth shall pass away:
Then, with golden harps, we'll sing,
"Glory, glory to our King!"

Enthronement. 137

246 *M. Bridges.*

Crown him with many crowns,
  The Lamb upon his throne!
Hark! how the heavenly anthem drowns
  All music but its own!
Awake, my soul, and sing
  Of him who died for thee;
And hail him as thy matchless King
  Through all eternity.

2 Crown him the Lord of love!
  Behold his hands and side,—
Those wounds, yet visible above,
  In beauty glorified.
No angel in the sky
  Can fully bear that sight,
But downward bends his wondering eye
  At mysteries so bright.

3 Crown him the Lord of life!
  Who triumphed o'er the grave,
And rose victorious in the strife
  For those he came to save.
His glories now we sing,
  Who died and rose on high;
Who died eternal life to bring,
  And lives that death may die.

4 Crown him the Lord of heaven!
  Enthroned in worlds above,
The King to whom alone is given
  The wondrous name of Love!
All hail, Redeemer, hail!
  For thou hast died for me;
Thy praise shall never, never fail
  Throughout eternity.

138 CHRIST.

NEWBOLD. C. M. — G. KINGSLEY.

1. Come, let us join our cheerful songs With an-gels round the throne; Ten thousand thousand are their tongues, But all their joys are one, But all their joys are one.

247
I. Watts.

Come, let us join our cheerful songs
 With angels round the throne;
Ten thousand thousand are their tongues,
 But all their joys are one.

2 "Worthy the Lamb that died," they cry,
 "To be exalted thus!"
"Worthy the Lamb!" our lips reply,
 "For he was slain for us."

3 Jesus is worthy to receive
 Honor and power divine;
And blessings, more than we can give,
 Be, Lord, forever thine!

4 Let all that dwell above the sky,
 And air, and earth, and seas,
Conspire to lift thy glories high,
 And speak thine endless praise.

5 The whole creation join in one,
 To bless the sacred name
Of him who sits upon the throne,
 And to adore the Lamb!

248
T. Kelly.

The head, that once was crowned with
 Is crowned with glory now;   [thorns,
A royal diadem adorns
 The mighty Victor's brow.

2 The highest place that heaven affords
 Is his by sovereign right,—
The King of kings, and Lord of lords,
 And heaven's eternal Light.

3 The joy of all who dwell above,
 The joy of all below,
To whom he manifests his love,
 And grants his name to know.

4 The cross he bore is life and health,
 Though shame and death to him;
His people's hope, his people's wealth,
 Their everlasting theme.

249
A. Steele.

Christ, with eternal glory crowned,
 The Lord, the Conqueror, reigns;
His praise the heavenly choirs resound
 In their immortal strains.

2 Amid the splendors of his throne,
 Unchanging love appears;
The names he purchased for his own,
 Still on his heart he bears.

3 O the rich depths of love divine!
 Of bliss, a boundless store!
Dear Saviour, let me call thee mine;
 I cannot wish for more.

4 On thee alone my hope relies;
 Beneath thy cross I fall,—
My Lord, my life, my sacrifice,
 My Saviour, and my all!

Enthronement.

CORONATION C. M.   O. HOLDEN.

1. All hail the power of Jesus' name! Let angels prostrate fall; Bring forth the royal di-a-dem,

And crown him Lord of all, Bring forth the roy-al di-a-dem, And crown him Lord of all.

250   *E. Perronet.*

ALL hail the power of Jesus' name!
  Let angels prostrate fall;
Bring forth the royal diadem,
  And crown him Lord of all.

2 Ye chosen seed of Israel's race,
  Ye ransomed from the fall;
Hail him, who saves you by his grace,
  And crown him Lord of all.

3 Hail him, ye heirs of David's line,—
  Whom David, Lord did call,—
The God incarnate, Man divine,
  And crown him Lord of all.

4 Sinners, whose love can ne'er forget
  The wormwood and the gall;
Go, spread your trophies at his feet,
  And crown him Lord of all.

5 Let every kindred, every tribe,
  On this terrestrial ball,
To him all majesty ascribe,
  And crown him Lord of all.

6 O that with yonder sacred throng,
  We at his feet may fall;
We'll join the everlasting song,
  And crown him Lord of all.

251   *I. Watts.*

MY Saviour, my Almighty Friend,
  When I begin thy praise,
Where will the growing numbers end,
  The numbers of thy grace?

2 Thou art my everlasting trust,
  Thy goodness I adore;
And since I knew thy graces first,
  I speak thy glories more.

3 My feet shall travel all the length
  Of the celestial road,
And march with courage in thy strength
  To see my Father, God.

4 How will my lips rejoice to tell
  The victories of my King!
My soul, redeemed from sin and hell,
  Shall thy salvation sing.

CHRIST.

ARIEL. C. P. M.   L. MASON.

O could I speak the matchless worth, O could I sound the glories forth, Which in my Saviour shine, I'd soar and touch the heavenly strings, And vie with Gabriel while he sings In notes almost divine, In notes almost divine.

252   *S. Medley.*

O could I speak the matchless worth,
O could I sound the glories forth,
  Which in my Saviour shine,
I'd soar and touch the heavenly strings,
And vie with Gabriel while he sings
  In notes almost divine.

2 I'd sing the precious blood he spilt,
My ransom from the dreadful guilt
  Of sin, and wrath divine;
I'd sing his glorious righteousness,
In which all-perfect, heavenly dress
  My soul shall ever shine.

3 I'd sing the characters he bears,
And all the forms of love he wears,
  Exalted on his throne;
In loftiest songs of sweetest praise,
I would to everlasting days
  Make all his glories known.

4 Well, the delightful day will come
When my dear Lord will bring me home,
  And I shall see his face:

Then with my Saviour, Brother, Friend,
A blest eternity I'll spend,
  Triumphant in his grace.

253   *C. Wesley.*

O LOVE divine, how sweet thou art!
When shall I find my willing heart
  All taken up by thee?
My thirsty spirit faints to prove
The greatness of redeeming love,
  The love of Christ to me.

2 Stronger his love than death and hell:
Its riches are unsearchable:
  The first-born sons of light
Desire in vain its depths to see;
They cannot reach the mystery,—
  The length and breadth and height.

3 God only knows the love of God;
O that it now were shed abroad
  In this poor, stony heart!
For love I sigh, for love I pine;
This only portion, Lord, be mine—
  Be mine this better part.

Songs of Adoration and Love.

DUKE STREET. L. M. — J. HATTON.

1. Now to the Lord a noble song! A-wake, my soul! a-wake, my tongue! Ho-san-na to th'e-ter-nal name, And all his bound-less love pro-claim.

254 *I. Watts.*
Now to the Lord a noble song!
Awake, my soul! awake, my tongue!
Hosanna to the eternal name,
And all his boundless love proclaim.

2 See where it shines in Jesus' face,
The brightest image of his grace;
God, in the person of his Son,
Hath all his mightiest works outdone.

3 Grace! 'tis a sweet, a charming theme;
My thoughts rejoice at Jesus' name:
Ye angels, dwell upon the sound;
Ye heavens, reflect it to the ground!

4 O may I reach that happy place,
Where he unveils his lovely face,
Where I his beauties shall behold,
And sing his name to harps of gold.

255 *I. Watts.*
Now for a song of lofty praise
To great Jehovah's equal Son!
Awake, my voice, in heavenly lays,
And sing the wonders he hath done.

2 Sing how he left the worlds of light,
And the bright robes he wore above;
How swift and joyful was his flight
On wings of everlasting love.

3 Deep in the shades of gloomy death,
Th' almighty Captive prisoner lay;
Th' almighty Captive left the earth,
And rose to everlasting day.

4 Among a thousand harps and songs,
Jesus, the God, exalted reigns:
His sacred name fills all their tongues,
And echoes thro' the heavenly plains.

VENETIA. C. P. M. — L. T. B.

1. O love divine, how sweet thou art! When shall I find my willing heart All taken up by thee? My thirsty spirit faints to prove The greatness of redeeming love, The love of Christ to me.

CHRIST.

ROSEHILL. L. M.
J. E. SWEETSER.

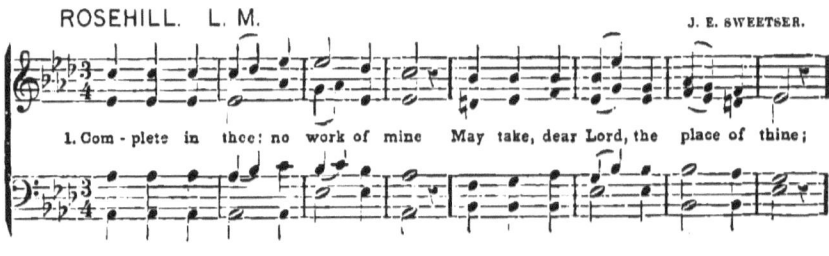

256
A. R. Wolfe.

Complete in thee! no work of mine
May take, dear Lord, the place of thine;
Thy blood has pardon bought for me,
And I am now complete in thee.

2 Complete in thee! no more shall sin
Thy grace has conquered reign within;
Thy voice will bid the tempter flee,
And I shall stand complete in thee.

3 Complete in thee! each want supplied,
And no good thing to me denied;
Since thou my portion, Lord, wilt be,
I ask no more, complete in thee.

4 Dear Saviour! when, before thy bar,
All tribes and tongues assembled are,
Among thy chosen may I be
At thy right hand, complete in thee.

257
S. Medley.

Jesus, engrave it on my heart,
That thou the one thing needful art;
I could from all things parted be,
But never, never, Lord, from thee.

2 Needful is thy most precious blood,
To reconcile my soul to God;
Needful is thy indulgent care;
Needful thy all-prevailing prayer.

3 Needful thy presence, dearest Lord,
True peace and comfort to afford;
Needful thy promise to impart
Fresh life and vigor to my heart.

4 Needful art thou, my guide, my stay,
Through all life's dark and weary way;
Nor less in death thou'lt needful be,
To bring my spirit home to thee.

5 Then needful still, my God, my King,
Thy name eternally I'll sing!
Glory and praise be ever his,
The one thing needful Jesus is!

258
J. Edmeston.

Fountain of grace, rich, full, and free,
What need I that is not in thee?
Full pardon, strength to meet the day,
And peace which none can take away.

2 Doth sickness fill my heart with fear?
'Tis sweet to know that thou art near;
Am I with dread of justice tried?
'Tis sweet to know that Christ hath died.

3 In life, thy promises of aid
Forbid my heart to be afraid;
In death, peace gently veils the eyes;
Christ rose, and I shall surely rise.

4 O all-sufficient Saviour, be
This all-sufficiency to me;
Nor pain, nor sin, nor death can harm
The weakest, shielded by thine arm.

Songs of Adoration and Love. 143

MISSIONARY CHANT. L. M.   CH. ZEUNER.

1. He lives! the great Redeemer lives! What joy the blest assurance gives! And now, before his Father, God, Pleads the full merits of his blood.

259   *A. Steele.*

He lives! the great Redeemer lives!
What joy the blest assurance gives!
And now, before his Father, God,
Pleads the full merits of his blood.

2 Repeated crimes awake our fears,
And justice armed with frowns appears;
But in the Saviour's lovely face
Sweet mercy smiles and all is peace.

3 In every dark, distressful hour,
When sin and Satan join their power,
Let this dear hope repel the dart,
That Jesus bears us on his heart.

4 Great Advocate, Almighty Friend!
On him our humble hopes depend;
Our cause can never, never fail,
For Jesus pleads, and must prevail.

260   *J. Wesley, tr.*

Jesus! thy blood and righteousness
My beauty are, my glorious dress;
'Mid flaming worlds, in these arrayed,
With joy shall I lift up my head.

2 When from the dust of earth I rise
To claim my mansion in the skies;
Ev'n then shall this be all my plea:
"Jesus hath lived and died for me."

3 This spotless robe the same appears,
When ruined nature sinks in years;
No age can change its glorious hue,—
The robe of Christ is ever new.

4 Oh, let the dead now hear thy voice
Now bid thy banished ones rejoice;
Their beauty this, their glorious dress—
Jesus! thy blood and righteousness!

261

There is none other name than thine,
Jehovah Jesus! Name divine!
On which to rest for sins forgiven—
For peace with God, for hope of heaven.

2 There is none other name than thine,
When cares, and fears, and griefs are mine,
That, with a gracious power, can heal
Each care, and fear, and grief I feel.

3 There is none other name than thine,
When called my spirit to resign,
To bear me through that latest strife
And ev'n in death to be my life.

4 Name above every name! thy praise
Shall fill the remnant of my days:
Jehovah Jesus! Name divine,
Rock of salvation! thou art mine.

144 CHRIST.

RATHBUN. 8s, 7s.   I. CONKEY.

262   *J. Bowring.*

In the cross of Christ I glory,
  Towering o'er the wrecks of time;
All the light of sacred story
  Gathers round its head sublime.

2 When the woes of life o'ertake me,
  Hopes deceive, and fears annoy,
Never shall the cross forsake me;
  Lo, it glows with peace and joy.

3 When the sun of bliss is beaming
  Light and love upon my way,
From the cross the radiance streaming
  Adds new lustre to the day.

4 Bane and blessing, pain and pleasure,
  By the cross are sanctified;
Peace is there, that knows no measure,
  Joys that through all time abide.

HOPE. 8s, 7s.   BEETHOVEN.

263   *R. Robinson.*

Come, thou Fount of every blessing,
  Tune my heart to sing thy grace;
Streams of mercy never ceasing,
  Call for songs of loudest praise.

2 Jesus sought me when a stranger,
  Wandering from the fold of God;
He, to rescue me from danger,
  Interposed his precious blood.

3 Oh, to grace how great a debtor
  Daily I'm constrained to be!
Let thy goodness, like a fetter,
  Bind my wandering heart to thee.

4 Prone to wander, Lord, I feel it;
  Prone to leave the God I love;
Here's my heart; O take and seal it,—
  Seal it for thy courts above!

Songs of Adoration and Love. 145

ATTLEFIELD. L. M.   SCHUBERT.

1. A-wake, my soul, to joy-ful lays, And sing the great Re-deem-er's praise;
He just-ly claims a song from me: His lov-ing-kind-ness, O how free!

264   *S. Medley.*

AWAKE, my soul, to joyful lays,
And sing the great Redeemer's praise;
He justly claims a song from me:
His loving-kindness, O how free!

2 He saw me ruined in the fall,
Yet loved me, notwithstanding all;
He saved me from my lost estate:
His loving-kindness, O how great!

3 When trouble, like a gloomy cloud,
Has gathered thick and thundered loud,
He near my soul hath always stood;
His loving-kindness, O how good!

4 Soon shall I pass the gloomy vale;
Soon all my mortal powers must fail:
O may my last expiring breath
His loving-kindness sing in death!

265   *T. Kelly*

AROUND the Saviour's lofty throne,
Ten thousand times ten thousand sing;
They worship him as God alone,
And crown him—everlasting King.

2 Approach, ye saints! this God is yours;
'T is Jesus fills the throne above:
Ye cannot fail while God endures;
Ye cannot want while God is love.

3 Jesus, thou everlasting King!
To thee the praise of heaven belongs;
Yet smile on us who fain would bring
The tribute of our humbler songs.

4 Though sin defile our worship here,
We hope ere long thy face to view,
In heaven with angels to appear,
And praise thy name as angels do.

LOVING-KINDNESS. L. M.

1. Awake, my soul, to joyful lays, And sing the great Redeemer's praise; He justly claims a song from me: His
loving-kindness, O how free! Loving-kindness, loving-kindness, His loving-kindness, O how free!

CHRIST.

MARIAN. C. M. — J. P. HOLBROOK.

1. To thee, my Shep-herd and my Lord, A grate-ful song I'll raise;

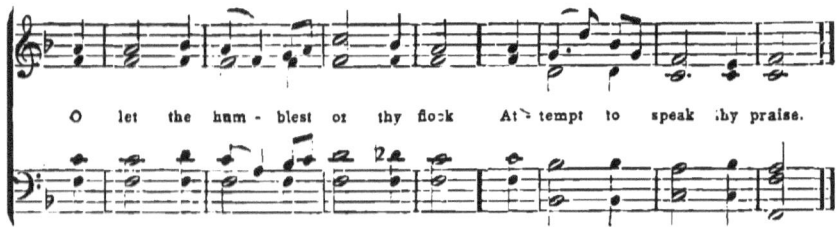

O let the hum-blest of thy flock At-tempt to speak thy praise.

266
O. Heginbotham.

To THEE, my Shepherd and my Lord,
A grateful song I'll raise;
O let the humblest of thy flock
Attempt to speak thy praise.

2 My life, my joy, my hope, I owe
To thine amazing love;
Ten thousand thousand comforts here,
And nobler bliss above.

3 To thee my trembling spirit flies,
With sin and grief oppressed;
Thy gentle voice dispels my fears,
And lulls my cares to rest.

4 Lead on, dear Shepherd!—led by thee,
No evil shall I fear;
Soon shall I reach thy fold above,
And praise thee better there.

267

COME, let us join in songs of praise
To our ascended Priest;
He entered heaven, with all our names
Engraven on his breast.

2 Below he washed our guilt away,
By his atoning blood;
Now he appears before the throne,
And pleads our cause with God.

3 Clothed with our nature still, he knows
The weakness of our frame,
And how to shield us from the foes
Which he himself o'ercame.

4 Nor time, nor distance, e'er shall quench
The fervors of his love;
For us he died in kindness here,
Nor is less kind above.

268
I. Watts.

WITH joy we meditate the grace
Of our High Priest above;
His heart is made of tenderness,
His bosom glows with love.

2 Touched with a sympathy within,
He knows our feeble frame;
He knows what sore temptations mean,
For he hath felt the same.

3 He, in the days of feeble flesh,
Poured out his cries and tears;
And, in his measure, feels afresh
What every member bears.

4 Then let our humble faith address
His mercy and his power;
We shall obtain delivering grace
In the distressing hour.

Songs of Adoration and Love. 147

NOEL. C. M.   L. MASON.

1. Ma - jes - tic sweet - ness sits enthroned Up - on the Sav - iour's brow;

His head with ra - diant glo - ries crowned, His lips with grace o'er - flow.

269
S. Stennett.

MAJESTIC sweetness sits enthroned
  Upon the Saviour's brow;
His head with radiant glories crowned,
  His lips with grace o'erflow.

2 No mortal can with him compare
  Among the sons of men;
Fairer is he than all the fair
  That fill the heavenly train.

3 He saw me plunged in deep distress,
  He flew to my relief;
For me he bore the shameful cross,
  And carried all my grief.

4 To him I owe my life and breath,
  And all the joys I have;
He makes me triumph over death,
  He saves me from the grave.

5 To heaven, the place of his abode,
  He brings my weary feet,
Shows me the glories of my God,
  And makes my joy complete.

6 Since from his bounty I receive
  Such proofs of love divine,
Had I a thousand hearts to give,
  Lord, they should all be thine.

270
I. Watts.

FATHER! how wide thy glory shines!
  How high thy wonders rise! [signs,
Known through the earth by thousand
  By thousand through the skies.

2 Those mighty orbs proclaim thy power,
  Their motions speak thy skill;
And, on the wings of every hour,
  We read thy patience still.

3 But, when we view thy strange design
  To save rebellious worms,
Where vengeance and compassion join
  In their divinest forms,—

4 Here the whole Deity is known;
  Nor dares a creature guess,
Which of the glories brightest shone,
  The justice, or the grace.

5 Now the full glories of the Lamb
  Adorn the heavenly plains;
Bright seraphs learn Immanuel's name,
  And try their choicest strains.

6 O may I bear some humble part,
  In that immortal song;
Wonder and joy shall tune my heart,
  And love command my tongue.

CHRIST.

CHRISTMAS. C. M. — HANDEL.

1. To our Redeemer's glorious name, A-wake the sa-cred song; O may his love—im-mor-tal flame— Tune eve-ry heart and tongue, Tune eve-ry heart and tongue.

271 *A. Steele.*

To our Redeemer's glorious name,
 Awake the sacred song;
O may his love—immortal flame—
 Tune every heart and tongue.

2 His love, what mortal thought can reach?
 What mortal tongue display?
Imagination's utmost stretch
 In wonder dies away.

3 Dear Lord, while we adoring pay
 Our humble thanks to thee,
May every heart with rapture say,
 "The Saviour died for me!"

4 O may the sweet, the blissful theme,
 Fill every heart and tongue,
Till strangers love thy charming name,
 And join the sacred song.

272 *C. Wesley.*

O for a thousand tongues to sing
 My dear Redeemer's praise;
The glories of my God and King,
 The triumphs of his grace!

2 My gracious Master and my God,
 Assist me to proclaim,
To spread through all the earth abroad,
 The honors of thy name.

3 Jesus, the name that calms our fears,
 That bids our sorrows cease;
'Tis music in the sinner's ears,
 'Tis life, and health, and peace.

4 He breaks the power of cancelled sin,
 He sets the prisoner free;
His blood can make the foulest clean,
 His blood availed for me.

AZMON. C. M. — C. G. GLÄSER.

1. O for a thous-and tongues to sing My dear Re-deem-er's praise; The glo-ries of my God and King, The tri-umphs of his grace!

Songs of Adoration and Love. 149

BEMERTON. C. M.   H. W. GREATOREX.

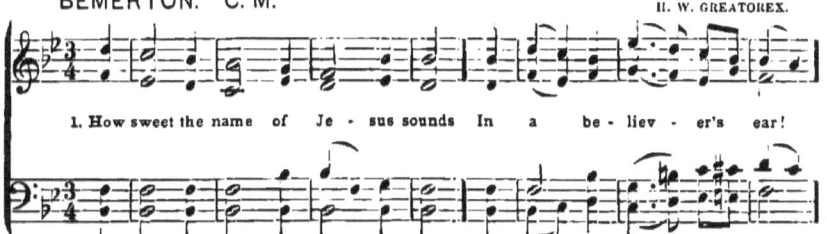

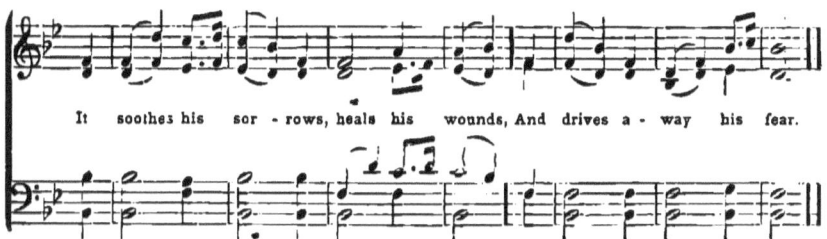

273   *J. Newton.*

How sweet the name of Jesus sounds
  In a believer's ear!
It soothes his sorrows, heals his wounds,
  And drives away his fear.

2 It makes the wounded spirit whole,
  And calms the troubled breast;
'Tis manna to the hungry soul,
  And to the weary, rest.

3 Jesus, my Shepherd, Saviour, Friend,
  My Prophet, Priest, and King;
My Lord, my Life, my Way, my End,
  Accept the praise I bring.

4 Weak is the effort of my heart,
  And cold my warmest thought;
But when I see thee as thou art,
  I'll praise thee as I ought.

5 Till then I would thy love proclaim,
  With every fleeting breath;
And may the music of thy name
  Refresh my soul in death.

274   *G. W. Bethune.*

O Jesus, when I think of thee,
  Thy manger, cross, and throne,
My spirit trusts exultingly
  In thee, and thee alone.

2 I see thee in thy weakness first;
  Then, glorious from thy shame,
I see thee death's strong fetters burst,
  And reach heaven's mightiest name.

3 For me thou didst become a man,
  For me didst weep and die;
For me achieve thy wondrous plan,
  For me ascend on high.

4 O let me share thy holy birth,
  Thy faith, thy death to sin!
And, strong amidst the toils of earth,
  My heavenly life begin.

5 Then shall I know what means the strain
  Triumphant of Saint Paul:
"To live is Christ, to die is gain;"
  "Christ is my all in all."

CHRIST.

CHESTERFIELD. C. M   T. HAWEIS.

1. Sal-va-tion! O the joy-ful sound! 'Tis pleas-ure to our ears;
A sove-reign balm for ev-ery wound, A cor-dial for our fears.

275
I. Watts.

SALVATION! O the joyful sound!
  'Tis pleasure to our ears;
A sovereign balm for every wound,
  A cordial for our fears.

2 Buried in sorrow and in sin,
  At hell's dark door we lay;
But we arise, by grace divine,
  To see a heavenly day.

3 Salvation! let the echo fly
  The spacious earth around,
While all the armies of the sky
  Conspire to raise the sound.

276
I. Watts.

PLUNGED in a gulf of dark despair,
  We wretched sinners lay,
Without one cheerful beam of hope,
  Or spark of glimmering day.

2 With pitying eyes the Prince of grace
  Beheld our helpless grief;
He saw, and (O amazing love!)
  He ran to our relief.

3 Down from the shining seats above,
  With joyful haste he fled,
Entered the grave in mortal flesh,
  And dwelt among the dead.

4 O for this love, let rocks and hills
  Their lasting silence break;
And all harmonious human tongues
  The Saviour's praises speak.

5 Angels, assist our mighty joys,
  Strike all your harps of gold;
But when you raise your highest notes,
  His love can ne'er be told.

277
I. Watts.

IN vain we seek for peace with God
  By methods of our own;
Blest Saviour! nothing but thy blood
  Can bring us near the throne.

2 The threatenings of thy broken law
  Impress the soul with dread:
If God his sword of vengeance draw,
  It strikes the spirit dead.

3 But thine atoning sacrifice
  Hath answered all demands;
And peace and pardon from the skies
  Are offered by thy hands.

4 'Tis by thy death we live, O Lord!
  'Tis on thy cross we rest:
For ever be thy love adored,
  Thy name for ever blest.

Songs of Adoration and Love. 151

MANOAH. C. M.   ROSSINI.

1. Christ is my Proph-et, Priest, and King; My Proph-et full of light; My great High Priest be-fore the throne; My King of heaven-ly might.

278   *J. Mason.*

CHRIST is my Prophet, Priest, and King;
My Prophet full of light;
My great High Priest before the throne;
My King of heavenly might.

2 For he, indeed, is Lord of lords,
And he the King of kings;
He is the Sun of Righteousness,
With healing in his wings.

3 Christ is my Peace: he died for me,
For me he gave his blood;
And, as my wondrous sacrifice,
Offered himself to God.

4 Christ Jesus is my All in All,
My comfort and my love;
My life below, and he shall be
My joy and crown above.

279   *G. W. Doane.*

THOU art the Way: to thee alone
From sin and death we flee;
And he who would the Father seek,
Must seek him, Lord, by thee.

2 Thou art the Truth: thy word alone
True wisdom can impart;
Thou only canst inform the mind,
And purify the heart.

3 Thou art the Life: the rending tomb
Proclaims thy conquering arm,
And those who put their trust in thee
Nor death, nor hell shall harm.

4 Thou art the Way, the Truth, the Life;
Grant us that Way to know,
That Truth to keep, that Life to win,
Whose joys eternal flow.

280   *J. G. Deck.*

LORD Jesus, are we one with thee?
O height, O depth of love!
With thee we died upon the tree;
In thee we live above.

2 Our sins, our guilt, in love divine,
Were borne on earth by thee;
The gall, the curse, the wrath were thine
To set thy members free.

3 Ascended now in glory bright,
Still one with us thou art;
Nor life, nor death, nor depth, nor height,
Thy saints and thee can part.

4 Soon, soon shall come that glorious day,
When, seated on thy throne,
Thou shalt to wondering worlds display
That thou with us art one!

CHRST.

281

O ONE with God the Father
 In majesty and might,
The brightness of his glory
 Eternal Light of Light;
O'er this our home of darkness
 Thy rays are streaming now;
The shadows flee before thee,
 The world's true Light art Thou.

2 Yet, Lord, we see but darkly;—
 O heavenly Light arise,
Dispel these mists that shroud us,
 And hide thee from our eyes!
We long to trace the footprints
 That thou thyself hast trod,
We long to see the pathway
 That leads to thee, our God.

3 O Jesus, shine around us
 With radiance of thy grace;
O Jesus turn upon us
 The brightness of thy face.
We need no star to guide us,
 As on our way we press,
If thou thy light vouchsafest,
 O Sun of righteousness.

282   H. M.   *T. Kelly.*

THE atoning work is done,
 The victim's blood is shed,
And Jesus now is gone
 His people's cause to plead:
He stands in heaven their great High Priest,
And bears their names upon his breast.

2 No temple made with hands
 His place of service is;
In heaven itself he stands,
 A heavenly priesthood his:
In him the shadows of the law,
Are all fulfilled, and now withdraw.

3 And though awhile he be
 Hid from the eyes of men,
His people look to see
 Their great High Priest again:
In brightest glory he will come,
And take his waiting people home.

Dox. To God the Father's throne
 Your highest honors raise;
Glory to God the Son;
 To God, the Spirit, praise;
With all our powers, Eternal King,
Thy name we sing, while faith adores.

Songs of Adoration and Love. 153

FRANKLIN. H. M.   J. P. HOLBROOK.

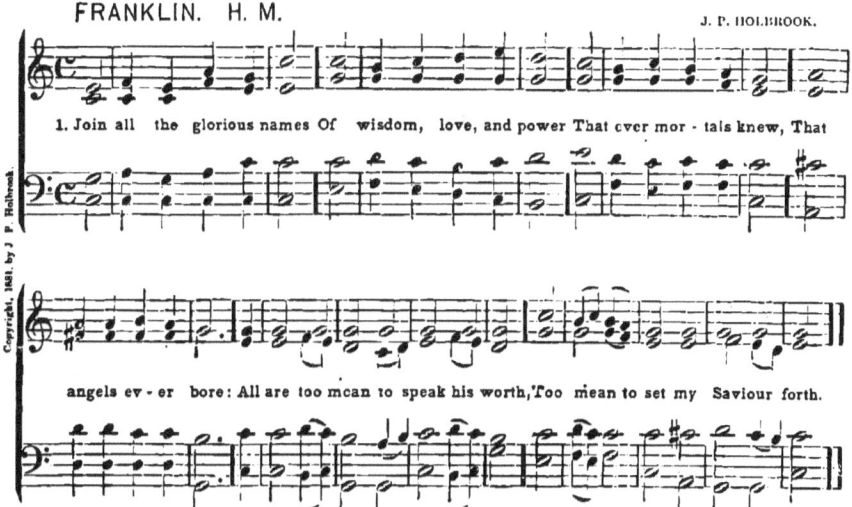

1. Join all the glorious names Of wisdom, love, and power That ever mor-tals knew, That angels ev-er bore: All are too mean to speak his worth, Too mean to set my Saviour forth.

Copyright, 1881, by J. P. Holbrook

283   *I. Watts.*

Join all the glorious names
  Of wisdom, love, and power
That ever mortals knew,
  That angels ever bore:
All are too mean to speak his worth,
Too mean to set my Saviour forth.

2 Great Prophet of our God!
  My tongue would bless thy name;
By thee the joyful news
  Of our salvation came:
The joyful news of sins forgiven,
Of hell subdued, and peace with heaven.

3 Jesus, our great High Priest,
  Offered his blood and died;
My guilty conscience seeks
  No sacrifice beside:
His powerful blood did once atone,
And now it pleads before the throne.

4 O thou Almighty Lord,
  My Conqueror and my King,
Thy sceptre and thy sword,
  Thy reigning grace I sing:
Thine is the power; behold, I sit,
In willing bonds, beneath thy feet.

284   *C. Wesley.*

Rejoice, the Lord is King,
  Your Lord and King adore;
Mortals, give thanks and sing,
  And triumph evermore:
Lift up your heart, lift up your voice,
Rejoice, again I say, rejoice.

2 Jesus the Saviour reigns,
  The God of truth and love;
When he had purged our stains,
  He took his seat above:
Lift up your heart, lift up your voice,
Rejoice, again I say, rejoice.

3 His kingdom cannot fail,
  He rules o'er earth and heaven;
The keys of death and hell
  Are to our Jesus given.
Lift up your heart, lift up your voice,
Rejoice, again I say, rejoice.

4 Rejoice in glorious hope;
  Jesus, the Judge, shall come,
And take his servants up
  To their eternal home:
We soon shall hear the archangel's voice,
The trump of God shall sound, Rejoice.

First Lines of Hymns.

HYMNS.	HYMNS.
285 Creator Spirit, by whose aid	294 My God, my reconciled God,
286 Spirit of power, and truth, and love,	295 Come, Holy Spirit, come,
287 Eternal Spirit, we confess	296 Lord God, the Holy Ghost,
288 Come, gracious Spirit, heavenly Dove,	297 Our blest Redeemer, ere he breathed
289 The Spirit came! that mighty Breath	298 Holy Ghost, the infinite,
290 Let songs of praises fill the sky!	299 Granted is the Saviour's prayer;
291 Spirit of life, and light, and love,	300 Gracious Spirit, Love divine!
292 Come, Holy Spirit, heavenly Dove,	301 Gracious Spirit, dwell with me;
293 Can aught beneath a power divine,	302 Source divine of strength and power,

SCHAFF. L. M. 6l.

1. Cre-a-tor Spir-it, by whose aid The world's founda-tions first were laid,
Come, vis-it ev-ery wait-ing mind, Come, pour thy joys on hu-man kind;
From sin and sor-row set us free, And make thy tem-ples wor-thy thee.

285   *J. Dryden, tr.*

CREATOR Spirit, by whose aid
The world's foundations first were laid,
Come, visit every waiting mind,
Come, pour thy joys on human kind;
From sin and sorrow set us free,
And make thy temples worthy thee.

2 O source of uncreated light,
The Father's promised Paraclete;
Thrice holy fount, thrice holy fire,
Our hearts with heavenly love inspire;
Come, and thy sacred unction bring,
To sanctify us while we sing.

3 Refine and purge our earthly parts;
But, O inflame and fire our hearts;
Make us eternal truths receive,
And practice all that we believe;
Give us thyself, that we may see
The Father and the Son, by thee.

4 Immortal honors, endless fame,
Attend the almighty Father's name!
The Saviour Son be glorified,
Who for lost man's redemption died!
And equal adoration be,
Eternal Comforter, to thee!

Invocations. 155

JANES. L. M.   MOZART.

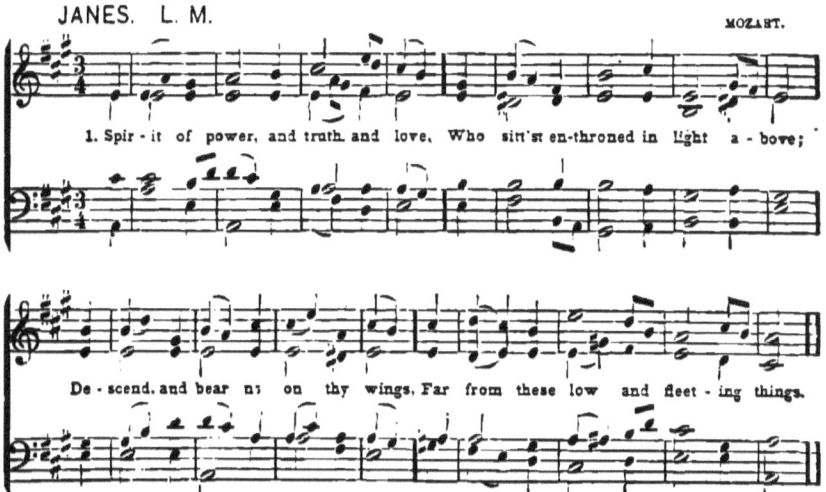

1. Spirit of power, and truth, and love, Who sitt'st enthroned in light above; Descend, and bear us on thy wings, Far from these low and fleeting things.

286
W. L. Alexander.

Spirit of power, and truth, and love,
Who sitt'st enthroned in light above;
Descend, and bear us on thy wings,
Far from these low and fleeting things.

2 'Tis thine the wounded soul to heal;
'Tis thine to make the hardened feel;
Thine to give light to blinded eyes,
And bid the earth-bound spirit rise.

3 When faith is weak, and courage fails,
When grief or doubt our soul assails,
Who can, like thee, our spirits cheer?
Great Comforter, be ever near.

4 Come, Holy Spirit, like the fire:
With burning zeal our souls inspire;
Come, like the south wind, breathing balm,
Our joys refresh, our passions calm.

5 Come, like the sun's enlightening beam;
Come, like the cooling, cleansing stream;
With all thy graces present be:
Spirit of God! we wait for thee.

287
I. Watts.

Eternal Spirit, we confess
And sing the wonders of thy grace:
Thy power conveys our blessings down
From God the Father and the Son.

2 Enlightened by thy heavenly ray,
Our shades and darkness turn to day;
Thine inward teachings make us know
Our danger and our refuge too.

3 Thy power and glory work within,
And break the chains of reigning sin;
All our imperious lusts subdue,
And form our wretched hearts anew.

4 The troubled conscience knows thy voice;
Thy cheering words awake our joys;
Thy words allay the stormy wind,
And calm the surges of the mind.

288
S. Browne.

Come, gracious Spirit, heavenly Dove,
With light and comfort from above;
Be thou our guardian, thou our guide,
O'er every thought and step preside.

2 The light of truth to us display,
And make us know and choose thy way;
Plant holy fear in every heart,
That we from thee may ne'er depart.

3 Lead us to Christ, the living way,
Nor let us from his precepts stray;
Lead us to holiness, the road
That we must take to dwell with God.

4 Lead us to heaven, that we may share
Fullness of joy for ever there;
Lead us to God, our final rest,
To be with him for ever blest.

MERTON. C. M.
H. K. OLIVER.

1. The Spir-it came! that might-y Breath From heaven's e-ter-nal shores;
His un-cre-a-ted fresh-ness fills His Bride, as she a-dores.

289
F. W. Faber.

The Spirit came! that mighty Breath
From heaven's eternal shores;
His uncreated freshness fills
His Bride, as she adores.

2 The Spirit came into the Church
With his unfailing power;
He is the living Heart that beats
Within her at this hour.

3 Most tender Spirit, mighty God,
Sweet must thy presence be,
If loss of Jesus can be gain,
So long as we have thee!

290
T. Cotterill.

Let songs of praises fill the sky!
Christ, our ascended Lord,
Sends down his Spirit from on high,
According to his word.

2 The Spirit, by his heavenly breath,
New life creates within;
He quickens sinners from their death
Of trespasses and sin.

3 The things of Christ the Spirit takes,
And to our hearts reveals;
Our bodies he his temple makes,
And our redemption seals.

4 Come, Holy Spirit, from above,
With thy celestial fire;
Come, and with flames of zeal and love
Our hearts and tongues inspire!

291
T. Haweis.

Spirit of life, and light, and love,
Thy heavenly influence give;
Quicken our souls, born from above,
In Christ that we may live.

2 To our benighted minds reveal
The glories of his grace,
And bring us where no clouds conceal
The brightness of his face.

3 His love within us shed abroad,
Life's ever-springing well;
Till God in us, and we in God,
In love eternal dwell.

ST. BERNARD. C. M.
ST. ALBAN'S TUNE BOOK.

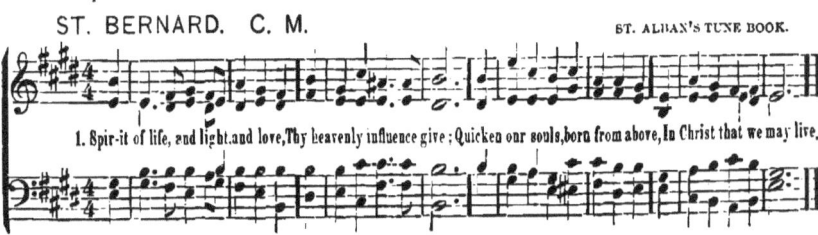

1. Spir-it of life, and light, and love, Thy heavenly influence give; Quicken our souls, born from above, In Christ that we may live.

Invocations. 157

SIMPSON. C. M.   L. SPOHR.

292
I. Watts.

Come, Holy Spirit, heavenly Dove,
  With all thy quickening powers,
Kindle a flame of sacred love
  In these cold hearts of ours.

2 In vain we tune our formal songs,
  In vain we strive to rise;
Hosannas languish on our tongues,
  And our devotion dies.

3 Dear Lord, and shall we ever live
  At this poor dying rate?
Our love so faint, so cold to thee,
  And thine to us so great?

4 Come, Holy Spirit, heavenly Dove,
  With all thy quickening powers;
Come, shed abroad a Saviour's love,
  And that shall kindle ours.

293
A. Steele.

Can aught, beneath a power divine,
  The stubborn will subdue?
'T is thine, almighty Spirit, thine,
  To form the heart anew.

2 'T is thine, the passions to recall,
  And upward bid them rise;
To make the scales of error fall,
  From reason's darkened eyes;—

3 To chase the shades of death away,
  And bid the sinner live;

A beam of heaven, a vital ray,
  'T is thine alone to give.

4 O change these wretched hearts of ours,
  And give them life divine;
Then shall our passions and our powers,
  Almighty Lord, be thine.

294
J. Mason.

My God, my reconciled God,
  Creator of my peace,
Thee will I love, and praise, and sing,
  Till life and breath shall cease.

2 My soul doth magnify the Lord,
  My spirit doth rejoice
In God, my Saviour and my God;
  I hear his joyful voice.

3 I need not go abroad for joy,
  Who have a feast at home;
My sighs are turned into songs,
  The Comforter is come!

4 Down from above, the blessèd Dove
  Is come into my breast,
To witness God's eternal love:
  This is my heavenly feast.

5 My God, my reconcilèd God,
  Creator of my peace,
Thee will I love, and praise, and sing,
  Till life and breath shall cease.

THE HOLY SPIRIT.

LEIGHTON. S. M. H. W. GREATOREX.

1. Come, Holy Spirit, come! Let thy bright beams arise: Dispel the sorrow from our minds, The darkness from our eyes.

295 *J. Hart.*

COME, Holy Spirit, come!
Let thy bright beams arise:
Dispel the sorrow from our minds,
The darkness from our eyes.

2 Revive our drooping faith,
Our doubts and fears remove,
And kindle in our breasts the flame
Of never-dying love.

3 'Tis thine to cleanse the heart,
To sanctify the soul,
To pour fresh life in every part,
And new-create the whole.

4 O dwell within our hearts;
Our minds from bondage free;
Then shall we know, and praise, and love,
The Father, Son, and Thee.

296 *J. Montgomery.*

LORD God, the Holy Ghost,
In this accepted hour,
As on the day of Pentecost,
Descend in all thy power.

2 Like mighty rushing wind
Upon the waves beneath,
Move with one impulse every mind,
One soul, one feeling breathe.

3 The young, the old inspire
With wisdom from above;
And give us hearts and tongues of fire
To pray, and praise, and love.

4 Spirit of truth, be thou,
In life and death, our guide;
O Spirit of adoption, now
May we be sanctified.

MARTH. 7s, 5s. J. P. HOLBROOK.

1. Holy Ghost, the infinite, Shine upon our nature's night With thy blessed inward light, Comforter Divine!

Invocations.

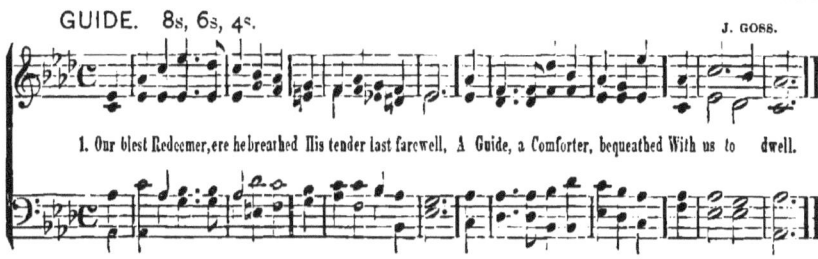

GUIDE. 8s, 6s, 4s. J. GOSS.

1. Our blest Redeemer, ere he breathed His tender last farewell, A Guide, a Comforter, bequeathed With us to dwell.

297 *H. Auber.*

Our blest Redeemer, ere he breathed
His tender last farewell,
A Guide, a Comforter, bequeathed
With us to dwell.

2 He came in tongues of living flame,
To teach, convince, subdue;
All powerful as the wind he came,
As viewless too.

3 He came sweet influence to impart,
A gracious willing guest,
While he can find one humble heart
Wherein to rest.

4 And his that gentle voice we hear,
Soft as the breath of even,
That checks each thought, that calms each
And speaks of heaven.   [fear,

5 And every virtue we possess,
And every conquest won,
And every thought of holiness,
Are his alone.

6 Spirit of purity and grace,
Our weakness, pitying, see:
O make our hearts thy dwelling-place,
And worthier thee.

COMFORTER 7s, 5s. J. BARNBY.

1. Holy Ghost, the in-fi-nite, Shine upon our nature's night With thy blessed inward light, Comforter Di-vine!

298 *G. Rawson.*

Holy Ghost, the infinite,
Shine upon our nature's night
With thy blesséd inward light,
  Comforter Divine!

2 We are sinful, cleanse us, Lord;
We are faint, thy strength afford;
Lost, until by thee restored,
  Comforter Divine!

3 Like the dew, thy peace distil;
Guide, subdue our wayward will,
Things of Christ unfolding still,
  Comforter Divine!

4 In us, for us, intercede,
And with voiceless groaning plead
Our unutterable need,
  Comforter Divine!

5 In us "Abba, Father," cry,
Earnest of our bliss on high,
Seal of immortality,
  Comforter Divine!

6 Search for us the depths of God;
Bear us up the starry road,
To the height of thine abode,
  Comforter Divine!

THE HOLY SPIRIT.

299   *C. Wesley.*

Granted is the Saviour's prayer;
Hail, O gracious Comforter,
Promise of our parting Lord,
To his throne in heaven restored!

2 God, the everlasting God,
Makes with mortals his abode;
Whom the heavens cannot contain,
He vouchsafes to dwell with man,

3 Never will he thence depart,
Inmate of a humble heart;
Carrying on his work within,
Striving till he cast out sin.

4 Come, divine and peaceful Guest,
Make thy home within my breast;
Day by day my life renew,
Thou the Gift and Giver too!

300   *J. Stocker.*

Gracious Spirit, Love divine!
Let thy light within me shine;
All my guilty fears remove,
Fill me with thy heavenly love.

2 Speak thy pardoning grace to me,
Set the burdened sinner free;
Lead me to the Lamb of God,
Wash me in his precious blood.

3 Life and peace to me impart,
Seal salvation on my heart;
Breathe thyself into my breast,—
Earnest of immortal rest.

4 Let me never from thee stray,
Keep me in the narrow way,
Fill my soul with joy divine,
Keep me, Lord! forever thine.

Invocations. 161

CUTLER. 7s, 6l. (A.)

1. Gracious Spirit, dwell with me; I myself would gracious be,
And with words that help and heal, Would thy life in mine reveal,
And with actions bold and meek, Would for Christ, my Saviour speak.

301 *T. T. Lynch.*

Gracious Spirit, dwell with me;
 I myself would gracious be,
And with words that help and heal,
 Would thy life in mine reveal,
And with actions bold and meek,
 Would for Christ, my Saviour speak.

2 Truthful Spirit, dwell with me;
 I myself would truthful be,
And with wisdom kind and clear
 Let thy life in mine appear,
And with actions brotherly
 Speak my Lord's sincerity.

3 Mighty Spirit, dwell with me;
 I myself would mighty be,
Mighty so as to prevail
 Where unaided man must fail,
Ever by a mighty hope
 Pressing on and bearing up.

4 Holy Spirit, dwell with me;
 I myself would holy be;
Separate from sin, I would
 Choose and cherish all things good,
And whatever I can be
 Give to him, who gave me thee.

302 *C. Winkworth, tr.*

Source Divine of strength and power,
 Thou blest Spirit God hath given,
Aid us in temptation's hour,
 Train and perfect us for heaven;
Though the flesh resist thy will,
 Let thy grace be stronger still.

2 Witness in our hearts that God
 Counts us children through his Son;
That our Father's gentle rod
 Smites us for our good alone;
So when tried, perplexed, distrest,
 In his love we still may rest.

3 Quicken us to seek his face
 Freely, with a trusting heart;
In our prayers O breathe thy grace,
 And thy help to us impart:
So shall our requests be heard,
 And our faith to joy be stirred.

4 Guide us, Lord, from day to day,
 Keep us in the path of grace;
Clear all hindrances away
 That might stay us in the race:
Let thy words of cheer and balm
 Bring us courage, patience, calm.

THE SCRIPTURES.
First Lines of Hymns.

HYMNS.
303 O Word of God incarnate,
304 The heavens declare thy glory, Lord!
305 God, in the gospel of his Son,
306 A glory gilds the sacred page,
307 How precious is the book divine,
308 Lamp of our feet, whereby we trace,
309 Laden with guilt, and full of fears,

HYMNS.
310 Lord I have made thy word my choice,
311 Father of mercies, in thy word,
312 Begin, my tongue, some heavenly theme,
313 The mercies of my God and King,
314 Lord, thy Word abideth,
315 Ever would I fain be reading,
316 What a strange and wondrous story,

MIRIAM. 7s, 6s.   J P. HOLBROOK.

1. O Word of God In-car-nate, O Wis dom from on high, O Truth unchanged unchanging, O Light of our dark sky;

We praise thee for the radiance That from the hallowed page, A lantern to our foot-steps Shines on from age to age.

303   W. W. How.

O WORD of God Incarnate,
　O Wisdom from on high,
O Truth unchanged, unchanging,
　O Light of our dark sky;
We praise thee for the radiance
　That from the hallowed page,
A lantern to our footsteps,
　Shines on from age to age.

2 The Church from thee, her Master,
　Received the gift divine;
And still that light she lifteth
　O'er all the earth to shine.
It is the golden casket
　Where gems of truth are stored;
It is the heaven-drawn picture
　Of Thee, the living Word.

3 It floateth like a banner
　Before God's host unfurled;
It shineth like a beacon
　Above the darkling world;
It is the chart and compass,
　That o'er life's surging sea,
Mid mists, and rocks, and quicksands,
　Still guide, O Christ, to thee.

4 O make thy Church, dear Saviour,
　A lamp of burnished gold,
To bear before the nations
　Thy true light, as of old.
O teach thy wandering pilgrims
　By this their path to trace,
Till, clouds and darkness ended,
* They see thee face to face.

The Word of God. 163

MELCOMBE. L. M. — S. WEBBE

1. The heavens declare thy glory, Lord; In every star thy wisdom shines;
But when our eyes behold thy word, We read thy name in fairer lines.

304
I. Watts.

The heavens declare thy glory, Lord;
In every star thy wisdom shines;
But when our eyes behold thy word,
We read thy name in fairer lines.

2 The rolling sun, the changing light
And nights and days thy power confess,
But the blest volume thou hast writ
Reveals thy justice and thy grace.

3 Sun, moon and stars convey thy praise
Round the whole earth, and never stand;
So, when thy truth began its race,
It touched and glanced on every land.

4 Nor shall thy spreading gospel rest
Till through the world thy truth has run,
Till Christ has all the nations blest
That see the light or feel the sun.

5 Great Sun of Righteousness, arise;
Bless the dark world with heavenly light;
Thy gospel makes the simple wise,
Thy laws are pure, thy judgments right.

6 Thy noblest wonders here we view
In souls renewed and sins forgiven;
Lord, cleanse my sins, my soul renew,
And make thy word my guide to heaven.

305
B. Beddome.

God, in the gospel of his Son,
Makes his eternal counsels known,
Where love in all its glory shines,
And truth is drawn in fairest lines.

2 Here, sinners of an humble frame
May taste his grace, and learn his name;
May read, in characters of blood,
The wisdom, power, and grace of God.

3 Here faith reveals to mortal eyes,
A brighter world beyond the skies;
Here shines the light which guides our way
From earth to realms of endless day.

4 O grant us grace, almighty Lord,
To read and mark thy holy word,
Its truths with meekness to receive,
And by its holy precepts live.

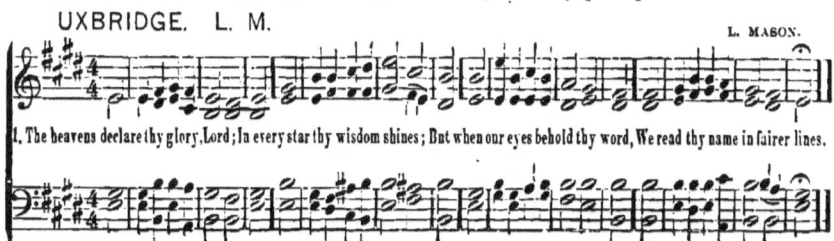

UXBRIDGE. L. M. — L. MASON.

1. The heavens declare thy glory, Lord; In every star thy wisdom shines; But when our eyes behold thy word, We read thy name in fairer lines.

THE SCRIPTURES.

BURLINGTON. C. M. — J. F. BURROWES.

1. A glory gilds the sacred page, Majestic like the sun;
It gives a light to every age— It gives but borrows none.

306
W. Cowper.

A glory gilds the sacred page,
  Majestic like the sun;
It gives a light to every age—
  It gives but borrows none.

2 The hand that gave it still supplies
  The gracious light and heat;
His truths upon the nations rise—
  They rise, but never set.

3 Let everlasting thanks be thine
  For such a bright display
As makes a world of darkness shine
  With beams of heavenly day.

4 My soul rejoices to pursue
  The steps of him I love,
Till glory breaks upon my view
  In brighter worlds above.

307
J. Fawcett.

How precious is the book divine
  By inspiration given!
Bright as a lamp its doctrines shine
  To guide our souls to heaven.

2 It sweetly cheers our drooping hearts
  In this dark vale of tears;
Life, light and joy it still imparts,
  And quells our rising fears.

3 This lamp through all the tedious night
  Of life shall guide our way,
Till we behold the clearer light
  Of an eternal day.

308
B. Barton.

Lamp of our feet, whereby we trace
  Our path when wont to stray;
Stream from the Fount of heavenly grace,
  Brook by the traveller's way;

2 Bread of our souls, whereon we feed,
  True manna from on high;
Our guide and chart, wherein we read
  Of realms beyond the sky.

3 Word of the everlasting God,
  Will of his glorious Son;
Without thee how could earth be trod,
  Or heaven itself be won?

4 Lord, grant us all aright to learn
  The wisdom it imparts;
And to its heavenly teaching turn,
  With simple, child-like hearts.

309
I. Watts.

Laden with guilt, and full of fears,
  I fly to thee, my Lord!
And not a glimpse of hope appears,
  But in thy written word.

2 This is the judge that ends the strife,
  Where wit and reason fail;
My guide to everlasting life,
  Through all this gloomy vale.

3 O may thy counsels, mighty God!
  My roving feet command;
Nor I forsake the happy road,
  That leads to thy right hand.

The Word of God. 165

BEMERTON. C. M. — H. W. GREATOREX

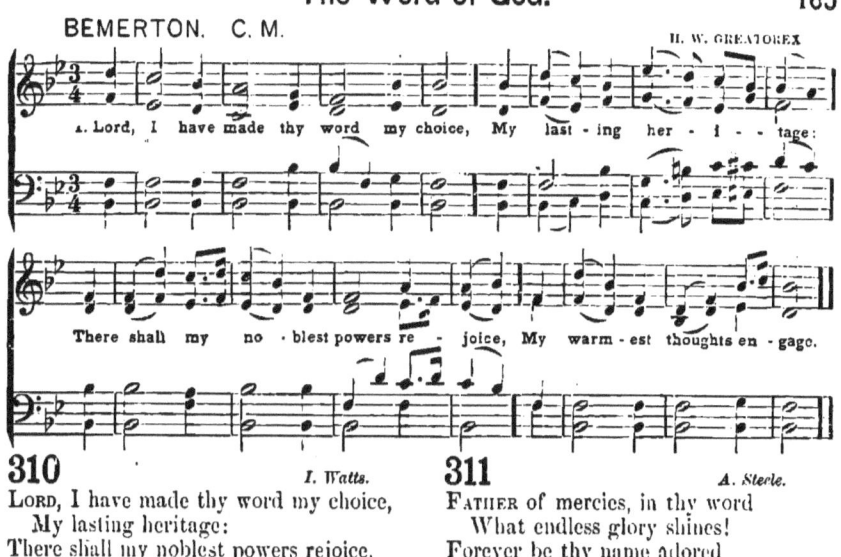

1. Lord, I have made thy word my choice, My last-ing her-i-tage: There shall my no-blest powers re-joice, My warm-est thoughts en-gage.

310 *I. Watts.*

Lord, I have made thy word my choice,
My lasting heritage:
There shall my noblest powers rejoice,
My warmest thoughts engage.

2 I'll read the histories of thy love,
And keep thy laws in sight;
While through the promises I rove
With ever fresh delight.

3 'Tis a broad land of wealth unknown,
Where springs of life arise,
Seeds of immortal bliss are sown,
And hidden glory lies.

4 The best relief that mourners have:
It makes our sorrows blest;
Our fairest hope beyond the grave,
And our eternal rest.

311 *A. Steele.*

Father of mercies, in thy word
What endless glory shines!
Forever be thy name adored
For these celestial lines.

2 Here the Redeemer's welcome voice
Spreads heavenly peace around;
And life and everlasting joys
Attend the blissful sound.

3 O may these heavenly pages be
My ever dear delight;
And still new beauties may I see,
And still increasing light.

4 Divine Instructor, gracious Lord,
Be thou forever near;
Teach me to love thy sacred word,
And view my Saviour there.

DOWNS. C. M. — L. MASON.

1. Fa-ther of mer-cies, in thy word What end-less glo-ry shines! For-ev-er be thy name a-dored For these ce-les-tial lines.

THE SCRIPTURES.

166

MANOAH. C. M. — ROSSINI.

1. Be-gin, my tongue, some heaven-ly theme, And speak some boundless thing; The might-y works, or might-ier name, Of our e-ter-nal King.

312   I. Watts.

Begin, my tongue, some heavenly theme,
And speak some boundless thing;
The mighty works, or mightier name,
Of our eternal King.

2 Tell of his wondrous faithfulness,
And sound his power abroad;
Sing the sweet promise of his grace,
And the performing God.

3 His every word of grace is strong,
As that which built the skies;
The voice that rolls the stars along,
Speaks all the promises.

4 O might I hear thy heavenly tongue
But whisper, "Thou art mine!"
Those gentle words should raise my song
To notes almost divine.

313   H. F. Lyte.

The mercies of my God and King
My tongue shall still pursue;
O happy they who, while they sing
Those mercies, share them too!

2 As bright and lasting as the sun,
As lofty as the sky,
From age to age thy word shall run,
And change and change defy.

3 The cov'nant of the King of kings
Shall stand forever sure;
Beneath the shadow of thy wings
Thy saints repose secure.

4 In earth below, in heaven above,
Who, who is Lord like thee?
O spread the gospel of thy love
Till all thy glories see!

CLARK. 6s. — R. R. CHOPE.

1. Lord, thy Word a-bid-eth, And our footsteps guideth: Who its truth believeth Light and joy receiveth.

314   H. W. Baker.

Lord, thy Word abideth,
And our footsteps guideth;
Who its truth believeth
Light and joy receiveth.

2 When our foes are near us,
Then thy word doth cheer us,
Word of consolation,
Message of salvation.

3 When the storms are o'er us,
And dark clouds before us,
Then its light directeth
And our way protecteth.

4 Word of mercy, giving
Succor to the living;
Word of life, supplying
Comfort to the dying!

The Word of God. 167

CHAPMAN. 8s, 7s. D. J. P. HOLBROOK.

315
C. Winkworth, tr.

Ever would I fain be reading
In the ancient holy Book,
Of my Saviour's gentle pleading,
Truth in every word and look.

2 How when children came he bless'd them,
Suffered no man to reprove,
Took them in his arms, and press'd them
To his heart with words of love.

3 How to all the sick and tearful
Help was ever gladly shown;
How he sought the poor and fearful,
Called them brothers and his own.

4 How no contrite soul e'er sought him,
And was bidden to depart,
How with gentle words he taught him,
Took the death from out his heart.

5 How the flock he gently leadeth
Whom his Father gave him here;
How his arms he widely spreadeth
To his heart to draw us near.

6 Still I read the ancient story,
And my joy is ever new,
How for us he left his glory,
How he still is kind and true

316

What a strange and wondrous story,
From the Book of God is read:
How the Lord of life and glory
Had not where to lay his head.

2 How he left his throne in heaven,
Here to suffer, bleed, and die,
That my soul might be forgiven,
And ascend to God on high.

3 Father, let thy Holy Spirit
Still reveal a Saviour's love,
And prepare me to inherit
Glory where he reigns above;

4 There, with saints and angels dwelling,
May I that great love proclaim,
And with them be ever telling
All the wonders of his name.

First Lines of Hymns.

FOUNDATION.
HYMNS.
317 Christ is made the sure foundation,
318 The church's one foundation,
319 Glorious things of thee are spoken,
320 Hark, the church proclaims her honor,

BAPTISM.
321 Sound aloud Jehovah's praises,
322 We praise thee, Saviour, for the grace,
323 He who, a little child, began,
324 Saviour, who thy flock art feeding,
325 How large the promise! how divine,
326 See Israel's gentle Shepherd stand,

CONFESSION OF THE FAITH.
327 Thy servants now, O Triune Lord,

HYMNS
328 Blest Trinity, from mortal sight,
329 Come, ever blessed Spirit, come,
330 Lord, I am thine, entirely thine,
331 O happy day, that fixed my choice,
332 My God, accept my heart this day,
333 The promise of my Father's love,
334 What shall I render to my God,
335 We saw thee not when thou didst tread,
336 Jesus, my Saviour, who could dare,

MINISTRY.
337 "Go preach my gospel," saith the Lord,
338 Ye Christian heralds, go, proclaim,
339 Pour out thy Spirit from on high,
340 How beauteous are their feet,
341 Jesus, the name high over all,

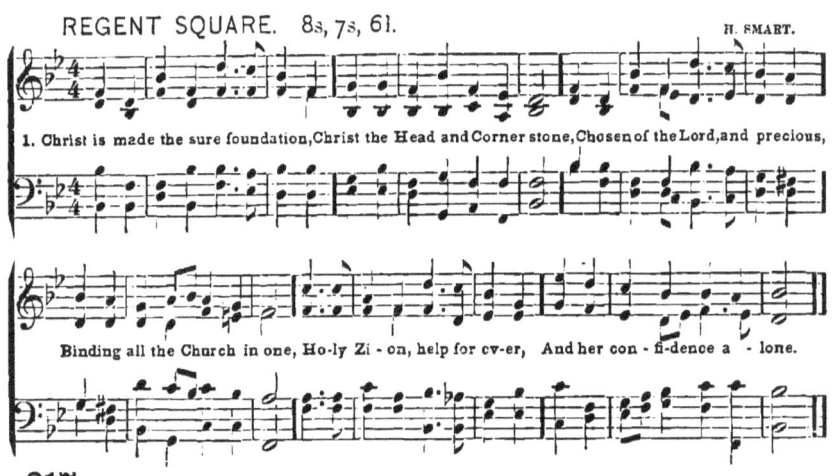

REGENT SQUARE. 8s, 7s, 6l.   H. SMART.

1. Christ is made the sure foundation, Christ the Head and Corner stone, Chosen of the Lord, and precious,
Binding all the Church in one, Ho-ly Zi-on, help for ev-er, And her con-fi-dence a-lone.

317   J. M. Neale, tr.

Christ is made the sure foundation,
  Christ the Head and Corner-stone,
Chosen of the Lord, and precious,
  Binding all the Church in one,
Holy Zion's help for ever,
  And her confidence alone.

2 All that dedicated City,
  Dearly loved of God on high,
In exultant jubilation
  Pours perpetual melody;
God the One in Three adoring
  In glad hymns eternally.

3 To this temple, where we call thee,
  Come, O Lord of hosts, to-day:
With thy wonted loving kindness,
  Hear thy servants as they pray;
And thy fullest benediction
  Shed within its walls alway.

4 Here vouchsafe to all thy servants
  What they ask of thee to gain,
What they gain from thee for ever
  With the blessed to retain,
And hereafter in thy glory
  Evermore with thee to reign.

Christ the Foundation. 169

AURELIA. 7s, 6s. — S. S. WESLEY.

1. The Church's one foundation Is Jesus Christ her Lord; She is his new creation By water and the word: From heaven he came and sought her To be his holy bride: With his own blood he bought her, And for her life he died.

318 S. J. Stone.

The Church's one foundation
 Is Jesus Christ her Lord;
She is his new creation
 By water and the word:
From heaven he came and sought her
 To be his holy bride;
With his own blood he bought her,
 And for her life he died.

2 Elect from every nation,
 Yet one o'er all the earth,
Her charter of salvation
 One Lord, one faith, one birth;
One holy Name she blesses,
 Partakes one holy food,
And to one hope she presses,
 With every grace endued.

3 Though with a scornful wonder,
 Men see her sore opprest,
By schisms rent asunder,
 By heresies distrest;
Yet saints their watch are keeping,
 Their cry goes up, "How long?"
And soon the night of weeping
 Shall be the morn of song.

4 'Mid toil and tribulation,
 And tumult of her war,
She waits the consummation
 Of peace for evermore;
Till with the vision glorious
 Her longing eyes are blest,
And the great Church victorious
 Shall be the Church at rest.

5 Yet she on earth hath union
 With God the Three in One,
And mystic sweet communion
 With those whose rest is won:
O happy ones and holy!
 Lord, give us grace that we
Like them, the meek and lowly,
 On high may dwell with thee.

THE CHURCH.

STOUGHTON. 8s, 7s. J. P. HOLBROOK.

319
J. Newton.

Glorious things of thee are spoken,
 Zion, city of our God;
He whose word cannot be broken,
 Formed thee for his own abode:
On the Rock of ages founded,
 What can shake thy sure repose?
With salvation's walls surrounded,
 Thou mayst smile at all thy foes.

2 See, the streams of living waters,
 Springing from eternal love,
Well supply thy sons and daughters,
 And all fear of want remove:
Who can faint, while such a river
 Ever flows their thirst t'assuage?
Grace, which like the Lord, the Giver,
 Never fails from age to age.

3 Round each habitation hovering,
 See the cloud and fire appear,
For a glory and a covering,
 Showing that the Lord is near:
Thus deriving from their banner
 Light by night, and shade by day,
Safe they feed upon the manna
 Which he gives them when they pray.

320
C. Winkworth, tr.

Hark, the Church proclaims her honor
 And her strength is only this:
God hath laid his choice upon her,
 And the work she doth is His.
He his church hath firmly founded,
 He will guard what he began;
We, by sin and foes surrounded,
 Build her bulwarks as we can.

2 Frail and fleeting are our powers,
 Short our days, and foresight dim,
And we own the choice not ours,
 We were chosen first by him.
Onward then! for naught despairing,
 Calm we follow at his word,
Thus through joy and sorrow bearing
 Faithful witness to our Lord.

3 Though we here must strive with meek-
 Though in tears we often bend, [ness,
What his might began in weakness,
 Shall achieve a glorious end.
Thus the Church proclaims her honor
 And her strength is only this:
God hath laid his choice upon her,
 And the work she doth is His.

Baptism into the Name. 171

IRENÆUS. 8s, 7s. C. C. SCHOLEFIELD.

321

Sound aloud Jehovah's praises,
  Tell abroad the glorious Name;
Heaven the ceaseless anthem raises,
  Let the earth her God proclaim:
God, the hope of every nation,
God, the source of consolation,
  Holy, Blessèd Trinity!

2 This the Name from ancient ages
  Hidden in its dazzling light;
This the Name that kings and sages
  Prayed and strove to know aright,
Through God's wondrous Incarnation
Now revealed the world's Salvation,
  Ever Blessèd Trinity!

3 Into this great Name and holy
  We all tribes and tongues baptize;
Thus the Highest owns the lowly,
  Homeward, heavenward, bids them rise,
Gathers them from every nation,
Bids them join in adoration
  Of the Blessèd Trinity!

4 In this Name the heart rejoices,
  Pouring forth its secret prayer:
In this Name we lift our voices,
  And our common faith declare;
Offering humble supplication,
Thanks, and praise, and adoration
  To the Blessèd Trinity! Amen.

THE CHURCH.

HURSLEY. L. M.   ARR. W. H. MONK.

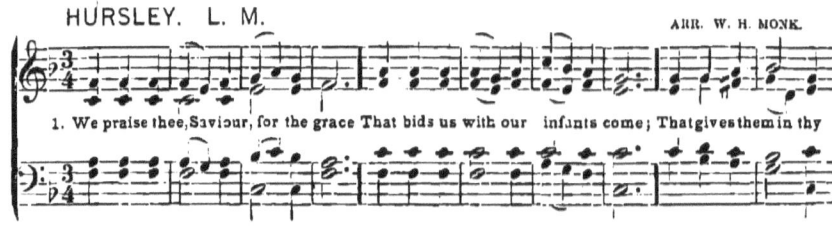

322   *Ray Palmer.*

WE praise thee, Saviour, for the grace
That bids us with our infants come;
That gives them in thy heart a place,
And in thy kingdom grants them room.

2 We bring them to thine altar, Lord,
And here the holy seal apply;

O make them clean,—their names record
In thine own Book of Life on high.

3 When storms shall beat, or gathering foes
Beset the path their feet must tread,
Dear Shepherd, let thine arms enclose,
Or o'er them for defence be spread.

4 If thou hast marked them for the tomb,
Ere morning brightens into day,
As in thy bosom bear them home,
And gently wipe our tears away.

5 Or if when gathered to thy rest,
'T is ours to leave them pilgrims still,
Guide thou their steps till with us blest,
They reach thine everlasting hill.

DWIGHT. L. M.   ARR. J. P. HOLBROOK.

323   *W. Robertson.*

HE who, a little child, began
The life divine to show to man,
Proclaims from heaven the message free,
"Let little children come to me."

2 We bring them, Lord, and with the sign
Of sprinkled water name them thine:
Their souls with saving grace endow,
Baptize them with thy Spirit now.

3 O give thine angels charge, good Lord,
Them safely in thy way to guard;
Thy blessing on their lives command,
And write their names upon thy hand.

4 O thou, who by an infant's tongue
Dost hear thy perfect glory sung,
May these with all the heavenly host
Praise Father, Son, and Holy Ghost.

Baptism of Infants. 173

WESTMINSTER. 8s, 7s.   J. P. HOLBROOK.

1. Saviour! who thy flock art feeding, With the shepherd's kindest care, All the feeble gently leading, While the lambs thy bosom share.

324   W. A. Muhlenberg.

Saviour! who thy flock art feeding
With the shepherd's kindest care,
All the feeble gently leading,
While the lambs thy bosom share.

2 Now, these little ones receiving,
Fold them in thy gracious arm;
There we know, thy word believing,
Only there secure from harm.

3 Never, from thy pasture roving,
Let them be the lion's prey;
Let thy tenderness, so loving,
Keep them all life's dangerous way.

4 Then, within thy fold eternal,
Let them find a resting-place;
Feed in pastures ever vernal,
Drink the rivers of thy grace.

CLINTON. C. M.   J. P. HOLBROOK.

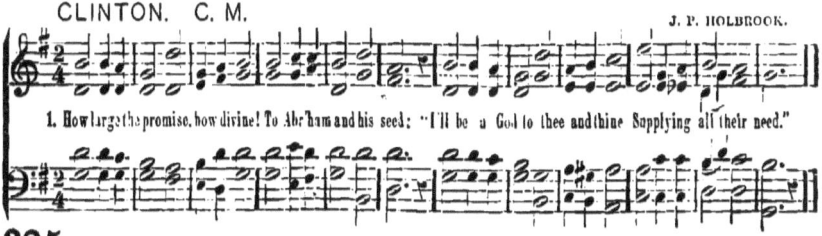

1. How large the promise, how divine! To Abraham and his seed: "I'll be a God to thee and thine Supplying all their need."

325   I. Watts.

How LARGE the promise, how divine!
To Abraham and his seed:
"I'll be a God to thee and thine,
Supplying all their need."

2 The words of his extensive love
From age to age endure:
The Angel of the covenant proves,
And seals the blessings sure.

3 Jesus the ancient faith confirms,
To our great fathers given;
He takes young children to his arms,
And calls them heirs of heaven.

4 Our God!—how faithful are his ways!
His love endures the same;

Nor from the promise of his grace
Blots out the children's name.

326   P. Doddridge.

SEE Israel's gentle Shepherd stand
With all-engaging charms;
Hark, how he calls the tender lambs,
And folds them in his arms!

2 "Permit them to approach," he cries,
"Nor scorn their humble name;
For 'twas to bless such souls as these,
The Lord of angels came."

3 We bring them, Lord, in thankful hands,
And yield them up to thee;
Joyful that we ourselves are thine,—
Thine let our offspring be.

THE CHURCH.

JANES. L. M.   MOZART.

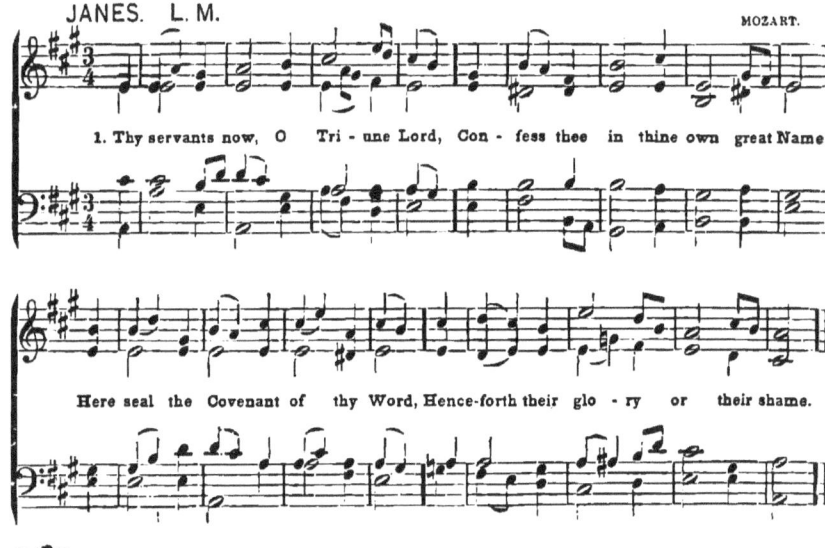

1. Thy servants now, O Triune Lord, Confess thee in thine own great Name: Here seal the Covenant of thy Word, Henceforth their glory or their shame.

327

Thy servants now, O Triune Lord,
  Confess thee in thine own great Name;
Here seal the Covenant of thy Word,
  Henceforth their glory or their shame.

2 Grant them, O Father, power to do
  The work which thou hast laid on each;
Grant them, O blessèd Son, to know
  The heavenly wisdom thou dost teach.

3 And thou, O Holy Ghost, inspire
  Their wills thy counsels to approve,
What thou desirest to desire,
  And love whatever thou dost love.

4 To Father, Son, and Holy Ghost,
  The God whom heaven and earth adore,
Be glory as it was of old,
  Is now, and shall be evermore.

328
H. W. Baker, tr.

Blest Trinity, from mortal sight
Veiled in thine own eternal light,
We thee confess, in thee believe,
To thee with loving hearts we cleave.

2 Eternal Father, thee we praise;
To thee, O Son, our hymns we raise;
O Holy Ghost, we thee adore:
One mighty God for evermore.

329
C. Wordsworth.

Come, ever blessèd Spirit, come,
And make thy servants' hearts thy home;
Thus consecrated, Lord, to thee,
May each a living temple be.

2 Arm these thy soldiers, mighty Lord,
With shield of faith, and Spirit's sword;
Forth to the battle may they go,
And boldly fight against the foe.

3 With banner of the cross unfurled,
O may they overcome the world;
And so at last receive from thee
The palm and crown of victory.

4 O grant us so to use thy grace
That we may see thy glorious face;
And ever with the heavenly host,
Praise Father, Son, and Holy Ghost.

Confession of Faith. 175

HAMBURG. L. M.   ARR. L. MASON.

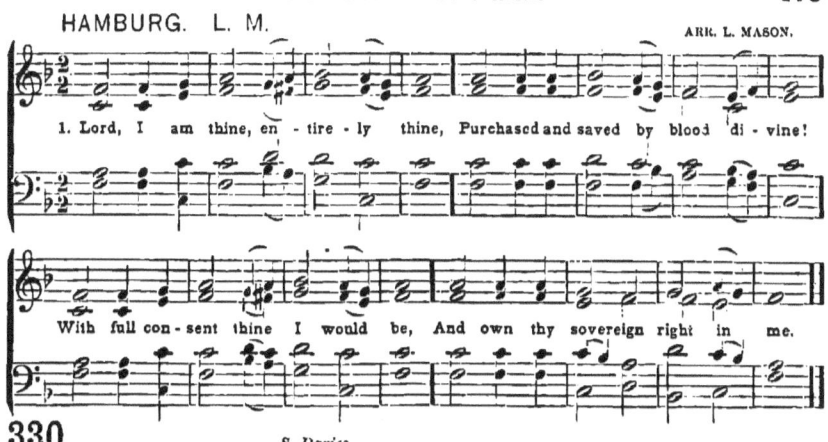

330
S. Davies.

Lord, I am thine, entirely thine,
Purchased and saved by blood divine!
With full consent thine I would be,
And own thy sovereign right in me.

2 Here, O my Lord, my soul, my all,
I yield to thee beyond recall;
Accept thine own,—so long withheld,
Accept what I so freely yield.

3 Grant one poor sinner more a place
Among the children of thy grace;
A wretched sinner lost to God,
But ransomed by Immanuel's blood.

4 The vow is past beyond repeal;
Now will I set the solemn seal:
Thine would I live, thine would I die,
Be thine through all eternity.

ODEON. L. M.
Andante.   ARR. MENDELSSOHN.

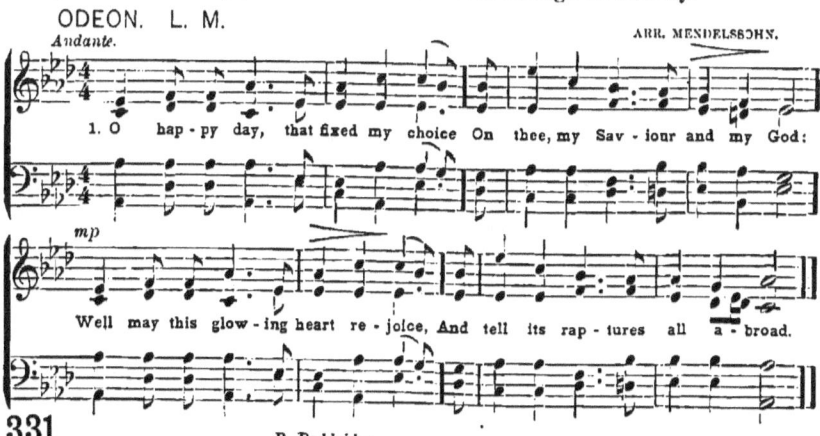

331
P. Doddridge.

O happy day, that fixed my choice
  On thee, my Saviour and my God:
Well may this glowing heart rejoice,
  And tell its raptures all abroad.

2 O happy bond, that seals my vows
  To him who merits all my love:
Let cheerful anthems fill his house,
  While to that sacred shrine I move.

3 'Tis done; the great transaction's done;
  I am my Lord's, and he is mine;
He drew me, and I followed on,
  Charmed to confess the voice divine.

4 High heaven, that heard the solemn vow,
  That vow renewed shall daily hear,
Till in life's latest hour I bow,
  And bless in death a bond so dear.

176 THE CHURCH.

BURLINGTON. C. M.   J. F. BURROWES.

1. My God, ac-cept my heart this day, And make it al-ways thine,

That I from thee no more may stray, No more from thee de-cline.

332   *M. Bridges.*
My God, accept my heart this day,
  And make it always thine,
That I from thee no more may stray,
  No more from thee decline.

2 Before the Cross of him who died,
  Behold, I prostrate fall;
Let every sin be crucified,
  And Christ be all in all.

3 Anoint me with thy heavenly grace,
  And seal me for thine own;
That I may see thy glorious face,
  And worship near thy throne.

4 Let every thought, and work and word,
  To thee be ever given;
Then life shall be thy service, Lord,
  And death the gate of heaven.

333   *I. Watts.*
"THE promise of my Father's love
  Shall stand for ever good!"—
He said, and gave his soul to death,
  And sealed the grace with blood.

2 To this dear covenant of thy word,
  I set my worthless name;
I seal th'engagement to my Lord,
  And make my humble claim.

3 Thy light, and strength, and pardoning
  And glory shall be mine;   [grace,

My life and soul, my heart and flesh,
  And all my powers are thine.

4 I call that legacy my own,
  Which Jesus did bequeath;
'Twas purchased with a dying groan,
  And ratified in death.

5 Sweet is the memory of his name,
  Who blessed us in his will,
And, to his testament of love,
  Made his own life the seal.

334   *I. Watts.*
WHAT shall I render to my God
  For all his kindness shown?
My feet shall visit thine abode,
  My songs address thy throne.

2 How much is mercy thy delight,
  Thou ever blessèd God!
How dear thy servants in thy sight!
  How precious is their blood!

3 How happy all thy servants are!
  How great thy grace to me!
My life, which thou hast made thy care,
  Lord, I devote to thee.

4 Here in thy courts I leave my vow,
  And thy rich grace record;
Witness, ye saints, who hear me now,
  If I forsake the Lord.

Confession of Faith. 177

CUMMINS. L. M. 6 l. KREUTZER.

1. We saw thee not when thou didst tread, O Saviour, this our sinful earth, Nor heard thy voice restore the dead And wake them to a second birth; But we believe that thou didst come, And leave for us thy glorious home, And leave for us thy glorious home.

335
J. H. Gurney.

WE saw thee not when thou didst tread,
O Saviour, this our sinful earth,
Nor heard thy voice restore the dead
And wake them to a second birth;
But we believe that thou didst come,
And leave for us thy glorious home.

2 We were not with the faithful few
Who stood thy bitter cross around,
Nor heard thy prayer for those that slew,
Nor felt the earthquake rock the ground;
We saw no spear-wound in thy side;
Yet we believe that thou hast died.

3 We did not see the chosen few
When thou didst through the clouds ascend,
First lift to heaven their wondering view,
Then to the earth all prostrate bend;
But we believe that mortal eyes
Beheld that journey to the skies.

4 And, now that thou dost reign on high,
Although, our longing sight to bless,
No ray of glory from the sky
Shines down upon our wilderness:
Yet we believe that thou art there,
And seek thee, Lord, in praise and prayer.

336
C. Winkworth, tr.

JESUS, my Saviour, who could dare
Bid thee such bitter anguish bear,
What evil heart entreat thee thus?
For thou art good, hast wronged none,
As we and ours too oft have done,
Thou hast not sinned, dear Lord, like us.

2 My grievous sins, that number more
Than yonder sands upon the shore,
Have brought to pass this agony.
'T is I have caused the floods of woe
That now thy dying soul o'erflow,
And those sad hearts that watch by thee.

3 And thou dost suffer for my sake;
Thou dost in love the burdens take
That weighed my spirit to the ground;
Yes, thou art made a curse for me,
That I might yet be blest through thee,
My healing in thy wounds is found.

4 Whate'er my utmost powers can do,
To thee to render service true,
Here at thy feet I lay it low;
From henceforth there is naught of mine
But I would seek to make it thine,
Since all myself to thee I owe

THE CHURCH.

MISSIONARY CHANT. L. M. CH. ZEUNER.

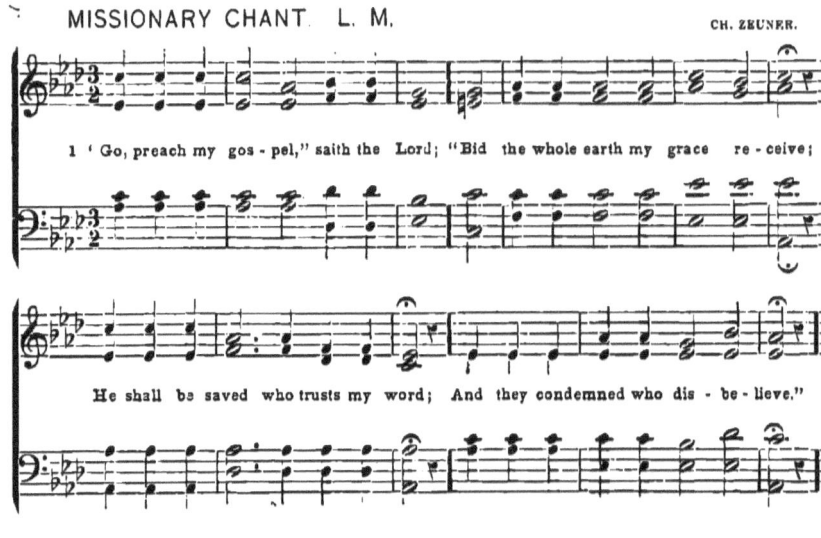

1 " Go, preach my gos-pel," saith the Lord; "Bid the whole earth my grace re-ceive;
He shall be saved who trusts my word; And they condemned who dis-be-lieve."

337
I. Watts.

"Go, preach my gospel," saith the Lord;
 Bid the whole earth my grace receive;
He shall be saved who trusts my word;
 And they condemned who disbelieve.

2 "I'll make your great commission known,
 And ye shall prove my gospel true
By all the works that I have done,
 By all the wonders ye shall do.

3 "Teach all the nations my commands;
 I'm with you till the world shall end;
All power is trusted in my hands;
 I can destroy, and I defend."

4 He spake, and light shone round his head;
 On a bright cloud to heaven he rode;
They to the farthest nations spread
 The grace of their ascended God.

338

Ye Christian heralds, go, proclaim
Salvation through Immanuel's name;
To distant climes the tidings bear,
And plant the Rose of Sharon there.

2 He'll shield you with a wall of fire,
With flaming zeal your breast inspire,
Bid raging winds their fury cease,
And hush the tempest into peace.

3 And when our labors all are o'er,
 Then we shall meet to part no more;
Meet, with the blood-bought throng to fall,
 And crown our Jesus Lord of all.

339
J. Montgomery.

Pour out thy Spirit from on high;
 Lord, thine assembled servants bless;
Graces and gifts to each supply,
 And clothe thy priests with righteousness.

2 Within thy temple, where we stand
 To teach the truth, not ours, but thine,
May we, like stars in thy right hand,
 The angels of the churches, shine!

3 Wisdom, and zeal, and faith impart,
 Firmness with meekness from above,
To bear thy people on our heart,
 And love the souls whom thou dost love.

4 To watch and pray, and never faint;
 By day and night strict guard to keep,
To warn the sinner, cheer the saint,
 Nourish thy lambs, and feed thy sheep;

5 Then, when our work is finished here,
 In humble hope our charge resign;
When the chief Shepherd shall appear,
 O God, may they and we be thine!

The Ministry. 179

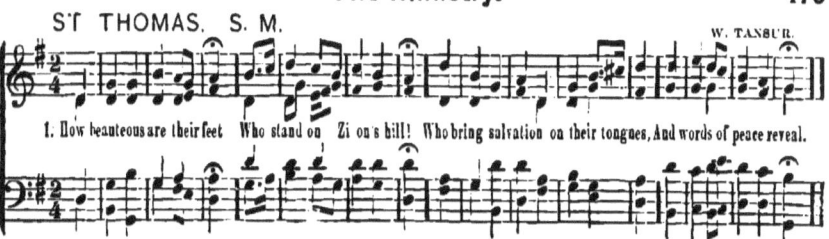

340   *I. Watts.*

How BEAUTEOUS are their feet
Who stand on Zion's hill!
Who bring salvation on their tongues,
And words of peace reveal.

2 How charming is their voice!
How sweet their tidings are!
"Zion, behold thy Saviour King!
He reigns and triumphs here."

3 How happy are our ears,
That hear this joyful sound,
Which kings and prophets waited for,
And sought, but never found!

4 How blessèd are our eyes,
That see this heavenly light!
Prophets and kings desired it long,
But died without the sight.

5 The watchmen join their voice,
And tuneful notes employ;
Jerusalem breaks forth in songs,
And deserts learn the joy.

6 The Lord makes bare his arm
Through all the earth abroad;
Let every nation now behold
Their Saviour and their God.

341   *C. Wesley.*

JESUS, the name high over all,
In hell, or earth, or sky;
Angels and men before it fall,
And devils fear and fly.

2 Jesus, the name to sinners dear,
The name to sinners given;
It scatters all their guilty fear,
And turns their hell to heaven.

3 Jesus the prisoner's fetters breaks,
And bruises Satan's head;
Power into strengthless souls he speaks,
And life into the dead.

4 O that the world might taste and see
The riches of his grace;
The arms of love that compass me,
Would all mankind embrace.

5 His only righteousness I show,
His saving truth proclaim:
'Tis all my business here below,
To cry, Behold the Lamb!

6 Happy, if with my latest breath
I may but speak his name;
Preach him to all, and cry in death,
Behold, behold the Lamb!

180 "THE SPIRIT and the BRIDE say COME."

First Lines of Hymns.

REASONING AND INVITATION.

HYMNS.
342 Blow ye the trumpet, blow,
343 Come ye sinners, poor and
344 The voice of free grace cries, Escape
345 Art thou weary, art thou languid,
346 That holy One,
347 Behold the Lamb of God, who bears
348 Peace, troubled soul, whose plaintive
349 Return, O wanderer, now return,
350 Come, humble sinner; in whose heart
351 Come, weary souls, with sin distressed,
352 Behold, a stranger at the door,

HYMNS.
353 Come unto me, ye weary,

EXPOSTULATION AND WARNING.

354 Sinners, turn, why will ye die?
355 To-day the Saviour calls:
356 While life prolongs its precious light,
357 Life is the time to serve the Lord,
358 Why will ye waste on trifling cares
359 And will the Judge descend,
360 Ah, how shall fallen man
361 Oh, where shall rest be found
362 Hasten, sinner! to be wise

LENOX. H. M.   L. EDSON.

1. Blow ye the trumpet, blow, The gladly solemn sound! Let all the nations know, To earth's remot-est bound:
The year of ju-bi-lee is come; The year of ju-bi-lee is come; Re-turn, ye ransomed sin-ners, home.

342   C. Wesley.

Blow ye the trumpet, blow,
  The gladly solemn sound!
Let all the nations know,
  To earth's remotest bound:
The year of jubilee is come;
Return, ye ransomed sinners, home.

2 Jesus, our great High Priest,
  Hath full atonement made:
Ye weary spirits, rest;
  Ye mournful souls, be glad:
The year of jubilee is come;
Return, ye ransomed sinners, home.

3 Exalt the Lamb of God,
  The sin-atoning Lamb;
Redemption in his blood
  To all the world proclaim:
The year of jubilee is come;
Return, ye ransomed sinners, home.

4 Ye who have sold for naught
  Your heritage above,
Come, take it back unbought,
  The gift of Jesus' love:
The year of jubilee is come;
Return, ye ransomed sinners, home.

Reasoning and Invitation.

INVITATION. 8s, 7s, 4s.   J. P. HOLBROOK.

1. Come, ye sinners, poor and wretched, Now is your accepted hour: Jesus ready stands to save you, Full of pity, love and power: He is able, He is willing; doubt no more.

343 J. Hart.

Come, ye sinners, poor and wretched,
 Now is your accepted hour:
Jesus ready stands to save you,
 Full of pity, love, and power:
  He is able,
He is willing; doubt no more.

2 Let not conscience make you linger,
 Nor of fitness fondly dream;
All the fitness he requireth
 Is to feel your need of him;
  This he gives you;
'T is the Spirit's rising beam.

3 Come, ye weary, heavy-laden,
 Lost and ruined by the fall;
If you tarry till you're better,
 You will never come at all.
  Not the righteous,
Sinners, Jesus came to call.

4 Agonizing in the garden,
 Your Redeemer prostrate lies;
On the bloody tree behold him!
 Hear him cry, before he dies,
  It is finish'd!
Sinners, will not this suffice?

5 Lo! the incarnate God ascended
 Pleads the merit of his blood;
Venture on him, venture wholly
 Let no other trust intrude;
  None but Jesus
Can do helpless sinners good.

ZION. 8s, 7s, 4s.   T. HASTINGS.

1. {Come, ye sinners, poor and wretched, Now is your accepted hour: / Jesus ready stands to save you, Full of pity, love, and power:} He is a-ble, He is willing; doubt no more, He is a-ble, He is willing; doubt no more.

"COME!"

SCOTTLAND. 12s. — J. CLARKE.

1. The voice of free grace cries, Escape to the mountain; For Adam's lost race Christ hath opened a fountain; For sin and uncleanness and every transgression, His blood flows most freely, in streams of salvation, His blood flows most freely in streams of salvation. Hallelujah to the Lamb, who hath purchased our pardon! We'll praise him again, when we pass over Jordan, We'll praise him again, when we pass over Jordan.

344   *R. Birdsall.*

The voice of free grace cries, Escape to the mountain;
For Adam's lost race Christ hath opened a fountain;
For sin and uncleanness and every transgression,
His blood flows most freely in streams of salvation,
Hallelujah to the Lamb, who hath purchased our pardon!
We'll praise him again, when we pass over Jordan.

2 Ye souls that are wounded, O flee to the Saviour;
He calls you in mercy, 'tis infinite favor;
Your sins are increasing, escape to the mountain;
His blood can remove them, it flows from the fountain.

3 With joy shall we stand, when escaped to the shore;
With harps in our hands, we will praise him the more;
We'll range the sweet plains on the banks of the river,
And sing of salvation for ever and ever.

Reasoning and Invitation.

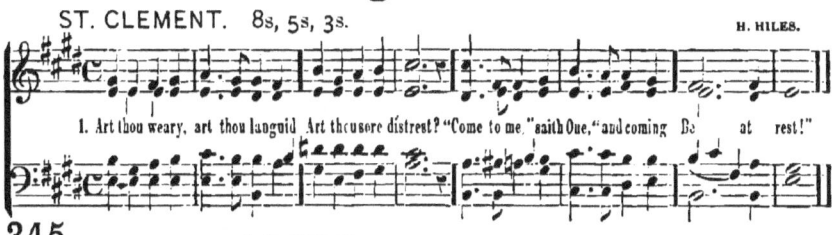

345
J. M. Neale, tr.

Art thou weary, art thou languid,
  Art thou sore distrest?
"Come to me," saith One, "and coming
  Be at rest!"

2 Hath he marks to lead me to him,
  If he be my guide?
"In his feet and hands are wound-prints,
  And his side."

3 Is there diadem as monarch,
  That his brow adorns?
"Yea, a crown in very surety,
  But of thorns!"

4 If I find him, if I follow,
  What his guerdon here?
"Many a sorrow, many a labor,
  Many a tear."

5 If I still hold closely to him,
  What hath he at last?
"Sorrow vanquished, labor ended,
  Jordan past!"

6 If I ask him to receive me,
  Will he say me nay?
"Not till earth, and not till heaven
  Pass away!"

346
A. D. F. Randolph.

That holy One,
Who came to earth for thee,—
  O strangest thing beneath the sun,
  That He, by any mortal one,
Forgotten e'er should be!

2 The Son of God,
Who pity had on thee;
  Who turned aside the smiting rod,
  And all alone the Garden trod,—
Forgotten shall He be?

3 The blessèd Lord,
Who came to die for thee,
  Whom Jew and Gentile then abhorred,
  While heavenly hosts his name adored,—
Forgotten can He be?

4 That Brother, Friend,
Who daily waits on thee;
  Who every want doth comprehend
  With love divine that has no end,
Forgotten can He be?

"COME!"

184 BROWNELL. L. M. 6l. — HAYDN.

1. Behold the Lamb of God, who bears The sins of all.... the world away! A servant's form he meekly wears, He sojourns in a house of clay. His glory is no longer seen But God with God is man with men.

347 *C. Wesley.*

Behold the Lamb of God, who bears
The sins of all the world away!
A servant's form he meekly wears,
He sojourns in a house of clay,
His glory is no longer seen,
But God with God is man with men.

2 See where the lame, the halt, the blind,
The deaf, the dumb, the sick, the poor,
Flock to the Friend of human kind,
And freely all accept their cure;
To whom did he his help deny?
Whom in his days of flesh pass by?

3 See where the God incarnate stands,
And calls his wandering creatures home,
He all day long spreads out his hands—
Come, weary souls, to Jesus come!
Come ye with all your guilt opprest,
Believe, and he will give you rest.

4 Oh, do not of his goodness doubt;
His saving grace for all is free;
He will in no wise cast him out
Who comes a sinner, trustingly.
Come, then, with all your needs opprest,
Trust him, and he will give you rest.

348 *W. Shirley.*

Peace, troubled soul, whose plaintive moan
Hath taught each scene the notes of woe;
Cease thy complaint, suppress thy groan,
And let thy tears forget to flow:
Behold, the precious balm is found,
To lull thy pain, to heal thy wound.

2 Come, freely come, by sin oppressed;
On Jesus cast thy weighty load;
In him thy refuge find, thy rest,
Safe in the mercy of thy God:
Thy God's thy Saviour—glorious word!
O hear, believe, and bless the Lord.

Reasoning and Invitation.

BEMERTON. C. M.   H. W. GREATOREX.

1. Return, O wanderer, now return, And seek thy Father's face! Those new desires, which in thee burn, Were kindled by his grace.

349   *W. B. Collyer.*

RETURN, O wanderer, now return,
And seek thy Father's face!
Those new desires which in thee burn,
Were kindled by his grace.

2 Return, O wanderer, now return!
He hears thy humble sigh;
He sees thy softened spirit mourn,
When no one else is nigh.

3 Return, O wanderer, now return!
Thy Saviour bids thee live:
Go to his bleeding feet, and learn
How freely he'll forgive.

4 Return, O wanderer, now return,
And wipe the falling tear!
Thy Father calls—no longer mourn:
His love invites thee near.

350   *E. Jones.*

COME, humble sinner, in whose breast,
A thousand thoughts revolve;
Come with your guilt and fear oppressed,
And make this last resolve:

2 "I'll go to Jesus; though my sin
Hath like a mountain rose:
I know his courts, I'll enter in,
Whatever may oppose.

3 "Prostrate I'll lie before his throne,
And there my guilt confess;
I'll tell him I'm a wretch undone,
Without his sovereign grace.

4 "I can but perish if I go,
I am resolved to try;
For if I stay away, I know
I must forever die."

EVAN. C. M.   W. H. HAVERGAL.

1. Come, humble sinner, in whose breast, A thousand thoughts revolve; Come with your guilt and fear oppressed, And make this last resolve:

"COME!"

DWIGHT. L. M. — ARR. J. P. HOLBROOK.

1. Come, weary souls, with sin distressed, Come, and accept the promised rest; The Saviour's gracious call obey, And cast your gloomy fears away.

351
A. Steele.

Come, weary souls, with sin distressed,
Come, and accept the promised rest;
The Saviour's gracious call obey,
And cast your gloomy fears away.

2 Oppressed with guilt,—a painful load,—
O come and bow before your God!
Divine compassion, mighty love
Will all the painful load remove.

3 Here mercy's boundless ocean flows,
To cleanse your guilt and heal your woes;
Pardon, and life, and endless peace—
How rich the gift, how free the grace!

4 Dear Saviour! let thy powerful love
Confirm our faith, our fears remove;
O sweetly reign in every breast,
And guide us to eternal rest.

GRACE CHURCH. L. M. — I. PLEYEL.

1. Be-hold, a Stran-ger at the door! He gen-tly knocks, has knocked be-fore; Has wait-ed long, is wait-ing still: You treat no oth-er friend so ill.

352
J. Grigg.

Behold, a Stranger at the door;
He gently knocks, has knocked before;
Has waited long, is waiting still:
You treat no other friend so ill.

2 O lovely attitude! he stands
With melting heart, and laden hands,
O matchless kindness! and he shows
This matchless kindness to his foes.

3 Rise, touched with gratitude divine,
Turn out his enemy and thine,
That soul-destroying monster, Sin;
And let the heavenly Stranger in.

4 Admit him, ere his anger burn;
His feet, departed, ne'er return!
Admit him, or the hour's at hand
When at his door denied you'll stand.

Reasoning and Invitation. 187

353   *W. C. Dix.*

"Come unto me, ye weary,
  And I will give you rest."
O blessed voice of Jesus,
  Which comes to hearts oppressed!
It tells of benediction,
  Of pardon, grace and peace,
Of joy that hath no ending,
  Of love that cannot cease.

2 "Come unto me, ye wanderers,
  And I will give you light."
O loving voice of Jesus,
  Which comes to cheer the night!
Our hearts were filled with sadness,
  And we had lost our way;
But he has brought us gladness,
  And songs at break of day.

3 "Come unto me, ye fainting,
  And I will give you life."
O cheering voice of Jesus,
  Which comes to aid our strife!
The foe is stern and eager,
  The fight is fierce and long;
But thou hast made us mighty,
  And stronger than the strong.

4 "And whosoever cometh,
  I will not cast him out."
O welcome voice of Jesus,
  Which drives away our doubt,
Which calls us, very sinners,
  Unworthy though we be
Of love so free and boundless,
  To come, dear Lord, to thee!

"COME!"

BLUMENTHAL. 7s.
J. BLUMENTHAL.

1. Sinners, turn, why will ye die? God, your Maker, asks you why;
God, who did your being give, Made you (*Omit*)......... with himself to live; He the fa-tal cause demands, Why, ye thankless creatures why Will you cross his love and die?

354 *C. Wesley.*

Sinners, turn, why will ye die?
God, your Maker, asks you why;
God, who did your being give,
Made you with himself to live;
He the fatal cause demands,
Asks the work of his own hands,
Why, ye thankless creatures, why
Will you cross his love and die?

2 Sinners, turn, why will ye die?
God, your Saviour, asks you why;
He who did your souls retrieve,
Died himself that ye might live:
Will you let him die in vain?
Crucify your Lord again?
Why, ye ransomed sinners, why
Will you slight his grace and die?

3 Sinners, turn, why will ye die?
God, the Spirit, asks you why;
He, who all your lives hath strove,
Wooed you to embrace his love:
Will you not his grace receive?
Will you still refuse to live?
Why, ye long-sought sinners, why
Will you grieve your God, and die?

WOOD. 6s, 4s.
J. P. HOLBROOK.

1. To-day the Saviour calls: Ye wanderers come; O ye benighted souls, Why longer roam?

355

To-day the Saviour calls:
 Ye wanderers come;
O ye benighted souls,
 Why longer roam?

2 To-day the Saviour calls:
 O hear him now;
Within these sacred walls
 To Jesus bow.

3 To-day the Saviour calls:
 For refuge fly;
The storm of justice falls,
 And death is nigh.

4 The Spirit calls to-day:
 Yield to his power;
O grieve him not away:
 'Tis mercy's hour.

Expostulation and Warning.

ROSE HILL. L. M. — J. E. SWEETSER.

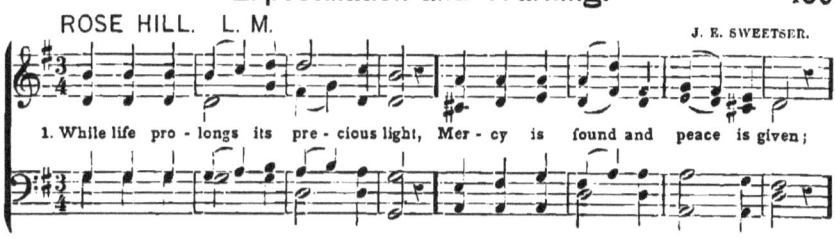

1. While life pro-longs its pre-cious light, Mer-cy is found and peace is given;

But soon, ah, soon ap-proaching night Shall blot out eve-ry hope of heaven.

356
T. Dwight.

WHILE life prolongs its precious light,
Mercy is found and peace is given;
But soon, ah, soon approaching night
Shall blot out every hope of heaven.

2 While God invites, how blest the day!
How sweet the gospel's charming sound!
Come, sinners, haste, O haste away,
While yet a pardoning God he's found.

3 Soon, borne on time's most rapid wing,
Shall death command you to the grave,
Before his bar your spirits bring,
And none be found to hear or save.

4 Now God invites, how blest the day!
How sweet the gospel's charming sound!
Come, sinners, haste, O haste away,
While yet a pardoning God is found.

357
I. Watts.

LIFE is the time to serve the Lord,
The time t'insure the great reward;
And while the lamp holds out to burn,
The vilest sinner may return.

2 Life is the hour that God has given
T'escape from hell and fly to heaven;
The day of grace,—and mortals may
Secure the blessings of the day.

3 Then what my thoughts design to do,
My hands, with all your might pursue,
Since no device, nor work is found,
Nor faith, nor hope, beneath the ground.

4 There are no acts of pardon passed
In the cold grave to which we haste;
But darkness, death, and long despair
Reign in eternal silence there.

358
P. Doddridge.

WHY will ye waste on trifling cares
That life which God's compassion spares
While, in the various range of thought,
The one thing needful is forgot?

2 Shall God invite you from above?
Shall Jesus urge his dying love?
Shall troubled conscience give you pain?
And all these pleas unite in vain?

3 Not so your eyes will always view
Those objects which you now pursue:
Not so will heaven and hell appear,
When death's decisive hour is near.

4 Almighty God, thy grace impart;
Fix deep conviction on each heart;
Nor let us waste on trifling cares
That life which thy compassion spares.

EDWARDS. S. M.

ARR. G. KINGSLEY

359 *P. Doddridge.*

And will the Judge descend,
And must the dead arise,
And not a single soul escape
His all-discerning eyes?

2 How will my heart endure
The terrors of that day,
When earth and heaven before his face
Astonished shrink away?

3 But ere that trumpet shakes
The mansions of the dead,
Hark, from the gospel's cheering sound
What joyful tidings spread.

4 Ye sinners, seek his grace
Whose wrath ye cannot bear;
Fly to the shelter of his cross,
And find salvation there.

360 *I. Watts.*

Ah, how shall fallen man
Be just before his God!
If he contend in righteousness,
We fall beneath his rod.

2 If he our ways should mark,
With strict inquiring eyes,
Could we for one of thousand faults
A just excuse devise?

3 All-seeing, powerful God!
Who can with thee contend?
Or who that tries th'unequal strife,
Shall prosper in the end?

4 Ah, how shall guilty man
Contend with such a God!
None, none can meet him and escape,
But through the Saviour's blood.

BOYLSTON. S. M.

L. MASON.

Expostulation and Warning. 191

WILKES. S. M.   J. B. WILKES.

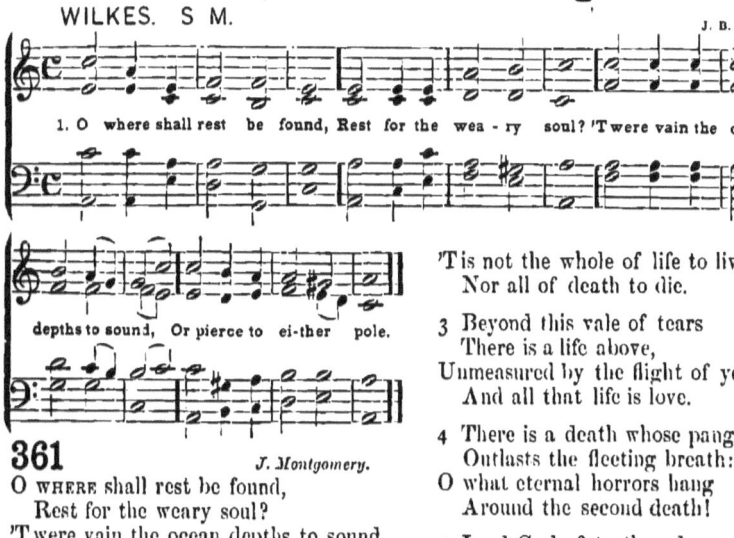

1. O where shall rest be found, Rest for the weary soul? 'Twere vain the ocean depths to sound, Or pierce to either pole.

'Tis not the whole of life to live,
Nor all of death to die.

3 Beyond this vale of tears
There is a life above,
Unmeasured by the flight of years;
And all that life is love.

361   J. Montgomery.

O WHERE shall rest be found,
Rest for the weary soul?
'Twere vain the ocean depths to sound,
Or pierce to either pole.

2 The world can never give
The bliss for which we sigh:

4 There is a death whose pang
Outlasts the fleeting breath:
O what eternal horrors hang
Around the second death!

5 Lord God of truth and grace,
Teach us that death to shun;
Lest we be banished from thy face,
And evermore undone.

SEYMOUR. 7s.   WEBER.

1. Hasten, sinner! to be wise, Stay not for the morrow's sun: Wisdom, if thou still despise, Harder is it to be won.

362   F. Scott.

HASTEN, sinner! to be wise,
Stay not for the morrow's sun:
Wisdom, if thou still despise,
Harder is it to be won.

2 Hasten mercy to implore,
Stay not for the morrow's sun,
Lest thy season should be o'er,
Ere this evening's stage be run.

3 Hasten, sinner! now return,
Stay not for the morrow's sun,
Lest thy lamp should cease to burn,
Ere salvation's work is done.

4 Hasten, sinner! to be blest,
Stay not for the morrow's sun,
Lest perdition thee arrest,
Ere the morrow is begun.

First Lines of Hymns.

PENITENCE—SELF-SURRENDER.
HYMNS.
363 From deep distress and troubled thoughts,
364 Show pity, Lord, O Lord forgive,
365 A broken heart, my God, my King,
366 God calling yet? shall I not hear,
367 With broken heart and contrite sigh,
368 Depth of mercy, can there be
369 Thou who didst on Calvary bleed,
370 Just as I am, without one plea,
371 Lord, I approach the mercy-seat
372 O God of mercy, hear my call
373 Did Christ o'er sinners weep,
374 Jesus, I come to thee,
375 Out of the deep I call,
376 Like Noah's weary dove
377 O Jesus, thou art standing
378 O Jesus, I have promised
379 Weary of earth, and laden with my sin,
380 I come, O Lord, to thee,

GLADNESS—GRATITUDE.
381 Hallelujah! Christ is mine;
382 When this passing world is done,
383 I heard the voice of Jesus say
384 My Saviour, what thou didst of old,
385 Blessed be God, forever blest,
386 My God, fill thou my life with praise,
387 I was a wandering sheep,
388 Once blind with sin and self,
389 Jesus, too late I thee have sought,
390 Jesus, and shall it ever be,

FAITH—TRUST.
391 Art thou not mine, my living Lord,
392 No more, my God, I boast no more,
393 Faith is a living power from heaven,
394 Forever here my rest shall be,
395 O for a faith that will not shrink,
396 O Father, compass me about
397 Thou art my hiding place, O Lord,
398 I'm not ashamed to own my Lord,
399 O holy Saviour, Friend unseen,
400 I cannot always trace the way
401 To him who hears I whisper all,
402 O thou, the contrite sinner's friend,
403 O Gift of gifts, O grace of faith,
404 My God, 'tis to thy mercy-seat
405 My God, the covenant of thy love,
406 None loves me, Saviour with thy love
407 Lord, when I quit this earthly stage

ASPIRATION.
408 Jesus, thou Joy of loving hearts,
409 Away from earth my spirit turns,

HYMNS.
410 My spirit longs for thee
411 There is a blessed home
412 As pants the hart for cooling streams
413 O for a heart to praise my God,
414 Father, whate'er of earthly bliss
415 O could I find from day to day,
416 O for a closer walk with God,
417 Father of love, our Guide and Friend,
418 O everlasting strength!
419 O that the Lord would guide my ways
420 O Lord, impart thyself to me,
421 O Jesus, Light of all below,
422 O Lord, I would delight in thee,
423 Father, I know that all my life
424 Father! replenish with thy grace,
425 Nearer, my God, to thee,
426 More love to thee, O Christ,
427 Here behold me, as I cast me
428 Love divine, all love excelling,
4 9 Purer yet and purer
430 Brighter still, and brighter,
431 Light of life, seraphic Fire!
432 Christ, of all my hopes the ground,

ASSURANCE.
433 A debtor to mercy alone,
434 This God is the God we adore,
435 My hope is built on nothing less
436 Jesus, my boast, my light, my joy,
437 Now I have found the ground
438 I bless the Christ of God,
439 I would not walk alone,
440 I love thee, Saviour mine, and still
441 And wilt thou now forsake me, Lord,
442 I know that my Redeemer lives,
443 I lay my sins on Jesus,
444 Jesus! thy name I love,
445 Now I have found a friend,
446 My God! the spring of all my joys,
447 The Lord has promised good to me,
448 Compared with Christ, in all beside
449 Jesus, the very thought of thee
450 Jesus these eyes have never seen
451 The Lord my Shepherd is,
452 Grace, 'tis a charming sound,
453 If Jesus be my friend,
454 Here I can firmly rest,
455 Rest of the weary,
456 Sounding loud or low,
457 Whate'er my God ordains is right,
458 I once was a stranger to grace
459 How firm a foundation,

First Lines of Hymns.—Concluded.

CONSECRATION.

HYMNS
460 Jesus, I my cross have taken,
461 My spirit, on thy care,
462 We pray for childlike hearts,
463 How gentle God's commands!
464 Jesus, I live to thee,
465 Blest be thy love, dear Lord.
466 This is the sweetness of my life,
467 I worship thee, sweet Will of God,
468 My Jesus, as thou wilt!
469 Thy way, not mine, O Lord,
470 Not what I am, O Lord,
471 O Thou great Friend to all

DUTY—TOIL.

472 Go, labor on; spend, and be spent,
473 My gracious Lord, I own thy right
474 So let our lips and lives express
475 Jesus, Master, whom I serve,
476 Workman of God, O lose not heart,
477 A charge to keep I have,
478 Sow in the morn thy seed,
479 Serve we our God in faith,
480 Ye servants of the Lord,

SPIRITUAL CONFLICT.

481 Children of God, who, faint and slow,
482 Almighty God! I call to thee,
483 My soul, be on thy guard,
484 Soldiers of Christ! arise,
485 Stand up, my soul, shake off thy fears,
486 I send the joys of earth away,
487 Awake, our souls, away our fears,
488 Awake, my soul, lift up thine eyes,
489 Awake my soul, stretch every nerve,
490 Am I soldier of the cross,
491 Must Jesus bear the cross alone,
492 The Son of God goes forth to war,
493 Thou only Sovereign of my heart,
494 O thou, to whose all-searching sight
495 Rest for my soul I long to find,
496 Those eternal bowers
497 Temptation cannot come to me
498 Onward, Christian soldiers!
499 Forward! be our watchword,
500 O Lamb of God, still keep me
501 Quiet, Lord, my froward heart,
502 Go forward, Christian soldier,
503 Stand up! stand up for Jesus!

BURDENS AND SORROWS.

504 Jesus, lover of my soul,
505 Though in a foreign land
506 Thou very present aid
507 If through unruffled seas
508 Commit thou all thy griefs

HYMNS
509 Give to the winds thy fears,
510 I close my weary eye,
511 When day's shadows lengthen,
512 It is thy hand, my God,
513 Come, ye disconsolate
514 From lips divine, like healing balm
515 O Lord, my best desires fulfil,
516 Thy way is on the deep, O Lord,
517 When languor and disease invade,
518 Dear Refuge of my weary soul,
519 God of my life, to thee I call,
520 Be still, my heart, these anxious cares
521 O Love Divine, that stooped to share
522. When time seems short and death is near,
523 Is it not strange, the darkest hour
524 When the dark waves round us roll,
525 Cast thy burden on the Lord.
526 With tearful eyes I look around,
527 My God, my Father, while I stray,
528 Jesus, my Saviour, look on me,
529 When our heads are bowed with woe,

PILGRIM SONGS.

530 In heavenly love abiding,
531 Our yet unfinished story
532 Life can bring with it nothing.
533 A pilgrim and a stranger,
534 O happy band of pilgrims,
535 Through the night of doubt and sorrow,
536 Rise, my soul, and stretch thy wings,
537 This is not my place of resting,
538 When along life's thorny road,
539 My days are gliding swiftly by
540 I'm but a stranger here,
541 If on our daily course our mind,
542 All as God wills, who wisely heeds
543 How vain is all beneath the skies,
544 By faith in Christ I walk with God,
545 A stranger in the world below,
546 The Lord's my Shepherd, I'll not want,
547 The King of love my Shepherd is,
548 He who on the accursed tree
549 The Lord is my shepherd, no want
550 Tho' faint, yet pursuing, we go
551 Thou knowest, Lord, the weariness
552 I journey through a desert
553 I do not ask, O Lord! that life
554 Lead, kindly light, amid
555 A few more years shall roll
556 One sweetly solemn thought
557 Abide with me, fast falls
558 I've wrestled on toward heaven,

194. THE CHRISTIAN.
RICHARDS. L. M. 81. QUARTET & CHORUS CHOIR.

363
I. Watts.

From deep distress and troubled thoughts,
To thee, my God, I raise my cries;
If thou severely mark our faults,
No flesh can stand before thine eyes.

2 But thou hast built thy throne of grace,
Free to dispense thy pardons there;
That sinners may approach thy face,
And hope and love, as well as fear.

3 My trust is fixed upon thy word,
Nor shall I trust thy word in vain;
Let mourning souls address the Lord,
And find relief from all their pain.

4 Great is his love, and large his grace,
Through the redemption of his Son;
He turns our feet from sinful ways,
And pardons what our hands have done.

364
I. Watts.

Show pity, Lord! O Lord, forgive;
Let a repenting rebel live;
Are not thy mercies large and free?
May not a sinner trust in thee?

2 My crimes are great, but can't surpass
The power and glory of thy grace:
Great God! thy nature hath no bound,
So let thy pardoning love be found.

3 My lips with shame my sins confess,
Against thy law, against thy grace;
Lord, should thy judgment grow severe,
I am condemned, but thou art clear.

4 Yet save a trembling sinner, Lord!
Whose hope, still hovering round thy word,
Would light on some sweet promise there,
Some sure support against despair.

Penitence—Self-Surrender. 195

WARNER. L. M. — ARR. GEO. KINGSLEY.

1. A broken heart, my God, my King, Is all the sacrifice I bring; The God of grace will ne'er despise A broken heart for sacrifice.

365 *I. Watts.*

A BROKEN heart, my God, my King,
Is all the sacrifice I bring;
The God of grace will ne'er despise
A broken heart for sacrifice.

2 My soul lies humbled in the dust,
And owns thy dreadful sentence just;
Look down, O Lord, with pitying eye,
And save the soul condemned to die.

3 Then will I teach the world thy ways;
Sinners shall learn thy sovereign grace;
I'll lead them to my Saviour's blood,
And they shall praise a pardoning God.

4 O may thy love inspire my tongue!
Salvation shall be all my song;
And all my powers shall join to bless
The Lord, my strength and righteousness.

366 *J. Borthwick, tr.*

GOD calling yet! shall I not hear?
Earth's pleasures shall I still hold dear?
Shall life's swift passing years all fly,
And still my soul in slumber lie?

2 God calling yet! and shall he knock,
And I my heart the closer lock?
He still is waiting to receive,
And shall I dare his Spirit grieve?

3 God calling yet! and shall I give
No heed, but still in bondage live?
I wait, but he does not forsake;
He calls me still; my heart, awake!

4 God calling yet! I cannot stay;
My heart I yield without delay:
Vain world, farewell, from thee I part;
The voice of God hath reached my heart!

367 *C. Elven.*

WITH broken heart and contrite sigh,
A trembling sinner, Lord, I cry:
Thy pardoning grace is rich and free;
O God, be merciful to me.

2 I smite upon my troubled breast,
With deep and conscious guilt opprest,
Christ and his cross my only plea;
O God, be merciful to me.

3 Far off I stand with tearful eyes,
Nor dare uplift them to the skies;
But thou dost all my anguish see;
O God, be merciful to me.

4 Nor alms, nor deeds that I have done,
Can for a single sin atone;
To Calvary alone I flee;
O God, be merciful to me.

THE CHRISTIAN.

MERCY. 7s.   GOTTSCHALK.

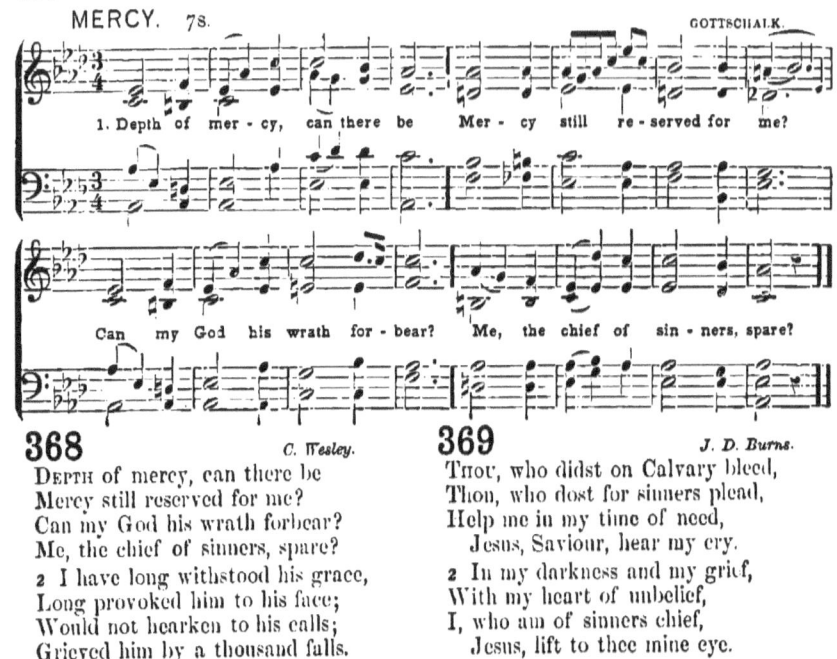

368   *C. Wesley.*

DEPTH of mercy, can there be
Mercy still reserved for me?
Can my God his wrath forbear?
Me, the chief of sinners, spare?

2 I have long withstood his grace,
Long provoked him to his face;
Would not hearken to his calls;
Grieved him by a thousand falls.

3 Kindled his relentings are;
Me he now delights to spare;
Cries; "How shall I give thee up?"
Lets the lifted thunder drop.

4 Still for me the Saviour stands,
Shows his wounds, and spreads his hands;
God is love: I know, I feel;
Jesus weeps, and loves me still.

369   *J. D. Burns.*

THOU, who didst on Calvary bleed,
Thou, who dost for sinners plead,
Help me in my time of need,
   Jesus, Saviour, hear my cry.

2 In my darkness and my grief,
With my heart of unbelief,
I, who am of sinners chief,
   Jesus, lift to thee mine eye.

3 Foes without and fears within,
With no plea thy grace to win,
But that thou canst save from sin,
   Jesus, to thy cross I fly.

4 There on thee I cast my care,
There to thee I raise my prayer,
Jesus, save me from despair,
   Save me, save me, or I die.

FISK. 7s.

Penitence—Self-Surrender. 197

KIMBALL. 8s, 6s.   QUARTET & CHORUS CHOIR.

1. Just as I am, with-out one plea, But that thy blood was shed for me, And that thou bidst me come to thee, O Lamb of God, I come! O Lamb of God, I come!

370
C. Elliott.

Just as I am, without one plea,
But that thy blood was shed for me,
And that thou bidst me come to thee,
O Lamb of God, I come!

2 Just as I am, and waiting not
To rid my soul of one dark blot,
To thee, whose blood can cleanse each spot,
O Lamb of God, I come!

3 Just as I am, poor, wretched, blind,
Sight, riches, healing of the mind,
Yea, all I need, in thee to find,
O Lamb of God, I come!

4 Just as I am, thou wilt receive,
Wilt welcome, pardon, cleanse, relieve,
Because thy promise I believe,
O Lamb of God, I come!

5 Just as I am, thy love unknown
Hath broken every barrier down;
Now, to be thine, yea, thine alone,
O Lamb of God, I come!

6 Just as I am, of that free love
"The breadth, length, depth and height"
Here for a season, then above,— [to prove,-
O Lamb of God, I come!

AUSTEN. L. M.   DONIZETTI.

1. Just as I am, with-out one plea; But that thy blood was shed for me, And that thou bidst me come to thee, O Lamb of God, I come, I come!

THE CHRISTIAN.

FINCH. C. M. — J. P. HOLBROOK.

1. Lord, I approach the mercy-seat, Where thou dost answer prayer;
There humbly fall before thy feet, For none can perish there.

371
J. Newton.

Lord, I approach the mercy-seat,
　Where thou dost answer prayer;
There humbly fall before thy feet,
　For none can perish there.

2 Thy promise is my only plea;
　With this I venture nigh:
Thou callest burdened souls to thee,
　And such, O Lord, am I.

3 Bowed down beneath a load of sin,
　By Satan sorely pressed,
By war without and fear within,
　I come to thee for rest.

4 O wondrous love!—to bleed and die,
　To bear the cross and shame,

That guilty sinners, such as I,
　Might plead thy gracious name.

372
I. Watts.

O God of mercy! hear my call,
　My load of guilt remove;
Break down this separating wall,
　That bars me from thy love.

2 Give me the presence of thy grace;
　Then my rejoicing tongue
Shall speak aloud thy righteousness,
　And make thy praise my song.

3 A soul oppressed with sin's desert,
　My God will ne'er despise;
An humble groan, a broken heart,
　Is our best sacrifice.

SHAWMUT. S. M. — ARR. L. MASON.

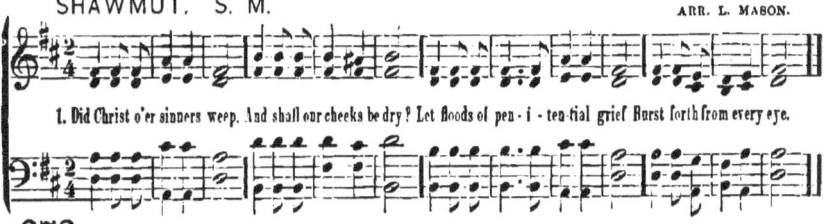

1. Did Christ o'er sinners weep. And shall our cheeks be dry? Let floods of pen-i-ten-tial grief Burst forth from every eye.

373
B. Beddome.

Did Christ o'er sinners weep,
　And shall our cheeks be dry?
Let floods of penitential grief
　Burst forth from every eye.

2 The Son of God in tears
　Angels with wonder see

Be thou astonished, O my soul,
　He shed those tears for thee.

3 He wept that we might weep;
　Each sin demands a tear;
In heaven alone no sin is found,
　And there's no weeping there.

Penitence—Self-Surrender.

BEMAN. S. M.   G. P. MERRICK.

1. Je-sus! I come to thee, A sinner doomed to die; My only refuge is thy cross,—Here at thy feet I lie.

374   *N. S. S. Beman.*

Jesus! I come to thee,
 A sinner doomed to die;
My only refuge is thy cross,—
 Here at thy feet I lie.

2 O Lord! my heart is fixed,—
  I hope in thee alone;
Break off the chains of sin and death,
 And bind me to thy throne.

3 Thy blood can cleanse my heart,
 Thy hand can wipe my tears;—
O send thy blessed Spirit down,
 To banish all my fears.

4 Then shall my soul arise,
 From sin and Satan free;
Redeemed from hell and every foe,
 I'll trust alone in thee.

375   *H. W. Baker.*

Out of the deep I call
 To thee, O Lord, to thee;
Before thy throne of grace I fall,
 Be merciful to me.

2 Out of the deep I cry,
 The woeful deep of sin,
Of evil done in days gone by,
 Of evil now within.

3 Out of the deep of fear,
 And dread of coming shame,
From morning watch till night is near,
 I plead the precious Name.

4 Lord, there is mercy now,
 As ever was, with thee;
Before thy throne of grace I bow,
 Be merciful to me.

GREENWOOD S. M.   J. E. SWEETSER.

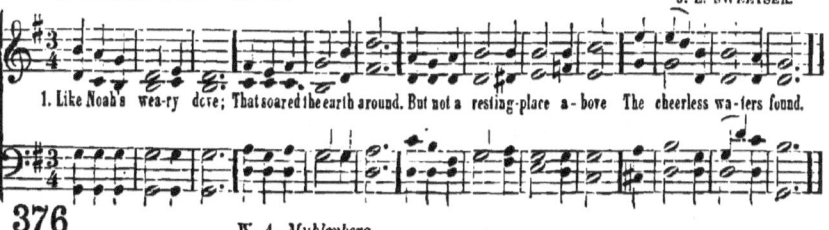

1. Like Noah's weary dove; That soared the earth around, But not a resting-place above The cheerless waters found.

376   *W. A. Muhlenberg.*

Like Noah's weary dove,
 That soared the earth around,
But not a resting-place above
 The cheerless waters found;

2 O cease, my wandering soul,
 On restless wing to roam;
All the wide world, to either pole,
 Has not for thee a home.

3 Behold the Ark of God,
 Behold the open door;
O haste to gain that dear abode,
 And rove, my soul, no more.

4 There, safe thou shalt abide,
 There, sweet shall be thy rest,
And every longing satisfied,
 With full salvation blest.

THE CHRISTIAN.

ST. HILDA. 7s, 6s. H. HUSBAND.

1. O Jesus, thou art standing
Outside the fast-closed door,
In lowly patience waiting
To pass the threshold o'er:
We bear the name of Christians,
His name and sign we bear;
O shame, thrice shame upon us,
To keep him standing there!

2 O Jesus, thou art knocking:
And lo! that hand is scarred,
And thorns thy brow encircle,
And tears thy face have marred:
O love that passeth knowledge
So patiently to wait!
O sin that hath no equal
So fast to bar the gate!

3 O Jesus, thou art pleading
In accents meek and low,
"I died for you, my children,
And will ye treat me so?"
O Lord, with shame and sorrow
We open now the door:
Dear Saviour, enter, enter,
And leave us never more.

377 W. W. How.

378 J. E. Bode.

O Jesus, I have promised
To serve thee to the end;
Be thou forever near me,
My Master and my Friend!
My foes are ever near me,
Around me and within;
But Jesus, draw thou nearer
And shield my soul from sin.

2 O let me hear thee speaking
In accents clear and still,
Above the storms of passion,
The murmurs of self-will.
O speak to re-assure me,
My stubborn heart control;
O speak, and make me listen,
Thou Master of my soul!

3 O Jesus, I have promised
To serve thee to the end;
Then give me grace to follow
My Master and my Friend.
O guide me, call me, draw me,
Uphold me to the end;
And then in heaven receive me,
My Saviour and my Friend!

Penitence—Self-Surrender. 201

379 *S. J. Stone.*
Weary of earth and laden with my sin,
I look at heaven and long to enter in,
But there no evil thing may find a home:
And yet I hear a voice that bids me "Come."

2 So vile I am, how dare I hope to stand
In the pure glory of that holy land?
Before the whiteness of that throne appear?
Yet there are hands stretched out to draw me near.

3 It is the voice of Jesus that I hear,
His are the hands stretched out to draw me near,
And his the blood that can for all atone,
And set me faultless there before the throne.

4 Yea, thou wilt answer for me, righteous Lord,
Thine all the merits, mine the great reward;
Thine the sharp thorns, and mine the golden crown,
Mine the life won, and thine the life laid down.

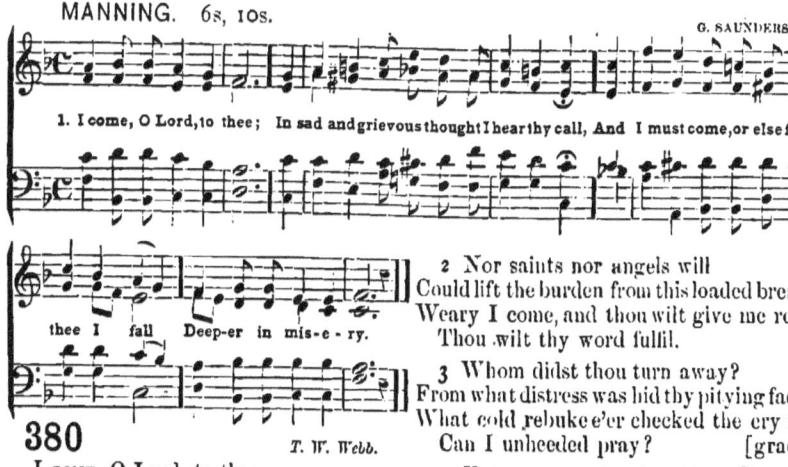

380 *T. W. Webb.*
I come, O Lord, to thee;
In sad and grievous thought I hear thy call,
And I must come, or else from thee I fall
Deeper in misery.

2 Nor saints nor angels will
Could lift the burden from this loaded breast:
Weary I come, and thou wilt give me rest;
Thou wilt thy word fulfil.

3 Whom didst thou turn away?
From what distress was hid thy pitying face?
What cold rebuke e'er checked the cry for grace?
Can I unheeded pray?

4 Enter my opening heart! [heaven!
Fill it with love and peace, and light from
Give me thyself, for all in thee is given!
Come, never to depart!

THE CHRISTIAN.

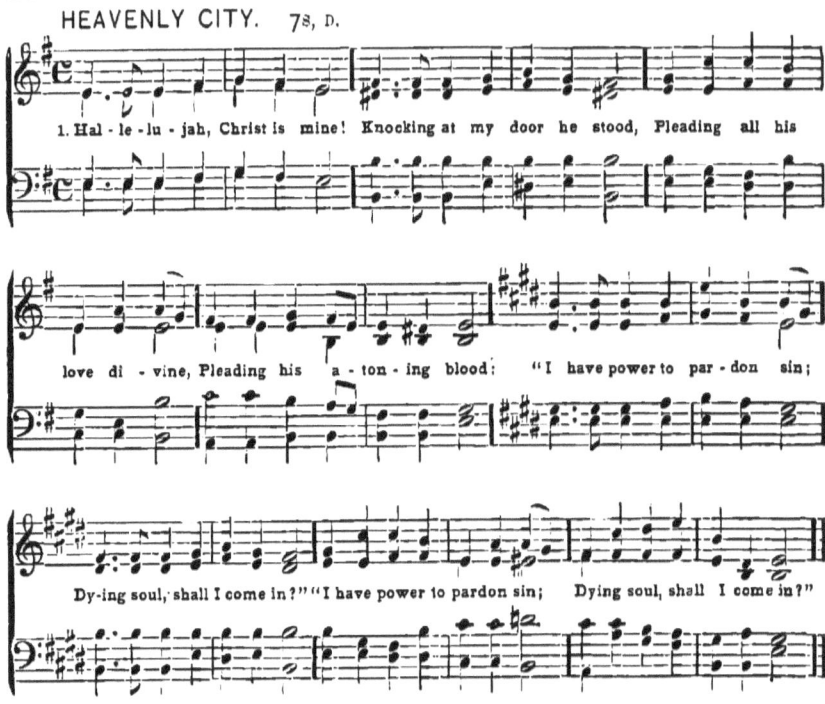

HEAVENLY CITY. 7s, D.

1. Hal-le-lu-jah, Christ is mine! Knocking at my door he stood, Pleading all his love di-vine, Pleading his a-ton-ing blood: "I have power to par-don sin; Dy-ing soul, shall I come in?" "I have power to pardon sin; Dying soul, shall I come in?"

381   E. P. Barrows.

HALLELUJAH, Christ is mine!
Knocking at my door, he stood,
Pleading all his love divine,
Pleading his atoning blood:
"I have power to pardon sin;
Dying soul, shall I come in?"

4 As those gracious words he spoke,
Lo! I felt a power divine,
Mightier than the lightning's stroke,
Breaking this hard heart of mine:
Straight the door I opened wide;
"Jesus, Lord, come in," I cried.

3 Then my soul, long tempest-tossed,
Entered into glorious rest:
All my powers in joy were lost;
Holy gladness filled my breast;
'Twas a trance of heavenly love,
Like the bliss of those above.

4 Sinful pleasures in that day
Vanished like a dream from view;
Earthly things I cast away,
My Redeemer to pursue.
'T is enough—his love divine!
Hallelujah, Christ is mine.

382   R. M. McCheyne.

WHEN this passing world is done,
When has sunk yon glorious sun;
When we stand with Christ in light,
All our finished life in sight;
Then, Lord, shall we fully know—
Not till then—how much we owe.

2 When we stand before the throne,
Dressed in beauty not our own;
When we see thee as thou art,
Love thee with unsinning heart:
Then, Lord, shall we fully know—
Not till then—how much we owe.

3 When the praise of heaven we hear,
Loud as thunders to the ear,
Loud as many waters' noise,
Sweet as harp's melodious voice:
Then, Lord, shall we fully know—
Not till then—how much we owe.

Gladness—Gratitude. 203

TRUMAN. C. M.   J. P. HOLBROOK.

1. I heard the voice of Jesus say, "Come unto me and rest; Lay down, thou weary one, lay down Thy head upon my breast." I came to Jesus as I was, Weary, and worn, and sad; I found in him a resting place, And he has made me glad.

383   *H. Bonar.*

I HEARD the voice of Jesus say,
  "Come unto me and rest;
Lay down, thou weary one, lay down
  Thy head upon my breast."
I came to Jesus as I was,
  Weary, and worn, and sad;
I found in him a resting place,
  And he has made me glad.

2 I heard the voice of Jesus say,
  "Behold, I freely give
The living water; thirsty one,
  Stoop down and drink, and live."
I came to Jesus, and I drank
  Of that life-giving stream;
My thirst was quenched, my soul revived,
  And now I live in him.

3 I heard the voice of Jesus say,
  "I am this dark world's light;
Look unto me, thy morn shall rise,
  And all thy day be bright."
I looked to Jesus, and I found
  In him my Star, my Sun;
And in that light of life I'll walk
  Till all my journey's done.

384   *C. Winkworth, tr.*

My Saviour, what thou didst of old,
  When thou wast dwelling here,
Thou doest yet for them, who bold
  In faith to thee draw near.
As thou hadst pity on the blind,
  According to thy word,
Thou sufferedst me thy grace to find,
  Thy light hast on me poured.

2 I heard the music of the psalms
  Thy people sang to thee,
I felt the waving of their palms,
  And yet I could not see.
My pain grew more than I could bear,
  Too keen my grief became,
Then I took heart in my despair
  To call upon thy name.

3 Thou saidst to me, "What wouldst thou
  "That I receive my sight, [have?"
To see thy face, O Lord, I crave."
  Thou saidst, "Receive thy sight!"
Since words of thine can never fail,
  My fears are past and o'er;
My soul is glad with light, the veil
  Is on my heart no more.

THE CHRISTIAN.

MANOAH. C. M. — ROSSINI.

1. Bless-ed be God! for-ev-er blest, And glo-rious be his name: His Son he gave our souls to save From ev-er-last-ing shame.

385

Blessed be God! for ever blest,
　And glorious be his name:
His Son he gave our souls to save
　From everlasting shame.

2 Our flesh he took, our sins he bore,
　Himself for us he gave;
His cross was ours, and we with him
　Were buried in one grave.

3 With him we rose, with him we live,
　With him we sit above;
With him for ever we shall share
　The Father's boundless love.

4 Bless, then, Jehovah's blessèd name;
　And bless our blessèd King!
And songs of glad deliverance
　For ever, ever sing!

386
H. Bonar.

My God, fill thou my life with praise;
　Let all my being speak
Of thee and of thy love, O Lord,
　Poor though I be, and weak!

2 Praise in the common things of life,
　Its goings out and in,
Praise in each duty, and each deed,
　However small and mean.

3 So shall no part of day or night
　From sacredness be free,
But all my life, in every step,
　Be fellowship with thee.

4 So too, shalt thou, dear Lord, from me
　Receive the offering due,
And so shall I begin on earth
　The song forever new.

LEBANON. S. M. D. — J. ZUNDEL.

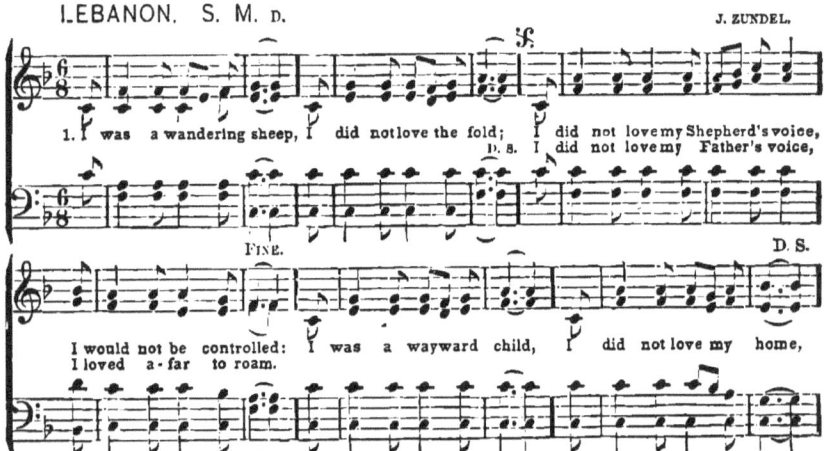

1. I was a wandering sheep, I did not love the fold; I did not love my Shepherd's voice,
D. S. I did not love my Father's voice,
I would not be controlled: I was a wayward child, I did not love my home,
I loved a-far to roam.

Gladness—Gratitude. 205

BONAR S. M. D. J. P. HOLBROOK.

1 I was a wandering sheep, I did not love the fold; I did not love my Shepherd's voice, I would not be con-trolled: I was a way-ward child, I did not love my home, I did not love my Fa-ther's voice, I loved a-far to roam.

387
H. Bonar.

I WAS a wandering sheep,
  I did not love the fold;
I did not love my Shepherd's voice
  I would not be controlled:
I was a wayward child,
  I did not love my home,
I did not love my Father's voice,
  I loved afar to roam.

2 Jesus my Shepherd is,
  'Twas he that loved my soul,
'Twas he that washed me in his blood,
  'Twas he that made me whole;
'Twas he that sought the lost,
  That found the wandering sheep,
'Twas he that brought me to the fold,
  'Tis he that still doth keep.

3 I was a wandering sheep,
  I would not be controlled;
But now I love my Shepherd's voice,
  I love, I love the fold:
I was a wayward child;
  I once preferred to roam;
But now I love my Father's voice,
  I love, I love his home.

388
C. Winkworth, tr

ONCE blind with sin and self,
  Along the treacherous way
That ends in ruin at the last,
  I hastened far astray;
Then God revealed his Son,
  For with a love most deep,
Most undeserved, his heart still yearned
  O'er me, poor wandering sheep!

2 Christ with his life of love,
  To me was far and strange;
My heart clung only to the world
  Of sight and sense and change.
Now found by him who sought,
  And through his blood forgiven,
In him my heart hath peace with God,
  And hope through him of heaven.

3 Then keep me near to thee
  Thou Saviour of my soul;
Bind me by cords of love; my name
  Among thy saints enroll.
Deign thou to take my heart,
  And let thy heart be mine,
Let all my love flow out to thee
  And lose itself in thine.

THE CHRISTIAN.

389
H. Collins.

Jesus, too late I thee have sought,
How can I love thee as I ought;
And how extol thy matchless fame,
The glorious beauty of thy Name?

2 Jesus, what didst thou find in me,
That thou hast dealt so lovingly?
How great the joy that thou hast brought,
So far exceeding hope or thought!

3 Jesus, my Lord, I thee adore,
O make me love thee more and more,
And ever from thy dwelling place
Pour down the riches of thy grace.

4 Jesus, thy name shall be my song,
To thee my heart and soul belong;
All that I have or am is thine,
And thou, blest Saviour, thou art mine.

390
J. Grigg.

Jesus! and shall it ever be,
A mortal man ashamed of thee?
Ashamed of thee, whom angels praise,
Whose glories shine through endless days?

2 Ashamed of Jesus! that dear Friend
On whom my hopes of heaven depend?
No; when I blush—be this my shame,
That I no more revere his name.

3 Ashamed of Jesus! yes, I may,
When I've no guilt to wash away;
No tear to wipe, no good to crave,
No fears to quell, no soul to save.

4 Till then—nor is my boasting vain—
Till then I boast a Saviour slain!
And O may this my glory be,
That Christ is not ashamed of me!

Faith—Trust. 207

SEASONS. L. M.   PLEYEL.

1. Art thou not mine, my liv-ing Lord? And can my hope, my com-fort die? Fixed on thine ev-er-last-ing word, That word which built the earth and sky?

391   *A. Steele.*

Art thou not mine, my living Lord?
  And can my hope, my comfort die?
Fixed on thine everlasting word,
  That word which built the earth and sky?

2 If my immortal Saviour lives,
  Then my immortal life is sure;
His word a firm foundation gives;
  Here let me build, and rest secure.

3 Here let my faith unshaken dwell;
  Immovable the promise stands;
Not all the powers of earth or hell
  Can e'er dissolve the sacred bands.

4 Here, O my soul, thy trust repose;
  If Jesus is forever mine,
Not death itself, that last of foes,
  Shall break a union so divine.

392   *I. Watts.*

No more, my God, I boast no more
  Of all the duties I have done;
I quit the hopes I held before,
  To trust the merits of thy Son.

2 Now for the love I bear his name,
  What was my gain I count my loss;
My former pride I call my shame,
  And nail my glory to his cross.

3 Yes, and I must and will esteem
  All things but loss for Jesus' sake;
O may my soul be found in him,
  And of his righteousness partake.

4 The best obedience of my hands
  Dares not appear before thy throne;
But faith can answer thy demands,
  By pleading what my Lord has done.

393   *C. Winkworth, tr.*

Faith is a living power from heaven
Which grasps the promise God has given;
A trust that cannot be o'erthrown,
Securely fixed on Christ alone.

2 Faith finds in Christ whate'er we need
To save and strengthen, guide and feed;
Strong in his grace, it joys to share
His cross, in hope his crown to wear.

3 Faith to the conscience whispers peace,
And bids the mourner's sighing cease;
By faith the children's right we claim,
And call upon our Father's name.

4 Faith feels the Spirit's kindling breath
In love and hope that conquer death;
Faith brings us to delight in God,
And trusts and blesses e'en his rod.

208 THE CHRISTIAN.

SIMPSON. C. M.   L. SPOHR.

394
C. Wesley.
For ever here my rest shall be,
  Close to thy bleeding side;
This all my hope, and all my plea—
  For me the Saviour died.

2 My dying Saviour, and my God,
  Fountain for guilt and sin,
Sprinkle me ever with thy blood,
  And cleanse and keep me clean.

3 Wash me, and make me thus thine own,
  Wash me, and mine thou art;
Wash me, but not my feet alone,—
  My hands, my head, my heart.

4 Th' atonement of thy blood apply,
  Till faith to sight improve;
Till hope in full fruition die,
  And all my soul be love.

395
W. H. Bathurst.
O for a faith that will not shrink
  Though pressed by every foe;
That will not tremble on the brink
  Of any earthly woe!—

2 That will not murmur nor complain
  Beneath the chastening rod,
But, in the hour of grief or pain,
  Will lean upon its God;—

3 A faith that shines more bright and clear
  When tempests rage without;
That, when in danger, knows no fear,
  In darkness, feels no doubt;—

4 Lord, give us such a faith as this,
  And then, whate'er may come,
We'll taste ev'n here, the hallowed bliss
  Of an eternal home.

396
C. Winkworth, tr.
O Father, compass me about
  With love, for I am weak;
Forgive, forgive my sinful doubt,
  Thy pitying glance I seek.

2 Art thou not evermore the same,
  Hath not thy word revealed
Thyself to us, that we may claim
  Thee for our strength and shield?

3 I know thy thoughts are peace toward me,
  Safe am I in thy hands,
And I may firmly build on thee,
  For sure thy counsel stands!

4 Whate'er thy word hath promised, all
  Wilt thou full surely give;
Wherefore from thee I will not fall,
  Thy word doth make me live.

5 Though mountains crumble into dust,
  Thy covenant standeth fast;
Who follows thee in faithful trust,
  Shall reach the goal at last.

6 Though strange and winding seem the way
  While yet on earth I dwell,
In heaven my heart shall gladly say,
  Thou, God, dost all things well!

Faith—Trust. 209

PACKER. C. M. — J. P. HOLBROOK.

1. Thou art my hiding-place, O Lord! In thee I put my trust, Encouraged by thy holy word,—A feeble child of dust. 2. I have no argument beside, I urge no other plea; And 'tis enough the Saviour died, The Saviour died for me.

397 T. Raffles.

Thou art my hiding-place, O Lord!
In thee I put my trust,
Encouraged by thy holy word,—
A feeble child of dust.

2 I have no argument beside,
I urge no other plea;
And 'tis enough the Saviour died,
The Saviour died for me!

3 When storms of fierce temptation beat,
And furious foes assail,
My refuge is the mercy-seat,
My hope within the vail.

4 From strife of tongues and bitter words,
My spirit flies to thee;
Joy to my heart the thought affords,
My Saviour died for me!

398 I. Watts.

I'am not ashamed to own my Lord,
Or to defend his cause,
Maintain the honor of his word,
The glory of his cross.

2 Jesus, my God! I know his Name,
His Name is all my trust;
Nor will he put my soul to shame,
Nor let my hope be lost.

3 Firm as his throne his promise stands,
And he can well secure
What I've committed to his hands,
Till the decisive hour.

4 Then will he own my worthless name
Before his Father's face,
And in the new Jerusalem
Appoint my soul a place.

HUMMEL. C. M. — C. ZEUNER.

1. I'm not ashamed to own my Lord, Or to defend his cause, Maintain the honor of his word. The glory of his cross,

210 THE CHRISTIAN.

HURLBUT. 8s, 6s.   F. FLEMMING.

1. O Holy Saviour, Friend unseen! The faint, the weak, on thee may lean; Help me throughout life's changing scene, By faith to cling to thee.

399
C. Elliott.

O Holy Saviour, Friend unseen!
The faint, the weak, on thee may lean;
Help me, throughout life's changing scene,
  By faith to cling to thee.

2 Blest with communion so divine,
Take what thou wilt, shall I repine,
When, as the branches to the vine,
  My soul may cling to thee?

3 Far from my home, fatigued, opprest,
Here have I found a place of rest;
An exile still, yet not unblest,
  While I can cling to thee.

4 Though faith and hope awhile be tried,
I ask not, need not, aught beside:
How safe, how calm, how satisfied,
  The souls that cling to thee!

5 They fear not life's rough storms to brave,
Since thou art near, and strong to save;
Nor shudder e'en at death's dark wave;
  Because they cling to thee!

6 Blest is my lot, whate'er befall;
What can disturb me, who appall,
While, as my Strength, my Rock, my All,
  Saviour! I cling to thee?

ELLIOTT. 8s, 4s.   J. B. DYKES.

1. I can not always trace the way Where thou, almighty One, dost move; But I can always, always say That God is love.

400

I can not always trace the way
  Where thou, almighty One, dost move;
But I can always, always say
  That God is love.

2 When fear her chilling mantle flings
  O'er earth, my soul to heaven above,
As to her native home, upsprings;
  For God is love.

3 When myst'ry clouds my darkened path,
  I'll check my dread, my doubts reprove;
In this my soul sweet comfort hath,
  That God is love.

4 O may this truth my heart employ,
  Bid every gloomy thought remove,
And turn all tears, all woes to joy—
  Thou, God, art love.

Faith—Trust.

KIMBALL. 8s, 6s. — J. P. HOLBROOK.

1. To Him who hears I whisper all, And soft-lier than the dews of heaven The tears of Christ's compassion fall, I know I am for-given, I know I am for-given.

401 *H. M. Kimball.*

To HIM who hears I whisper all,
 And softlier than the dews of heaven,
The tears of Christ's compassion fall,
 I know I am forgiven.

2 Wrapped in the peace that follows prayer,
 I fold my hands in perfect trust,
Forgetful of the cross I bear,
 Through noon-day heat and dust.

3 No more life's mysteries vex my thought,
 No cruel doubts disturb my breast,
My heavy-laden spirit sought
 And found the promised rest.

402 *C. Elliott.*

O THOU, the contrite sinner's Friend!
 Who, loving, lov'st them to the end,
On this alone my hopes depend,
 That thou wilt plead for me.

2 When weary in the Christian race,
Far off appears my resting place,
And, fainting, I mistrust thy grace,
 Then, Saviour, plead for me.

3 When I have erred and gone astray,
Afar from thine and wisdom's way,
And see no glimmering, guiding ray,
 Still, Saviour, plead for me.

4 When Satan, by my sins made bold,
Strives from thy cross to loose my hold,
Then with thy pitying arms enfold,
 And plead, O plead for me!

INTERCESSION. 8s, 6s. — T. MOUNTAIN.

1. O thou, the con-trite sin-ner's Friend! Who, lov-ing lov'st them to the end, On this a-lone my hopes de-pend, That thou wilt plead for me.

212 THE CHRISTIAN.

VALENTIA. C. M.   ARR. G. KINGSLEY.

1. O gift of gifts! O grace of faith! My God! how can it be
That thou, who hast dis-cern-ing love, Shouldst give that gift to me?

403   *F. W. Faber.*

O GIFT of gifts! O grace of faith!
  My God! how can it be
That thou, who hast discerning love,
  Shouldst give that gift to me?

2 Ah, grace! into unlikeliest hearts
  It is thy boast to come,
The glory of thy light to find
  In darkest spots a home.

3 How can they live, how will they die,
  How bear the cross of grief,
Who have not got the light of faith,
  The courage of belief?

4 The crowd of cares, the weightiest cross,
  Seem trifles less than light;
Earth looks so little, and so low,
  When faith shines full and bright.

5 O happy, happy that I am!
  If thou canst be, O Faith!
The treasure, that thou art in life,
  What wilt thou be in death?

6 Thy choice, O God of goodness! then
  I lovingly adore;
O give me grace to keep thy grace,
  And grace to love thee more.

404   *A. Steele.*

My God! 't is to thy mercy-seat
  My soul for shelter flies;
'T is here I find a safe retreat
  When storms and tempests rise.

2 My cheerful hope can never die
  If thou, my God, art near;
Thy grace can raise my comforts high
  And banish every fear.

3 My great Protector and my Lord!
  Thy constant aid impart;
And let thy kind, thy gracious word
  Sustain my trembling heart.

4 O never let my soul remove
  From this divine retreat;
Still let me trust thy power and love,
  And dwell beneath thy feet.

405   *P. Doddridge.*

My God, the covenant of thy love
  Abides for ever sure;
And in its matchless grace I feel
  My happiness secure.

2 Since thou, the everlasting God,
  My Father art become,
Jesus my Guardian and my Friend,
  And heaven my final home;

3 I welcome all thy sovereign will,
  For all that will is love;
And when I know not what thou dost,
  I wait the light above.

4 Thy covenant in the darkest gloom
  Shall heavenly rays impart,
And when my eyelids close in death,
  Sustain my fainting heart.

NORWOOD. L. M. — W. H. HART.

1. None loves me, Sav-iour, with thy love, None else can meet such needs as mine; O grant me, as thou shalt ap-prove, All that be-fits a child of thine.

406   *G. Duffield, tr.*

NONE loves me, Saviour, with thy love,
None else can meet such needs as mine;
O grant me, as thou shalt approve,
All that befits a child of thine.

2 Give me a faith shall never fail,
One that shall always work by love;
And then whatever foes assail,
They shall but higher courage move.

3 A heart, that, when my days are glad
May never from thy way decline,
And when the sky of life grows sad
May still submit its will to thine.

4 A heart that loves to trust in thee,
A patient heart create in me;
From every doubt and fear release,
And give me confidence and peace.

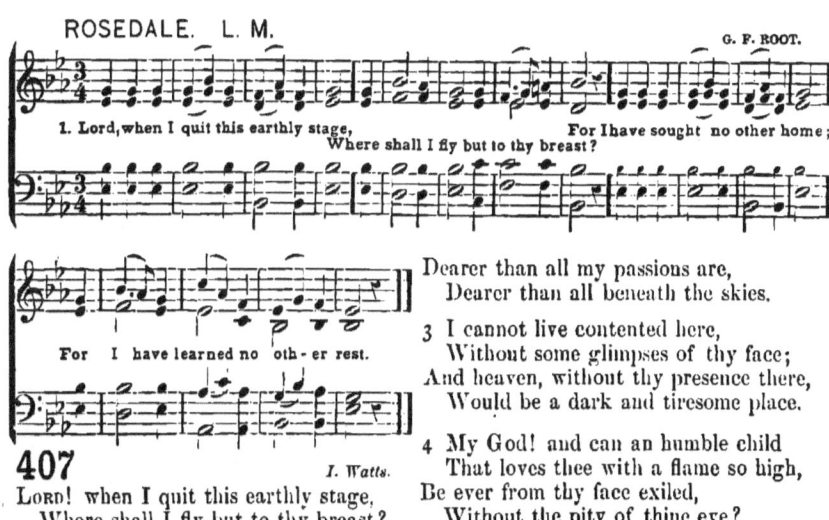

ROSEDALE. L. M. — G. F. ROOT.

1. Lord, when I quit this earthly stage, Where shall I fly but to thy breast? For I have sought no other home; For I have learned no oth-er rest.

407   *I. Watts.*

LORD! when I quit this earthly stage,
Where shall I fly but to thy breast?
For I have sought no other home;
For I have learned no other rest.

2 Christ is my light, my life, my care,
My blessèd hope, my heavenly prize,
Dearer than all my passions are,
Dearer than all beneath the skies.

3 I cannot live contented here,
Without some glimpses of thy face;
And heaven, without thy presence there,
Would be a dark and tiresome place.

4 My God! and can an humble child
That loves thee with a flame so high,
Be ever from thy face exiled,
Without the pity of thine eye?

5 Impossible!—for thine own hands
Have tied my heart so fast to thee;
And in thy book the promise stands,
That where thou art thy friends must be.

THE CHRISTIAN.

DAWSON. L. M.
J. P. HOLBROOK.

408 *Ray Palmer, tr.*

Jesus, thou Joy of loving hearts,
  Thou Fount of life, thou Light of men,
From the best bliss that earth imparts,
  We turn unfilled to thee again.

2 Thy truth unchanged hath ever stood;
  Thou savest those that on thee call;
To them that seek thee, thou art good,
  To them that find thee, All in all.

3 We taste thee, O thou living Bread,
  And long to feast upon thee still;

We drink of thee, the Fountain Head,
  And thirst our souls from thee to fill.

4 Our restless spirits yearn for thee,
  Where'er our changeful lot is cast;
Glad, when thy gracious smile we see,
  Blest, when our faith can hold thee fast.

5 O Jesus, ever with us stay;
  Make all our moments calm and bright;
Chase the dark night of sin away;
  Shed o'er the world thy holy light.

PERCY. L. M.
H. PERCY SMITH.

409 *Ray Palmer.*

Away from earth my spirit turns,
  Away from every transient good;
With strong desire my bosom burns
  To feast on heaven's diviner food.

2 Thou, Saviour, art the living bread;
  Thou wilt my every want supply:
By thee sustained and cheered and led,
  I'll press through dangers to the sky.

3 What though temptations oft distress,
  And sin assails, and breaks my peace;
Thou wilt uphold and save and bless,
  And bid the storms of passion cease.

4 Then let me take thy gracious hand,
  And walk beside thee onward still;
Till my glad feet shall safely stand
  Forever firm on Zion's hill.

Aspiration.

410 *J. Byrom.*

My spirit longs for thee
Within my troubled breast,
Unworthy though I be
Of so divine a guest.
Of so divine a guest
Unworthy though I be,
Yet hath my heart no rest
Unless it come from thee.

2 Unless it come from thee,
In vain I look around;
In all that I can see
No rest is to be found.
No rest is to be found
But in thy blessèd love:
O let my wish be crowned,
And send it from above.

411 *H. W. Baker.*

There is a blessèd home
Beyond this land of woe,
Where trials never come,
Nor tears of sorrow flow;
Where faith is lost in sight,
And patient hope is crowned,
And everlasting light
Its glory throws around.

2 Look up, ye saints of God,
Nor fear to tread below
The path your Saviour trod
Of daily toil and woe;
Wait but a little while
In uncomplaining love,
His own most gracious smile
Shall welcome you above.

THE CHRISTIAN.

SIMPSON. C. M. — L. SPOHR.

1. As pants the hart for cool-ing streams When heat-ed in the chase;
So longs my soul, O God, for thee, And thy re-fresh-ing grace.

412 *Tate-Brady.*

As PANTS the hart for cooling streams
When heated in the chase;
So longs my soul, O God, for thee,
And thy refreshing grace.

2 For thee, my God, the living God,
My thirsty soul doth pine;
O when shall I behold thy face,
Thou Majesty divine?

3 Why restless, why cast down, my soul?
Trust God; and he'll employ
His aid for thee, and change these sighs
To thankful hymns of joy.

4 Why restless, why cast down, my soul?
Hope still; and thou shalt sing
The praise of him who is thy God,
Thy health's eternal spring.

413 *C. Wesley.*

O FOR a heart to praise my God,
A heart from sin set free;
A heart that's sprinkled with the blood
So freely shed for me!

2 O for a lowly, contrite heart,
Believing, true, and clean!
Which neither life nor death can part
From him that dwells within.

3 A heart in every thought renewed,
And filled with love divine;
Perfect, and right, and pure, and good;
An image, Lord, of thine.

4 Thy nature, gracious Lord! impart;
Come quickly from above;
Write thy new name upon my heart,—
Thy new, best name of Love.

CHURCH. C. M. — J. P. HOLBROOK.

1. O for a heart to praise my God, A heart from sin set free;
A heart that's sprinkled with the blood So free-ly shed for me!

Aspiration. 217

NAOMI. C. M. — ARR. L. MASON.

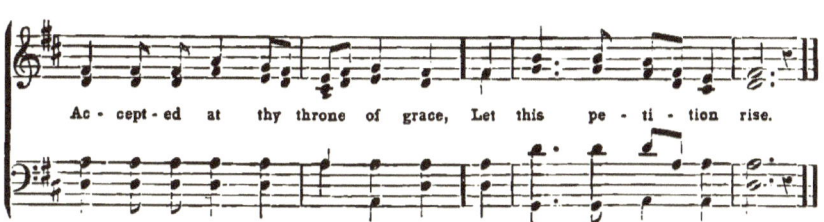

1. Father, whate'er of earthly bliss Thy sovereign will denies,
Accepted at thy throne of grace, Let this petition rise.

414 *A. Steele.*
Father, whate'er of earthly bliss
Thy sovereign will denies,
Accepted at thy throne of grace,
Let this petition rise:

2 Give me a calm, a thankful heart,
From every murmur free;
The blessings of thy grace impart,
And make me live to thee.

3 Let the sweet hope that thou art mine
My life and death attend;
Thy presence through my journey shine,
And crown my journey's end.

415 *B. Cleaveland.*
O could I find, from day to day,
A nearness to my God,
Then would my hours glide sweet away
While leaning on his word.

2 Lord, I desire with thee to live
Anew from day to day,
In joys the world can never give,
Nor ever take away.

3 Blest Jesus, come and rule my heart,
And make me wholly thine,
That I may never more depart,
Nor grieve thy love divine.

4 Thus, till my last, expiring breath,
Thy goodness I'll adore;
And when my frame dissolves in death,
My soul shall love thee more.

416 *W. Cowper.*
O for a closer walk with God,
A calm and heavenly frame,
A light to shine upon the road
That leads me to the Lamb!

2 Return, O Holy Dove, return,
Sweet messenger of rest;
I hate the sins that made thee mourn,
And drove thee from my breast.

3 The dearest idol I have known,
Whate'er that idol be;
Help me to tear it from thy throne,
And worship only thee.

4 So shall my walk be close with God,
Calm and serene my frame;
So purer light shall mark the road
That leads me to the Lamb.

417 *W. J. Irons.*
Father of love, our Guide and Friend,
O lead us gently on,
Until life's trial time shall end,
And heavenly peace be won.

2 And if some darker lot be good,
O teach us to endure
The sorrow, pain, or solitude
That makes the spirit pure.

3 We know not what the path may be
As yet by us untrod;
But we can trust our all to thee,
Our Father and our God.

THE CHRISTIAN.

MAYO. S. M. — C. W. JORDAN.

1. O ev-er-last-ing Strength! Up-hold me in the way;
Bring me, in spite of foes, at length, To joy, and light, and day.

418
H. Bonar.

O EVERLASTING Strength!
 Uphold me in the way;
Bring me, in spite of foes, at length,
 To joy, and light, and day.

2 O everlasting Love;
 Well-spring of grace and peace,
Pour down thy fullness from above;
 Bid doubt and trouble cease.

3 O everlasting Rest!
 Lift off life's load of care;
Relieve, revive this burdened breast,
 And every sorrow bear.

4 Thou art in heaven our All;
 Our All on earth art thou:
Upon thy glorious name we call;
 Lord Jesus bless us now!

BURLINGTON. C. M. — J. F. BURROWES.

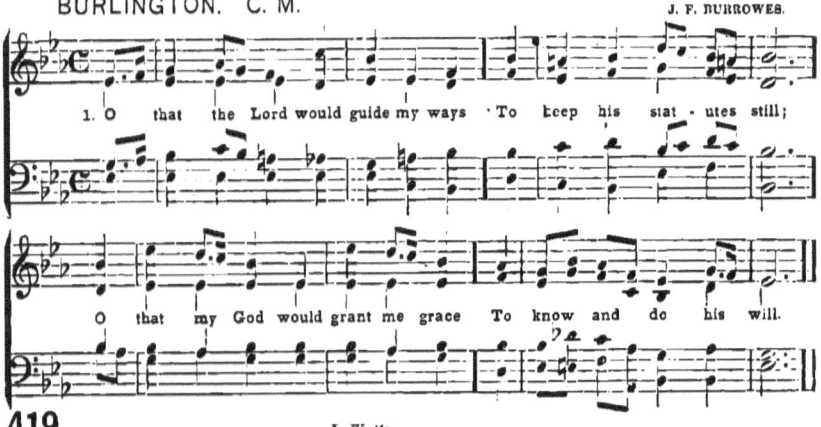

1. O that the Lord would guide my ways To keep his stat-utes still;
O that my God would grant me grace To know and do his will.

419
I. Watts.

O THAT the Lord would guide my ways
 To keep his statutes still;
O that my God would grant me grace
 To know and do his will.

2 Order my footsteps by thy word,
 And make my heart sincere;
Let sin have no dominion, Lord!
 But keep my conscience clear.

3 My soul hath gone too far astray,
 My feet too often slip;
Yet, since I've not forgot thy way,
 Restore thy wandering sheep.

4 Make me to walk in thy commands—
 'Tis a delightful road;
Nor let my head, or heart, or hands,
 Offend against my God.

Aspiration. 219

PALMER. C. M.   J. P. HOLBROOK.

1. O Lord, im-part thy-self to me, No oth-er good I need; When thou, the Son, shalt make me free, I shall be free in-deed.

420   *C. Wesley.*

O LORD, impart thyself to me,
  No other good I need;
When thou, the Son, shalt make me free,
  I shall be free indeed.

2 I cannot rest till in thy blood
  I full redemption have;
But thou, through whom I come to God,
  Canst to the utmost save.

3 From sin, the guilt, the power, the pain,
  Thou wilt redeem my soul:
Lord, I believe, and not in vain;
  My faith shall make me whole.

4 I too with thee shall walk in white;
  With all thy saints shall prove
The length, and depth, and breadth, and
  Of everlasting love.   [height

421   *E. Caswall, tr.*

O JESUS, Light of all below!
  Thou Fount of life and fire!
Surpassing all the joys we know,
  All that we can desire,—

2 When once thou visitest the heart,
  Then truth begins to shine;
Then earthly vanities depart;
  Then kindles love divine.

3 May every heart confess thy name,
  And ever thee adore;
And, seeking thee, itself inflame
  To seek thee more and more.

4 Thee may our tongues for ever bless;
  Thee may we love alone;
And ever in our lives express
  The image of thine own.

422   *J. Ryland.*

O LORD, I would delight in thee,
  And on thy care depend;
To thee in every trouble flee,
  My best, my only Friend.

2 When all created streams are dried,
  Thy fulness is the same:
May I with this be satisfied,
  And glory in thy name!

3 O that I had a stronger faith,
  To look within the vail,—
To credit what my Saviour saith,
  Whose word can never fail.

4 He who has made my heaven secure,
  Will here all good provide:
While Christ is rich, can I be poor?
  What can I want beside?

5 O Lord, I cast my care on thee;
  I triumph and adore:
Henceforth my great concern shall be
  To love and please thee more.

THE CHRISTIAN.

KITTREDGE. 8s, 6s.   ABR. D. R. STANFORD.

423
A. L. Waring.

Father, I know that all my life
  Is portioned out for me;
The changes that will surely come
  I do not fear to see:
I ask thee for a present mind,
  Intent on ever pleasing thee.

2 I would not have the restless will
  That hurries to and fro,
That seeks for some great thing to do,
  Or secret thing to know:
I would be treated as a child,
  And led and guided where I go.

3 Wherever in the world I am,
  In whatsoe'er estate,
I have a fellowship with hearts,
  To keep and cultivate;
A work of lowly love to do
  For him on whom I lowly wait.

4 I ask thee for the daily strength,
  To none that ask denied,
A mind to blend with outward life,
  While keeping at thy side;
Content to fill a little space,
  If thou, my Lord, art glorified.

Aspiration. 221

VINCENT. 8s, 6s. (L. T. B.)

424
C. Winkworth, tr.

FATHER! replenish with thy grace
 This longing heart of mine,
Make it thy quiet dwelling-place,
 Thy sacred inmost shrine!
Forgive that oft my spirit wears
Her time and strength in trivial cares,
Enfold me in thy changeless peace,
That I from all but thee may cease.

2 O God the Son! thy wisdom's light
 On my dark reason pour;
Forgive that things of sense and sight
 Were all her joy of yore;
Henceforth let every thought and deed
On thee be fix'd, from thee proceed,
Draw me to thee, for I would rise
Above these earthly vanities!

3 O Holy Ghost! thou fire of love,
 Enkindle thou my will;
Gird me with strength, Lord, from above,
 Thy bidding to fulfil:
Forgive that I so oft have done
The grievous things I ought to shun;
Let me with pure and quenchless fire
Thy favor and thyself desire.

4 Most high and holy Trinity!
 Draw me from ways of time,
And let thine own eternity
 Make all my aims sublime;
Make me at peace within; at one
With thee on earth; when life is done
Take me to dwell in light with thee,
Most high and holy Trinity!

222 THE CHRISTIAN.

NEARER, MY GOD, TO THEE. 6s, 4s.
J. P. HOLBROOK.

425
S. F. Adams.

NEARER, my God, to thee,
Nearer to thee !
Ev'n though it be a cross
That raiseth me !
Still all my song shall be,
Nearer, my God, to thee,
Nearer to thee !

2 Though like the wanderer,
The sun gone down,
Darkness be over me,
My rest a stone,
Yet in my dreams I'd be
Nearer, my God, to thee,
Nearer to thee !

3 There let the way appear,
Steps unto heaven;
All that thou sendest me,
In mercy given;
Angels to beckon me
Nearer, my God, to thee,
Nearer to thee !

4 Then, with my waking thoughts
Bright with thy praise,
Out of my stony griefs
Bethel I'll raise;
So by my woes to be
Nearer, my God, to thee,
Nearer to thee !

5 Or if on joyful wing
Cleaving the sky,
Sun, moon and stars forgot,
Upward I fly,
Still all my song shall be,
Nearer, my God, to thee,
Nearer to thee.

BETHANY. 6s, 4s.
L. MASON.

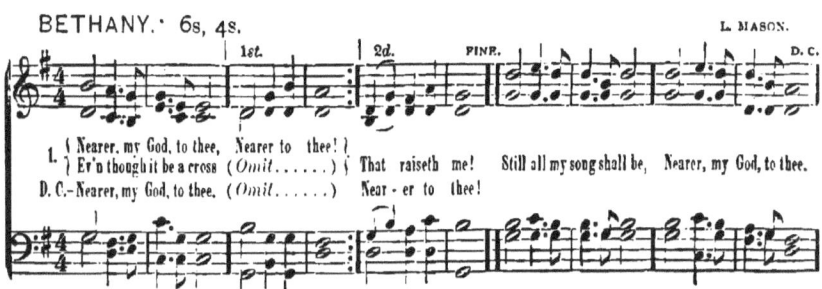

Aspiration. 223

SUMNER. 6s, 4s. J. P. HOLBROOK.

1. More love to thee, O Christ! More love to thee! Hear thou the prayer I make, On bended knee; This is my earnest plea.— More love, O Christ, to thee, More love to thee.

426
E. P. Prentiss.

MORE love to thee, O Christ!
More love to thee!
Hear thou the prayer I make,
On bended knee;
This is my earnest plea,—
More love, O Christ, to thee,
More love to thee.

2 Once earthly joy I craved,
Sought peace and rest;
Now thee alone I seek,
Give what is best:
This all my prayer shall be,—
More love, O Christ, to thee,
More love to thee.

3 Let sorrow do its work,
Send grief and pain;
Sweet are thy messengers,
Sweet their refrain,
When they can sing with me,—
More love, O Christ, to thee,
More love to thee.

4 Then shall my latest breath
Whisper thy praise;
This be the parting cry
My heart shall raise,—
This still its prayer shall be,—
More love, O Christ, to thee,
More love to thee!

ELY. 6s, 4s. J. P. HOLBROOK.

1. Near-er, my God, to thee, Near-er to thee! Ev'n though it be a cross That raiseth me! Still all my song shall be, Near-er, my God, to thee, Near-er to thee!

THE CHRISTIAN.

FRASER. 8s, 7s. 6l.
A. F. C. KOLLMANN.

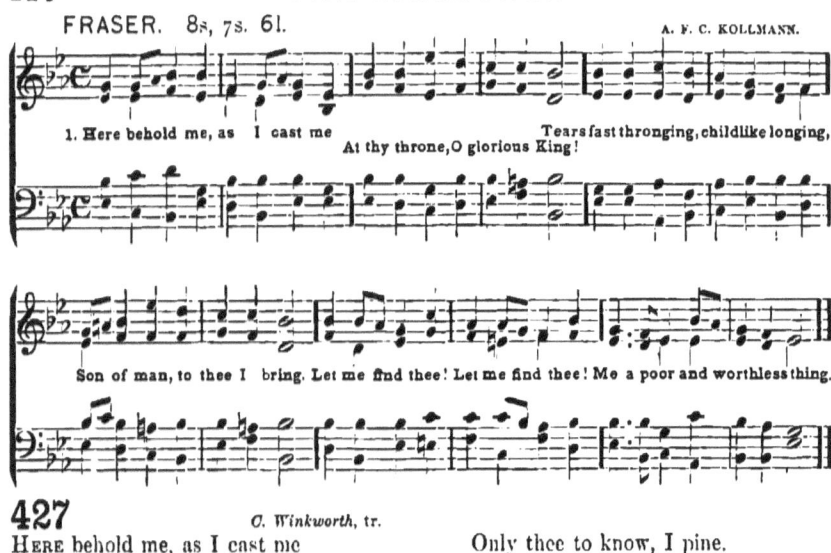

427   *C. Winkworth, tr.*

Here behold me, as I cast me
  At thy throne, O glorious King!
Tears fast thronging, childlike longing,
  Son of man, to thee I bring.
Let me find thee! Let me find thee!
  Me a poor and worthless thing.

2 Look upon me, Lord, I pray thee,
  Let thy spirit dwell in mine;
Thou hast sought me, thou hast bought me,
  Only thee to know, I pine.
Let me know thee! Let me find thee!
  Take my heart and grant me thine!

3 Nought I ask for, nought I strive for,
  But thy grace so rich and free,
That thou givest whom thou lovest,
  And who truly cleave to thee.
Let me find thee! Let me find thee!
  He hath all things who hath thee.

LOVE DIVINE. 8s, 7s.
J. ZUNDEL.

Aspiration.

LOVE DIVINE. CONCLUDED.

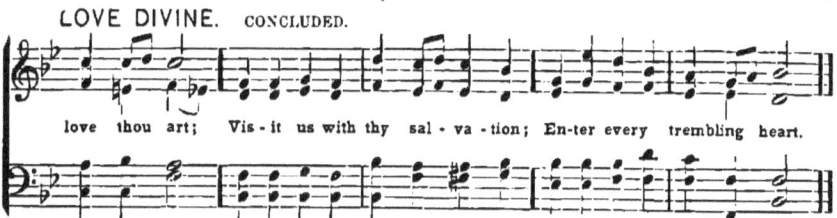

love thou art; Vis-it us with thy sal-va-tion; En-ter every trembling heart.

428
C. Wesley.

Love divine, all love excelling,
  Joy of heaven, to earth come down!
Fix in us thy humble dwelling,
  All thy faithful mercies crown;
Jesus, thou art all compassion,
  Pure unbounded love thou art;
Visit us with thy salvation;
  Enter every trembling heart.

2 Breathe, O breathe thy loving Spirit
  Into every troubled breast;
Let us all in thee inherit,
  Let us find the promised rest:

Thee we would be always blessing,
  Serve thee as thy hosts above,
Pray, and praise thee without ceasing,
  Glory in thy perfect love.

3 Finish then thy new creation;
  Pure and spotless let us be;
Let us see our whole salvation,
  Perfectly secured in thee;
Changed from glory into glory,
  Till in heaven we take our place,
Till we cast our crowns before thee,
  Lost in wonder, love and praise.

BAYLEY. 8s, 7s. D. *T. H. BAYLEY.*

1. Love di-vine, all love ex-cell-ing, Joy of heaven, to earth come down!

Fix in us thy hum-ble dwell-ing; All thy faith-ful mer-cies crown;
D. S. Vis-it us with thy sal-va-tion; En-ter ev-ery trem-bling heart.

Je-sus, thou art all com-pas-ion, Pure, un-bound-ed love thou art;

THE CHRISTIAN.

PHELPS. 6s, 5s. J. P. HOLBROOK.

429

Purer yet and purer
  I would be in mind,
Dearer yet and dearer
  Every duty find;
Hoping still and trusting
  God without a fear,
Patiently believing
  He will make all clear.

2 Calmer yet and calmer
  Trial bear and pain,
Surer yet and surer
  Peace at last to gain;
Suffering still and doing,
  To his will resigned,
And to God subduing
  Heart and will and mind.

3 Higher yet and higher
  Out of clouds and night,
Nearer yet and nearer
  Rising to the light—
Light serene and holy,
  Where my soul may rest,
Purified and lowly,
  Sanctified and blest.

430 G. Thring.

Brighter still, and brighter,
  Glows the western sun,
Shedding all its gladness
  O'er our work that's done;
Time will soon be over,
  Toil and sorrow past,
May we, Blessèd Saviour,
  Find a rest at last!

2 Onward, ever onward,
  Journeying o'er the road
Worn by saints before us,
  Journeying on to God;
Leaving all behind us,
  May we hasten on,
Backward never looking
  Till the prize is won.

3 Higher then, and higher,
  Bear the ransomed soul,
Earthly toils forgotten,
  Saviour, to its goal;
Where, in joys unthought of,
  Saints with angels sing,
Never weary, raising
  Praises to their King.

Aspiration. 227

431
C. Wesley.

LIGHT of life, seraphic Fire!
Love divine! thyself impart;
Every fainting soul inspire;
Shine in every drooping heart.

2 Every mournful sinner cheer;
Scatter all our guilty gloom;
Saviour, Son of God! appear;
To thy human temples come.

3 Come in this accepted hour,
Bring thy heavenly kingdom in;
Fill us with thy glorious power,
Rooting out the love of sin.

4 Nothing more can we require,
We will covet nothing less;
Be thou all our heart's desire,
All our joy and all our peace.

432
R. Wardlaw.

CHRIST, of all my hopes the ground,
Christ, the spring of all my joy,
Still in thee may I be found,
Still for thee my powers employ.

2 Fountain of o'erflowing grace,
Freely from thy fulness give;
Till I close my earthly race,
May I prove it, "Christ to live."

3 When I touch the blessed shore,
Back the closing waves shall roll;
Death's dark stream shall never more
Part from thee my ravished soul.

4 Thus, O thus an entrance give
To the land of cloudless sky;
Having known it, "Christ to live,"
Let me know it, "gain to die."

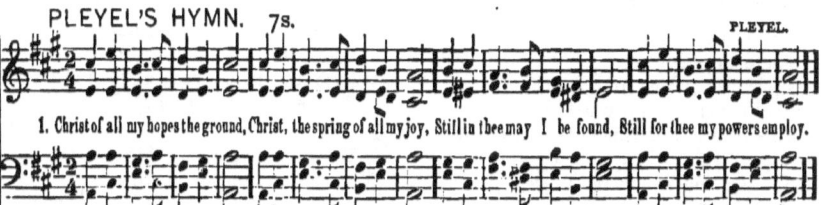

THE CHRISTIAN.

PAXTON. 8s.   A. H. Mann.

433   *A. M. Toplady.*
A Debtor to mercy alone,
 Of Covenant mercy I sing;
Nor fear with thy righteousness on,
 My person and offerings to bring:
The terrors of law and of God
 With me can have nothing to do;
My Saviour's obedience and blood
 Hide all my transgressions from view.

2 The work which his goodness began,
 The arm of his strength will complete,
His promise is Yea and Amen,
 And never was forfeited yet;
Things future, nor things that are now,
 Not all things below or above
Can make him his purpose forego,
 Or sever my soul from his love.

3 My name from the palms of his hands
 Eternity will not erase;
Impressed on his heart it remains,
 In marks of indelible grace:
Yes—I to the end shall endure,
 As sure as the earnest is given;
More happy, but not more secure,
 The glorified spirits in heaven.

434   *J. Hart.*
This God is the God we adore,
 Our faithful unchangeable friend,
Whose love is as great as his power,
 And neither knows measure nor end:
2 'Tis Jesus, the first and the last,
 Whose Spirit shall guide us safe home;
We'll praise him for all that is past,
 And trust him for all that's to come.

Assurance.

EVANSTON. L. M. 6 l. — J. P. HOLBROOK.

1. My hope is built on nothing less Than Jesus' blood and righteousness;
I dare not trust the sweetest frame, But wholly lean on Jesus' name:
On Christ, the solid rock, I stand; All other ground is sinking sand.

435
E. Mote.

My hope is built on nothing less
Than Jesus' blood and righteousness;
I dare not trust the sweetest frame,
But wholly lean on Jesus' name:
On Christ, the solid rock, I stand;
All other ground is sinking sand.

2 When darkness seems to veil his face,
I rest on his unchanging grace;
In every high and stormy gale,
My anchor holds within the veil:
On Christ, the solid rock, I stand;
All other ground is sinking sand.

3 His oath, his covenant, and blood,
Support me in the whelming flood:
When all around my soul gives way,
He then is all my hope and stay:
On Christ, the solid rock, I stand;
All other ground is sinking sand.

436
C. Winkworth, tr.

Jesus, my boast, my light, my joy,
The treasure nought can e'er destroy,
No words, no song that I can frame
Speak half the sweetness of thy name;
They only all its power shall prove,
Whose hearts have learnt thy faith and love.

2 Whene'er I do but think of thee,
Thy dews drop down and solace me;
Whene'er I hope in thee, my Friend,
Thy comfort and thy peace descend;
Whene'er in grief I pray and sing,
I feel new courage in me spring.

3 The world can show no truth like thine,
And therefore I will not repine;
I know thou wilt forsake me not,
Thy truth is fixed, whate'er my lot;
Then while I live this life of care,
The cross for thee I'll gladly bear.

437
J. A. Rothe.

Now I have found the ground wherein
 Sure my soul's anchor may remain:
The wounds of Jesus, for my sin
 Before the world's foundation slain;
Whose mercy shall unshaken stay
When heaven and earth are fled away.

2 Fixed on this ground will I remain,
 Though heart may fail and flesh decay;
This anchor shall my soul sustain,
 When earth's foundations melt away:
Mercy's full power I then shall prove,
Loved with an everlasting love.

THE CHRISTIAN.

LANGTON. S. M.   ARR. C. STREATFIELD.

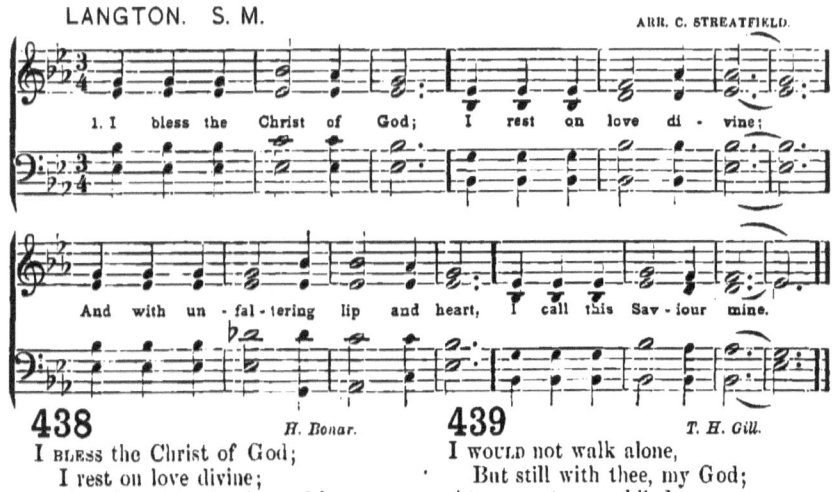

438   *H. Bonar.*

I BLESS the Christ of God;
  I rest on love divine;
And with unfaltering lip and heart,
  I call this Saviour mine.

2 His cross dispels each doubt;
  I bury in his tomb
Each thought of unbelief and fear,
  Each lingering shade of gloom.

3 I praise the God of grace;
  I trust his truth and might;
He calls me his, I call him mine,
  My God, my joy, my light.

4 'Tis he who saveth me,
  And freely pardon gives;
I love because he loveth me,
  I live because he lives.

439   *T. H. Gill.*

I WOULD not walk alone,
  But still with thee, my God;
At every step my blindness own,
  And ask of thee the road.

2 I love thy yoke to wear,
  To feel thy gracious bands,
Sweetly restrained by thy care,
  And happy in thy hands.

3 The weakness I enjoy
  That casts me on thy breast;
The conflicts that thy strength employ
  Make me divinely blest.

4 Dear Lord and Master mine,
  Still keep thy servant true;
My Guardian and my Guide divine;
  Bring, bring thy pilgrim through.

BRADFORD. C. M.   HANDEL.

Assurance. 231

BELMONT. C. M.   S. WEBBE.

1. I love thee, Saviour mine, and still I ever will love thee,
Solely because my God thou art, Who first hast loved me.

440   F. Xavier.

I LOVE thee, Saviour mine, and still
  I ever will love thee,
Solely because my God thou art,
  Who first hast lovéd me.

2 For me to lowest depths of woe
  Thou didst thyself abase;
For me didst bear the cross and shame
  And manifold disgrace:

3 For me didst suffer pains unknown,
  Blood-sweat and agony,
Yea, death itself,—all, all for me,
  Who was thine enemy.

4 For this I love thee, and will love,
  And in thy praise will sing,
Because thou first loved me, my God,
  My Saviour and my King!

441

AND wilt thou now forsake me, Lord?
  I know it cannot be;
No earthly tongue can ever tell
  What thou hast been to me.

2 Through all the changing scenes of life
  Thy love hath sheltered me;
I've trusted in thy promises,
  And thou wilt faithful be.

3 In life or death, I take my stand
  Where I have ever stood,
Beneath the shelter of thy cross,
  And trusting in thy blood.

4 And when in all the helplessness
  Of death I turn to thee,
Thou wilt not then forsake me, Lord!
  I know it cannot be.

442   C. Wesley.

I KNOW that my Redeemer lives,
  And ever prays for me:
A token of his love he gives,
  A pledge of liberty.

2 I find him lifting up my head;
  He brings salvation near:
His presence makes me free indeed,
  And he will soon appear.

3 He wills that I should holy be:
  What can withstand his will?
The counsel of his grace in me
  He surely shall fulfill.

4 Jesus, I hang upon thy word;
  I steadfastly believe
Thou wilt return and claim me, Lord,
  And to thyself receive.

232 THE CHRISTIAN.

VOX JESU. 7s, 6s. J. P. HOLBROOK.

1. I lay my sins on Jesus, The spotless Lamb of God; He bears them all, and frees us From the ac-curs-ed load: I bring my guilt to Jesus, To wash my crimson stains White in his blood most precious, Till not a stain remains.

443
H. Bonar.

1 I LAY my sins on Jesus,
  The spotless Lamb of God;
 He bears them all, and frees us
  From the accursèd load:
 I bring my guilt to Jesus,
  To wash my crimson stains
 White in his blood most precious,
  Till not a stain remains.

2 I lay my wants on Jesus;
  All fullness dwells in him;
 He heals all my diseases,
  He doth my soul redeem:
 I lay my griefs on Jesus,
  My burdens and my cares;
 He from them all releases,
  He all my sorrow shares.

3 I rest my soul on Jesus,
  This weary soul of mine;
 His right hand me embraces,
  I on his breast recline.
 I love the name of Jesus,
  Immanuel, Christ, the Lord;
 Like fragrance on the breezes,
  His name abroad is poured.

4 I long to be like Jesus,
  Meek, loving, lowly, mild;
 I long to be like Jesus,
  The Father's holy child:
 I long to be with Jesus
  Amid the heavenly throng,
 To sing with saints his praises,
  To learn the angels' song.

Assurance. 233

LYTE. 6s, 4s.   J. P. HOLBROOK.

1. Je-sus! thy name I love, All oth-er names above, Je-sus, my Lord! Oh! thou art all to me; Nothing to please I see, Nothing a-part from thee, Je-sus, my Lord!

444

Jesus! thy name I love,
All other names above,
   Jesus, my Lord!
Oh! thou art all to me;
Nothing to please I see,
Nothing apart from thee,
   Jesus, my Lord!

2 Thou, blessèd Son of God!
Hast bought me with thy blood,
   Jesus, my Lord!
Oh! how great is thy love,
All other loves above,—
Love that I daily prove,
   Jesus, my Lord!

3 When unto thee I flee,
Thou wilt my Refuge be,
   Jesus, my Lord!
What need I now to fear?
What earthly grief or care?
Since thou art ever near,
   Jesus, my Lord!

4 Soon thou wilt come again;
I shall be happy then,
   Jesus, my Lord!
Then thine own face I'll see,
Then I shall like thee be,
Then evermore with thee,
   Jesus, my Lord!

445   H. Hope.

Now I have found a friend,
Whose love shall never end,
   Jesus is mine.
Though earthly joys decrease,
Though earthly friendships cease,
Now I have lasting peace,
   Jesus is mine.

2 When death is sent to me,
Welcome eternity,
   Jesus is mine.
He my redemption is,
Wisdom and righteousness,
Life, light, and holiness,
   Jesus is mine.

3 When earth shall pass away,
In the great judgment-day,
   Jesus is mine.
When that glad day shall bring
Me to behold my King,
Then evermore I'll sing,
   Jesus is mine!

THE CHRISTIAN.

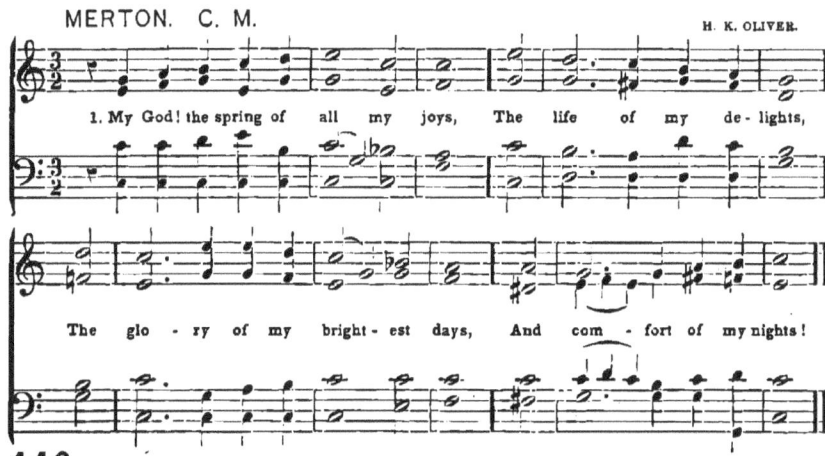

446 *I. Watts.*
My God! the spring of all my joys,
  The life of my delights,
The glory of my brightest days,
  And comfort of my nights!

2 In darkest shades if he appear,
  My dawning is begun:
He is my soul's bright morning star,
  And he my rising sun.

3 The opening heavens around me shine
  With beams of sacred bliss,
While Jesus shows his heart is mine,
  And whispers, I am his!

4 My soul would leave this heavy clay
  At that transporting word,
Run up with joy the shining way,
  To meet my dearest Lord.

447 *J. Newton.*
The Lord has promised good to me,
  His word my hope secures;
He will my shield and portion be,
  As long as life endures.

2 His grace first taught my heart to fear,
  And grace my fears relieved:
How precious did that grace appear,
  The hour I first believed!

3 Thro' many dangers, toils and snares,
  I have already come;
'Tis grace has brought me safe thus far,
  And grace will lead me home.

448 *A. M. Toplady.*
Compared with Christ, in all beside
  No comeliness I see;
The one thing needful, dearest Lord,
  Is to be one with thee.

2 Less than thyself will not suffice
  My comfort to restore;
More than thyself I cannot crave,
  And thou canst give no more.

3 Whate'er consists not with thy love,
  O teach me to resign!
I'm rich to all th' intents of bliss,
  Since thou, O Lord, art mine.

Assurance. 235

LESLIE. C. M. *Andante.* (A.)

449
E. Caswall, tr.

Jesus, the very thought of thee
With sweetness fills my breast;
But sweeter far thy face to see,
And in thy presence rest.

2 O Hope of every contrite heart,
O Joy of all the meek,
To those who fall, how kind thou art!
How good to those who seek!

3 But what to those who find? Ah, this
Nor tongue nor pen can show:
The love of Jesus, what it is,
None but his loved ones know.

4 Jesus, our only Joy be thou,
As thou our Prize wilt be;
Jesus, be thou our glory now,
And through eternity.

FINCH. C. M. J. P. HOLBROOK.

450
Ray Palmer.

Jesus, these eyes have never seen
That radiant form of thine;
The veil of sense hangs dark between
Thy blessèd face and mine.

2 I see thee not, I hear thee not,
Yet art thou oft with me;
And earth hath ne'er so dear a spot,
As where I meet with thee.

3 Yet though I have not seen, and still
Must rest in faith alone,
I love thee, dearest Lord,—and will,
Unseen, but not unknown.

4 When death these mortal eyes shall seal,
And still this throbbing heart,
The rending veil shall thee reveal,
All-glorious as thou art.

THE CHRISTIAN.

GREENWOOD S. M.   J. E. SWEETSER.

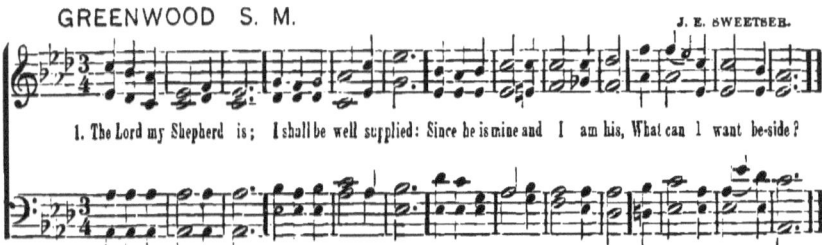

1. The Lord my Shepherd is; I shall be well supplied: Since he is mine and I am his, What can I want beside?

451   *I. Watts.*

The Lord my Shepherd is;
  I shall be well supplied:
Since he is mine, and I am his,
  What can I want beside?

2 He leads me to the place
  Where heavenly pasture grows;
Where living waters gently pass,
  And full salvation flows.

3 If e'er I go astray,
  He doth my soul reclaim;
And guides me, in his own right way,
  For his most holy name.

4 While he affords his aid,
  I cannot yield to fear;
Though I should walk through death's dark
  My Shepherd's with me there. [shade,

5 In sight of all my foes,
  Thou dost my table spread;
My cup with blessings overflows,
  And joy exalts my head.

6 The bounties of thy love
  Shall crown my future days;
Nor from thy house will I remove,
  Nor cease to speak thy praise.

LEIGHTON. S. M.   H. W. GREATOREX.

1. Grace, 'tis a charming sound, Harmonious to the ear: Heaven with the echo shall resound, And all the earth shall hear.

452   *P. Doddridge.*

Grace, 'tis a charming sound,
  Harmonious to the ear;
Heaven with the echo shall resound,
  And all the earth shall hear.

2 Grace first contrived a way
  To save rebellious man,
And all the steps that grace display,
  Which drew the wondrous plan.

3 Grace taught my wandering feet
  To tread the heavenly road;
And new supplies each hour I meet,
  While pressing on to God.

4 Grace all the work shall crown,
  Through everlasting days;
It lays in heaven the topmost stone,
  And well deserves the praise.

Assurance. 237

MAYO. S. M.
C. W. JORDAN.

1. If Jesus be my Friend, And I to him belong,

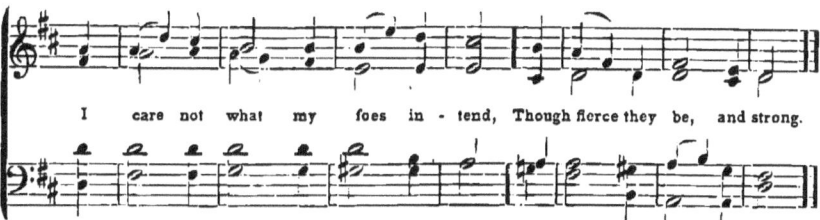

I care not what my foes in-tend, Though fierce they be, and strong.

453   *C. Winkworth, tr.*

If Jesus be my Friend,
 And I to him belong,
I care not what my foes intend,
 Though fierce they be, and strong.

2 I rest upon the ground
 Of Jesus and his blood;
For I in him alone have found
 The true, eternal good.

3 He whispers in my breast
 Sweet words of holy cheer,
How all who seek in God their rest
 Shall ever find him near;

4 How God hath built above
 A city fair and new,
Where eye and heart shall see and prove
 What faith has counted true.

5 My heart for gladness springs;
 It can not more be sad;
For very joy it smiles and sings,—
 Sees naught but sunshine glad.

6 The sun that lights mine eyes,
 Is Christ, the Lord I love;
I sing for joy of that which lies
 Stored up for me above.

454   *C. Winkworth, tr.*

Here I can firmly rest;
 I dare to boast of this,
That God, the highest and the best,
 My Friend and Father is.

2 Naught have I of my own,
 Naught in the life I lead;
What Christ hath given, that alone
 I dare in faith to plead.

3 From dangerous snares he saves:
 Where'er he bids me go
He checks the storms and calms the waves,
 That naught can work me woe.

4 At cost of all I have,
 At cost of life and limb,
I cling to God who yet shall save;—
 I will not turn from him.

5 His spirit in me dwells,
 O'er all my mind he reigns;
All care and sadness he dispels,
 And soothes away all pains.

6 He prospers day by day
 His work within my heart,
Till I have strength and faith to say,
 Thou, God, my Father art!

THE CHRISTIAN.

DANNER. 5s, 4s.

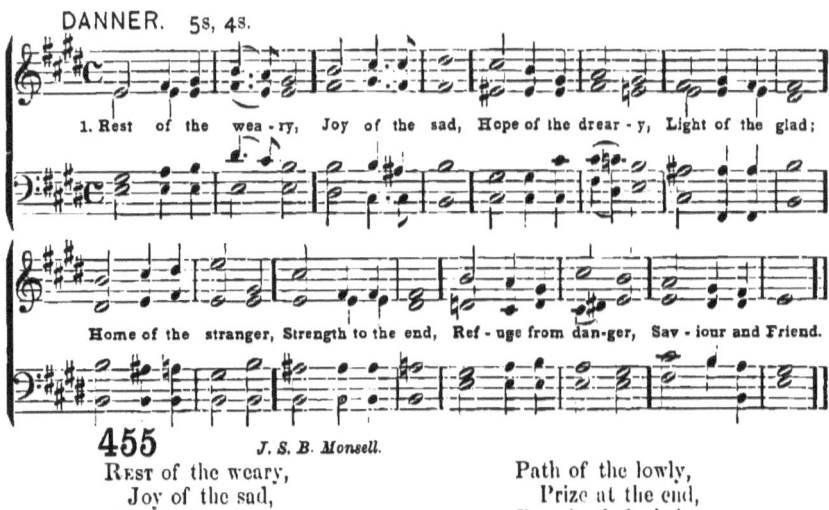

1. Rest of the weary, Joy of the sad, Hope of the dreary, Light of the glad; Home of the stranger, Strength to the end, Refuge from danger, Saviour and Friend.

455 *J. S. B. Monsell.*

Rest of the weary,
Joy of the sad,
Hope of the dreary,
Light of the glad;
Home of the stranger,
Strength to the end,
Refuge from danger,
Saviour and Friend.

2 Pillow where, lying,
Love rests its head;
Peace of the dying,
Life of the dead;

Path of the lowly,
Prize at the end,
Breath of the holy,
Saviour and Friend!

3 Ever confessing
Thee, I will raise
Unto thee blessing,
Glory and praise;
All my endeavor,
World without end,
Thine to be ever,
Saviour and Friend!

PASSPORT. 5s, 7s.   E. MOSS.

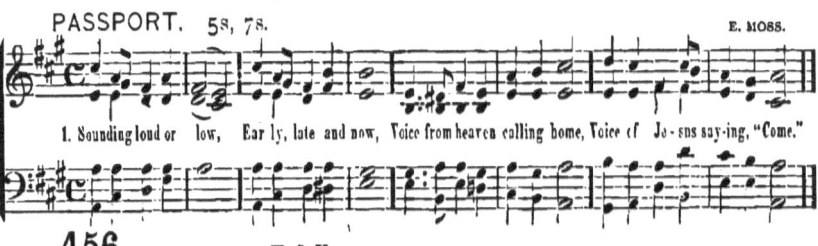

1. Sounding loud or low, Early, late and now, Voice from heaven calling home, Voice of Jesus saying, "Come."

456 *H. S. H.*

Sounding loud or low,
Early, late and now,
Voice from heaven calling home,
Voice of Jesus saying "Come."

2 Sinful, weak and weary,
There is hope for me!
Claim nor worth have I, O Lord,
Save my portion in that word.

3 On that word I cast me,
Plead it, Lord, to thee;

All my hope is written there,
All the plea that makes my prayer.

4 On that word I rest,
Truest, tenderest, best,
Pledge of all I need, and ground
Where my anchored hope is found.

5 Worthless though my name,
Crimsoned o'er with shame,
Calling still thou sayest, "Come!"
Blessed word! my passport home.

Assurance. 239

457   *C. Winkworth, tr.*

WHATE'ER my God ordains is right;
  His will is ever just;
  Howe'er he orders now my cause,
    I will be still and trust.
      He is my God;
      Though dark my road,
  He holds me that I shall not fall,
  Wherefore to Him I leave it all.

2 Whate'er my God ordains is right;
  He never will deceive:
  He leads me by the proper path,
    And so to Him I cleave,
      And take content
      What He hath sent:
  His hand can turn my griefs away,
  And patiently I wait his day.

3 Whate'er my God ordains is right;
  Though I the cup must drink,
  That bitter seems to my faint heart,
    I will not fear nor shrink;
      Tears pass away
      With dawn of day;
  Sweet comfort yet shall fill my heart,
  And pain and sorrow all depart.

4 Whate'er my God ordains is right;
  My Light, my Life is He,
  Who cannot will me aught but good;
    I trust him utterly;
      For well I know,
      In joy or woe,
  He holds me that I shall not fall;
  And so to Him I leave it all.

THE CHRISTIAN

CROSBY. 11s.   J. P. HOLBROOK.

1. I once was a stranger to grace and to God; I knew not my danger, and felt not my load; Tho' friends spoke in rapture of Christ on the tree, Je-ho-vah, my Saviour, seemed nothing to me.

458
R. M. McCheyne.

I once was a stranger to grace and to God;
I knew not my danger, and felt not my load;
Though friends spoke in rapture of Christ on the tree,
Jehovah, my Saviour, seemed nothing to me.

2 When free grace awoke me by light from on high,
Then legal fears shook me; I trembled to die;
No refuge, no safety, in self could I see:
Jehovah, thou only my Saviour must be.

3 My terrors all vanished before his sweet name;
My guilty fears banished, with boldness I came
To drink at the fountain, so copious and free;
Jehovah, my Saviour, is all things to me.

4 Jehovah, the Lord, is my treasure and boast;
Jehovah, my Saviour,—I ne'er can be lost:
In thee I shall conquer, by flood and by field,
Jehovah my anchor, Jehovah my shield!

MURRAY. 11s.   J. P. HOLBROOK.

1. I once was a stranger to grace and to God; I knew not my danger, and felt not my load; Though friends spoke in rapture of Christ on the tree, Je-ho-vah, my Saviour, seemed nothing to me.

Assurance. 241

PORTUGUESE HYMN. 11s. J. READING.

1. How firm a foun-da-tion, ye saints of the Lord, Is laid fo-your faith in his ex-cel-lent word! What more can he say, than to you he hath said, To you, who for re-fuge to Je-sus have fled? To you, who for re-fuge to Je-sus have fled?

459   *G. Keith.*

How firm a foundation, ye saints of the Lord,
Is laid for your faith in his excellent word!
What more can he say, than to you he hath said,
To you, who for refuge to Jesus have fled?

2 "Fear not, I am with thee, O be not dismayed,
For I am thy God, I will still give thee aid;
I'll strengthen thee, help thee, and cause thee to stand,
Upheld by my gracious, omnipotent hand.

3 "When through the deep waters I call thee to go,
The rivers of sorrow shall not overflow;
For I will be with thee thy trials to bless,
And sanctify to thee thy deepest distress.

4 "E'en down to old age all my people shall prove
My sovereign, eternal, unchangeable love;
And when hoary hairs shall their temples adorn,
Like lambs they shall still in my bosom be borne.

5 "The soul that on Jesus hath leaned for repose,
I will not, I will not desert to his foes?
That soul, though all hell should endeavor to shake,
I'll never, no never, no never forsake!"

THE CHRISTIAN.

CONSECRATION. 8s, 7s. D. — J. P. HOLBROOK.

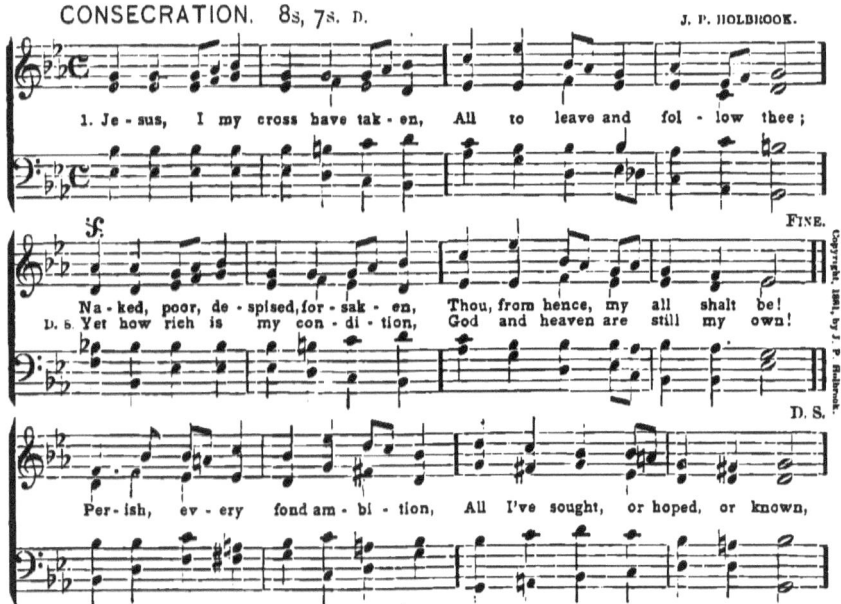

460
H. F. Lyte.

Jesus, I my cross have taken,
 All to leave and follow thee;
Naked, poor, despised, forsaken,
 Thou, from hence, my all shalt be!
Perish, every fond ambition,
 All I've sought, or hoped, or known,
Yet how rich is my condition,
 God and heaven are still my own!

2 Man may trouble and distress me,
 'T will but drive me to thy breast;
Life with trials hard may press me,
 Heaven will bring me sweeter rest!
I have called thee, Abba, Father!
 I have stayed my heart on thee!
Storms may rise, and clouds may gather,
 All must work for good to me.

3 Take, my soul, thy full salvation,
 Rise o'er sin, and fear, and care;
Joy to find in every station
 Something still to do or bear.
Think what Spirit dwells within thee;
 What a Father's smile is thine;
What a Saviour died to win thee!
 Child of heaven, shouldst thou repine?

4 Haste thee on from grace to glory,
 Armed by faith, and winged by prayer;
Heaven's eternal day's before thee,
 God's own hand shall guide thee there:
Soon shall close thy earthly mission,
 Swift shall pass thy pilgrim days,
Hope soon change to glad fruition,
 Faith to sight, and prayer to praise.

AUTUMN. 8s, 7s. D. — SPANISH MELODY.

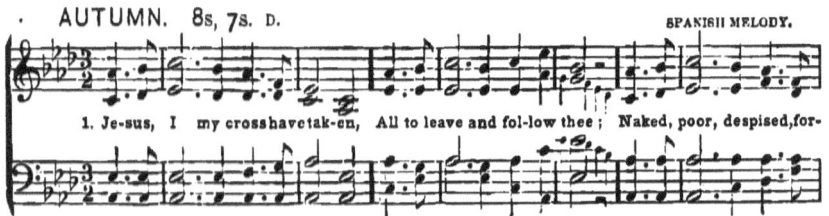

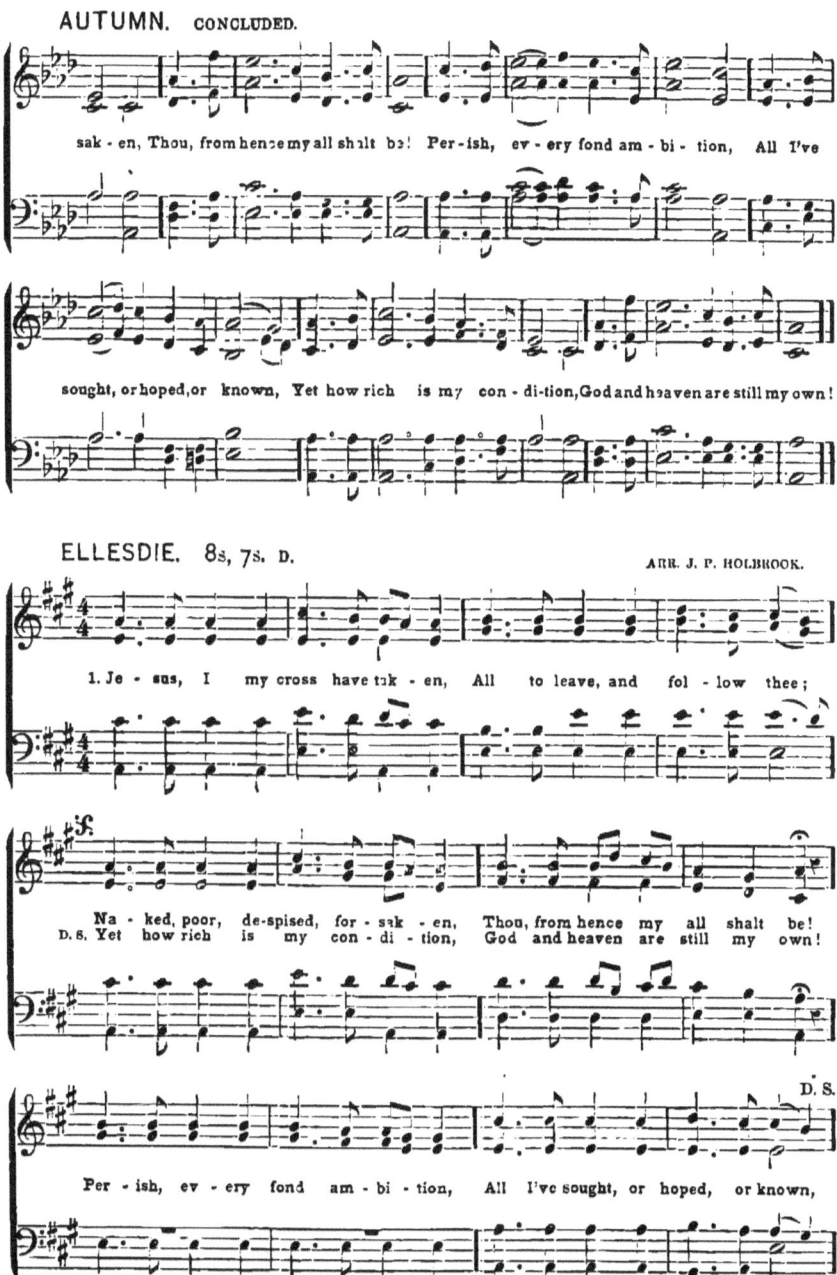

THE CHRISTIAN.

DENNIS. S. M.   NAGELI.

1. My spirit, on thy care, Blest Saviour, I recline;
Thou wilt not leave me to despair, For thou art Love divine.

461   *H. F. Lyte.*

My spirit, on thy care,
  Blest Saviour, I recline;
Thou wilt not leave me to despair,
  For thou art Love divine.

2 In thee I place my trust,
  On thee I calmly rest;
I know thee good, I know thee just,
  And count thy choice the best.

3 Whate'er events betide,
  Thy will they all perform;
Safe in thy breast my head I hide,
  Nor fear the coming storm.

4 Let good or ill befall,
  It must be good for me;
Secure of having thee in all,
  Of having all in thee.

462

We pray for childlike hearts,
  For gentle holy love,
For strength, dear Lord, to do thy will,
  As angels do above.

2 We pray for simple faith,
  For hope that never faints,
For true communion evermore,
  With all thy blessed saints.

3 On friends around us here,
  O let thy blessing fall!
We pray for grace to love them well,
  But thee beyond them all.

4 O joy to live for thee!
  O joy in thee to die.
O very joy of joys, to see
  Thy face eternally!

463   *P. Doddridge.*

How gentle God's commands!
  How kind his precepts are!
Come, cast your burden on the Lord,
  And trust his constant care.

2 Beneath his watchful eye
  His saints securely dwell;
That hand which bears all nature up,
  Shall guard his children well.

3 Why should this anxious load
  Press down your weary mind?
Haste to your heavenly Father's throne,
  And sweet refreshment find.

4 His goodness stands approved,
  Unchanged from day to day:
I'll drop my burden at his feet,
  And bear a song away.

Consecration.

464
H. Harbaugh.

Jesus, I live to thee,
  The loveliest and best;
My life in thee, thy life in me,
  In thy blest love I rest.

2 Jesus, I die to thee,
  Whenever death shall come;
To die in thee is life to me,
  In my eternal home.

3 Whether to live or die,
  I know not which is best;
To live in thee is bliss to me,
  To die is endless rest.

4 Living or dying, Lord,
  I ask but to be thine;
My life in thee, thy life in me,
  Makes heaven forever mine.

465
J. Austin.

Blest be thy love, dear Lord,
  That taught us this sweet way,
Only to love thee for thyself
  And for that love obey.

2 O Thou, our souls' chief hope,
  We to thy mercy fly;
Where'er we are, thou canst protect,
  Whate'er we need, supply.

3 Whether we sleep or wake,
  To thee we both resign;
By night we see, as well as day,
  If thy light on us shine.

4 Whether we live or die,
  Both we submit to thee;
In death we live, as well as life,
  If thine in death we be.

THE CHRISTIAN.

466   A.

This is the sweetness of my life,
  Jesus, that I love thee;
And this my strength in every strife,
  My God, thou lovest me.

2 Thy tender love on me that falls,
  And mine to thee that flows,
Each for my grateful worship calls;
  For each thy grace bestows.

3 There is no doubting in pure love,
  No weariness, no fear:
The saints its fullness know above,
  We have a foretaste here.

4 Dear Lord, this sweetness and this strength
  Into my being pour,
Till perfect love I know at length,
  And doubt and fear no more.

467   F. W. Faber.

I worship thee, sweet Will of God,
  And all thy ways adore;
And every day I live, I seem
  To love thee more and more.

2 I have no cares, O blessèd Will,
  For all my cares are thine;
I live in triumph, Lord, for thou
  Hast made thy triumphs mine.

3 He always wins who sides with God,
  To him no chance is lost;
God's will is sweetest to him when
  It triumphs at his cost.

4 Ill that he blesses is our good,
  And unblest good is ill;
And all is right that seems most wrong,
  If it be his sweet will.

JEWETT. 6s. D — ARR. J. P. HOLBROOK.

1. My Jesus, as thou wilt! O may thy will be mine! Into thy hand of love I would my all resign: Through sorrow, or through joy, Conduct me as thine own, And help me still to say, My Lord, thy will be done!

468
J. Borthwick, tr.

My Jesus, as thou wilt!
  O may thy will be mine!
Into thy hand of love
  I would my all resign:
Through sorrow, or through joy,
  Conduct me as thine own,
And help me still to say,
  My Lord, thy will be done!

2 My Jesus, as thou wilt!
  Though seen through many a tear,
Let not my star of hope
  Grow dim or disappear:
Since thou on earth hast wept,
  And sorrowed oft alone,
If I must weep with thee,
  My Lord, thy will be done!

3 My Jesus, as thou wilt!
  All shall be well for me:
Each changing future scene,
  I gladly trust with thee:
Then to my home above
  I travel calmly on,
And sing, in life or death,
  My Lord, thy will be done!

469
H. Bonar.

Thy way, not mine, O Lord,
  However dark it be!
Lead me by thine own hand,
  Choose out the path for me.
I dare not choose my lot;
  I would not, if I might;
Choose thou for me, my God,
  So shall I walk aright.

2 The kingdom that I seek,
  Is thine: so let the way
That leads to it be thine,
  Else I must surely stray.
Take thou my cup, and it
  With joy or sorrow fill,
As best to thee may seem;
  Choose thou my good and ill.

3 Choose thou for me my friends,
  My sickness or my health;
Choose thou my cares for me,
  My poverty or wealth.
Not mine, not mine the choice,
  In things or great or small;
Be thou my guide, my strength,
  My wisdom, and my all.

THE CHRISTIAN.

BERLIN. 10s. MENDELSSOHN.

1. Not what I am, O Lord but what thou art! That, that a-lone can be my soul's truerest; Thy love, not mine, bids fear and doubt depart. And stills the tempest of my toss-ing breast.

470 *H. Bonar.*

Nor what I am, O Lord, but what thou art!
That, that alone can be my soul's true rest;
Thy love, not mine, bids fear and doubt depart,
And stills the tempest of my tossing breast.

2 It blesses now, and shall forever bless,
It saves me now, and shall for ever save;
It holds me up in days of helplessness,
It bears me safely o'er each swelling wave.

3 'Tis what I know of thee, my Lord and God,
That fills my soul with peace, my lips with song;
Thou art my health, my joy, my staff and rod,
Leaning on thee, in weakness I am strong.

4 More of thyself, O show me hour by hour,
More of thy glory, O my God and Lord;
More of thyself in all thy grace and power,
More of thy love and truth, Incarnate Word!

471 *T. Parker.*

O thou great Friend to all the sons of men,
Who once appeared in humblest guise below,
Sin to rebuke, to break the captive's chain,
And call thy brethren forth from want and woe,

2 We look to thee: thy truth is still the light
Which guides the nations, groping on their way,
Stumbling and falling in disastrous night,
Yet hoping ever for the perfect day.

3 Yes: thou art still the Life; thou art the Way
The holiest know,—Light, Life and Way of heaven;
And they who deepest hope, and deepest pray,
Toil by the light, life, way, which thou hast given.

Duty—Toil. 249

BISHOP. L. M.   J. P. HOLBROOK.

1. Go, labor on; spend and be spent,— Thy joy to do the Father's will: It is the way the Master went; Should not the servant tread it still?

472   *H. Bonar.*

Go, LABOR on; spend and be spent,—
Thy joy to do the Father's will:
It is the way the Master went;
Should not the servant tread it still?

2 Go, labor on, while it is day;
The world's dark night is hastening on;
Speed, speed thy work,—cast sloth away!
It is not thus that souls are won.

3 Toil on, faint not, keep watch, and pray!
Be wise the erring soul to win;
Go forth into the world's highway;
Compel the wanderer to come in.

4 Toil on, and in thy toil rejoice;
For toil comes rest, for exile home;
Soon shalt thou hear the Bridegroom's voice,
The midnight peal: "Behold, I come!"

473   *P. Doddridge.*

My gracious Lord, I own thy right
To every service I can pay,
And call it my supreme delight
To hear thy dictates and obey.

2 What is my being, but for thee,
Its sure support, its noblest end?
Thine ever smiling face to see,
And serve the cause of such a Friend.

3 I would not breathe for worldly joy,
Or to increase my worldly good;
Nor future days nor powers employ
To spread a sounding name abroad.

4 'Tis to my Saviour I would live,
To him who for my ransom died;
Nor could the bowers of Eden give
Such bliss as blossoms at his side.

474   *I. Watts.*

So LET our lips and lives express
The holy gospel we profess;
So let our works and virtues shine,
To prove the doctrine all divine.

2 Thus shall we best proclaim abroad
The honors of our Saviour God;
When his salvation reigns within,
And grace subdues the power of sin.

3 Our flesh and sense must be denied,
Passion and envy, lust and pride;
While justice, temperance, truth, and love,
Our inward piety approve.

4 Religion bears our spirits up,
While we expect that blessèd hope,
The bright appearance of the Lord,
And faith stands leaning on his word.

THE CHRISTIAN.

250

HULLAH. 7s. 6l.   HULLAH.

1. Je-sus, Mas-ter, whom I serve, Though so fee-bly and so ill,
D. C. O-pen thou mine eyes to see, All the work thou hast for me.

Strength-en hand and heart and nerve, All thy bid-ding to ful-fil;

---

475 F. R. Havergal.

Jesus, Master, whom I serve,
Though so feebly and so ill,
Strengthen hand and heart and nerve,
All thy bidding to fulfil;
Open thou mine eyes to see,
All the work thou hast for me.

2 Lord, thou needest not, I know,
Service such as I can bring;
Yet I long to prove and show
Full allegiance to my King.
Thou an honor art to me,
Let me be a praise to thee.

3 Jesus, Master! wilt thou use
One who owes thee more than all?
As thou wilt! I would not choose,
Only let me hear thy call.
Jesus! let me always be
In thy service glad and free.

COLMAN. C. M.   G. KINGSLEY.

1. Workmen of God, O lose not heart, But learn what God is like; And in the darkest battle-field, Thou shalt know where to strike.

---

476 F. W. Faber.

Workman of God, O lose not heart,
But learn what God is like;
And in the darkest battle-field,
Thou shalt know where to strike.

2 O blest is he to whom is given
The instinct that can tell
That God is on the field, when he
Is most invisible!

3 He hides himself so wondrously,
As though there were no God;
He is least seen when all the powers
Of ill are most abroad.

4 And blest is he who can divine
Where real right doth lie,
And dares to take the side that seems
Wrong to man's blindfold eye.

5 For right is right, since God is God;
And right the day must win;
To doubt would be disloyalty,
To falter would be sin.

6 O learn to scorn the praise of men;
O learn to lose with God!
For Jesus won the world through shame,
And beckons thee his road.

Duty—Toil. 251

BOYLSTON S. M.   L. MASON.

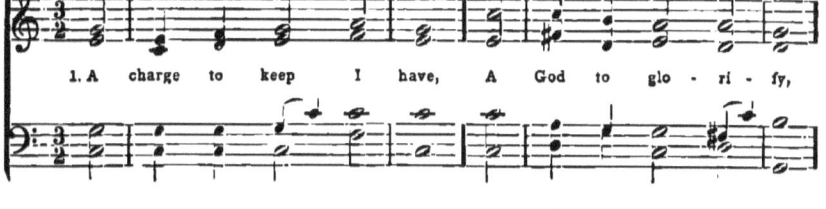

477   *J. Wesley.*
A CHARGE to keep I have,
  A God to glorify;
A never-dying soul to save,
  And fit it for the sky;

2 To serve the present age,
  My calling to fulfil;
O may it all my powers engage
  To do my Master's will.

3 Arm me with jealous care,
  As in thy sight to live,
And O thy servant, Lord, prepare
  A strict account to give.

4 Help me to watch and pray,
  And on thyself rely,
Assured, if my trust betray,
  I shall for ever die.

478   *J. Montgomery*
Sow in the morn thy seed,
  At eve hold not thy hand;
To doubt and fear give thou no heed,
  Broadcast it o'er the land.

2 Thou canst not toil in vain;
  Cold, heat, the moist and dry,
Shall foster and mature the grain
  For garners in the sky.

3 Then, when the glorious end,
  The day of God, shall come,
The angel-reapers shall descend,
  And heaven sing, "Harvest home!"

479   *H. Bonar.*
SERVE we our God in faith,
  No work for him is vain;
Blesséd and holy is the toil,
  And infinite the gain.

2 Spend and be spent would we,
  While lasteth time's brief day;
No turning back in coward fear,
  No lingering by the way.

3 Onward we press in haste,
  Upward our journey still;
Ours is the path the Master trod
  Through good report and ill.

4 The way may rougher grow,
  The weariness increase;
We gird our loins, and hasten on;
  The end, the end is peace.

480   *P. Doddridge.*
YE servants of the Lord,
  Each in his office wait,
Observant of his heavenly word,
  And watchful at his gate.

2 Let all your lamps be bright,
  And trim the golden flame;
Gird up your loins as in his sight,
  For awful is his name.

3 Watch! 'tis your Lord's command;
  And while we speak, he's near:
Mark the first signal of his hand,
  And ready all appear.

252 THE CHRISTIAN.

DURYEA. C. M.

481
J. Bowdler.

Children of God, who, faint and slow,
Your pilgrim-path pursue,
In strength and weakness, joy and woe,
To God's high calling true!—

2 Why move ye thus, with lingering tread,
A doubting, mournful band?
Why faintly hangs the drooping head?
Why fails the feeble hand?

3 O weak to know a Saviour's power,
To feel a Father's care;
A moment's toil, a passing shower,
Is all the grief ye share.

4 The orb of light, though clouds awhile
May hide his noon-tide ray,
Shall soon in lovelier beauty smile
To gild the closing day,—

5 And, bursting through the dusky shroud
That dared his power invest,
Ride throned in light o'er every cloud,
Triumphant to his rest.

6 Then, Christian, dry the falling tear,
The faithless doubt remove;
Redeemed at last from guilt and fear,
O wake thy heart to love!

Spiritual Conflict. 253

LUTHER'S. 8s, 7s. — M. LUTHER.

1. Almighty God! I call to thee, By sore tempta-tion shak-en; Incline thy gracious ear to me, And leave me not for-sak-en; For who that feels the power with-in Of past re-morse and present sin, Can stand, O Lord, be-fore thee?

482 *Luther.*

Almighty God! I call to thee,
By sore temptation shaken;
Incline thy gracious ear to me,
And leave me not forsaken;
For who that feels the power within
Of past remorse and present sin,
Can stand, O Lord, before thee?

2 On thee alone my stay I place,
All human help rejecting;
Relying on thy sovereign grace,
Thy sovereign aid expecting,
I rest upon thy sacred word,
That thou'lt repel him not, O Lord,
Who to thy mercy fleeth.

3 And though I travail all the night,
And travail all the morrow,
My trust is in Jehovah's might,
My triumph in my sorrow;
Forgetting not that thou of old
Didst Israel, though weak, uphold;
When weakest then most loving!

4 What though my sinfulness be great,
Redeeming love is greater;
What though all hell should lie in wait,
Supreme is my Creator;
And He my rock and fortress is,
And when most helpless, most I'm His,
My strength and my Redeemer.

ELIZABETHTOWN. C. M. — GEO. KINGSLEY.

1. Chil-dren of God, who, faint and slow, Your pil-grim-path pur-sue, In strength and weak-ness, joy and woe, To God's high call-ing true!—

THE CHRISTIAN.

LABAN. S. M. — L. MASON.

1. My soul, be on thy guard, Ten thousand foes arise; And hosts of sin are pressing hard To draw thee from the skies.

483 G. Heath.

My soul, be on thy guard;
Ten thousand foes arise;
And hosts of sin are pressing hard
To draw thee from the skies,

2 O watch, and fight, and pray,
The battle ne'er give o'er;
Renew it boldly every day,
And help divine implore.

3 Ne'er think the victory won,
Nor once at ease sit down;
Thine arduous work will not be done
Till thou receive thy crown.

4 Fight on, my soul, till death
Shall bring thee to thy God;
He'll take thee at thy parting breath,
To his divine abode.

484 C. Wesley.

Soldiers of Christ! arise,
And put your armor on,
Strong in the strength which God supplies,
Through his eternal Son.

2 Strong in the Lord of hosts,
And in his mighty power:
Who in the strength of Jesus trusts,
Is more than conqueror.

3 Stand, then, in his great might,
With all his strength endued;
But take, to arm you for the fight,
The panoply of God;

4 That, having all things done,
And all your conflicts past,
Ye may o'ercome, through Christ alone,
And stand complete at last.

MISSIONARY CHANT. L. M. — CH. ZEUNER.

1. I send the joys of earth away; Away, ye tempters of the mind, False as the smooth, deceitful sea, And empty as the whistling wind!

Spiritual Conflict.

LONG. L. M. — J. P. HOLBROOK.

1. Stand up, my soul, shake off thy fears, And gird the gos-pel ar-mor on; March to the gates of end-less joy, Where Jesus thy great Captain's gone, Where Jesus thy great Captain's gone.

485 — I. Watts.

Stand up, my soul, shake off thy fears,
  And gird the gospel armor on;
March to the gates of endless joy,
  Where Jesus thy great Captain's gone.

2 Hell and thy sins resist thy course,
  But hell and sin are vanquished foes;
Thy Jesus nailed them to the cross,
  And sung the triumph when he rose.

3 Then let my soul march boldly on,
  Press forward to the heavenly gate;
There peace and joy eternal reign,
  And glittering robes for conquerors wait.

4 There shall I wear a starry crown,
  And triumph in almighty grace;
While all the armies of the skies
  Join in my glorious Leader's praise.

486 — I. Watts.

I send the joys of earth away;
  Away, ye tempters of the mind,
False as the smooth, deceitful sea,
  And empty as the whistling wind!

2 Now to the shining realms above
  I stretch my hands and glance my eyes;
O for the pinions of a dove
  To bear me to the upper skies!

3 There, from the bosom of my God,
  Oceans of endless pleasure roll!
There would I fix my last abode,
  And drown the sorrows of my soul!

487 — I. Watts.

Awake, our souls, away our fears,
  Let every trembling thought be gone;
Awake, and run the heavenly race,
  And put a cheerful courage on.

2 True, 'tis a strait and thorny road,
  And mortal spirits tire and faint;
But they forget the mighty God,
  Who feeds the strength of every saint:

3 The mighty God, whose matchless
  Is ever new, and ever young, [power
And firm endures, while endless years
  Their everlasting circles run.

4 Swift as an eagle cuts the air,
  We'll mount aloft to thine abode;
On wings of love our souls shall fly,
  Nor tire amidst the heavenly road.

488 — A. L. Barbauld.

Awake, my soul, lift up thine eyes:
  See where thy foes against thee rise,
Put on the armor from above
  Of heavenly truth and heavenly love.

2 Thou tread'st upon enchanted ground,
  Perils and snares beset thee round;
Beware of all, guard every part,
  But most, the traitor in thy heart.

3 The terrors and the charm repel,
  The powers of earth, and powers of hell;
The Man of Calvary triumphed here:
  Why should his faithful followers fear?

THE CHRISTIAN.

CHRISTMAS. C. M.
HANDEL.

1. A-wake, my soul, stretch ev-ery nerve, And press with vig-or on: A heavenly race de-mands thy zeal, And an im-mor-tal crown, And an im-mor-tal crown.

489　　　P. Doddridge.

AWAKE, my soul, stretch every nerve,
　And press with vigor on;
A heavenly race demands thy zeal,
　And an immortal crown.

2 A cloud of witnesses around
　Hold thee in full survey:
Forget the steps already trod,
　And onward urge thy way.

3 'Tis God's all-animating voice
　That calls thee from on high;
'Tis his own hand presents the prize
　To thine aspiring eye.

4 Blest Saviour, introduced by thee,
　Have I my race begun;
And crowned with victory, at thy feet
　I'll lay my honors down.

490　　　I. Watts.

AM I a soldier of the cross,
　A follower of the Lamb,
And shall I fear to own his cause,
　Or blush to speak his name!

2 Must I be carried to the skies
　On flowery beds of ease,
While others fought to win the prize,
　And sailed through bloody seas?

3 Are there no foes for me to face?
　Must I not stem the flood?
Is this vile world a friend to grace,
　To help me on to God?

4 Sure I must fight, if I would reign:
　Increase my courage, Lord!
I'll bear the toil, endure the pain,
　Supported by thy word.

NEWBOLD. C. M.
G. KINGSLEY.

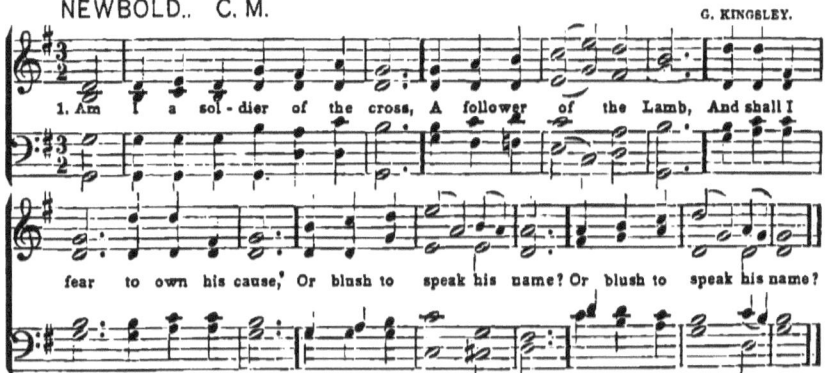

1. Am I a sol-dier of the cross, A follower of the Lamb, And shall I fear to own his cause, Or blush to speak his name? Or blush to speak his name?

Spiritual Conflict.

MAITLAND. C. M.

1. Must Jesus bear the cross alone, And all the world go free?
No, there's a cross for every one, And there's a cross for me.

491

Must Jesus bear the cross alone,
   And all the world go free?
No, there's a cross for every one,
   And there's a cross for me.

2 This consecrated cross I'll bear,
   Till death shall set me free,
And then go home my crown to wear,
   For there's a crown for me.

3 Upon the crystal pavement down
   At Jesus' pierced feet,
Joyful I'll cast my golden crown,
   And his dear name repeat.

4 And palms shall wave, and harps shall ring
   Beneath heaven's arches high;
The Lord that lives, the ransomed sing,
   That lives no more to die.

492
R. Heber.

The Son of God goes forth to war,
   A kingly crown to gain;
His blood-red banner streams afar,
   Who follows in his train?

2 Who best can drink his cup of woe,
   Triumphant over pain;
Who patient bears his cross below,
   He follows in his train.

3 The martyr first, whose eagle eye
   Could pierce beyond the grave;
Who saw his Master in the sky,
   And called on him to save.

4 Like him, with pardon on his tongue,
   In midst of mortal pain,
He prayed for them that did the wrong:
   Who follows in his train?

5 A glorious band, the chosen few,
   On whom the Spirit came:
The martyred saints, their hope they knew,
   And mocked the cross and flame.

6 They climbed the steep ascent to heaven
   Through peril, toil and pain;
O God, to us may grace be given
   To follow in their train.

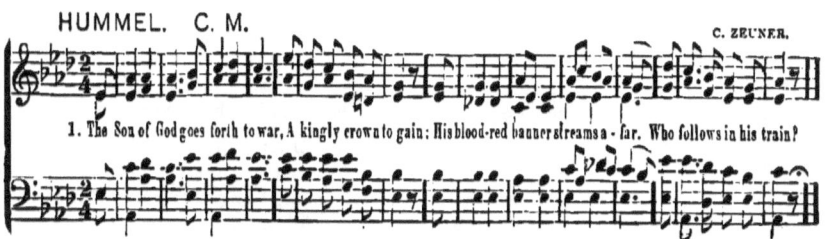

HUMMEL. C. M. — C. ZEUNER.

1. The Son of God goes forth to war, A kingly crown to gain: His blood-red banner streams afar. Who follows in his train?

258 THE CHRISTIAN.

BLAKE. L. M. — J. P. HOLBROOK.

1. Thou on-ly Sov-'reign of my heart, My Ref-uge, my al-might-y Friend— And can my soul from thee de-part, On whom a-lone my hopes de-pend!

493 *A. Steele.*

Thou only Sovereign of my heart,
 My Refuge, my almighty Friend—
And can my soul from thee depart,
 On whom alone my hopes depend!

2 Eternal life thy words impart;
 On these my fainting spirit lives;
Here sweeter comforts cheer my heart,
 Than all the round of nature gives.

3 Thy name my inmost powers adore;
 Thou art my life, my joy, my care;
Depart from thee—'tis death, 'tis more;
 'Tis endless ruin, deep despair!

4 Low at thy feet my soul would lie;
 Here safety dwells, and peace divine;
Still let me live beneath thine eye,
 For life, eternal life, is thine.

494 *J. Wesley,* tr.

O thou, to whose all-searching sight
The darkness shineth as the light!
Search, prove my heart, it pants for thee;
O burst these bonds, and set it free.

2 If in this darksome wild I stray,
Be thou my light, be thou my way;
No foes, no violence I fear,
No harm, while thou, my God, art near.

3 When rising floods my soul o'erflow,
When sinks my heart in waves of woe,

Jesus, thy timely aid impart,
And raise my head, and cheer my heart.

4 Saviour, where'er thy steps I see,
Dauntless, untired, I follow thee;
O let thy hand support me still,
And lead me to thy holy hill.

5 If rough and thorny be the way,
My strength proportion to my day;
Till toil and grief and pain shall cease,
Where all is calm and joy and peace.

495 *C. Wesley.*

Rest for my soul I long to find:
 Saviour of all, if mine thou art,
Give me thy meek and lowly mind,
 And stamp thine image on my heart.

2 Break off the yoke of inbred sin,
 And fully set my spirit free:
I cannot rest, till pure within,
 Till I am wholly lost in thee.

3 Fain would I learn of thee, my God;
 Thy light and easy burden prove,
The cross all stained with hallowed blood,
 The labor of thy dying love.

4 I would—but thou must give the power;
 My heart from every sin release;
Bring near, bring near the joyful hour,
 And fill me with thy perfect peace!

Spiritual Conflict. 259

GREEK HYMN. 6s, 5s. ARR. J. P. HOLBROOK.

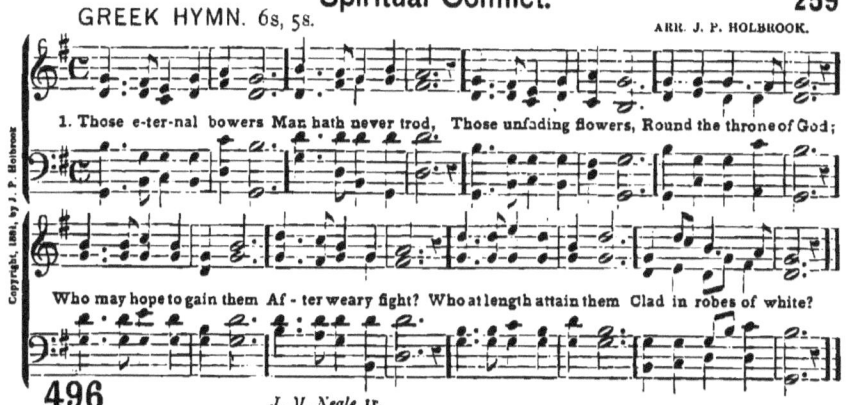

496
J. M. Neale, tr.

Those eternal bowers
  Man hath never trod,
Those unfading flowers,
  Round the throne of God;
Who may hope to gain them
  After weary fight?
Who at length attain them
  Clad in robes of white?

2 He, who gladly barters
  All on earthly ground;
He, who like the martyrs
  Says, "I will be crowned;"
He, whose one oblation
  Is a life of love;
Clinging to the nation
  Of the blest above.

3 While I do my duty,
  Struggling through the tide,
Whisper thou of beauty
  On the other side!
Soon forgot the story
  Of our brief distress;
O the future glory!
  O the loveliness!

PERCY. L. M. H. PERCY SM TH.

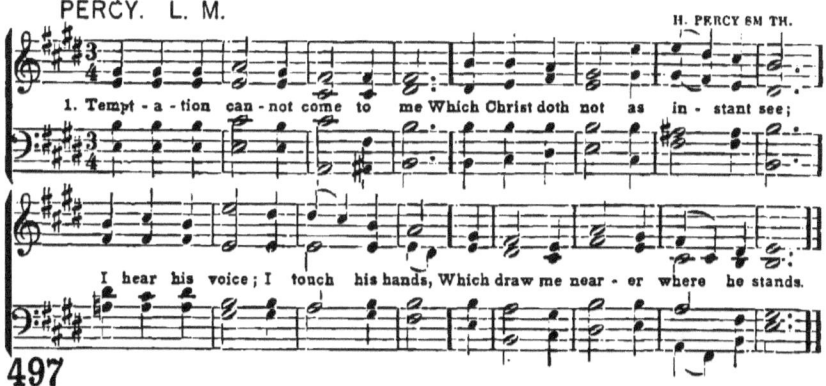

497

Temptation cannot come to me
Which Christ doth not as instant see;
I hear his voice; I touch his hands,
Which draw me nearer where he stands.

2 When I am tempted to deny,
If I but turn and meet his eye,
My heart doth break, and break again,
Before its speechless love and pain.

3 O grace, beyond my power of thought,
For me by my Redeemer bought!
O love, whose wondrous depth and height
Is far beyond my mortal sight!

4 O joy no language can express!
For me—for me the blessedness!
The stainless robe, the glorious crown,
For which He laid the ransom down!

260 THE CHRISTIAN.

ONWARD. 6s, 5s.   A. S. SULLIVAN.

1. Onward, Christian soldiers! Marching as to war, With the cross of Jesus Going on before. Christ, the royal Master, Leads against the foe; Forward into battle, See, his banners go! Onward, Christian soldiers! Marching as to war, With the cross of Jesus Going on before.

498
S. Baring-Gould.

Onward, Christian soldiers!
Marching as to war,
With the cross of Jesus
Going on before.
Christ the royal Master,
Leads against the foe;
Forward into battle,
See, his banners go!
  Onward, Christian soldiers!
  Marching as to war,
  With the cross of Jesus
  Going on before.

2 Like a mighty army
Moves the Church of God;
Brothers, we are treading
Where the saints have trod;
We are not divided,
All one body we,
One in hope and doctrine,
One in charity.
  Onward, &c.

3 Crowns and thrones may perish,
Kingdoms rise and wane,
But the Church of Jesus
Constant will remain;
Gates of hell can never
'Gainst that Church prevail;
We have Christ's own promise,
And that cannot fail.
  Onward, &c.

4 Onward, then, ye people!
Join our happy throng,
Blend with ours your voices
In the triumph-song;
Glory, laud, and honor
Unto Christ the King,
This through countless ages
Men and angels sing.
  Onward, Christian soldiers!
  Marching as to war,
  With the cross of Jesus
  Going on before.

Spiritual Conflict.

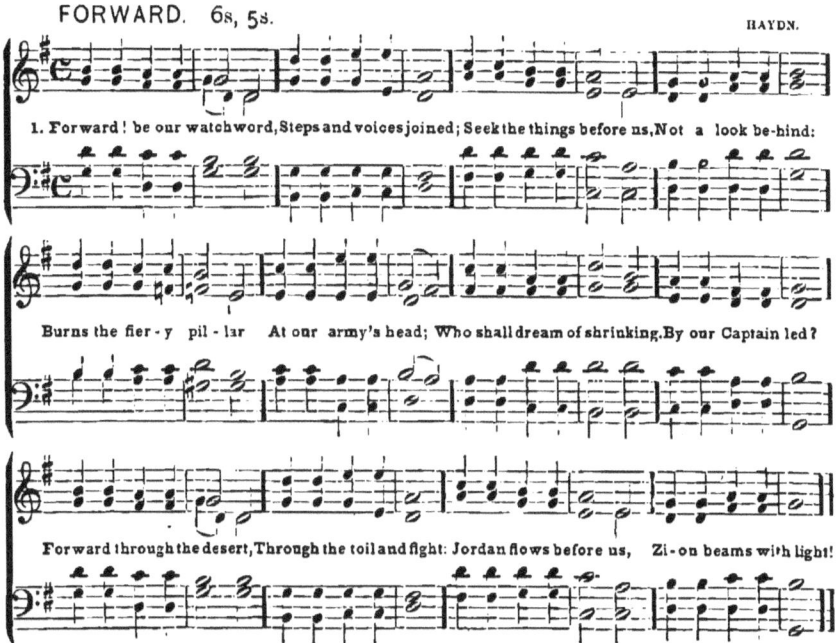

499 *H. Alford.*

Forward! be our watchword,
 Steps and voices joined;
Seek the things before us,
 Not a look behind:
Burns the fiery pillar
 At our army's head;
Who shall dream of shrinking,
 By our Captain led?
Forward through the desert,
 Through the toil and fight:
Jordan flows before us,
 Zion beams with light!

2 Forward! flock of Jesus,
 Salt of all the earth,
Till each yearning purpose
 Spring to glorious birth:
Sick, they ask for healing;
 Blind, they grope for day;
Pour upon the nations
 Wisdom's loving ray.
Forward, out of error,
 Leave behind the night;
Forward through the darkness,
 Forward into light!

3 Glories upon glories
 Hath our God prepared,
By the souls that love him
 One day to be shared:
Eye hath not beheld them,
 Ear hath never heard;
Nor of these hath uttered
 Thought or speech a word;
Forward, marching eastward
 Where the heaven is bright,
Till the veil be lifted,
 Till our faith be sight!

4 Far o'er yon horizon
 Rise the city towers,
Where our God abideth;
 That fair home is ours:
Flash the streets with jasper,
 Shine the gates with gold;
Flows the gladdening river
 Shedding joys untold;
Thither, onward thither,
 In the Spirit's might:
Pilgrims to your country,
 Forward into light!

THE CHRISTIAN.

262 MIRIAM. 7s, 6s. J. P. HOLBROOK.

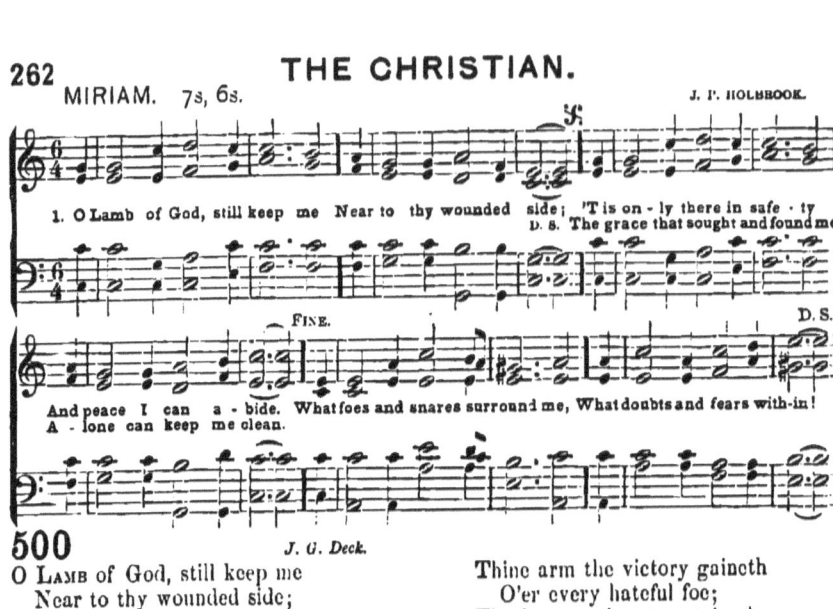

500 J. G. Deck.

O Lamb of God, still keep me
Near to thy wounded side;
'Tis only there in safety
And peace I can abide.
What foes and snares surround me,
What doubts and fears within!
The grace that sought and found me,
Alone can keep me clean.

2 'Tis only in thee hiding,
I know my life secure;
Only in thee abiding,
The conflict can endure:

Thine arm the victory gaineth
O'er every hateful foe;
Thy love my heart sustaineth,
In all its care and woe.

3 Soon shall my eyes behold thee
With rapture face to face;
One half hath not been told me
Of all thy power and grace;
Thy beauty, Lord, and glory,
The wonders of thy love,
Shall be the endless story
Of all thy saints above.

REPOSE. 7s. 6 l. ARR. J. P. HOLBROOK.

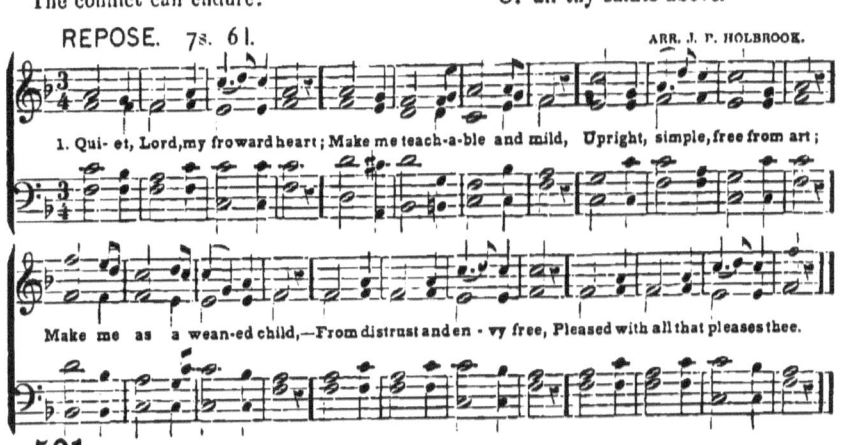

501 J. Newton.

Quiet, Lord, my froward heart;
Make me teachable and mild,
Upright, simple, free from art;

Make me as a weanéd child,—
From distrust and envy free,
Pleased with all that pleases thee.

Spiritual Conflict. 263

2 What thou shalt to-day provide,
   Let me as a child receive;
What to-morrow may betide,
   Calmly to thy wisdom leave:
'Tis enough that thou wilt care;
Why should I the burden bear?

3 As a little child relies
   On a care beyond his own,
Knows he's neither strong nor wise,
   Fears to stir a step alone;
Let me thus with thee abide,
As my Father, Guard, and Guide.

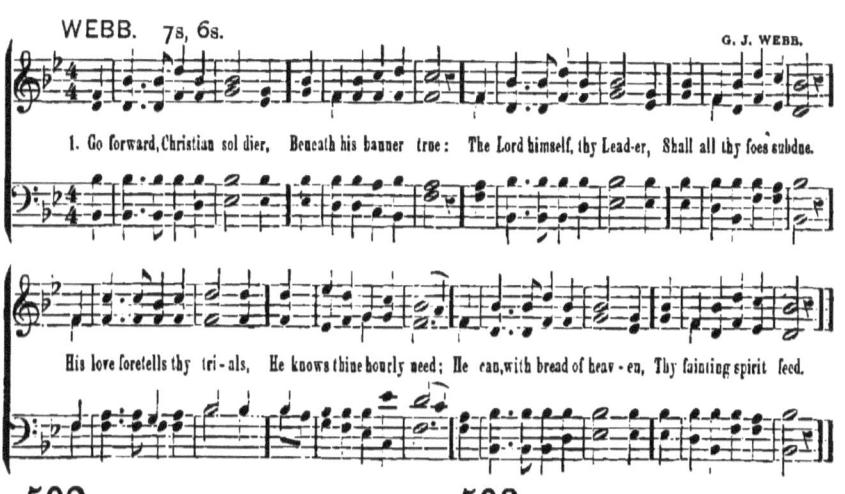

WEBB. 7s, 6s.   G. J. WEBB.

1. Go forward, Christian soldier, Beneath his banner true: The Lord himself, thy Leader, Shall all thy foes subdue. His love foretells thy trials, He knows thine hourly need; He can, with bread of heav-en, Thy fainting spirit feed.

502   *L. Tuttiett.*

Go forward, Christian soldier,
   Beneath his banner true:
The Lord himself, thy Leader,
   Shall all thy foes subdue.
His love foretells thy trials,
   He knows thine hourly need;
He can, with bread of heaven,
   Thy fainting spirit feed.

2 Go forward, Christian soldier,
   Fear not the secret foe;
Far more are o'er thee watching
   Than human eye can know.
Trust only Christ, thy Captain,
   Cease not to watch and pray;
Heed not the treach'rous voices,
   That lure thy soul astray.

3 Go forward, Christian soldier,
   Nor dream of peaceful rest
Till Satan's host is vanquished,
   And heaven is all possest;
Till Christ himself shall call thee
   To lay thine armor by,
And wear, in endless glory,
   The crown of victory.

503   *G. Duffield.*

Stand up! stand up for Jesus!
   Ye soldiers of the cross;
Lift high his royal banner,
   It must not suffer loss:
From vict'ry unto vict'ry
   His army he shall lead,
Till every foe is vanquished,
   And Christ is Lord indeed.

2 Stand up! stand up for Jesus!
   Stand in his strength alone;
The arm of flesh will fail you—
   Ye dare not trust your own!
Put on the gospel armor,
   And, watching unto prayer,
Where duty calls, or danger,
   Be never wanting there.

3 Stand up! stand up for Jesus!
   The strife will not be long;
This day the noise of battle,
   The next the victor's song:
To him that overcometh,
   A crown of life shall be;
He with the King of Glory
   Shall reign eternally!

264   THE CHRISTIAN.

REFUGE. 7s. D.   J. P. HOLBROOK.

1 Jesus! lover of my soul, Let me to thy bosom fly While the billows near me roll, While the tempest still is high. Hide me, O my Saviour! hide, Till the storm of life is past: Safe into the haven guide; Oh, receive my soul at last!

504   *C. Wesley.*

Jesus! Lover of my soul,
  Let me to thy bosom fly
While the billows near me roll,
  While the tempest still is high.
Hide me, O my Saviour! hide,
  Till the storm of life is past;
Safe into the haven guide;
  Oh, receive my soul at last!

2 Other refuge have I none;
  Hangs my helpless soul on thee;
Leave, ah! leave me not alone,
  Still support and comfort me.
All my trust on thee is stayed;
  All my help from thee I bring;
Cover my defenceless head
  With the shadow of thy wing.

3 Thou, O Christ! art all I want;
  More than all in thee I find;
Raise the fallen, cheer the faint,
  Heal the sick, and lead the blind.
Just and holy is thy name,
  I am all unrighteousness;
False and full of sin I am,
  Thou art full of truth and grace.

4 Plenteous grace with thee is found,—
  Grace to pardon all my sin;
Let the healing streams abound,
  Make and keep me pure within.
Thou of life the fountain art,
  Freely let me take of thee;
Spring thou up within my heart,
  Rise to all eternity.

HOLLINGSIDE. 7s. D.   J. B. DYKES.

1. Jesus! lover of my soul, Let me to thy bosom fly While the billows near me roll,

266 THE CHRISTIAN.

GREENWOOD. S. M. J. E. SWEETSER.

505
A. M. Toplady.

Though in a foreign land,
 We are not far from home;
And nearer to our house above
 We every moment come.

2 His grace will to the end
 Stronger and brighter shine;
Nor present things, nor things to come,
 Shall quench the spark divine.

3 Soon shall our doubts and fears
 Subside at his control;
His loving-kindness shall break through
 The midnight of the soul.

4 Blest is the man, O God,
 That stays himself on thee;
Who wait for thy salvation, Lord,
 Shall thy salvation see.

506
C. Wesley.

Thou very present aid
 In suffering and distress,
The soul which still on thee is stayed,
 Is kept in perfect peace.

2 The soul, by faith reclined
 On the Redeemer's breast,
'Mid raging storms exults to find
 An everlasting rest.

3 Jesus, to whom I fly,
 Doth all my wishes fill:
What though created streams are dry;
 I have the fountain still.

4 Stripped of my earthly friends,
 I find them all in One;
And peace and joy that never ends,
 And heaven in Christ begun.

507
A. M. Toplady.

If, through unruffled seas,
 Toward heaven we calmly sail,
With grateful hearts, O God, to thee,
 We'll own the favoring gale.

2 But should the surges rise,
 And rest delay to come,
Blest be the sorrow—kind the storm,
 Which drives us nearer home.

3 Soon shall our doubts and fears
 All yield to thy control:
Thy tender mercies shall illume
 The midnight of the soul.

4 Teach us, in every state,
 To make thy will our own;
And when the joys of sense depart,
 To live by faith alone.

Burdens and Sorrows. 267

SCHUMANN. S. M.   R. SCHUMANN.

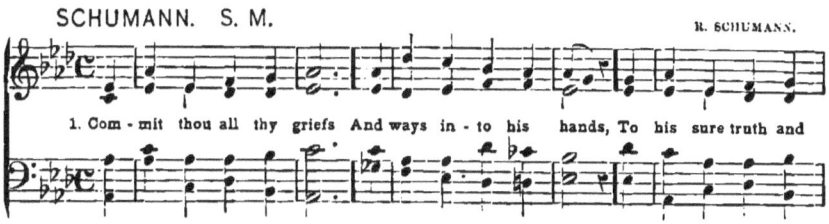

1. Com-mit thou all thy griefs And ways in-to his hands, To his sure truth and ten-der care, Who earth and heaven commands.

He shall direct thy wandering feet,
He shall prepare thy way.

3 Still heavy is thy heart?
Still sink thy spirits down?
Cast off the weight, let fear depart,
Bid every care be gone.

508   *J. Wesley, tr.*

Commit thou all thy griefs
And ways into his hands,
To his sure truth and tender care,
Who earth and heaven commands.

2 Who points the clouds their course,
Whom winds and seas obey,

4 No profit can'st thou gain
By self-consuming care;
To him commend thy cause; his ear
Attends the softest prayer.

5 Thou on the Lord rely;
So safe shalt thou go on;
Fix on his work thy steadfast eye,
So shall thy work be done.

OLMUTZ. S. M.   ARR. L. MASON.

1. Give to the winds thy fears; Hope, and be undismayed; God hears thy sighs and counts thy tears; God shall lift up thy head.

Wait thou his time; so shall thy night
Soon end in joyous day.

3 Far, far above thy thought
His counsel shall appear,
When fully he the work hath wrought,
That caused thy needless fear.

509   *J. Wesley, tr.*

Give to the winds thy fears;
Hope, and be undismayed;
God hears thy sighs and counts thy tears;
God shall lift up thy head.

2 Through waves, and clouds, and storms,
He gently clears thy way;

4 What though thou rulest not!
Yet heaven, and earth, and hell
Proclaim, God sitteth on the throne,
And ruleth all things well.

5 Leave to his sovereign sway
To choose and to command;
So shalt thou wondering own his way,
How wise, how strong his hand.

THE CHRISTIAN.

TRUST. 6s, 5s. IAMBIC.

1. I close my weary eye, Saviour, ever near! I lift my soul on high,

Through the darkness drear: Be thou my light, I cry, Saviour, ever dear!

510
H. Bonar.

I CLOSE my weary eye,
  Saviour, ever near!
I lift my soul on high,
  Through the darkness drear:
Be thou my light, I cry,
  Saviour, ever dear!

2 I feel thine arms around,
  Saviour, ever near!
With thee if I am found,
  Never can I fear,
Whatever ills abound;—
  Saviour, ever dear!

3 Thine is the day and night,
  Saviour, ever near;
Thine is the dark and light,
  Be my covert here:
O shield me with thy might,
  Saviour, ever dear!

511

WHEN day's shadows lengthen,
  Jesus, be thou near;
Pardon, comfort, strengthen;
  Chase away my fear;
Love and hope be deepened,
  Faith more strong and clear.

2 When the night grows darkest,
  Passing through the shade,
Let me hear the promise
  Once for ever made—
It is I, thy Saviour,
  Be not thou afraid.

3 Soon the warfare over,
  Burdens all laid down,
Tears no more nor sorrow,
  Endless rest alone:
Then the song of gladness,
  Round th' eternal Throne!

FAITH. 6s, 5s. TROCHAIC. E. MOSS.

1. When days' shadows lengthen, Jesus, be thou near; Pardon, comfort, strengthen;

Chase away my fear; Love and hope be deepened, Faith more strong and clear.

Burdens and Sorrows. 269

MAYO. S. M.   C. W. JORDAN.

1. It is thy hand my God; My sorrow comes from thee: I bow beneath thy chastening rod; 'Tis love that bruises me.

512   *J. G Deck*

It is thy hand, my God;
My sorrow comes from thee:
I bow beneath thy chastening rod;
'Tis love that bruises me.

2 I would not murmur, Lord;
Before thee I am dumb:
Lest I should breathe one murmuring word,
To thee for help I come.

3 I know thy will is right,
Though it may seem severe;
Thy path is still unsullied light,
Though dark it oft appear.

4 Here my poor heart can rest;
My God, it cleaves to thee;
Thy will is love, thine end is best;
All work for good to me.

COME, YE DISCONSOLATE. 11s, 10s.   S. WEBBE.

1. Come, ye dis-con-so-late, where'er ye languish; Come to the mer-cy-seat, fer-vent-ly kneel; Here bring your wounded hearts, here tell your anguish; Earth has no sorrow that heaven cannot heal.

513   *T. Moore.*

Come, ye disconsolate, where'er ye languish:
Come to the mercy-seat, fervently kneel;
Here bring your wounded hearts, here tell your anguish;
Earth has no sorrow that heaven cannot heal.

2 Joy of the comfortless, light of the straying,
Hope of the penitent, fadeless and pure;
Here speaks the Comforter, tenderly saying—
Earth has no sorrow that heaven cannot cure.

270 THE CHRISTIAN.

THALLON. C. M.   J. P. HOLBROOK.

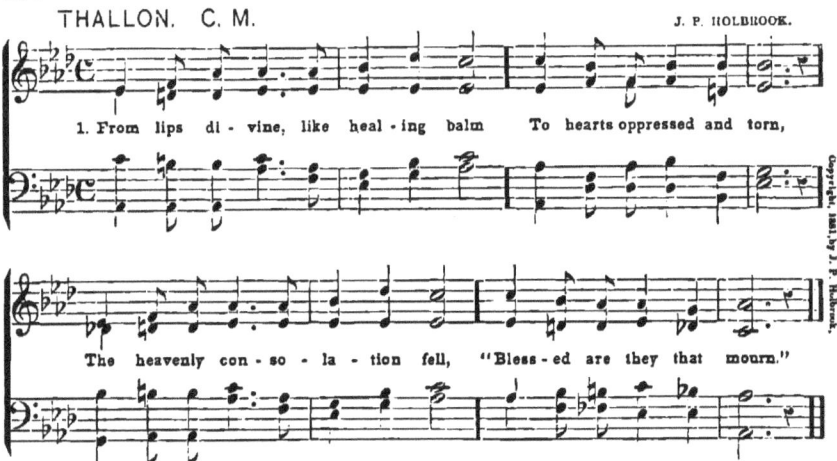

1. From lips di-vine, like heal-ing balm To hearts oppressed and torn, The heavenly con-so-la-tion fell, "Bless-ed are they that mourn."

514   *W. H. Burleigh.*

From lips divine, like healing balm
To hearts oppressed and torn,
The heavenly consolation fell,
"Blessed are they that mourn."

2 Unto the hopes by sorrow crushed
A noble faith succeeds;
And life, by trials furrowed, bears
The fruit of loving deeds.

3 How rich, how sweet, how full of strength,
Our human spirits are,
Baptized into the sanctities
Of suffering and prayer.

4 Yes, heavenly wisdom, love divine,
Breathed through the lips which said,
"O blessed are the hearts that mourn,
They shall be comforted."

515   *W. Cowper.*

O Lord, my best desires fulfil,
And help me to resign
Life, health, and comfort to thy will,
And make thy pleasure mine.

2 Why should I shrink at thy command,
Whose love forbids my fears?
Or tremble at the gracious hand
That wipes away my tears?

3 No, let me rather freely yield
What most I prize to thee,

Who never hast a good withheld,
Or wilt withhold from me.

4 Thy favor, all my journey through,
Thou art engaged to grant;
What else I want, or think I do,
'Tis better still to want.

5 But, ah, my inmost spirit cries,
Still bind me to thy sway;
Else the next cloud that veils my skies,
Drives all these thoughts away.

516

Thy way is on the deep, O Lord!
E'en there we'll go with thee,
To meet the tempest at thy word,
And walk upon the sea.

2 Poor tremblers at his rougher wind,
Why do we doubt him so?
Who gives the storm a path, will find
The way our feet should go.

3 A moment may his hand be lost,—
Drear moment of delay;—
We cry, Lord, help the tempest-tost!
And safe we're borne away.

4 The Lord yields nothing to our fears,
And flies from selfish care;
But comes himself where'er he hears
The voice of loving prayer.

Burdens and Sorrows.

BURLINGTON. C. M. — J. P. BURROWES.

1. When languor and disease invade This trembling house of clay,
'Tis sweet to look beyond my pain, And long to fly away

517 *A. M. Toplady.*

When languor and disease invade
This trembling house of clay,
'Tis sweet to look beyond my pain,
And long to fly away;

2 Sweet to look inward, and attend
The whispers of his love;
Sweet to look upward to the place
Where Jesus pleads above;

3 Sweet on his faithfulness to rest,
Whose love can never end;
Sweet on his covenant of grace
For all things to depend;

4 Sweet, in the confidence of faith,
To trust his firm decrees;
Sweet to lie passive in his hands,
And know no will but his.

518 *A. Steele.*

Dear Refuge of my weary soul,
On thee, when sorrows rise,
On thee, when waves of trouble roll,
My fainting hope relies.

2 To thee I tell each rising grief,
For thou alone canst heal;
Thy word can bring a sweet relief
For every pain I feel.

3 My gracious God, where shall I flee?
Thou art my only trust;
And still my soul would cleave to thee,
Though prostrate in the dust.

4 Thy mercy-seat is open still;
Here let my soul retreat,
With humble hope attend thy will,
And wait beneath thy feet.

CHURCH. C. M. — J. P. HOLBROOK.

1. Dear Refuge of my weary soul, On thee, when sorrows rise,
On thee, when waves of trouble roll, My fainting hope relies.

THE CHRISTIAN.

519   *W. Cowper.*

God of my life, to thee I call!
Afflicted, at thy feet I fall;
When the great water-floods prevail,
Leave not my trembling heart to fail.

2 Friend of the friendless and the faint,
Where should I lodge my deep complaint?
Where, but with thee, whose open door
Invites the helpless and the poor?

3 Did ever mourner plead with thee,
And thou refuse that mourner's plea?
Does not the word still fixed remain,
That none shall seek thy face in vain?

4 Poor though I am—despised, forgot,
Yet God, my God, forgets me not;
And he is safe, and must succeed,
For whom the Lord vouchsafes to plead.

520   *J. Newton.*

Be still my heart, these anxious cares
To thee are burdens, thorns, and snares,
They cast dishonor on thy Lord,
And contradict his gracious word.

2 When first before his mercy-seat,
Thou didst to him thy all commit,
He gave thee warrant from that hour
To trust his wisdom, love, and power.

3 Did ever trouble yet befall,
And he refuse to hear thy call?
And has he not his promise passed,
That thou shalt overcome at last?

4 Though rough and thorny be the road,
It leads thee home, apace, to God;
Then count thy present trials small,
For heaven will make amends for all.

Burdens and Sorrows.

DWIGHT. L. M.   ARR. J. P. HOLBROOK.

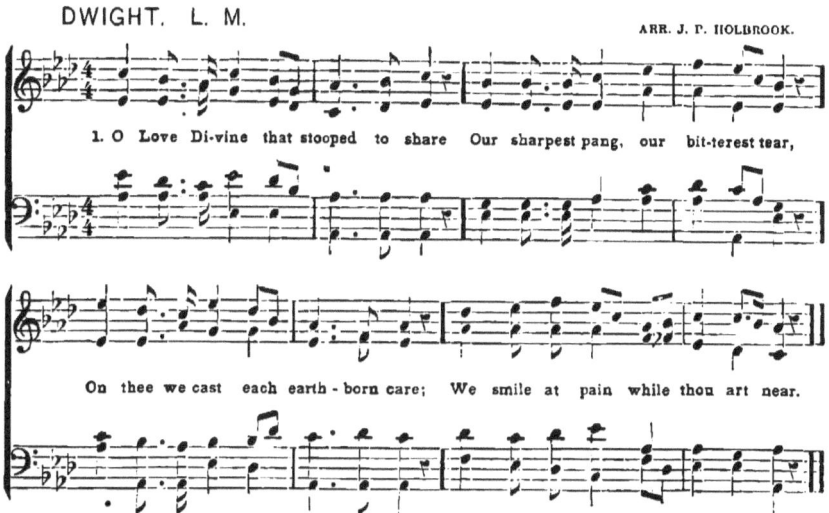

1. O Love Divine that stooped to share Our sharpest pang, our bitterest tear, On thee we cast each earth-born care; We smile at pain while thou art near.

521   *O. W. Holmes.*

O Love Divine, that stooped to share
  Our sharpest pang, our bitterest tear,
On thee we cast each earth-born care;
  We smile at pain while thou art near.

2 Though long the weary way we tread,
  And sorrow crown each lingering year,
No path we shun, no darkness dread,
  Our hearts still whispering, thou art near.

3 When drooping pleasure turns to grief,
  And trembling faith is changed to fear,
The murmuring wind, the quivering leaf,
  Shall softly tell us, thou art near.

4 On thee we fling our burdening woe,
  O Love Divine, forever dear;
Content to suffer while we know,
  Living or dying, thou art near!

522   RICHARDS. L.M.   *G. W. Bethune.*

When time seems short and death is near,
  And I am pressed by doubt and fear,
And sins, an overflowing tide,
  Assail my peace on every side,
This thought my refuge still shall be,
  I know the Saviour died for me.

2 His name is Jesus, and he died
  For guilty sinners crucified;
Content to die that he might win
  Their ransom from the death of sin:
No sinner worse than I can be,
  Therefore I know he died for me.

3 If grace were bought, I could not buy;
  If grace were coined, no wealth have I;
By grace alone I draw my breath,
  Held up from everlasting death;
Yet, since I know his grace is free,
  I know the Saviour died for me.

523   *J. Keble.*

Is it not strange, the darkest hour
  That ever dawned on sinful earth
Should touch the heart with softest power,
  And give our sweetest comforts birth?

2 That to the cross our eyes should turn
  For cheering light and strength to save,
Sooner than where the Easter sun
  Shines glorious on the open grave?

3 Yet so it is; for only there
  The storms of life are lulled to rest;
Stilled by the Saviour's trusting prayer,
  Soothed by the peace within his breast.

4 My Saviour, whom 'tis life to see,
  Thy promise in thy cross appears;
Its power, its peace, O grant to me,
  Its perfect love to still my fears.

THE CHRISTIAN.

274
DIJON. 7s.   GERMAN.

524
When the dark waves round us roll,
  And we look in vain for aid,
Speak, Lord, to the trembling soul,—
  "It is I; be not afraid."

2 When our brightest hopes depart,
    When our fairest visions fade,
  Whisper to the fainting heart,—
    "It is I; be not afraid."

3 When with wearing hopeless pain
    Sinks the spirit sore dismayed,
  Breathe Thou then the comfort-strain,—
    "It is I; be not afraid."

4 When we feel the end is near,
    Passing into death's dark shade,
  May the voice be strong and clear,—
    "It is I; be not afraid."

525   R. Hill.
Cast thy burden on the Lord,
  Only lean upon his word;
Thou wilt soon have cause to bless
  His eternal faithfulness.

2 He sustains thee by his hand,
  He enables thee to stand;
  Those whom Jesus once hath loved
  From his grace are never moved.

3 Heaven and earth may pass away,
  God's free grace shall not decay;
  He hath promised to fulfil
  All the pleasure of his will.

4 Jesus! Guardian of the flock,
  Be thyself our constant Rock;
  Make us, by thy powerful hand,
  Strong as Zion's mountain stand.

SCOTT. 7s.   J. P. HOLBROOK.

Burdens and Sorrows. 275

"COME TO ME." ARR. J. P. HOLBROOK.

526
C. Elliott.

With tearful eyes I look around;
  Life seems a dark and stormy sea;
Yet 'midst the gloom I hear a sound,
  A heavenly whisper, "Come to Me!"

2 It tells me of a place of rest,
  It tells me where my soul may flee:
O, to the weary, faint, opprest,
  How sweet the bidding, "Come to Me!"

3 "Come, for all else must fail and die;
  Earth is no resting-place for thee;
To heaven direct thy weeping eye;
  I am thy portion; Come to Me!"

4 O voice of mercy, voice of love,
  In conflict, grief, and agony,
Support me, cheer me from above,
  And gently whisper, "Come to Me!"

THE CHRISTIAN.

SUBMISSION. 8s, 4s.   CH. ZEUNER.

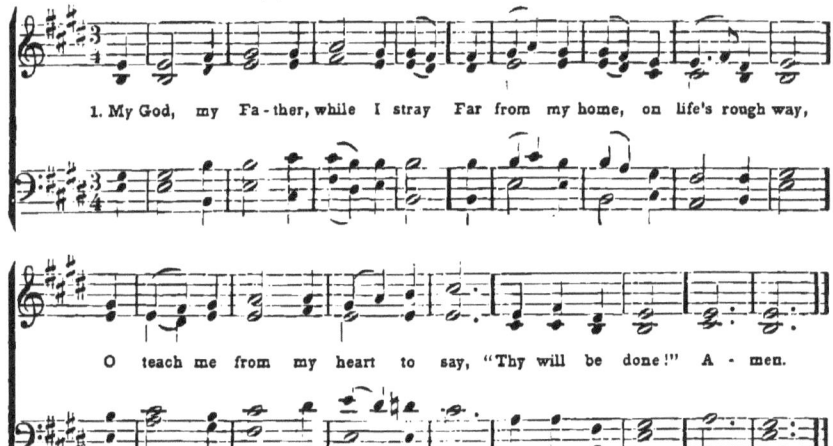

1. My God, my Father, while I stray Far from my home, on life's rough way, O teach me from my heart to say, "Thy will be done!" A-men.

527   *C. Elliott.*
My God, my Father, while I stray
Far from my home, on life's rough way,
O teach me from my heart to say,
  "Thy will be done!"

2 What though in lonely grief I sigh
For friends beloved no longer nigh;
Submissive still would I reply,
  "Thy will be done!"

3 If thou shouldst call me to resign
What most I prize,—it ne'er was mine;
I only yield thee what was thine:
  "Thy will be done!"

4 If but my fainting heart be blest
With thy sweet Spirit for its guest,
My God, to thee I leave the rest:
  "Thy will be done!"

5 Renew my will from day to day;
Blend it with thine, and take away
All that now makes it hard to say,
  "Thy will be done!"

6 Then when on earth I breathe no more,
The prayer oft mixed with tears before,
I'll sing upon a happier shore:
  "Thy will be done!"

528   *J. R. Macduff.*
Jesus, my Saviour, look on me,
For I am weary and opprest;
I come to cast myself on thee:
  Thou art my rest.

2 Look down on me, for I am weak,
I feel the toilsome journey's length;
Thine aid omnipotent I seek;
  Thou art my strength.

3 I am bewildered on my way,
Dark and tempestuous is the night;
O send thou forth some cheering ray:
  Thou art my light.

4 When Satan flings his fiery darts,
I look to thee: my terrors cease;
Thy cross a hiding-place imparts:
  Thou art my peace.

5 Standing alone on Jordan's brink,
In that tremendous latest strife,
Thou wilt not suffer me to sink:
  Thou art my life.

6 Thou wilt my every want supply,
E'en to the end, whate'er befall;
Through life, in death, eternally,
  Thou art my all

Burdens and Sorrows. 277

LEAVITT. 7s. D.   J. P. HOLBROOK.

1. When our heads are bowed with woe, When our bit-ter tears o'er-flow,

When we mourn the lost, the dear, Je-sus, Son of Ma-ry, hear.
D. S. Thou hast shed the hu-man tear, Je-sus, Son of Ma-ry, hear.

Thou our throb-bing flesh hast worn, Thou our mor-tal griefs hast borne,

529   *H. H. Milman.*

WHEN our heads are bowed with woe,
When our bitter tears o'erflow,
When we mourn the lost, the dear,
Jesus, Son of Mary, hear.
Thou our throbbing flesh hast worn,
Thou our mortal griefs hast borne,
Thou hast shed the human tear;
Jesus, Son of Mary, hear.

2 When the solemn death-bell tolls
For our own departing souls.
When our final doom is near,
Jesus, Son of Mary, hear.

Thou hast bowed the dying head,
Thou the blood of life hast shed,
Thou hast filled a mortal bier;
Jesus, Son of Mary, hear.

3 When the heart is sad within
With the thought of all its sin,
When the spirit shrinks with fear,
Jesus, Son of Mary, hear.
Thou, the shame, the grief hast known;
Though the sins were not thine own,
Thou hast deigned their load to bear;
Jesus, Son of Mary, hear.

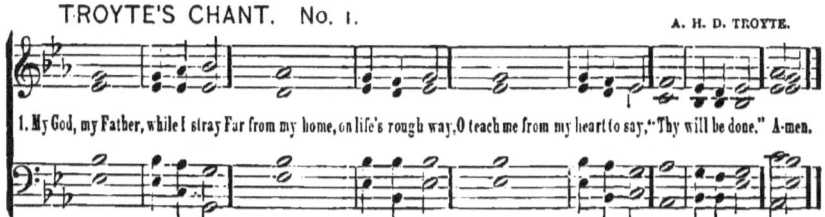

TROYTE'S CHANT. No. 1.   A. H. D. TROYTE.

1. My God, my Father, while I stray Far from my home, on life's rough way, O teach me from my heart to say, "Thy will be done." A-men.

278 THE CHRISTIAN.

MIRIAM. 7s, 6s. No. 2.   J. P. HOLBROOK.

530   A. L. Waring.

In heavenly love abiding,
  No change my heart shall fear,
And safe is such confiding,
  For nothing changes here:
The storm may roar without me,
  My heart may low be laid,
But God is round about me,
  And can I be dismayed?

2 Wherever he may guide me,
  No want shall turn me back;
My Shepherd is beside me,
  And nothing can I lack:
His wisdom ever waketh,
  His sight is never dim:
He knows the way he taketh,
  And I will walk with him.

3 Green pastures are before me,
  Which yet I have not seen;
Bright skies will soon be o'er me,
  Where darkest clouds have been:
My hope I can not measure;
  My path to life is free;
My Saviour has my treasure,
  And he will walk with me.

531   F. R. Havergal.

Our yet unfinished story
  Is tending all to this:
To God the greatest glory,
  To us the greatest bliss.

Our plans may be disjointed,
  But we may calmly rest:
What God has once appointed
  Is better than our best.

2 We cannot see before us,
  But our all-seeing Friend
Is always watching o'er us,
  And knows the very end;
And when amid our blindness
  His disappointments fall,
We trust His loving-kindness
  Whose wisdom sends them all.

532   W. Cowper.

Life can bring with it nothing,
  But he will bear us through;
Who gives the lilies clothing,
  Will clothe his people too:
Beneath the spreading heavens,
  No creature but is fed;
And he who feeds the ravens,
  Will give his children bread.

2 Though vine nor fig-tree neither,
  Their wonted fruit should bear,
Though all the fields should wither,
  Nor flocks nor herds be there;
Yet God the same abiding,
  His praise shall tune my voice,
For while in him confiding,
  I cannot but rejoice.

Pilgrim Songs.

ST. PAUL. 7s, 6s.

1. A pilgrim and a stranger, I journey here below; Far distant is my country, The home to which I go: Here I must toil and struggle, Oft weary and oppressed, But there my God shall lead me To everlasting rest.

533   *J. Borthwick, tr.*

A PILGRIM and a stranger,
  I journey here below;
Far distant is my country,
  The home to which I go:
Here I must toil and struggle,
  Oft weary and oppressed,
But there my God shall lead me
  To everlasting rest.

2 'Tis there my thoughts are dwelling,
  'Tis there I long to be;
Come, Lord! and call thy servant
  To blessedness with thee!
When all my toils are ended,
  When all my wanderings cease,
Call from the wayside lodging
  To the sweet home of peace!

3 There I shall dwell for ever,
  No more a stranger guest,
With all thy blood-bought children,
  In everlasting rest.
The pilgrim toils forgotten,
  The pilgrim conflicts o'er,
All earthly griefs behind us,
  Eternal joys before!

534   *J. M. Neale, tr.*

O HAPPY band of pilgrims,
  If onward ye will tread
With Jesus as your Leader
  To Jesus as your Head!
O happy, if ye labor
  As Jesus did for men;
O happy, if ye hunger
  As Jesus hungered then!

2 The trials that beset you,
  The sorrows ye endure,
The manifold temptations
  That death alone can cure,—
What are they but his jewels
  Of right celestial worth?
What are they but the ladder
  Set up to heaven on earth?

3 The cross that Jesus carried,
  He carried as your due;
The crown that Jesus weareth,
  He weareth it for you.
O happy band of pilgrims,
  Look upward to the skies,
Where soon your Kingly Leader
  Awards the heavenly prize!

280 THE CHRISTIAN.
BARING-GOULD. 8s, 7s. J. BARNBY.

535
S. Baring-Gould, tr.

Through the night of doubt and sorrow,
  Onward goes the pilgrim band,
Singing songs of expectation,
  Marching to the promised land.
Clear before us through the darkness
  Gleams and burns the guiding Light;
Brother clasps the hand of brother,
  Stepping fearless through the night.

2 One the light of God's own Presence,
  O'er his ransomed people shed,
Chasing far the gloom and terror,
  Brightening all the path we tread:
One the object of our journey,
  One the faith which never tires,
One the earnest looking forward,
  One the hope our God inspires.

3 One the strain the lips of thousands
  Lift as from the heart of one;
One the conflict, one the peril,
  One the march in God begun;
One the gladness of rejoicing
  On the far eternal shore,
Where the one Almighty Saviour
  Reigns in love for evermore.

4 Onward, therefore, pilgrim brothers,
  Onward, with the cross our aid;
Bear its shame, and fight its battle,
  Till we rest beneath its shade.
Soon shall come the great awaking,
  Soon the rending of the tomb;
Then, the scattering of all shadows,
  And the end of toil and gloom!

AMSTERDAM. 7s, 6s. J. NARES.

Pilgrim Songs.

AMSTERDAM. CONCLUDED.

to-ry things Toward heaven, thy native place: Sun, and moon, and stars decay; Time shall soon this earth re-move; Rise, my soul, and haste a-way To seats pre-pared a-bove.

536
R. Seagrave.

RISE, my soul! and stretch thy wings,
   Thy better portion trace;
Rise, from transitory things,
   Toward heaven, thy native place:
Sun, and moon, and stars decay,
   Time shall soon this earth remove;
Rise, my soul, and haste away
   To seats prepared above!

2 Rivers to the ocean run,
   Nor stay in all their course;
Fire ascending seeks the sun,—
   Both speed them to their source;
So a soul that's born of God,
   Pants to view his glorious face,
Upward tends to his abode,
   To rest in his embrace.

3 Cease, ye pilgrims! cease to mourn,—
   Press onward to the prize;
Soon your Saviour will return
   Triumphant in the skies:
Yet a season, and you know
   Happy entrance will be given,
All your sorrows left below,
   And earth exchanged for heaven.

MILLER. 8s, 7s. (A.)

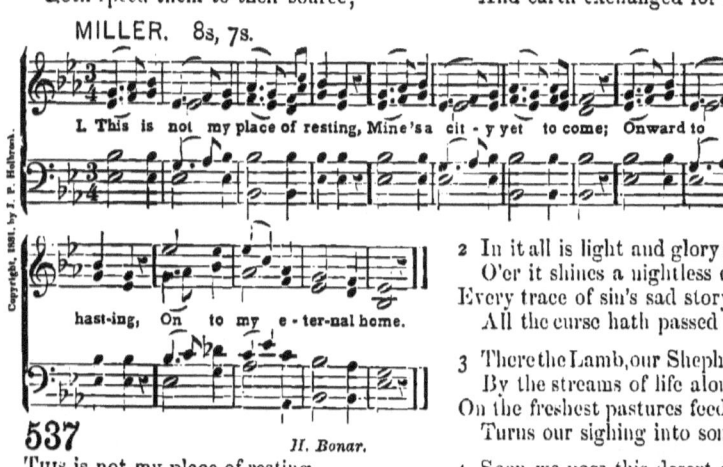

1. This is not my place of resting, Mine's a cit-y yet to come; Onward to it I am hast-ing, On to my e-ter-nal home.

537
H. Bonar.

THIS is not my place of resting,
   Mine's a city yet to come;
Onward to it I am hasting,
   On to my eternal home.

2 In it all is light and glory;
   O'er it shines a nightless day;
Every trace of sin's sad story,
   All the curse hath passed away.

3 There the Lamb, our Shepherd, leads us,
   By the streams of life along,
On the freshest pastures feeds us,
   Turns our sighing into song.

4 Soon we pass this desert dreary,
   Soon we bid farewell to pain;
Never more are sad or weary,
   Never, never sin again.

282 THE CHRISTIAN.

CAMP. 7s. D.   J. P. HOLBROOK.

1. When, a-long life's thorn-y road, Faints the soul beneath the load, By its cares and sins oppressed, Finds on earth no peace or rest; When the wi-ly tempter's near, Fill-ing us with doubts and fear: Jesus, to thy feet we flee; Je-sus, we will look to thee.

538

When, along life's thorny road,
Faints the soul beneath the load,
By its cares and sins oppressed,
Finds on earth no peace or rest;
When the wily tempter's near,
Filling us with doubts and fear:
Jesus, to thy feet we flee;
Jesus, we will look to thee.

2 Thou our Saviour, from the throne
List'nest to thy people's moan:
Thou, the living Head, dost share
Every pang thy members bear:
Full of tenderness thou art,
Thou wilt heal the broken heart;
Full of power, thine arm shall quell
All the rage and might of hell.

3 Mighty to redeem and save,
Thou hast overcome the grave;
Thou the bars of death hast riven,
Opened wide the gate of heaven:
Soon in glory thou shalt come,
Taking thy poor pilgrims home:
Jesus, then we all shall be
Ever, ever, Lord, with thee!

SHINING SHORE. P. M.

1. My days are gliding swiftly by, And I, a pilgrim stranger, Would not detain them as they fly,
D. S. just before, the shining shore,

Pilgrim Songs. 283

SHINING SHORE. CONCLUDED.

Those hours of toil and danger: For, O we stand on Jordan's strand; Our friends are passing over; And
We may almost dis-cov-er!

539
D. Nelson.

My days are gliding swiftly by,
And I, a pilgrim stranger,
Would not detain them, as they fly,
Those hours of toil and danger:
For, O we stand on Jordan's strand;
Our friends are passing over;
And just before, the shining shore
We may almost discover.

2 We'll gird our loins, my brethren dear,
Our heavenly home discerning;
Our absent Lord has left us word,
"Let every lamp be burning:"

3 Should coming days be cold and dark,
We need not cease our singing;
That perfect rest nought can molest,
Where golden harps are ringing:

4 Let sorrow's rudest tempest blow,
Each cord on earth to sever;
Our King says, "Come!" and there's our [home,
Forever, O forever.

HOME. 6s, 4s. A S. SULLIVAN.

1. I'm but a stranger here, Heaven is my home; Earth is a desert drear, Heaven is my home:
Danger and sorrow stand Round me on ev-ery hand; Heaven is my fatherland— Heaven is my home.

540
T. R. Taylor.

I'm but a stranger here,
Heaven is my home;
Earth is a desert drear,
Heaven is my home:
Danger and sorrow stand
Round me on every hand;
Heaven is my fatherland—
Heaven is my home.

2 What though the tempest rage,
Heaven is my home;
Short is my pilgrimage,
Heaven is my home:
Time's cold and wint'ry blast
Soon will be overpast;
I shall reach home at last—
Heaven is my home.

3 There, at my Saviour's side,
Heaven is my home;
I shall be glorified—
Heaven is my home:
There are the good and blest,
Those I loved most and best,
And there I, too, shall rest;—
Heaven is my home!

THE CHRISTIAN.

284

HURSLEY. L. M.   ARR. W. H. MONK.

541   *J. Keble.*

If on our daily course our mind
Be set, to hallow all we find,
New treasures still of countless price
God will provide for sacrifice.

2 Old friends, old scenes, will lovelier be,
As more of heaven in each we see;
Some softening gleam of love and prayer
Shall dawn on every cross and care.

3 The trivial round, the common task,
Will furnish all we ought to ask;
Room to deny ourselves; a road
To bring us daily nearer God.

4 Seek we no more, content with these
Let present rapture, comfort, ease,
As heaven shall bid them, come and go,—
The secret this, of Rest below.

5 Only, O Lord, in thy dear love,
Fit us for perfect rest above;
And help us this and every day
To live more nearly as we pray.

ELIZABETHTOWN. C. M.   G. KINGSLEY.

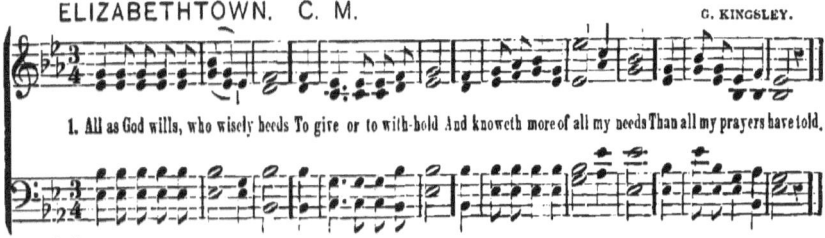

542   *J. G. Whittier.*

All as God wills, who wisely heeds
To give or to withhold,
And knoweth more of all my needs
Than all my prayers have told.

2 Enough that blessings undeserved
Have marked my erring track;
That wheresoe'er my feet have swerved
His chastening turned me back;

3 That more and more a providence
Of love is understood,
Making the springs of time and sense
Sweet with eternal good;

4 That death seems but a covered way
Which opens into light,
Wherein no blinded child can stray
Beyond a Father's sight.

5 No longer forward, nor behind,
I look in hope or fear;
But grateful take the good I find,
God's manna, now and here.

Pilgrim Songs.

NUNDA. L. M. D. — L. MASON.

1. { How vain is all beneath the skies, How transient ev-ery earthly bliss; }
   { How slender all the fondest ties, That bind us to a world like this. }
2. { The evening cloud, the morning dew, }
   { The withering grass, the fading flower, } Of earthly hopes are emblems true, The glo-ry of a pass-ing hour.

543   *D. E. Ford.*

How vain is all beneath the skies,
  How transient every earthly bliss;
How slender all the fondest ties,
  That bind us to a world like this.

2 The evening cloud, the morning dew,
  The withering grass, the fading flower,
Of earthly hopes are emblems true,
  The glory of a passing hour.

3 But though earth's fairest blossoms die,
  And all beneath the skies is vain,
There is a land, whose confines lie
  Beyond the reach of care and pain.

4 Then let the hope of joys to come
  Dispel our cares, and chase our fears:
If God be ours, we're travelling home,
  Though passing through a vale of tears.

544   *J. Newton.*

By faith in Christ I walk with God,
  With heaven, my journey's end, in view;
Supported by his staff and rod,
  My road is safe and pleasant too.

2 Tho' snares and dangers throng my path,
  And earth and hell my course withstand,
I triumph over all by faith,
  Guarded by his almighty hand.

3 The wilderness affords no food,
  But God for my support prepares,
Provides me every needful good,
  And frees my soul from wants and cares.

4 With him sweet converse I maintain;
  Great as he is, I dare be free;
I tell him all my grief and pain,
  And he reveals his love to me.

BEETHOVEN. L. M. — ARR. G. KINGSLEY.

1. By faith in Christ I walk with God, With heaven, my journey's end in view;
Sup-port-ed by his staff and rod, My road is safe and pleas-ant too.

286 THE CHRISTIAN.

GODWIN. C. M. 8 l or D.   ARR. J. P. HOLBROOK.

1. A stranger in the world below, I calmly sojourn here; Nor can its happiness or woe
Provoke my hope or fear: Provoke my hope and fear: Its evils in a moment end,
Its joys as soon are past; But O, the bliss to which I tend Eternally shall last!

545
C. Wesley.

A STRANGER in the world below,
  I calmly sojourn here;
Nor can its happiness or woe
  Provoke my hope or fear:
Its evils in a moment end,
  Its joys as soon are past;
But O, the bliss to which I tend
  Eternally shall last!

2 O what a blessed hope is ours!
  While here on earth we stay,
We more than taste the heavenly powers,
  And antedate that day:
We feel the resurrection near,
  Our life in Christ concealed,
And with his glorious presence here
  Our earthen vessels filled.

3 O would he more of heaven bestow,
  And let the vessels break,
And let our ransomed spirits go
  To grasp the God we seek;
In rapturous awe on him to gaze,
  Who bought the sight for me;
Adore and wonder at his grace
  Through all eternity!

546

THE Lord's my Shepherd, I'll not want:
  He makes me down to lie
In pastures green; he leadeth me
  The quiet waters by.

2 Yea, tho' I walk in death's dark vale,
  Yet will I fear no ill;
For thou art with me, and thy rod
  And staff me comfort still.

3 My table thou hast furnishéd
  In presence of my foes;
My head thou dost with oil anoint,
  And my cup overflows.

4 Goodness and mercy, all my life,
  Shall surely follow me;
And in God's house, for evermore
  My dwelling-place shall be.

Pilgrim Songs. 287

BEEBE. 8s, 7s. (IAMBIC.)

1. The King of love my Shepherd is, Whose goodness faileth never;
I nothing lack if I am his, And he is mine forever.

547
H. W. Baker.

THE King of love my Shepherd is,
Whose goodness faileth never;
I nothing lack if I am his,
And he is mine forever.

2 Where streams of living water flow
My ransomed soul he leadeth,
And where the verdant pastures grow,
With food celestial feedeth.

3 Perverse and foolish oft I strayed,
But yet in love he sought me,
And on his shoulder gently laid,
And home, rejoicing, brought me.

4 In death's dark vale I fear no ill
With thee, dear Lord, beside me;
Thy rod and staff my comfort still,
Thy cross before to guide me.

5 Thou spreadst a table in my sight,
Thy unction grace bestoweth,
And oh! what transport of delight
From thy pure chalice floweth.

6 And so through all the length of days
Thy goodness faileth never;
Good Shepherd, may I sing thy praise
Within thy house forever.

PLEYEL'S HYMN. 7s. PLEYEL.

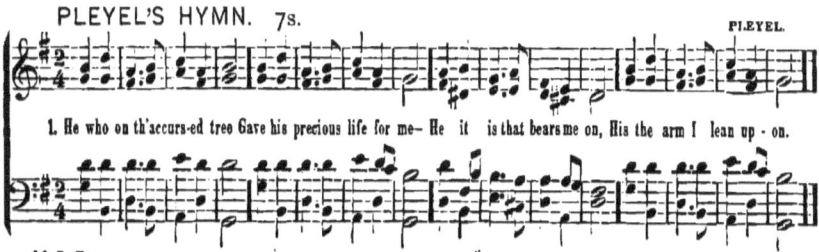

1. He who on th' accursed tree Gave his precious life for me— He it is that bears me on, His the arm I lean up-on.

548
J. R. Macduff.

HE who on th' accursed tree
Gave his precious life for me—
He it is that bears me on,
His the arm I lean upon.

2 He who now, enthroned above,
Still retains his heart of love,
Marking still each falling tear
Of his burdened pilgrims here.

3 He who wields creation's rod,
He my Brother, yet my God;
Faithful he, whate'er betide,
Is my everlasting Guide!

4 Scenes will vary, friends grow strange,
But the Changeless can not change,
Gladly will I journey on,
With his arm to lean upon.

288   THE CHRISTIAN.

PORTUGUESE HYMN. 11s.   J. READING.

1. The Lord is my shepherd, no want shall I know, I feed in green pastures, safe-folded I rest; He leadeth my soul where the still waters flow, Restores me when wandering, redeems when oppressed.

549
J. Montgomery.

The Lord is my shepherd, no want shall I know,
  I feed in green pastures, safe-folded I rest;
He leadeth my soul where the still waters flow,
  Restores me when wandering, redeems when oppressed.

2 Through the valley and shadow of death, though I stray,
  Since thou art my guardian, no evil I fear;
Thy rod shall defend me, thy staff be my stay;
  No harm can befall, with my comforter near.

3 Let goodness and mercy, my bountiful God!
  Still follow my steps till I meet thee above;
I seek—by the path which my forefathers trod,
  Through the land of their sojourn—thy kingdom of love.

550

Though faint, yet pursuing, we go on our way;
The Lord is our leader, his word is our stay;
Though suffering, and sorrow, and trial be near,
The Lord is our refuge, and whom can we fear?

2 He raiseth the fallen, he cheereth the faint;
The weak, and oppressed—he will hear their complaint;
The way may be weary, and thorny the road,
But how can we falter? our help is in God!

3 And to his green pastures our footsteps he leads;
His flock in the desert how kindly he feeds!
The lambs in his bosom he tenderly bears,
And brings back the wanderers all safe from the snares.

4 Though clouds may surround us, our God is our light;
Though storms rage around us, our God is our might;
So faint, yet pursuing, still onward we come;
The Lord is our Leader, and heaven is our home!

Pilgrim Songs.

BORTHWICK. 10s.   J. BARNBY.

1. Thou knowest Lord, the weariness and sorrow Of the sad heart that comes to thee for rest; Cares of to-day, and burdens for to-morrow, Blessings implored, and sins to be confessed; We come before thee at thy gracious word, And lay them at thy feet: thou knowest Lord.

551   *J. Borthwick.*

Thou knowest, Lord, the weariness and sorrow
  Of the sad heart that comes to thee for rest;
Cares of to-day, and burdens for to-morrow,
  Blessings implored, and sins to be confessed;
We come before thee at thy gracious word,
And lay them at thy feet : Thou knowest, Lord.

2 Thou knowest all the present; each temptation,
  Each toilsome duty, each foreboding fear;
All to each one assigned of tribulation,
  Or to beloved ones, than self more dear;
All pensive memories, as we journey on,
Longings for vanished smiles and voices gone.

3 Thou knowest all the future; gleams of gladness
  By stormy clouds too quickly overcast;
Hours of sweet fellowship and parting sadness,
  And the dark river to be crossed at last.
Oh! what could hope and confidence afford
To tread that path; but this, Thou knowest, Lord!

4 Therefore we come, thy gentle call obeying,
  And lay our sins and sorrows at thy feet;
On everlasting strength our weakness staying,
  Clothed in thy robe of righteousness complete:
Then rising and refreshed, we leave thy throne,
And follow on to know as we are known.

290 THE CHRISTIAN.
LANGRAN. 10s.   J. LANGRAN.

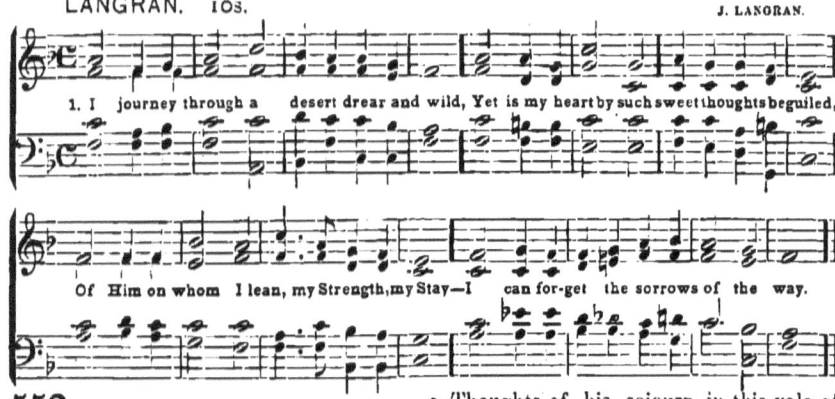

552
M. J. Walker.

I JOURNEY through a desert drear and wild,
Yet is my heart by such sweet thoughts beguiled,
Of Him on whom I lean, my Strength, my Stay—
I can forget the sorrows of the way.

2 Thoughts of his love—the root of every grace
Which finds in this poor heart a dwelling-place;
The sunshine of my soul, than day more bright,
And my calm pillow of repose at night.

3 Thoughts of his sojourn in this vale of tears;
The tale of love unfolded in those years
Of sinless suffering and of patient grace,
I love again, and yet again to trace.

4 Thoughts of his dying—on the cross I gaze,
And there behold its sad yet healing rays;
Beacon of hope, which lifted up on high,
Illumes with heav'nly light the tear-dimm'd eye.

5 Thoughts of his coming: for that joyful day
In patient hope I watch, and wait, and pray;
The day draws nigh, the midnight shadows flee;
O what a sunrise will that advent be!

ABBOTT. 10s, 4s.
R. ROGERS.

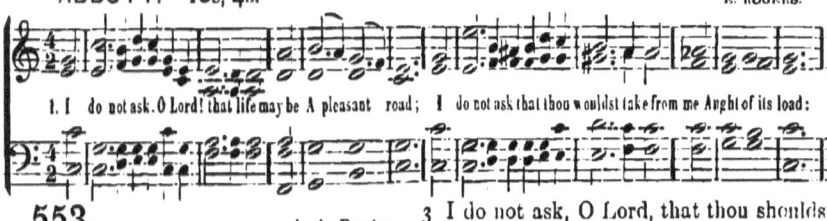

553
A. A. Proctor.

I DO not ask, O Lord! that life may be
   A pleasant road;
I do not ask that thou wouldst take from me
   Aught of its load:

2 For one thing only, Lord, dear Lord, I plead,
   Lead me aright—
Though strength should falter and though heart should bleed,—
   Through Peace to Light.

3 I do not ask, O Lord, that thou shouldst
   Full radiance here;   [shed
Give but a ray of peace that I may tread
   Without a fear.

4 I do not ask my cross to understand,
   My way to see;
Better in darkness just to feel thy hand,
   And follow thee.

5 Joy is like restless day; but peace divine
   Like quiet night;
Lead me, O Lord—till perfect day shall
   Through Peace to Light!   [shine—

Pilgrim Songs.

554
J. H. Newman.

LEAD, kindly Light, amid the encircling
    Lead thou me on;   [gloom
The night is dark, and I am far from home,
    Lead thou me on;
Keep thou my feet; I do not ask to see
The distant scene; one step enough for me.

2 I was not ever thus, nor prayed that thou
    Shouldst lead me on;
I loved to choose and see my path; but now
    Lead thou me on;
I loved the garish day, and, spite of fears
Pride ruled my will. Remember not past
    years!

3 So long thy power has blessed me, sure
    Will lead me on   [it still
O'er moor and fen, o'er crag and torrent
    The night is gone;   [till
And with the morn those angel faces smile
Which I have loved long since, and lost
    awhile!

292 THE CHRISTIAN.

ROSWELL. S. M. D.   I. ABRAM.

555   H. Bonar.

A FEW more years shall roll,
  A few more seasons come,
And we shall be with those that rest,
  Asleep within the tomb.

2 A few more struggles here,
  A few more partings o'er,
A few more toils, a few more tears,
  And we shall weep no more.

3 A few more storms shall beat
  On this wild rocky shore,
And we shall be where tempests cease,
  And surges swell no more.

4 A few more Sabbaths here
  Shall cheer us on our way,
And we shall reach the endless rest,
  Th' eternal Sabbath day.

5 'T is but a little while,
  And he shall come again
Who died that we might live, who lives
  That we with him may reign.

6 Then, O my Lord! prepare
  My soul for that glad day;
O wash me in thy precious blood,
  And take my sins away.

DENNIS. S. M.   NAGELI.

Pilgrim Songs.

556 ONE SWEETLY SOLEMN THOUGHT QUARTET & CHORUS CHOIR.

1. One sweetly solemn thought Comes to me .... | o'er · and | o'er;
2. Nearer the bound of life, Where we lay our ... | bur - dens | down;
3. Father, perfect my trust! Strengthen the ...... | might · of my | faith;

I am nearer home to-day Than I ever....... have | been · be- | fore.
Nearer leaving the cross; Near-........... er | gaining · the | crown;
Let me feel as I would When I stand on the rock of the | shore · of | death—

Nearer my Father's house, Where the... | many · mansions | be;
But lying darkly between, Winding.... | down · through the | night,
Feel as I would when my feet Are.... | slipping · over the | brink;

Nearer...................................the | great . white | throne,
Is the deep............................and | un - known | stream.
For it may be,........................I'm | near - er | home,

Nearer the.................................. | crys - tal | sea.
That leads at .... | last · to the | light.
Nearer...................................... | now · than I | think.

THE CHRISTIAN.

EVENTIDE. 10s. — W. H. MONK.

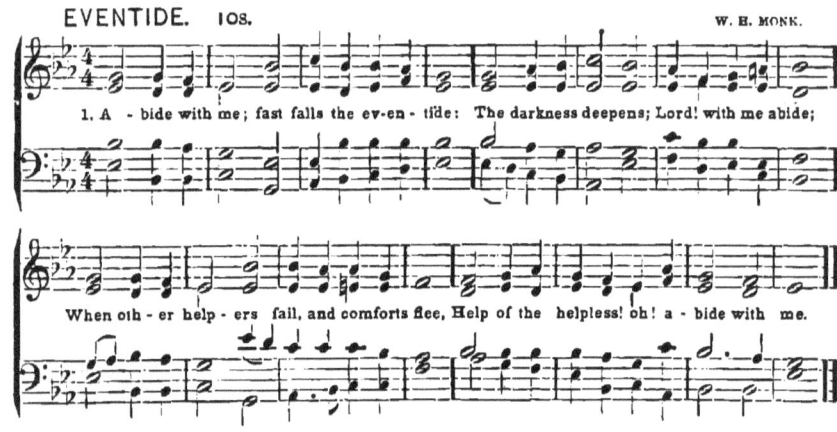

1. A-bide with me; fast falls the ev-en-tide: The darkness deepens; Lord! with me abide;
When oth-er help-ers fail, and comforts flee, Help of the helpless! oh! a-bide with me.

557 H. F. Lyte.

Abide with me; fast falls the eventide:
The darkness deepens; Lord! with me abide;
When other helpers fail, and comforts flee,
Help of the helpless! oh! abide with me.

2 Swift to its close ebbs out life's little day;
Earth's joys grow dim; its glories pass away;
Change and decay in all around I see:
O thou who changest not! abide with me.

3 I need thy presence every passing hour;
What, but thy grace, can foil the tempter's power?

Who, like thyself, my guide and stay can be?
Through cloud and sunshine, oh! abide with me.

4 I fear no foe with thee at hand to bless;
Ills have no weight, and tears no bitterness;
Where is death's sting? where, grave! thy victory?
I triumph still, if thou abide with me.

5 Hold thou thy cross before my closing eyes;
Shine through the gloom, and point me to [the skies.
Heaven's morning breaks, and earth's vain shadows flee:
In life and death, O Lord! abide with me.

BERLIN 10s. — MENDELSSOHN.

1. A-bide with me; fast falls the ev-en-tide: The darkness deepens; Lord! with me a-bide;
When other help-ers fail, and comforts flee, Help of the help-less! oh! a-bide with me.

Pilgrim Songs. 295

VOX JESU. 7s, 6s. J. P. HOLBROOK.

1. I've wrestled on toward heaven, 'Gainst storm, and wind, and tide; Now, like a weary traveler, That leaneth on his guide, Amid the shades of evening, While sinks life's lingering sand, I hail the glory dawning From our Immanuel's land!

Copyright, 1881, by J. P. Holbrook.

558
A. R. Cousin.

I 'VE wrestled on toward heaven,
　'Gainst storm, and wind, and tide;
Now, like a weary traveler,
　That leaneth on his guide,
Amid the shades of evening,
　While sinks life's lingering sand,
I hail the glory dawning
　From our Immanuel's land!

2 Deep waters crossed life's pathway,
　The hedge of thorns was sharp;
Now, these lie all behind me—
　O! for a well-tuned harp!
Join we our Hallelujah
　With yon triumphant band,
Who sing, where glory dwelleth,
　In our Immanuel's land!

3 With mercy and with judgment
　My web of time he wove,
And aye the dews of sorrow
　Were lustered with his love;
I'll bless the hand that guided,
　I'll bless the heart that planned,
When throned where glory dwelleth,
　In our Immanuel's land!

4 O Christ! He is the Fountain,
　The deep, sweet well of love!
The streams on earth I've tasted,
　More deep I'll drink above;
There, to an ocean fullness,
　His mercy doth expand,
And glory—glory dwelleth
　In our Immanuel's land!

296 THE LAST THINGS.

First Lines of Hymns.

DEATH.
HYMNS.
559 Thou who didst stoop below,
560 I would not live alway,
561 Thee we adore, eternal Name,
562 Beneath our feet and o'er our head
563 Why do we mourn departing friends
564 No, no, it is not dying,
565 It is not death to die,
566 Lowly and solemn be,
567 The moment comes when strength
568 Asleep in Jesus; blessed sleep,
569 How blest the righteous when he dies,
570 Unveil thy bosom, faithful tomb,
571 At evening time let there be light,
572 Jesus lives! no longer now
573 There is a land immortal
574 I know no life divided
575 Rejoice, rejoice, believers!
576 Behold the Bridegroom cometh
577 Stand we prepared to see and hear
578 Lord, thou hast joined my soul
579 Christ will gather in his own
580 So heaven is gathering, one by one,
581 We speak of the realms of the blest,
582 My Saviour, whom absent I love,
583 Time, thou speedest on but slowly,
584 Lo, the Day of Life approacheth,
585 We shall see Him in our nature,
586 Let me be with thee where thou art,
587 Jesus, blessed mediator,
588 Far beyond our skies of gladness,
589 Lo, the seal of death is breaking,

JUDGMENT.
HYMNS.
590 Before the throne
591 Lo, he comes with clouds
592 Day of judgment, day of wonders!
593 Great God, what do I see and hear
594 He reigns! the Lord, the Saviour reigns
595 That day of wrath! that dreadful

HEAVEN.
596 Hark, hark, my soul, angelic songs
597 Christian, the morn breaks
598 O Paradise! O Paradise!
599 When from far thy towers shall shine,
600 Brief life is here our portion
601 For thee, O dear, dear country,
602 Jerusalem, the golden,
603 Jerusalem, the glorious,
604 Who are these in bright array,
605 Ten thousand times ten thousand
606 Hark, the sound of holy voices,
607 King of Saints, to whom the number
608 Lord, it belongs not to my care
609 When I can read my title clear
610 There is an hour of peaceful rest,
611 O mother dear, Jerusalem,
612 There is a land of pure delight,
613 Jerusalem, my happy home,
614 There is no night in heaven,
615 Forever with the Lord,
616 What sinners value I resign,

FREDERICK. 11s.   G. KINGSLEY.

1. I would not live al-way; I ask not to stay Where storm after storm rises dark o'er the way;
The few lu-rid mornings that dawn on us here Are enough for life's woes, full enough for its cheer.

Through Death to Life. 297

PARK. 6s, 10s.   H. BAUMER.

559   *S. E. Miles.*

Thou, who didst stoop below
    To drain the cup of woe,
And wear the form of frail mortality;
    Thy blessèd labors done,
    Thy crown of victory won,
Hast passed from earth, passed to thy home on high.

2 Our eyes behold thee not,
    Yet hast thou not forgot
Those who have placed their hope, their trust, in thee;
    Before thy Father's face
    Thou hast prepared a place,
That where thou art, there they may also be.

3 It was no path of flowers,
    Through this dark world of ours,
Belovèd of the Father! thou didst tread;
    And shall we in dismay
    Shrink from the narrow way,
When clouds and darkness are around it spread?

4 And O, if thoughts of gloom
    Should hover o'er the tomb,
Thy light of love our guiding star shall be;
    Our spirits shall not dread
    The shadowy way to tread,
Friend, Guardian, Saviour! which doth lead to thee.

560   *W. A. Muhlenberg.*

I would not live alway: I ask not to stay
Where storm after storm rises dark o'er the way;
The few lurid mornings that dawn on us here
Are enough for life's woes, full enough for its cheer.

2 I would not live away: no, welcome the tomb!
Since Jesus hath lain there, I dread not its gloom;
There sweet be my rest, till he bids me arise
To hail him in triumph descending the skies.

3 Who, who would live away, away from his God,
Away from you heaven, that blissful abode,
Where the rivers of pleasure flow o'er the bright plains,
And the noontide of glory eternally reigns;

4 Where the saints of all ages in harmony meet,
Their Saviour and brethren transported to greet;
While the anthems of rapture unceasingly roll,
And the smile of the Lord is the feast of the soul!

DEATH.

561
I. Watts.

Thee we adore, eternal Name,
 And humbly own to thee
How feeble is our mortal frame,
 What dying worms are we.

2 Great God, on what a slender thread
 Hang everlasting things;
The eternal state of all the dead
 Upon life's feeble strings.

3 Infinite joy, or endless woe,
 Attend on every breath;
And yet how unconcerned we go
 Upon the brink of death.

4 Waken, O Lord, our drowsy sense,
 To walk this dangerous road;
And if our souls are hurried hence,
 May they be found with God.

562
R. Heber.

Beneath our feet and o'er our head
 Is equal warning given;
Beneath us lie the countless dead,
 Above us is the heaven!

2 Death rides on every passing breeze,
 And lurks in every flower;
Each season hath its own disease,
 Its peril every hour!

3 Turn, mortal, turn! thy danger know;
 Where'er thy foot can tread,
The earth rings hollow from below,
 And warns thee of her dead!

4 Turn, mortal, turn! thy soul apply
 To truths divinely given:
The dead who underneath thee lie,
 Shall live for hell or heaven!

563
I. Watts.

Why do we mourn departing friends,
 Or shake at death's alarms?
'Tis but the voice that Jesus sends,
 To call them to his arms.

2 Are we not tending upward, too,
 As fast as time can move?
Nor would we wish the hours more slow,
 To keep us from our love.

3 Why should we tremble to convey
 Their bodies to the tomb?
There the dear flesh of Jesus lay,
 And scattered all the gloom.

4 The graves of all the saints he blessed,
 And softened every bed;
Where should the dying members rest,
 But with the dying Head?

"Not Death to Die." 299

POMEROY. 7s, 6s. — J. P. HOLBROOK.

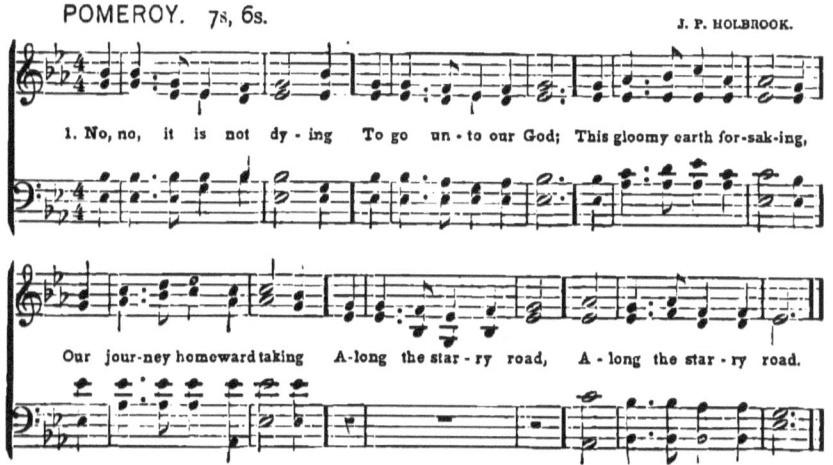

564 R. P Dunn. tr.

No, no, it is not dying
To go unto our God;
This gloomy earth forsaking,
Our journey homeward taking
Along the starry road.

2 No, no, it is not dying
Heaven's citizen to be;
A crown immortal wearing,
And rest unbroken sharing,
From care and conflict free.

3 No, no, it is not dying
To wear a heavenly crown;
Among God's people dwelling,
The glorious triumph swelling,
Of him whose sway we own.

4 O, no, this is not dying,
Thou Saviour of mankind!
There, streams of love are flowing,
No hindrance ever knowing;
Here, only drops we find.

LANGTON. S. M. — ABR. C. STREATFIELD.

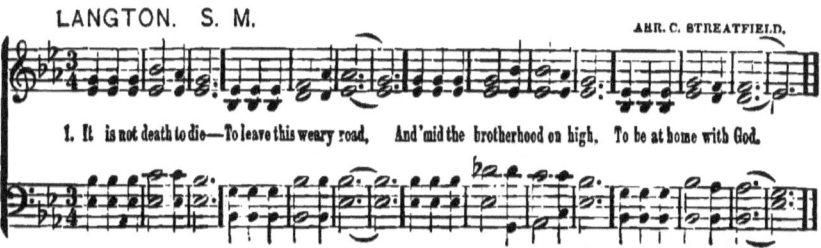

565 G. W. Bethune, tr.

It is not death to die—
To leave this weary road,
And 'mid the brotherhood on high,
To be at home with God.

2 It is not death to close
The eye long dimmed by tears,
And wake, in glorious repose
To spend eternal years.

3 It is not death to fling
Aside this sinful dust,
And rise, on strong exulting wing,
To live among the just.

4 Jesus, thou Prince of life!
Thy chosen cannot die;
Like thee, they conquer in the strife,
To reign with thee on high.

DEATH.

300 NOYES. 6s, 4s.   J. P. HOLBROOK.

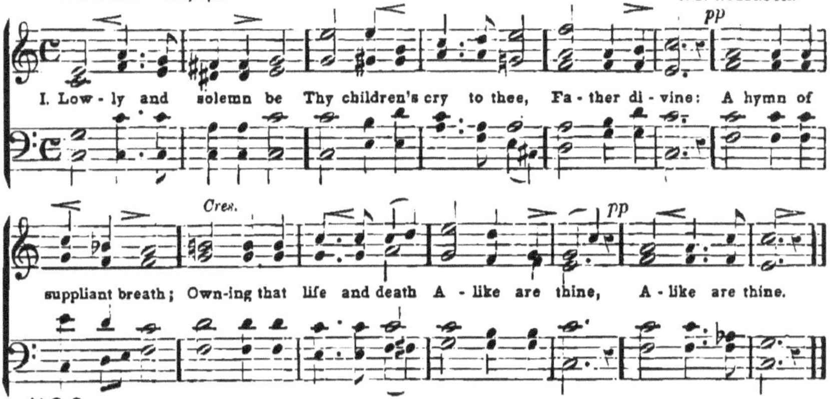

1. Lowly and solemn be Thy children's cry to thee, Father divine: A hymn of suppliant breath; Owning that life and death Alike are thine, Alike are thine.

566   *F. D. Hemans.*

Lowly and solemn be
Thy children's cry to thee,
  Father divine:
A hymn of suppliant breath;
Owning that life and death
  Alike are thine.

2 O Father, in that hour,
When earth all helping power
  Shall disavow;
When spear, and shield, and crown,
In faintness are cast down;
  Sustain us, Thou.

3 By Him who bowed to take
The death-cup for our sake,
  The thorn, the rod;
From whom the last dismay
Was not to pass away;
  Aid us, O God.

4 Tremblers beside the grave,
We call on thee to save,
  Father divine:
Hear, hear our suppliant breath,
Keep us in life and death,
  Thine, only thine.

CROSS. L. M.   J. B. DYKES.
Slow.

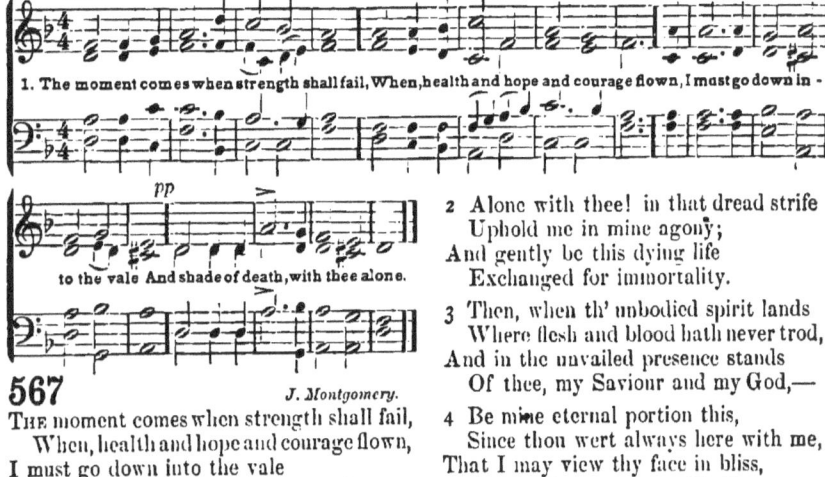

1. The moment comes when strength shall fail, When health and hope and courage flown, I must go down into the vale And shade of death, with thee alone.

567   *J. Montgomery.*

The moment comes when strength shall fail,
  When, health and hope and courage flown,
I must go down into the vale
  And shade of death, with thee alone.

2 Alone with thee! in that dread strife
  Uphold me in mine agony;
And gently be this dying life
  Exchanged for immortality.

3 Then, when th' unbodied spirit lands
  Where flesh and blood hath never trod,
And in the unvailed presence stands
  Of thee, my Saviour and my God,—

4 Be mine eternal portion this,
  Since thou wert always here with me,
That I may view thy face in bliss,
  And be for evermore with thee.

"Blessed are the Dead." 301

CALVARY. L. M. — J. P. HOLBROOK.

568 *M. Mackay.*

Asleep in Jesus: blessed sleep,
From which none ever wakes to weep,
A calm and undisturbed repose,
Unbroken by the last of foes.

2 Asleep in Jesus: O how sweet
To be for such a slumber meet;
With holy confidence to sing,
That death hath lost his venomed sting.

3 Asleep in Jesus: peaceful rest,
Whose waking is supremely blest;
No fear, no woe, shall dim that hour
That manifests the Saviour's power.

4 Asleep in Jesus: O for me
May such a blissful refuge be;
Securely shall my ashes lie,
Waiting the summons from on high.

569 *A. L. Barbauld.*

How blest the righteous, when he dies,
When sinks a weary soul to rest;
How mildly beam the closing eyes,
How gently heaves th' expiring breast.

2 So fades a summer cloud away;
So sinks the gale, when storms are o'er;
So gently shuts the eye of day;
So dies a wave along the shore.

3 A holy quiet reigns around,
A calm which life nor death destroys;
And naught disturbs the peace profound,
Which his unfettered soul enjoys.

4 Life's labor done, as sinks the clay,
Light from its load the spirit flies;
While heaven and earth combine to say,
"How blest the righteous when he dies!"

BERA. L. M. — J. E. GOULD.

302 DEATH.

SAUL. L. M. G. F. HANDEL.

570
I. Watts.

UNVEIL thy bosom, faithful tomb;
　Take this new treasure to thy trust,
And give these sacred relics room
　To slumber in the silent dust.

2 Nor pain, nor grief, nor anxious fear,
　Invade thy bounds; no mortal woes
Can reach the peaceful sleeper here,
　While angels watch the soft repose.

3 So Jesus slept; God's dying Son
　Passed thro' the grave, and blessed the bed:
Rest here, blest saint, till from his throne
　The morning break, and pierce the shade.

4 Break from his throne, illustrious morn!
　Attend, O earth! his sovereign word:
Restore thy trust: a glorious form
　Shall then ascend to meet the Lord!

Hope and Expectation. 303

HANDY. L. M. 6l. J. P. HOLBROOK.

571

At evening time, let there be light;
Life's little day draws near its close;
Around me fall the shades of night,
The night of death, the grave's repose;
To crown my joys, to end my woes,
At evening time let there be light.

2 At evening time, let there be light;
Stormy and dark hath been my day;
Yet rose the morn divinely bright—
Dews, birds, and blossoms cheered the way;
O for one sweet, one parting ray—
At evening time let there be light.

3 At evening time there shall be light,
For God hath spoken—it must be;
Fear, doubt, and anguish take their flight,
His glory now is risen on me;
Mine eyes shall His salvation see;
'Tis evening time—and there *is* light.

ST. ALBINUS. P. M. H. J. GAUNTLETT.

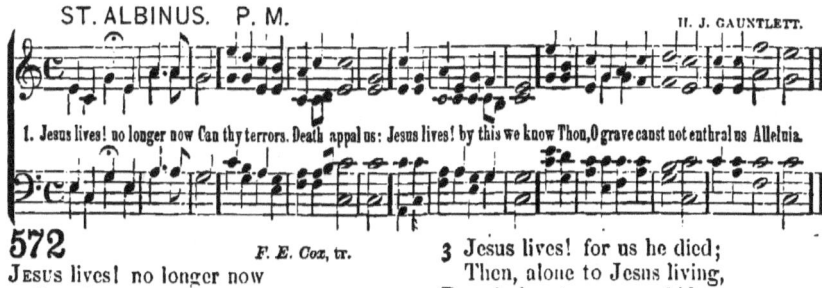

572
F. E. Cox, tr.

Jesus lives! no longer now
Can thy terrors, Death, appal us:
Jesus lives! by this we know
Thou, O grave canst not enthral us.

2 Jesus lives! henceforth is death
But the gate of life immortal;
This shall calm our trembling breath,
When we pass its gloomy portal.

3 Jesus lives! for us he died;
Then, alone to Jesus living,
Pure in heart may we abide,
Glory to our Saviour giving.

4 Jesus lives! our hearts know well
Nought from us his love shall sever;
Life, nor death, nor powers of hell
Tear us from his keeping ever.
Alleluia!

304 DEATH.

EWING. 7s, 6s.   ALEX. EWING.

1. There is a land immortal, The beautiful of lands; Beside its ancient portal A silent sentry stands; He only can undo it, And open wide the door; And mortals who pass through it, Are mortals nevermore.

573   *T. Mackellar.*

THERE is a land immortal,
　The beautiful of lands;
Beside its ancient portal
　A silent sentry stands;
He only can undo it,
　And open wide the door;
And mortals who pass through it,
　Are mortals nevermore.

2 Though dark and drear the passage
　That leadeth to the gate,
Yet grace comes with the message,
　To souls that watch and wait;
And at the time appointed
　A messenger comes down,
And leads the Lord's anointed
　From cross to glory's crown.

3 Their sighs are lost in singing,
　They're blessèd in their tears;
Their journey heavenward winging,
　They leave on earth their fears:
Death like an angel seemeth;
　"We welcome thee," they cry;
Their face with glory beameth—
　'Tis life for them to die!

574   *R. Massie, tr.*

I KNOW no life divided,
　O Lord of life! from thee;
In thee is life provided
　For all mankind and me;
I know no death, O Jesus!
　Because I live in thee;
Thy death it is which frees us
　From death eternally.

2 I fear no tribulation,
　Since, whatsoe'er it be,
It makes no separation
　Between my Lord and me;
If thou, my God and Teacher!
　Vouchsafe to be my own,
Though poor, I shall be richer
　Than monarch on his throne.

3 If, while on earth I wander,
　My heart is light and blest,
Ah, what shall I be yonder
　In perfect peace and rest?
O blessed thought in dying,
　We go to meet the Lord,
Where there shall be no sighing,
　His joy our full reward.

Hope and Expectation. 305

LANCASHIRE. 7s, 6s.　　　　　　　　　　　H. SMART.

575
J. Borthwick, tr.

REJOICE, rejoice, believers,
　And let your lights appear;
The evening is advancing,
　And darker night is near.
The Bridegroom is arising,
　And soon he will draw nigh;
Up, pray, and watch, and wrestle,
　At midnight comes the cry.

2 See that your lamps are burning,
　Replenish them with oil;
Look now for your salvation,
　The end of earthly toil.
The watchers on the mountain
　Proclaim the Bridegroom near,
Go meet him as he cometh,
　With hallelujahs clear.

3 O wise and holy virgins,
　Now raise your voices higher,
Till, in your songs of triumph,
　Ye meet the angel choir.

The marriage-feast is waiting;
　The gates wide open stand;
Up, up, ye heirs of glory,
　The Bridegroom is at hand.

4 Ye saints, who here in patience
　Your cross and sufferings bore,
Shall live and reign for ever,
　When sorrow is no more;
Around the throne of glory
　The Lamb ye shall behold,
In triumph cast before him
　Your diadems of gold.

5 Our Hope and Expectation,
　O Jesus! now appear;
Arise, thou Sun so longed for!
　O'er this benighted sphere;
With hearts and hands uplifted,
　We plead, O Lord! to see
The day of our redemption,
　That brings us unto thee.

306 DEATH.

MOULTRIE. 14s. G. A. MACFARREN.

1. Behold, the Bridegroom cometh in the middle of the night,
And blest is he whose loins are girt, whose lamp is burning bright;
But woe to that dull servant, whom his Master shall surprise,
With lamp untrimmed, unburning, and with slumber in his eyes.

576
G. Moultrie.

Behold, the Bridegroom cometh in the middle of the night,
And blest is he whose loins are girt, whose lamp is burning bright;
But woe to that dull servant, whom his Master shall surprise
With lamp untrimmed, unburning, and with slumber in his eyes.

2 Do thou, my soul, keep watch, beware lest thou in sleep sink down,
Lest thou be given o'er to death, and lose the golden crown;
But see that thou be sober, with a watchful eye, and thus
Cry "Holy, holy, holy God, have mercy upon us."

3 That day, the day of fear, shall come; my soul, slack not thy toil,
But light thy lamp, and feed it well, and make it bright with oil;
Thou knowest not how soon may sound the cry at eventide,
"Behold, the Bridegroom comes. Arise! He comes to meet the Bride."

4 Beware, my soul, take thou good heed, lest thou in slumber lie,
And, like the five, remain without, and knock, and vainly cry;
But watch, and bear thy lamp undimmed, and Christ shall gird thee on
His own bright wedding-robe of light, the glory of the Son.

Hope and Expectation. 307

WOOLSEY. 8s, 7s. W. H. HAVERGAL.

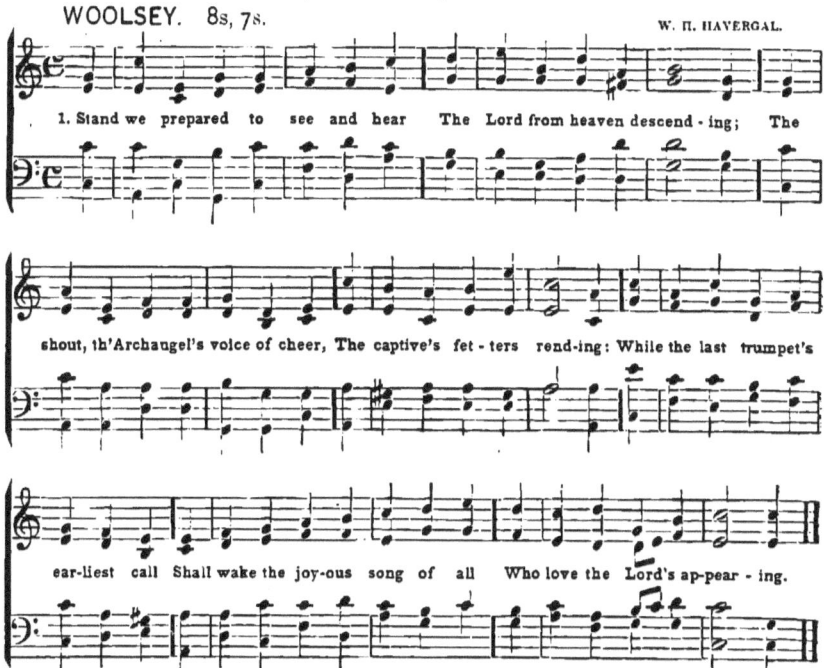

1. Stand we prepared to see and hear The Lord from heaven descending; The shout, th' Archangel's voice of cheer, The captive's fetters rending: While the last trumpet's earliest call Shall wake the joyous song of all Who love the Lord's appearing.

577

Stand we prepared to see and hear
  The Lord from heaven descending;
The shout, the Archangel's voice of cheer,
  The captive's fetters rending:
While the last trumpet's earliest call
Shall wake the joyous song of all
  Who love the Lord's appearing.

2 The dead in Christ shall first arise,
  From sweetest sleep awaking;
While living saints, with rapt surprise,
  The wondrous change partaking,
Shall hear the Bridegroom's coming feet,
And with their lamps go forth to meet
  The Lord for whom they waited.

3 Far spent the night, the morn is nigh,
  It is no time for sleeping;
A moment's twinkling of an eye
  May end the night of weeping;
Eternity of bliss begun,
Forever with the Bridegroom one,
  When time shall be no longer!

4 Grant us, O Christ, this grace to win,
  Thy ransomed flock implore thee;
With oil-fed lamps to enter in,
  And stand unblamed before thee.
So may we in thy triumph share,
Caught up to meet thee in the air,
  And come with thee in glory.

578 R. Massie, tr.

Lord, thou hast joined my soul to thine
  In bonds no power can sever;
Grafted in thee, the living Vine,
  I shall be thine for ever.
Lord, when I die, I die to thee,
Thy precious death hath won for me
  A life that never endeth.

2 Since thou hast risen from the grave,
  The grave cannot detain me;
"Christ died, Christ rose again," to save.
  These words shall now sustain me.
For where thou art, there I shall be,
That I may ever live with thee;
  This is my joy in dying.

DEATH.

SEYMOUR. 7s.

579 O. Winkworth, tr.

Christ will gather in his own
To the place where he is gone;
Where their heart and treasure lie,
Where our life is hid on high.
2 Day by day the voice saith "Come,
Enter this eternal home;"
Asking not if we can spare
This dear soul its summons there.

3 But the Lord doth naught amiss,
And, since he hath ordered this,
We have naught to do but still
Rest in silence on His will.
4 Many a heart no longer here,
Ah! was all too inly dear:
Yet, O Love, 'tis thou dost call,
Thou wilt be our All in all.

LESLIE. C. M.

580 E. H. Bickersteth.

So heaven is gathering, one by one,
  To its eternal rest,
All that is pure and permanent
  And beautiful and blest.
2 The family is scattered yet,
  Though of one home and heart:
Part militant in earthly gloom,
  In heavenly glory part.

3 But who can speak the rapture, when
  The number is complete;
And all the children sundered now
  Around one Father meet?
4 One fold, one Shepherd, one employ,
  One everlasting home,
Our Father's house, from whose dear rest,
  No wanderer e'er shall rove.

Hope and Expectation.

PAXTON. 8s. A. H. MANN.

1. We speak of the realms of the blest, That country so bright and so fair, And oft are its glories confessed; But what must it be to be there! We speak of its freedom from sin, From sorrow, temptation, and care, From trials without and within: But what must it be to be there!

581
E. Mills.

We speak of the realms of the blest,
 That country so bright and so fair,
And oft are its glories confessed;
 But what must it be to be there!
We speak of its freedom from sin,
 From sorrow, temptation, and care,
From trials without and within:
 But what must it be to be there!

2 We speak of its service of love,
 The robes which the glorified wear,
The church of the first-born above;
 But what must it be to be there!
Do thou, Lord, 'mid sorrow and woe,
 For heaven my spirit prepare,
And shortly I also shall know,
 And feel what it is to be there.

582
W. Cowper.

My Saviour, whom absent I love;
 Whom, not having seen, I adore;
Whose name is exalted above
 All glory, dominion and power.
Dissolve thou these bands that detain
 My soul from her portion in thee,
Ah! strike off this adamant chain,
 And make me eternally free.

2 When that happy era begins,
 When arrayed in thy glories I shine,
Nor grieve any more, by my sins,
 The bosom on which I recline,—
O then shall the vail be removed!
 And round me thy brightness be pour'd;
I shall meet him whom absent I loved,
 I shall see whom unseen I adored.

Hope and Expectation.

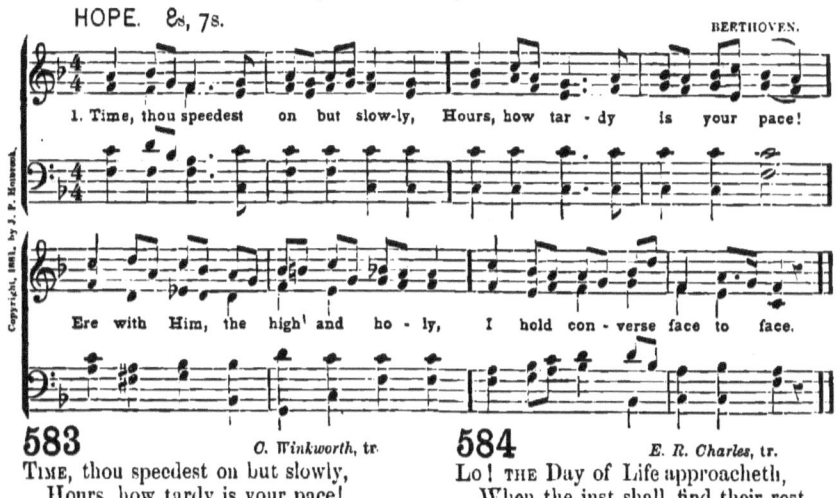

583 *C. Winkworth, tr.*

Time, thou speedest on but slowly,
Hours, how tardy is your pace!
Ere with Him, the high and holy,
I hold converse face to face.

2 Here is nought but care and mourning;
Comes a joy, it will not stay;
Fairly shines the sun at dawning,
Night will soon o'ercloud the day.

3 Onward then! not long I wander
Ere my Saviour comes for me,
And with him abiding yonder,
All his glory I shall see.

4 O the music and the singing
Of the host redeemed by love!
O the hallelujahs ringing
Through the halls of light above!

584 *E. R. Charles, tr.*

Lo! the Day of Life approacheth,
When the just shall find their rest,
When the wicked cease from troubling,
And the patient reign most blest.

2 O how past all utterance happy,
Sweet and joyful it will be,
When they who, unseen, have loved him,
Jesus face to face shall see!

3 There the peace will be unbroken,
Deep and solemn joy be shed,
Youth in fadeless flower and freshness,
And salvation perfected.

4 To those realms, just Judge, O call me,
Deign to open that blest gate,
Thou whom, seeking, looking, longing,
I with eager hope await!

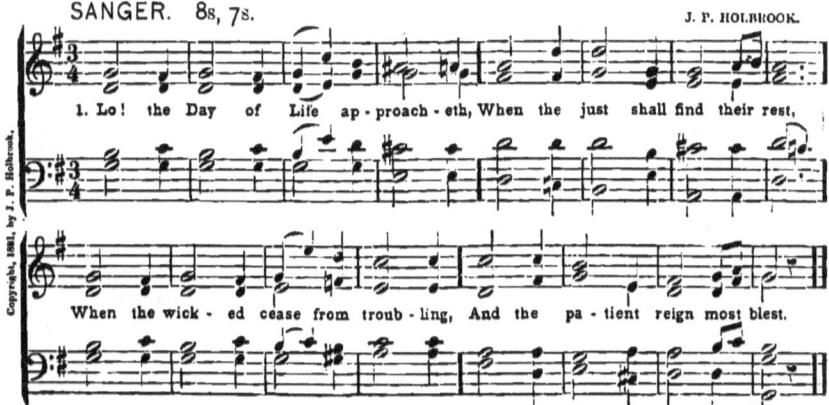

DEATH.

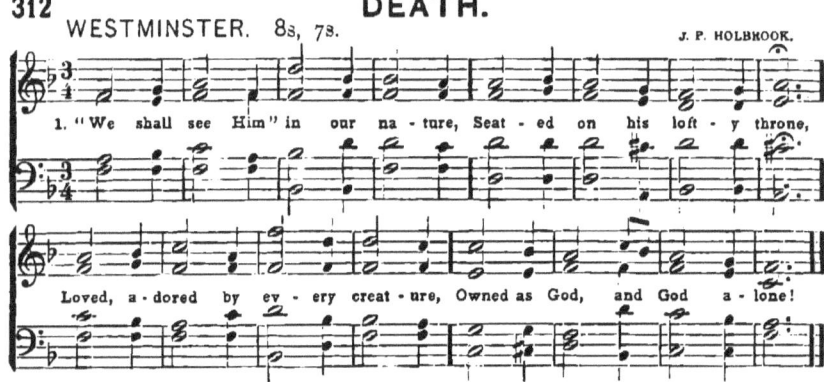

585

"We shall see Him" in our nature,
Seated on his lofty throne,
Loved, adored, by every creature,
Owned as God, and God alone!

2 There the hosts of shining spirits
Strike their harps, and loudly sing
To the praise of Jesus' merits,
To the glory of their King.

3 When we pass o'er death's dark river,
"We shall see him as he is,"
Resting in his love and favor,
Owning all the glory his.

4 There to cast our crowns before him,
O what bliss the thought affords!
There forever to adore him,
King of kings, and Lord of lords!

586
C. Elliott.

Let me be with thee where thou art,
My Saviour, my eternal Rest;
Then only will this longing heart
Be fully and for ever blest.

2 Let me be with thee where thou art,
Thine unvailed glory to behold;
Then only will this wandering heart
Cease to be false to thee and cold.

3 Let me be with thee where thou art,
Where spotless saints thy name adore;
Then only will this sinful heart
Be evil and defiled no more.

4 Let me be with thee where thou art,
Where none can die, where none remove;
There neither death nor life will part
Me from thy presence and thy love.

Hope and Expectation. 313

·587   *J. Conder.*

Jesus, blessèd Mediator,
  Thou the airy path hast trod;
Thou the Judge, the Consummator!
  Shepherd of the fold of God!
Can I trust a fellow-being?
  Can I trust an angel's care?
O thou merciful All-seeing!
  Beam around my spirit there.

2 Blessèd fold! no foe can enter;
  And no friend departeth thence;
Jesus is their sun, their centre,
  And their shield Omnipotence!
Blessèd, for the Lamb shall feed them,
  All their tears shall wipe away,
To the living fountains lead them,
  Till fruition's perfect day.

3 Lo, it comes, that day of wonder!
  Louder chorals shake the skies:
Hades' gates are burst asunder;
  See! the new-clothed myriads rise!
Thought, repress thy weak endeavor!
  Here must reason prostrate fall;
O the ineffable Forever!
  And the eternal All in All!

DEATH.

588 *H. Bonar.*
Far beyond our skies of gladness,
Far beyond our clouds of sadness,
Are the many mansions fair:
Far from pain and sin and folly,
In the palace of the holy—
  I would find my mansion there.

2 Where the glory brightly dwelleth,
Where the new song sweetly swelleth,
  And the discord never comes;
Where life's stream is ever laving,
And the palm is ever waving;—
  That must be the Home of homes.

3 Where the Lamb on high is seated,
By ten thousand voices greeted:
  Lord of lords, and King of kings.
Son of Man, they crown, they crown him,
Son of God, they own, they own him,
  With his Name the palace rings.

4 Blessing, honor, without measure,
Heav'nly riches, earthly treasure,
  Lay we at his blessèd feet.
Poor the praise that now we render,
Loud shall be our voices yonder,
  When before his throne we meet.

589
Lo, THE seal of death is breaking;
These who slept its sleep are waking;
  Heaven opes its portals fair!
Hark! the harps of God are ringing,
Hark! the seraph's hymn is flinging
  Music on immortal air.

2 There, no more at eve declining,
Suns without a cloud are shining
  O'er the land of life and love;
There the founts of life are flowing,
Flowers unknown to time are blowing,
  In that radiant scene above.

3 There no sigh of memory swelleth;
There no tear of misery welleth;
  Hearts will bleed or break no more;
Past is all the cold world's scorning,
Gone the night and broke the morning
  Over all the golden shore!

The Judgment. 315

BARROWS. 8s, 6s. J. P. HOLBROOK.

590 *E. P. Barrows.*

Before the throne
All will be known—
Each prayer to God above,
Each act of holy love,
Each visit to the fatherless,
And to the widow in distress.
  Then why, with anxious thought
  Seek'st thou to blazon forth
The righteous deeds thy hands have wrought,
And tell the world thy worth?
T'is thine to serve the Omniscient Lord;
T'is his to grant thee thy reward.

2 Before the throne
All will be known—
Each thought and word unclean,
Each hidden deed of sin,
Each venomed shaft, with malice fraught,
In secret at the righteous shot.
  The crimes which men have done
  In darkness and in night,
At the tribunal of God's Son,
Shall all be brought to light;
There sin no more shall be concealed,
But all things hid shall be revealed.

3 Before the throne
All will be known—
The Israelite indeed
Of faithful Abraham's seed,
With shouts of welcome shall be hailed,
While hypocrites shall stand unveiled.
  Christ from his judgment seat
  Shall fan the human race;
The chaff be driven from the wheat,
And each shall find its place.
Pray then, that grace may make thee here
Such as thou wouldst at last appear.

THE JUDGMENT.

WALDRON. 8s, 7s, 4s.   E. MOSS.

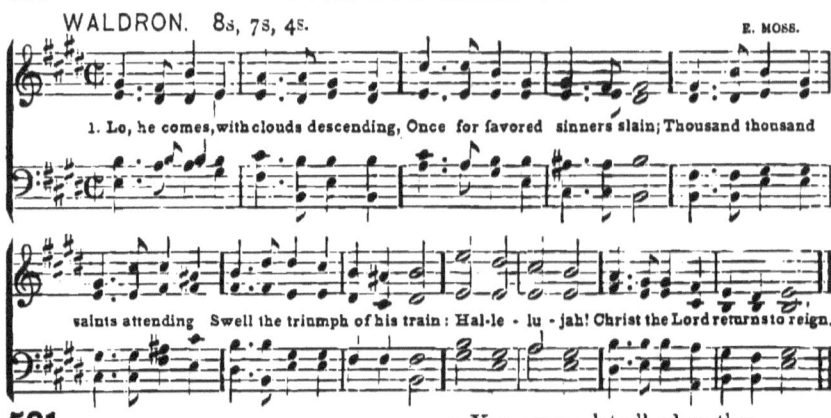

1. Lo, he comes, with clouds descending, Once for favored sinners slain; Thousand thousand saints attending Swell the triumph of his train: Hal-le-lu-jah! Christ the Lord returns to reign.

591   *C. Wesley.*
Lo, He comes, with clouds descending,
  Once for favored sinners slain;
Thousand thousand saints attending
  Swell the triumph of his train:
    Hallelujah!
  Christ the Lord returns to reign.

2 Every eye shall now behold him,
  Robed in dreadful majesty;
Those who set at nought and sold him,
  Pierced and nailed him to the tree,
    Deeply wailing,
  Shall the true Messiah see.

3 Now redemption, long expected,
  See in solemn pomp appear:
All his saints, by men rejected,
  Now shall meet Him in the air:
    Hallelujah!
  See the day of God appear.

4 Yea, amen; let all adore thee,
  High on thine eternal throne;
Saviour, take the power and glory;
  Claim the kingdom for thine own:
    Lord! Jehovah!
  Everlasting God, come down!

592   *J. Newton.*
Day of Judgment—day of wonders!
  Hark!—the trumpet's awful sound,
Louder than a thousand thunders,
  Shakes the vast creation round!
    How the summons
  Will the sinner's heart confound!

2 See the Judge our nature wearing,
  Clothed in majesty divine!
You, who long for his appearing,
  Then shall say "This God is mine!"
    Gracious Saviour,
  Own me in that day for thine!

BREST. 8s, 7s, 4s.   L. MASON.

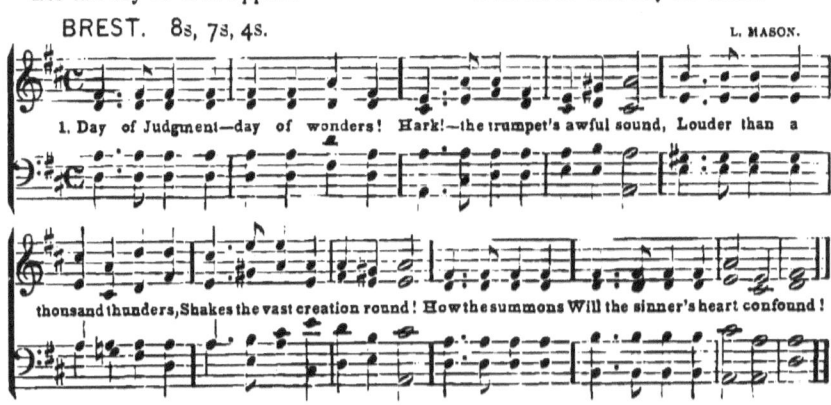

1. Day of Judgment—day of wonders! Hark!—the trumpet's awful sound, Louder than a thousand thunders, Shakes the vast creation round! How the summons Will the sinner's heart confound!

The Judgment. 317

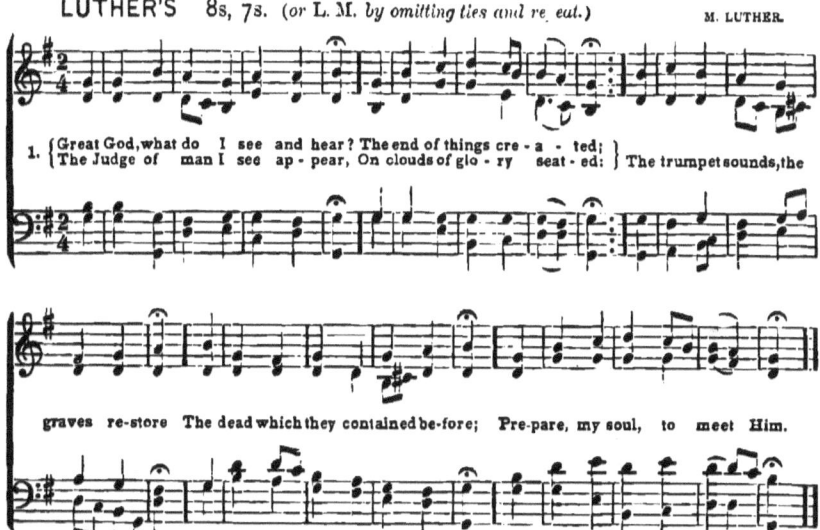

LUTHER'S 8s, 7s. (*or* L. M. *by omitting ties and re eat.*)   M. LUTHER.

1. Great God, what do I see and hear? The end of things cre-a-ted; The Judge of man I see ap-pear, On clouds of glo-ry seat-ed: The trumpet sounds, the graves re-store The dead which they contained be-fore; Pre-pare, my soul, to meet Him.

593
W. B. Collyer, tr.

GREAT God, what do I see and hear?
The end of things created;
The Judge of man I see appear,
On clouds of glory seated:
The trumpet sounds, the graves restore
The dead which they contained before;
Prepare, my soul, to meet Him.

2 The dead in Christ shall first arise,
At the last trumpet's sounding;
Caught up to meet him in the skies,
With joy their Lord surrounding;
No gloomy fears their souls dismay,
His presence sheds eternal day
On those prepared to meet Him.

3 Great God, what do I see and hear?
The end of things created;
The Judge of man I see appear,
On clouds of glory seated;
Beneath his cross I view the day,
When heaven and earth shall pass away,
And thus prepare to meet Him.

594
I. Watts.

HE reigns! the Lord, the Saviour reigns!
Sing to his name in lofty strains;
Let the whole earth in songs rejoice,
And in his praise exalt their voice!

2 Deep are his counsels, and unknown;
But grace and truth support his throne:
Tho' gloomy clouds his ways surround,
Justice is their eternal ground.

3 In robes of judgment, lo! he comes,—
Shakes the wide earth, and cleaves the tombs;
Then lift your heads, ye saints, on high,
And sing, for your redemption's nigh!

595
W. Scott.

THAT day of wrath! that dreadful day,
When heaven and earth shall pass away!
What power shall be the sinner's stay?
How shall he meet that dreadful day?—

2 When, shriveling like a parched scroll,
The flaming heavens together roll,
And louder yet, and yet more dread,
Swells the high trump that wakes the dead!

3 O, on that day, that wrathful day,
When man to judgment wakes from clay,
Be thou, O Christ, the sinner's stay,
Tho' heaven and earth shall pass away.

HEAVEN.

ANGELIC SONGS. 11s, 10s.

H. SMART.

1. Hark, hark, my soul! angelic songs are swelling O'er earth's green fields and ocean's wave-beat shore: How sweet the truth those blessed strains are telling Of that new life when sin shall be no more!

CHORUS. An-gels of Je-sus, an-gels of light, Sing-ing to wel-come the pilgrims of the night! Sing-ing to wel-come the pilgrims, the pilgrims of the night!

596
F. W. Faber.

Hark, hark, my soul! angelic songs are swelling
O'er earth's green fields and ocean's wave-beat shore:
How sweet the truth those blessed strains are telling
Of that new life when sin shall be no more!

2 Onward we go, for still we bear them singing,
"Come, weary souls, for Jesus bids you come;"
And through the dark, its echoes sweetly ringing,
The music of the gospel leads us home.

3 Rest comes at length, though life be long and dreary;
The day must dawn, and darksome night be past;
All journeys end in welcome to the weary,
And heaven, the heart's true home, will come at last.

4 Angels, sing on! your faithful watches keeping;
Sing us sweet fragments of the songs above;
Till morning's joy shall end the night of weeping,
And life's long shadows break in cloudless love.

The Eternal Day. 319

STORRS. 9s, 8s.
J. P. HOLBROOK.

1. Christian, the morn breaks sweetly o'er thee, And all the midnight shadows flee, Tinged are the distant skies with glory, A beacon light hung out for thee; Arise, arise! the light breaks o'er thee; Thy name is graven on the throne; Thy home is in the world of glory, Where thy Redeemer reigns alone.

597
I. B. Woodbury.

CHRISTIAN, the morn breaks sweetly o'er thee,
  And all the midnight shadows flee,
Tinged are the distant skies with glory,
  A beacon light hung out for thee;
Arise, arise! the light breaks o'er thee;
  Thy name is graven on the throne;
Thy home is in the world of glory,
  Where thy Redeemer reigns alone.

2 Tossed on times's rude, relentless surges,
  Calmly composed, and dauntless stand,
For lo! beyond those scenes emerges
  The height that bounds the promised land:

Behold! behold! the land is nearing,
  Where the wild sea-storm's rage is o'er;
Hark! how the heavenly hosts are cheering,
  See in what throngs they range the shore!
3 Cheer up! cheer up! the day breaks o'er thee,
  Bright as the summer's noon-tide ray,
The star-gemmed crowns and realms of glory
  Invite thy happy soul away;
Away! away! leave all for glory,
  Thy name is graven on the throne;
Thy home is in that world of glory,
  Where thy Redeemer reigns alone.

HEAVEN.

PARADISE. 8s, 6s, 6s.   J. BARNBY.

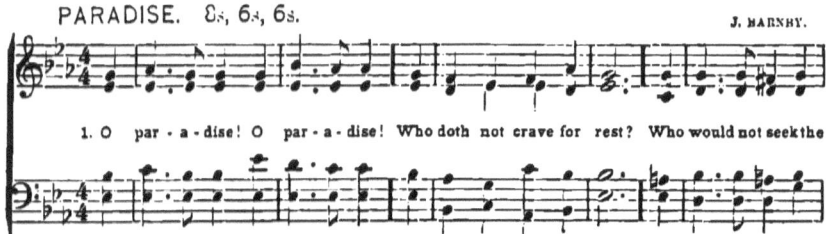

1. O par-a-dise! O par-a-dise! Who doth not crave for rest? Who would not seek the

hap-py land Where they that loved are blest? Where loy - - al hearts and true Stand

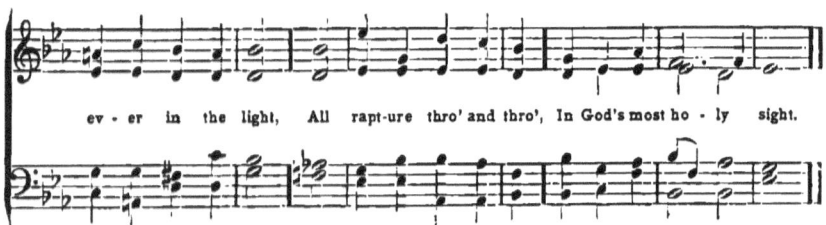

ev - er in the light, All rapt-ure thro' and thro', In God's most ho - ly sight.

---

598   *F. W. Faber.*

O PARADISE, O paradise,
  Who doth not crave for rest,
Who would not seek the happy land
  Where they that loved are blest?
    Where loyal hearts and true
    Stand ever in the light,
All rapture through and through,
  In God's most holy sight.

2 O paradise, O paradise,
  The world is growing old;
Who would not be at rest and free
  Where love is never cold?

3 O paradise, O paradise,
  'Tis weary waiting here;

I long to be where Jesus is,
  To feel, to see Him near;

4 O paradise, O paradise,
  I want to sin no more,
I want to be as pure on earth
  As on thy spotless shore;

5 O paradise, O paradise,
  I greatly long to see
The special place my dearest Lord
  In love prepares for me;

6 O paradise, O paradise,
  I feel 'twill not be long;
Patience! I almost think I hear
  Faint fragments of thy song.

The Eternal City. 321

HEAVENLY CITY. 7s, D.

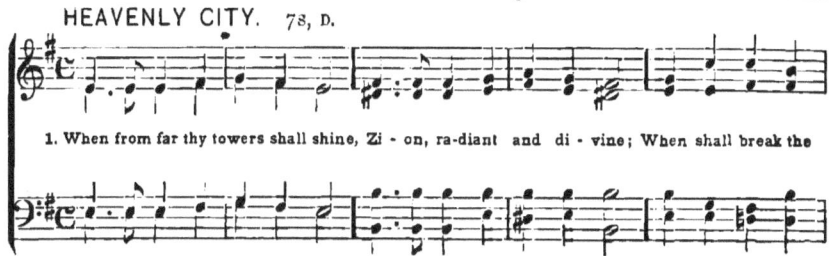

1. When from far thy towers shall shine, Zi-on, ra-diant and di-vine; When shall break the

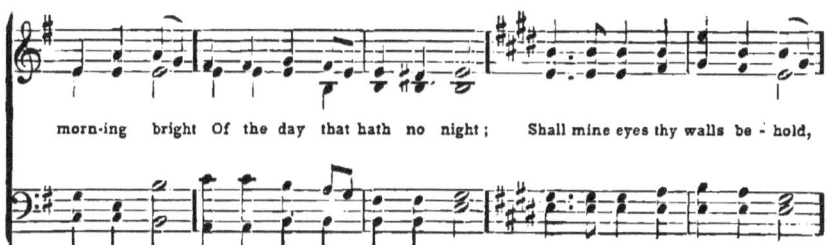

morn-ing bright Of the day that hath no night; Shall mine eyes thy walls be-hold,

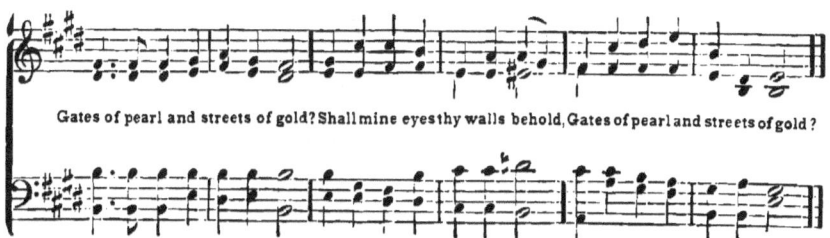

Gates of pearl and streets of gold? Shall mine eyes thy walls behold, Gates of pearl and streets of gold?

599   *H. Downton.*

WHEN from far thy towers shall shine,
Zion, radiant and divine;
When shall break the morning bright
Of the day that hath no night;
Shall mine eyes thy walls behold,
Gates of pearl and streets of gold?

2 At each portal keepeth ward,
Evermore, an angel guard;
Can my soul his dread glance bear,
When I claim to enter there?
Shall my feet be found in thee,
Glorious city of the free?

3 Needs no candle there, nor sun;
Shines in thee the Holy One!
While unnumbered harps proclaim
Glory to the Saviour's name,
Shall my weak and faltering tongue
Join the everlasting song?

4 Lamb of God! my ransomed soul
In thy book of life enrol;
Thy new name to me reveal;
On my forehead print thy seal;
So shall I thy glories see,
Zion, city of the free.

HEAVEN.

BERNARD. 7s, 6s.   J. P. HOLBROOK

1. Brief life is here our por-tion; Brief sor-row, short-lived care; The life that knows no end-ing, The tear-less life, is there. O hap-py re-tri-bu-tion: Short toil, e-ter-nal rest; For mor-tals and for sin-ners A mansion with the blest.

600   J. M. Neale, tr.

Brief life is here our portion;
  Brief sorrow, short-lived care;
The life that knows no ending,
  The tearless life, is there.
O happy retribution:
  Short toil, eternal rest;
For mortals and for sinners
  A mansion with the blest.

2 And now we fight the battle,
  But then shall wear the crown
Of full and everlasting
  And passionless renown.
And he whom now we trust in
  Shall then be seen and known;
And they that know and see him
  Shall have him for their own.

3 The morning shall awaken,
  The shadows shall decay,
And each true-hearted servant
  Shall shine as doth the day.
There God our king and portion,
  In fullness of his grace,
Shall we behold forever,
  And worship face to face.

601   J. M. Neale, tr.

For thee, O dear, dear country,
  Mine eyes their vigils keep;
For very love, beholding
  Thy happy name, they weep.
The mention of thy glory
  Is unction to the breast,
And medicine in sickness,
  And love, and life, and rest.

2 O one, O only mansion,
  O paradise of joy,
Where tears are ever banished,
  And smiles have no alloy;
The Lamb is all thy splendor,
  The Crucified thy praise;
His laud and benediction
  Thy ransomed people raise.

3 O sweet and blessèd country,
  The home of God's elect,
O sweet and blessèd country
  That eager hearts expect:
Jesus, in mercy bring us
  To that dear land of rest;
Who art with God the Father,
  And Spirit, ever blest.

Jerusalem Above. 323

EWING. 7s, 6s.   ALEXANDER EWING.

1. Je-ru-sa-lem the gold-en, With milk and hon-ey blest, Be-neath thy con-tem-pla-tion Sink heart and voice op-prest: I know not, O I know not What so-cial joys are there; What ra-dian-cy of glo-ry, What light beyond com-pare.

602   *J. M. Neale,* tr.

JERUSALEM, the golden,
  With milk and honey blest!
Beneath thy contemplation
  Sink heart and voice oppressed:
I know not, O, I know not
  What social joys are there,
What radiancy of glory,
  What light beyond compare.

2 O happy, holy portion,
  Refection for the blest,
True vision of true beauty,
  True cure of the distrest;
The home of fadeless splendor,
  Whose flowers for aye adorn,
Where they shall dwell as children,
  Who here as exiles mourn.

603   *J. M. Neale,* tr.

JERUSALEM, the glorious,
  The home of the elect,
O dear and future vision
  That eager hearts expect:
E'en now by faith I see thee,
  E'en here thy walls discern;
To thee my thoughts are kindled,
  And strive and pant and yearn.

2 They stand, those halls of Zion,
  All jubilant with song,
And bright with many an angel,
  And all the martyr throng:
The Prince is ever in them,
  The daylight is serene;
The pastures of the blessèd
  Are decked in glorious sheen

3 There is the throne of David;
  And there, from care released,
The shout of them that triumph,
  The song of them that feast;
And they who, with their Leader,
  Have conquered in the fight,
For ever and for ever
  Are clad in robes of white.

4 There all the halls of Zion
  For aye shall be complete,
And in the land of beauty
  All things of beauty meet.
Jerusalem! exulting
  On that securest shore,
I hope thee, wish thee, sing thee,
  And love thee evermore!

324 HEAVEN.

BEULAH. 7s, D.   ABB. E. IVES.

1. Who are these in bright array,
This innumerable throng,
Round the altar night and day,
Hymning one triumphant song:
"Worthy is the Lamb, once slain,
Blessing, honor, glory, power,
Wisdom, riches, to obtain,
New dominion every hour."

2 These through fiery trials trod;
These from great afflictions came;
Now, before the throne of God,
Sealed with his almighty Name;

604   J. Montgomery.

Clad in raiment pure and white,
Victor-palms in every hand,
Through their dear Redeemer's might,
More than conquerors they stand.

3 Hunger, thirst, disease unknown,
On immortal fruits they feed;
Them the Lamb amidst the throne,
Shall to living fountains lead;
Joy and gladness banish sighs,
Perfect love dispels all fear,
And forever from their eyes
God shall wipe away the tear.

The Innumerable Throng. 325

JUBILATE. 7s, 6s, 8s.   GERMAN.

605
H. Alford.

Ten thousand times ten thousand,
 In sparkling raiment bright
The armies of the ransomed saints
 Throng up the steeps of light:
Tis finished, all is finished,
 Their fight with death and sin:
Fling open wide the golden gates,
 And let the victors in.
  Ref.—O day, for which creation
   And all its tribes were made!
  O joy, for all its former woes
   A thousand fold repaid!

2 O then what raptured greetings
 On Canaan's happy shore,
What knitting severed friendships up,
 Where partings are no more!
Then eyes with joy shall sparkle,
 That brimmed with tears of late,
Orphans no longer fatherless,
 Nor widows desolate.—Ref.

3 Bring near thy great salvation
 Thou Lamb for sinners slain!
Fill up the roll of thine elect,
 Then take thy power and reign!
Appear, Desire of Nations,
 Thine exiles long for home!
Show in the heaven thy promised sign;
 Thou Prince and Saviour, Come!—Ref.

326 HEAVEN.

SMITH. 8s, 7s. HIMMEL.

1. Hark! the sound of holy voices, Chanting at the crystal sea,— Alleluia! alleluia! Alleluia! Lord! to thee. Multitude which none can number, Like the stars in glory stand, Clothed in white apparel, holding Palms of victory in their hands

606
C. Wordsworth.

Hark! the sound of holy voices,
　Chanting at the crystal sea,—
Alleluia! alleluia!
　Alleluia! Lord! to thee.
Multitude, which none can number,
　Like the stars in glory stand,
Clothed in white apparel, holding
　Palms of victory in their hands.

2 They have come from tribulation,
　And have washed their robes in blood,
Washed them in the blood of Jesus;
　Tried they were, and firm they stood.
Gladly, Lord! with thee they suffered;
　Gladly, Lord! with thee they died,
And, by death, to life immortal
　They were born and glorified.

3 God of God, the One-begotten,
　Light of Light, Emmanuel,
In whose body joined together
　All the saints for ever dwell.
Pour upon us of thy fullness,
　That we may for evermore
God the Father, God the Son, and
　God the Holy Ghost adore.

607

King of saints, to whom the number
　Of the starry host is known,
Many a name by man forgotten
　Lives forever round thy throne.
Lights which earth-born mists have darkened,
　There are shining full and clear—
Princes in the court of heaven,—
　Nameless, unremembered, here.

2 There, their record full is written,
　In the Lamb's great book of life—
All the faith, and prayer, and patience,
　All the toiling and the strife:
There are told thy hidden treasures:—
　Number us, O Lord, with them,
When thou makest up the jewels
　Of thy living diadem.

With Christ.

PALMER. C. M.   J. P. HOLBROOK.

1. Lord, it be-longs not to my care Wheth-er I die or live; To love and serve thee is my share, And this thy grace must give.

608   *R. Baxter.*

Lord, it belongs not to my care
Whether I die or live;
To love and serve thee is my share,
And this thy grace must give.

2 If life be long, I will be glad
That I may long obey;
If short, yet why should I be sad
To soar to endless day?

3 Christ leads me through no darker rooms
Than he went through before;
He that into God's kingdom comes
Must enter by this door.

4 Come, Lord, when grace hath made me meet
Thy blessèd face to see;
For if thy work on earth be sweet,
What will thy glory be?

5 Then I shall end my sad complaints,
And weary sinful days,
And join with the triumphant saints
That sing Jehovah's praise.

6 My knowledge of that life is small;
The eye of faith is dim;
But 'tis enough that Christ knows all,
And I shall be with him.

609   *I. Watts.*

When I can read my title clear
To mansions in the skies,
I bid farewell to every fear,
And wipe my weeping eyes.

2 Should earth against my soul engage,
And hellish darts be hurled,
Then I can smile at Satan's rage,
And face a frowning world.

3 Let cares like a wild deluge come,
And storms of sorrow fall;
May I but safely reach my home,
My God, my heaven, my all:

4 There shall I bathe my weary soul
In seas of heavenly rest,
And not a wave of trouble roll
Across my peaceful breast.

CLINTON. C. M.   J. P. HOLBROOK.

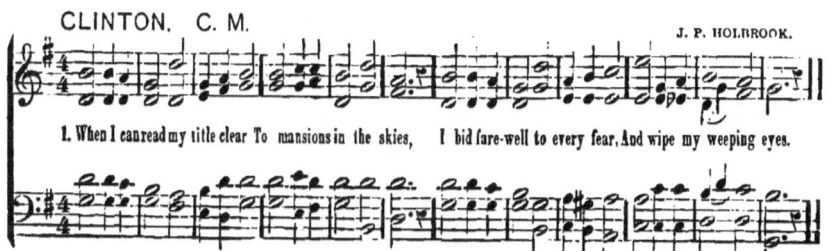

1. When I can read my title clear To mansions in the skies, I bid fare-well to every fear, And wipe my weeping eyes.

HEAVEN.

610
W. B. Tappan.

There is an hour of peaceful rest,
  To mourning wanderers given;
There is a joy for souls distressed,
  A balm for every wounded breast:
  'Tis found above—in heaven.

2 There is a home for weary souls,
  By sin and sorrow driven,—
When tossed on life's tempestuous shoals,
Where storms arise, and ocean rolls,
  And all is drear—but heaven.

3 There faith lifts up her cheerful eye
  To brighter prospects given;
And views the tempest passing by,
The evening shadows quickly fly,
  And all serene—in heaven.

611

O mother dear, Jerusalem!
  When shall I come to thee?
When shall my sorrows have an end?
  Thy joys when shall I see?

2 O happy harbor of God's saints!
  O sweet and pleasant soil!
In thee no sorrow may be found,
  Nor grief, nor care, nor toil.

3 No dimming cloud o'ershadows thee,
  Nor gloom, nor darksome night;
But every soul shines as the sun,
  For God himself is light.

4 Thy walls are made of precious stone,
  Thy bulwarks diamond-square;
Thy gates are all of orient pearl;
  O God! if I were there!

The Rest Eternal. 329

KELLOGG. C. M. D.   SCHUBERT.

1. There is a land of pure delight, Where saints immortal reign; Infinite day excludes the night, And pleasures banish pain. 2. There, everlasting spring abides, And never-withering flowers: Death, like a narrow sea, divides This heavenly land from ours.

612
I. Watts.

THERE is a land of pure delight,
  Where saints immortal reign;
Infinite day excludes the night,
  And pleasures banish pain.

2 There, everlasting spring abides,
  And never-withering flowers:
Death, like a narrow sea, divides
  This heavenly land from ours.

3 Sweet fields beyond the swelling flood,
  Stand dressed in living green:
So to the Jews old Canaan stood,
  While Jordan rolled between.

4 But timorous mortals start and shrink
  To cross this narrow sea,
And linger shivering on the brink,
  And fear to launch away.

5 O could we make our doubts remove,
  Those gloomy doubts that rise,
And see the Canaan that we love
  With unbeclouded eyes;

6 Could we but climb where Moses stood,
  And view the landscape o'er,
Not Jordan's stream, nor death's cold flood,
  Should fright us from the shore.

613

JERUSALEM, my happy home,
  Name ever dear to me,
When shall my labors have an end
  In joy, and peace, and thee?

2 When shall these eyes thy heaven-built
  And pearly gates behold;   [walls
Thy bulwarks with salvation strong,
  And streets of shining gold?

3 O when, thou City of my God,
  Shall I thy courts ascend,
Where congregations ne'er break up,
  And Sabbaths have no end?

4 There happier bowers than Eden's
  Nor sin nor sorrow know: [bloom,
Blest seats, through rude and stormy scenes
  I onward press to you.

5 Why should I shrink at pain and woe?
  Or feel at death dismay?
I've Canaan's goodly land in view,
  And realms of endless day.

6 Jerusalem, my happy home,
  My soul still pants for thee;
Then shall my labors have an end
  When I thy joys shall see.

HEAVEN.

STRICKLAND. S. M. D.   J. P. HOLBROOK

614

There is no night in heaven;
In that blest world above
Work never can bring weariness,
For work itself is love.

2 There is no grief in heaven;
For life is one glad day,
And tears are of those former things
Which all have passed away.

3 There is no want in heaven;
The Lamb of God supplies
Life's tree of twelve-fold fruitage still,
Life's spring which never dries.

4 There is no sin in heaven;
Behold that blessed throng!
All holy is their spotless robe,
All holy is their song.

5 There is no death in heaven;
For they who gain that shore
Have won their immortality,
And they can die no more.

6 Lord Jesus, be our guide,
O lead us safely on,
Till night and grief and sin and death
Are past, and heaven is won.

MAYO. S. M.   C. W. JORDAN.

Forever with the Lord. 331

OLMUTZ. S. M.   AEH. L. MASON.

615   *J. Montgomery.*

FOREVER with the Lord!
Amen, so let it be:
Life from the dead is in that word,
'Tis immortality.

2 Here in the body pent,
Absent from Him I roam,
Yet nightly pitch my moving tent
A day's march nearer home.

3 My Father's house on high,
Home of my soul, how near
At times to faith's far-seeing eye
The golden gates appear!

4 Ah, then my spirit faints
To reach the land I love,
The bright inheritance of saints,
Jerusalem above.

5 Knowing as I am known,
How shall I love that word,
And oft repeat before the throne,
"Forever with the Lord!"

AUSTEN. L. M.   DONIZETTI.

616   *I. Watts.*

WHAT sinners value I resign;
Lord 'tis enough that thou art mine:
I shall behold thy blissful face,
And stand complete in righteousness.

2 This life's a dream, an empty show;
But the bright world to which I go
Hath joys substantial and sincere:
When shall I wake and find me there!

3 O glorious hour, O blest abode,
I shall be near and like my God;
And flesh and sin no more control
The sacred pleasures of the soul.

4 My flesh shall slumber in the ground
Till the last trumpet's joyful sound;
Then burst the chains with sweet surprise,
And in my Saviour's image rise.

332 THE CHRISTIAN AND CHURCH.

First Lines of Hymns.

UNITY AND FELLOWSHIP.

HYMNS	
617	He is gone! and we remain,
618	One sole baptismal sign,
619	City of God, how broad and far
620	O where are kings and empires now
621	One holy Church of God appears
622	The City paved with gold,
623	For all the saints, who from
624	From all thy saints in warfare.
625	The saints of God! their conflict past,
626	Let saints below in concert sing
627	Happy the souls to Jesus joined
628	I love thy kingdom, Lord,
629	Far down the ages now
630	Blest be the tie that binds
631	Dear Saviour! we are thine,

PRAYER—REVIVAL.

632	From every stormy wind that blows,
633	And dost thou say, "Ask what thou?"
634	Sing to the Lord, and loud proclaim
635	Jesus, our best beloved Frien'!,
636	Prayer is the soul's sincere desire,
637	O for the happy hour
638	O Lord, thy work revive
639	Hark! through the courts of heaven
640	Saviour, visit thy plantation;
641	Hail, thou God of grace and glory.

CHARITIES—HELPFULNESS.

642	Thou to whom the sick and dying
643	O Fount of good, to own thy love
644	We give thee but thine own,
645	Thy life was given for me,
646	O Lord of heaven, and earth. and sea,
647	Mid the homes of want and woe,

MISSIONS.

648	Look from thy sphere of endless day,
649	Shine on our land, Jehovah, shine,
650	From Greenland's icy mountains,
651	Our country's voice is pleading,
652	The morning light is breaking,
653	Hail to the Lord's Anointed,
654	Jesus, we bow before thy throne,
655	Lord visit thy forsaken race,
656	Sovereign of worlds, display thy power
657	Soon may the last glad song arise
658	Arm of the Lord, awake!
659	O spirit of the living God,
660	Ascend thy throne, almighty King,
661	Now be the Gospel banner,
662	O that the Lord's salvation
663	Hasten the time appointed,
664	O Lord our God, arise!
665	O thou whom we adore!
666	Arise, O Lord, and shine
667	Gird on thy conquering sword,
668	Come, blessed Lord! let every shore
669	O God, the darkness roll away,
670	Let Zion and her sons rejoice
671	Onward speed thy conquering flight
672	Hark. the song of jubilee.
673	Hasten, Lord! the glorious time,
674	Shout the glad tidings,
675	Jesus shall reign where'er the sun
676	O Stone of God, by unseen hands
677	Triumphant Zion, lift thy head
678	Watchman! tell us of the night,
679	On the mountain's top appearing,
680	Souls in heathen darkness lying,
681	Lord, her watch thy Church is keeping,
682	Saviour, sprinkle many nations,
683	Sing, ye faithful, sing with gladness,
684	Come, kingdom of our God,
685	Come, Lord, and tarry not!

ST. EBBE. H. M.   R. REDHEAD.

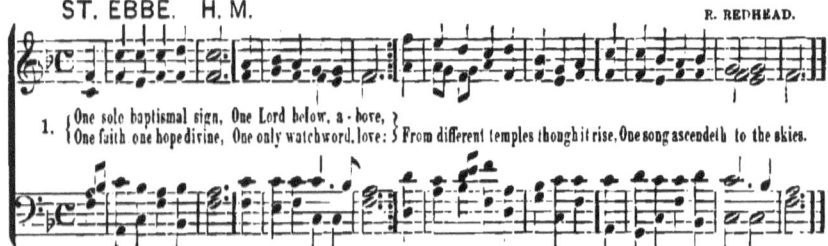

1. One sole baptismal sign, One Lord below, a-bove,
   One faith one hope divine, One only watchword, love: From different temples though it rise, One song ascendeth to the skies.

Unity and Fellowship. 333

HOLLINGSIDE. 7s. D. J. B. DYKES.

1. He is gone! and we re-main In this world of sin and pain: We have still his work to do, We can still his path pur-sue; Though himself we may not see. Com-fort-less we can-not be; For his Spir-it still is ours, Quickening, freshening all our powers.

617   *A. P. Stanley.*

He is gone! and we remain
In this world of sin and pain:
We have still his work to do,
We can still his path pursue;
Though himself we may not see,
Comfortless we cannot be;
For his Spirit still is ours,
Quickening, freshening all our powers.

2 He is gone! unto their goal
World and Church must onward roll;
Far behind we leave the past;
Forward all our glances cast:

Still his words before us range
Through the ages, as they change;
Wheresoe'er the truth shall lead,
He will give whate'er we need.

3 He is gone! but we once more
Shall behold him as before,
In the heaven of heavens the same
As on earth he went and came:
In the many mansions there,
Place for us he will prepare;
In that world unseen, unknown,
He and we shall yet be one.

618   H. M.   *G. Robinson.*

One sole baptismal sign,
  One Lord, below, above,
One faith, one hope divine,
  One only watchword—Love:
From different temples though it rise,
One song ascendeth to the skies.

2 Our sacrifice is one;
  One Priest before the throne;
The slain, the risen Son,
  Redeemer, Lord alone!
And sighs from contrite hearts that spring,
Our chief, our choicest offering.

3 Head of thy church beneath!
  The catholic, the true,
On all her members breathe;
  Her broken frame renew!
Then shall thy perfect will be done
When Christians love and live as one.

CHRISTIAN AND CHURCH.

DUNDEE. C. M.   *SCOTTISH.*

1. City of God, how broad and far
Out-spread thy walls sub-lime!
The true thy char-tered free-men are,
Of ev-ery age and clime.

619
S. Johnson.

City of God, how broad and far
 Outspread thy walls sublime!
The true thy chartered freemen are,
 Of every age and clime.

2 One holy Church, one army strong,
 One steadfast high intent,
One working band, one harvest-song,
 One King omnipotent!

3 How purely hath thy speech come down
 From man's primeval youth!
How grandly hath thine empire grown
 Of freedom, love, and truth!

4 How gleam thy watch-fires through the
 With never-fainting ray! [night
How rise thy towers serene and bright,
 To meet the dawning day!

5 In vain the surge's angry shock,
 In vain the drifting sands;
Unharmed, upon the Eternal Rock
 The Eternal City stands.

620
A. C. Coxe.

O where are kings and empires now
 Of old that went and came!
But, Lord, thy Church is praying yet,
 A thousand years the same.

2 We mark her goodly battlements,
 And her foundations strong;

We hear within the solemn voice
 Of her unending song.

3 For not like kingdoms of the world
 Thy holy Church, O God!
Though earthquake shocks are threaten-
 ing her,
And tempests are abroad;—

4 Unshaken as eternal hills,
 Immovable she stands,
A mountain that shall fill the earth,
 A house not made by hands.

621
S. Longfellow.

One holy Church of God appears
 Through every age and race,
Unwasted by the lapse of years,
 Unchanged by changing place.

2 From oldest time, on farthest shores,
 Beneath the pine or palm,
One unseen Presence she adores,
 With silence or with psalm.

3 Her priests are all God's faithful sons,
 To serve the world raised up;
The pure in heart her baptized ones,
 Love, her communion cup.

4 O living Church, thine errand speed;
 Fulfil thy task sublime;
With bread of life earth's hunger feed;
 Redeem the evil time!

Unity and Fellowship. 335

MALAN. H. M.

1. The cit-y paved with gold, Bright with each dazzling gem! When shall our eyes behold
The new Je-ru-sa-lem? Yet lo! e'en now in view-less might, Up-rise the
walls of liv-ing light! Yet lo! e'en now in viewless might Up-rise the walls of liv-ing light!

622

The City paved with gold,
 Bright with each dazzling gem!
When shall our eyes behold
 The new Jerusalem?
Yet lo! e'en now in viewless might
Uprise the walls of living light!

2 The kingdom of the Lord!
 It cometh not with show;
Nor throne, nor crown, nor sword,
 Proclaim its might below.
Though dimly scanned through mists of sin,
The Lord's true kingdom is within!

3 Not homeless wanderers here
 Our exile songs we sing;
Thou art our home most dear,
 Thou city of our King!
Thy future bliss we cannot tell,
Content in thee on earth we dwell.

4 Build, Lord, the mystic walls!
 Throw wide the unseen gates!
Fill all the golden halls,
 While yet thy triumph waits!
Make glad thy church with light and love,
Till glorified it shines above!

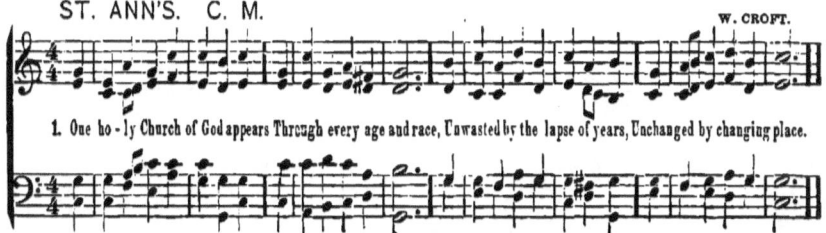

ST. ANN'S. C. M.   W. CROFT.

1. One ho-ly Church of God appears Through every age and race, Unwasted by the lapse of years, Unchanged by changing place.

CHRISTIAN AND CHURCH.

ALLELUIA. 10s. J. BARNBY.

623 W. W. How.

For all the saints, who from their | labors rest,
Who thee by faith before the | world confessed,
Thy name, O Jesus, be for | ever blest,
    Alleluia.

2 Thou wast their Rock, their Fortress | and their Might;
Thou Lord, their Captain in the | well-fought fight;
Thou, in the darkness drear, their | one true light. Alleluia.

3 O blest Communion, fellow | ship divine!
We feebly struggle; they in | glory shine;
Yet all are one in thee, for | all are thine.
    Alleluia.

4 And when the strife is fierce, the | warfare long,
Steals on the ear the distant | triumph song,
And hearts are brave again, and | arms are strong. Alleluia.

5 But lo, there breaks a yet more | glorious day;
The saints triumphant rise in | bright array;
The King of Glory passes | on his way.
    Alleluia.

6 From earth's wide bounds, from ocean's | farthest coast,
Through gates of pearl streams in the | countless host.
Singing to Father, Son, and | Holy Ghost. Alleluia,

CHANT. No. 2. A. H. D. TROYTE.

Unity and Fellowship.

BERNARD. 7s, 6s. J. P. HOLBROOK.

1. From all thy saints in warfare, For all thy saints at rest, To thee O blessed Jesus, All praises be addressed: Thou, Lord, didst win the battle That they might conquerors be; Their crowns of living glory Are lit with rays from thee.

624

From all thy saints in warfare,
 For all thy saints at rest,
To thee, O blessed Jesus,
 All praises be addressed:
Thou, Lord, didst win the battle
 That they might conquerors be;
Their crowns of living glory
 Are lit with rays from thee.

2 Apostles, prophets, martyrs,
 And all the sacred throng,
Who wear the spotless raiment,
 Who raise the ceaseless song;
For these passed on before us,
 Saviour, we thee adore,
And walking in their footsteps,
 Would serve thee more and more,

3 For grace which did in mercy
 For all their sins atone;
For love which hath ingathered
 The blessèd, one by one;
We praise thy name, O Saviour,
 And pray that we with them
May shine as precious jewels
 In thy bright diadem.

4 Then praise we God the Father,
 And praise we God the Son,
And God the Holy Spirit,
 Eternal Three in One;
Till all the ransomed number
 Fall down before the throne,
And honor, power, and glory
 Ascribe to God alone.

CHRISTIAN AND CHURCH.

EVANSTON. L. M. 6l. J. P. HOLBROOK.

1. The saints of God! their conflict past, And life's long battle won at last,
No more they need the shield or sword, They cast them down before their Lord:
O happy saints! for-ev-er blest, At Jesus' feet how safe their rest.

625

THE saints of God! their conflict past,
And life's long battle won at last,
No more they need the shield or sword,
They cast them down before their Lord;
 O happy saints! forever blest,
 At Jesus' feet how safe their rest!

2 The saints of God! their wanderings done,
No more their weary course they run,
No more they faint, no more they fall,
No foes oppress, no fears appal:
 O happy saints! for ever blest,
 In that dear home how sweet their rest.

3 The saints of God! life's voyage o'er,
Safe landed on that blissful shore,
No stormy tempests now they dread,
No whelming billows lift their head:
 O happy saints! forever blest,
 In that calm haven of their rest!

4 The saints of God their vigil keep
While yet their mortal bodies sleep,
Till from the dust they too shall rise
And soar triumphant to the skies:
 O happy saints! rejoice and sing,
 He quickly comes, your Lord and King

5 O God of saints! to thee we cry;
O Saviour! plead for us on high;
O Holy Ghost! our Guide and Friend,
Grant us thy grace till life shall end:
 That with all saints our rest may be
 In that bright Paradise with Thee!

Unity and Fellowship. 339

AZMON. C. M. — C. G. GLASER.

1. Let saints below in concert sing With those to glory gone;
For all the servants of our King In earth and heaven are one.

626 *C. Wesley.*

Let saints below in concert sing
With those to glory gone;
For all the servants of our King
In earth and heaven are one.

2 One family—we dwell in him—
One church above, beneath,
Though now divided by the stream,
The narrow stream of death;—

3 One army of the living God,
To his command we bow;
Part of the host have crossed the flood,
And part are crossing now.

4 Ev'n now to their eternal home
Some happy spirits fly;
And we are to the margin come,
And we expect to die.

5 Ev'n now, by faith, we join our hands
With those that went before,
And greet the ransomed blessèd bands
Upon the eternal shore.

6 Lord Jesus! be our constant guide:
And, when the word is given,
Bid death's cold flood its waves divide,
And land us safe in heaven.

627 *C. Wesley.*

Happy the souls to Jesus joined,
And saved by grace alone;
Walking in all his ways, they find
Their heaven on earth begun.

2 The church triumphant in thy love,
Their mighty joys we know:
They sing the Lamb in hymns above,
And we in hymns below.

3 Thee in thy glorious realm they praise,
And bow before thy throne;
We in the kingdom of thy grace:
The kingdoms are but one.

4 The holy to the holiest leads,
And thence our spirits rise;
For he that in thy statutes treads,
Shall meet thee in the skies.

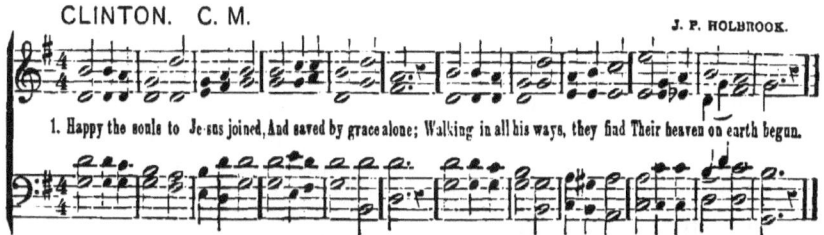

CLINTON. C. M. — J. P. HOLBROOK.

1. Happy the souls to Jesus joined, And saved by grace alone; Walking in all his ways, they find Their heaven on earth begun.

340 CHRISTIAN AND CHURCH.

SCHUMANN. S. M. — R. SCHUMANN.

628 *T. Dwight.*

I LOVE thy kingdom, Lord,—
 The house of thine abode,
The church our blest Redeemer saved
 With his own precious blood.

2 I love thy church, O God!
 Her walls before thee stand,
Dear as the apple of thine eye,
 And graven on thy hand.

3 For her my tears shall fall,
 For her my prayers ascend;
To her my cares and toils be given,
 Till cares and toils shall end.

4 Beyond my highest joy
 I prize her heavenly ways,
Her sweet communion, solemn vows,
 Her hymns of love and praise.

5 Jesus, thou Friend divine,
 Our Saviour and our King,
Thy hand from every snare and foe
 Shall great deliverance bring.

6 Sure as thy truth shall last,
 To Zion shall be given
The brightest glories earth can yield,
 And brighter bliss of heaven.

629 *H. Bonar.*

FAR down the ages now,
 Much of her journey done,
The pilgrim church pursues her way,
 Until her crown be won.

2 'Tis the same story still
 Of sin and weariness,
Of grace and love yet flowing down
 To pardon and to bless.

3 No wider is the gate,
 No broader is the way,
No smoother is the ancient path,
 That leads to light and day.

4 No sweeter is the cup,
 Nor less our lot of ill:
'Twas tribulation ages since,
 'Tis tribulation still.

5 No slacker grows the fight,
 No feebler is the foe,
Nor less the need of armor tried,
 Of shield and spear and bow.

6 Still faithful to our God,
 And to our Captain true,
We follow where He leads the way,
 The kingdom in our view.

Unity and Fellowship. 341

FERGUSON. S. M.   G. KINGSLEY.

1. Blest be the tie that binds Our hearts in Christian love: The fel-low-ship of kindred minds is like to that a - bove.

630   *J. Fawcett.*

BLEST be the tie that binds
  Our hearts in Christian love:
The fellowship of kindred minds
  Is like to that above.

2 Before our Father's throne
  We pour our ardent prayers;
Our fears, our hopes, our aims are one,
  Our comforts and our cares.

3 We share our mutual woes,
  Our mutual burdens bear;
And often for each other flows
  The sympathizing tear.

4 When we asunder part,
  It gives us inward pain;
But we shall still be joined in heart,
  And hope to meet again.

5 This glorious hope revives
  Our courage by the way;
While each in expectation lives,
  And longs to see the day.

6 From sorrow, toil, and pain,
  And sin, we shall be free,
And perfect love and friendship reign
  Through all eternity.

631   *P. Doddridge.*

DEAR Saviour! we are thine,
  By everlasting bands;
Our hearts, our souls, we would resign
  Entirely to thy hands.

2 Thy Spirit shall unite
  Our souls to thee, our Head;
Shall form in us thine image bright,
  And teach thy paths to tread.

3 Death may our souls divide
  From these abodes of clay;
But love shall keep us near thy side,
  Through all the gloomy way.

4 Since Christ and we are one,
  Why should we doubt or fear?
If he in heaven has fixed his throne,
  He'll fix his members there.

DENNIS. S. M.   NAGELI.

1. Dear Sav - iour! we are thine, By ev - er - last - ing bands;
Our hearts, our souls we would re - sign En - tire - ly to thy hands.

CHRISTIAN AND CHURCH.

ROSEDALE. L. M. — G. F. ROOT.

1. From every stormy wind that blows, From every swelling tide of woes, There is a calm, a sure retreat; 'Tis found beneath the mercy-seat.

632
H. Stowell.

From every stormy wind that blows,
From every swelling tide of woes,
There is a calm, a sure retreat;
'Tis found beneath the mercy-seat.

2 There is a place where Jesus sheds
The oil of gladness on our heads,—
A place, than all besides, more sweet;
It is the blood-bought mercy-seat.

3 There is a scene where spirits blend,
Where friend holds fellowship with friend;
Though sundered far, by faith they meet
Around one common mercy-seat.

4 There, there, on eagle wings we soar,
And sense and sin molest no more,
And heaven comes down our souls to greet,
And glory crowns the mercy-seat.

633
J. Newton.

And dost thou say, "Ask what thou wilt?"
Lord, I would seize the golden hour;
I pray to be released from guilt,
And freed from sin and Satan's power.

2 More of thy presence, Lord! impart;
More of thine image let me bear;
Erect thy throne within my heart,
And reign without a rival there.

3 Give me to read my pardon sealed,
And from thy joy to draw my strength;
To have thy boundless love revealed,
In all its height and breadth and length.

4 Grant these requests;—I ask no more,
But to thy care the rest resign;
Sick, or in health, or rich, or poor,
All shall be well, if thou art mine.

634
P. Doddridge.

Sing to the Lord, and loud proclaim
His mighty and his loving name!
O may he not be named alone,
But by our sure experience known.

2 Through every age his gracious ear
Is open to his children's prayer;
Nor can one humble soul complain
That it hath sought its God in vain.

3 What unbelieving heart shall dare
In whispers to suggest a fear,
While still he owns his ancient name,
The same his power, his love the same?

4 To thee our souls in faith arise,
To thee we lift expectant eyes,
And boldly through the desert tread,
For God will guard, where God shall lead

Prayer. 343

WHIPPLE. L. M.   J. P. HOLBROOK.

1. Jesus, our best beloved Friend! Draw out our souls in pure desire;
Jesus, in love to us descend, Baptize us with thy Spirit's fire.

635
J. Montgomery.

Jesus, our best belovéd Friend!
Draw out our souls in pure desire;
Jesus, in love to us descend,
Baptize us with thy Spirit's fire.

2 Our souls and bodies we resign,
To fear and follow thy commands;
O take our hearts, our hearts are thine,
Accept the service of our hands.

3 Firm, faithful, watching unto prayer,
May we thy blesséd will obey,
Toil in thy vineyard here, and bear
The heat and burden of the day.

4 Yet, Lord, for us a resting place,
In heaven, at thy right hand, prepare;
And, till we see thee face to face,
Be all our conversation there.

BYEFIELD. C. M.   T. HASTINGS.

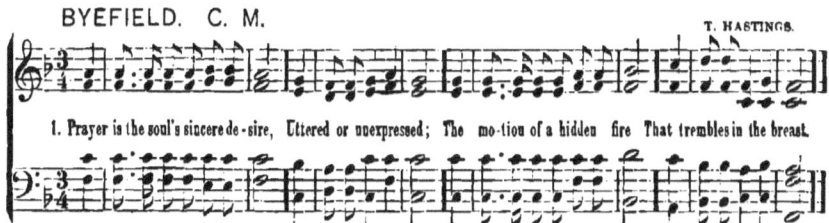

1. Prayer is the soul's sincere desire, Uttered or unexpressed; The motion of a hidden fire That trembles in the breast.

636
J. Montgomery.

Prayer is the soul's sincere desire,
Uttered or unexpressed;
The motion of a hidden fire,
That trembles in the breast.

2 Prayer is the burden of a sigh,
The falling of a tear,
The upward glancing of an eye,
When none but God is near.

3 Prayer is the simplest form of speech
That infant lips can try;
Prayer the sublimest strains that reach
The Majesty on high.

4 Prayer is the contrite sinner's voice,
Returning from his ways;
While angels in their songs rejoice,
And cry, " Behold, he prays!"

5 Prayer is the Christian's vital breath,
The Christian's native air,
His watchword at the gates of death:
He enters heaven with prayer.

6 O thou by whom we come to God,
The Life, the Truth, the Way!
The path of prayer thyself hast trod;
Lord! teach us how to pray.

344 CHRISTIAN AND CHURCH.

MORNINGTON. S. M.

637   *G. W. Bethune.*

O FOR the happy hour
When God will hear our cry,
And send with a reviving power,
His Spirit from on high.

2 While many crowd thy house,
How few around thy board
Meet to record their solemn vows,
And bless thee as their Lord.

3 Thou, thou alone canst give
Thy gospel sure success,
And bid the dying sinner live
Anew in holiness.

4 Come with thy power divine,
Spirit of life and love;
Then shall our people all be thine,
Our church like that above.

638   *P. Brown.*

O LORD, thy work revive
In Zion's gloomy hour,
And make her dying graces live
By thy restoring power.

2 Awake thy chosen few
To fervent, earnest prayer;
Again may they their vows renew,
Thy blessèd presence share,

3 Thy Spirit then will speak
Through lips of feeble clay,
And hearts of adamant will break,
And rebels will obey.

4 Lord, lend thy gracious ear;
O listen to our cry;
O come and bring salvation here;
Our hopes on thee rely.

639

HARK! through the courts of heaven
Angelic voices sound:
He that was dead now lives again;
He that was lost is found.

2 God of unfailing grace,
Send down thy Spirit now;
O raise the lowly soul to hope,
And make the lofty bow.

3 In countries far from home,
On earthly husks who feed,
Back to their Father's house, O Lord,
Their wandering footsteps lead.

4 Then at each soul's return,
The heavenly harp shall sound;
He that was dead now lives again;
He that was lost is found!

"Revive thy Work." 345

GAYLORD. 8s, 7s. ARR. J. P. HOLBROOK.

1. Saviour, vis-it thy plant-a-tion; Grant us, Lord, a gracious rain: All will come to des-o-la-tion,
D. S. Lest, for want of thine assistance,

FINE.   D. S.

Un-less thou re-turn a-gain. Keep no long-er at a distance, Shine up-on us from on high,
Ev-ery plant should droop and die.

640
J. Newton.

SAVIOUR, visit thy plantation;
  Grant us, Lord, a gracious rain:
All will come to desolation,
  Unless thou return again.
Keep no longer at a distance,
  Shine upon us from on high,
Lest, for want of thine assistance,
  Every plant should droop and die.

2 Let our mutual love be fervent;
  Make us prevalent in prayer;
Let each one esteemed thy servant
  Shun the world's bewitching snare.
Break the tempter's fatal power,
  Turn the stony heart to flesh,
And begin from this good hour
  To revive thy work afresh.

641
T. W. Aveling.

HAIL, thou God of grace and glory,
  Who thy name hast magnified,
By redemption's wondrous story,
  By the Saviour crucified;
Send the baptism of thy Spirit,
  Shed the pentecostal fire;
Let us all thy grace inherit,
  Waken, crown each good desire.

2 Bind thy people, Lord, in union,
  With the sevenfold cord of love;
Breathe a spirit of communion
  With the glorious hosts above;
Let thy work be seen progressing;
  Bow each heart, and bend each knee,
Till the world, thy truth possessing,
  Celebrates its jubilee.

HOPE. 8s, 7s. BEETHOVEN.

1. Hail, thou God of grace and glo-ry, Who thy name hast mag-ni-fied,

By re-demp-tion's wondrous sto-ry, By the Sav-iour cru-ci-fied.

CHRISTIAN AND CHURCH.

CHARITY. 8s, 7s, 7s. W. SCHULTES.

642

Thou to whom the sick and dying
  Ever came, nor came in vain,
Still with healing word replying
  To the weary cry of pain;
Hear us Jesus, as we meet,
Suppliants at thy mercy-seat.

2 Still the weary, sick, and dying
  Need a brother's, sister's care,
On thy higher help relying
  May we now their burden share,
Bringing all our offerings meet,
Suppliants at thy mercy-seat.

3 May each child of thine be willing,
  Willing both in hand and heart,
With the law of love fulfilling,
  Comfort ever to impart.
Ever bringing offerings meet,
Suppliants at thy mercy-seat.

LESLIE. C. M.
Andante. A.

643
P. Doddridge.

O Fount of good, to own thy love
  Our thankful hearts incline:
What can we render, Lord, to thee,
  When all the worlds are thine?

2 But thou hast needy brethren here,
  Partakers of thy grace,
Whose names thou wilt thyself confess
  Before the Father's face.

3 In each sad accent of distress
  Thy pleading voice is heard;
In them thou mayst be clothed and fed,
  And visited and cheered.

4 Help us, O Lord, thy yoke to wear,
  With joy to do thy will;
Each other's burdens gladly bear,
  And love's sweet law fulfil.

Charities—Helpfulness.

LANGTON. S. M. ARR. C. STREATFIELD.

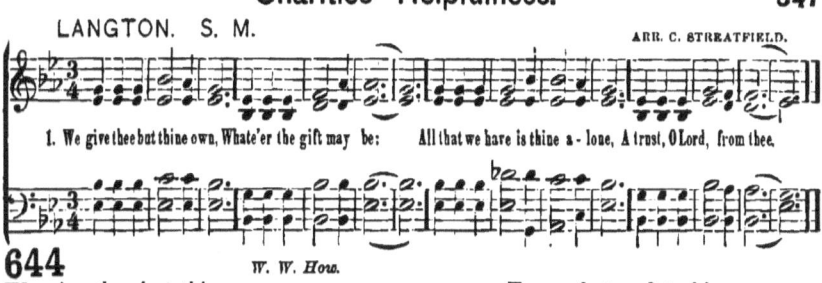

644
W. W. How.

We give thee but thine own,
  Whate'er the gift may be:
All that we have is thine alone,
  A trust, O Lord, from thee.

2 May we thy bounties thus
    As stewards true receive,
  And gladly, as thou blessest us,
    To thee our first-fruits give.

3 O, hearts are bruised and dead,
    And homes are bare and cold,
  And lambs, for whom the Shepherd bled,
    Are straying from the fold.

4 To comfort and to bless,
    To find a balm for woe,
  To tend the lone and fatherless,
    Is angels' work below.

5 The captive to release,
    To God the lost to bring,
  To teach the way of life and peace,
    It is a Christ-like thing.

6 And we believe thy word,
    Though dim our faith may be;
  Whate'er for thine we do, O Lord,
    We do it unto thee.

MACY. 6s. ARR. J. P. HOLBROOK.

645
F. R. Havergal.

Thy life was given for me,
  Thy blood, O Lord, was shed,
That I might ransomed be,
  And quickened from the dead.
Thy life was given for me:—
  What have I given for thee?

2 And thou hast brought to me,
    Down from thy home above,
  Salvation full and free,
    Thy pardon and thy love.
  Great gifts thou broughtest me;—
    What have I brought to thee?

3 O let my life be given,
    My years for thee be spent;
  World-fetters all be riven
    And joy with suffering blent;—
  To thee my all I bring,
    My Saviour and my King.

CHRISTIAN AND CHURCH.

DAWSON. L. M.
J. P. HOLBROOK.

646   *C. Wordsworth.*

O Lord of heaven and earth and sea,
  To thee all praise and glory be;
  How shall we show our love to thee,
    Who givest all—who givest all?
2 For souls redeemed, for sins forgiven,
  For means of grace and hopes of heaven,
  What can to thee, O Lord, be given,
    Who givest all—who givest all?

3 We lose what on ourselves we spend,
  We have, as treasures without end,
  Whatever, Lord, to thee we lend,
    Who givest all—who givest all.
4 Whatever, Lord, we lend to thee,
  Repaid a thousand fold will be;
  Then gladly may we give to thee,
    Who givest all—who givest all.

ALLEN. 7s.
BEETHOVEN.

647   *W. W. How.*

'Mid the homes of want and woe,
  Strangers to the living Word,
  Let the Saviour's herald go,
    Let the voice of hope be heard.
2 Where the shadows deepest lie,
  Carry truth's unsullied ray;
  Where are crimes of blackest dye,
    There the saving word display

3 To the weary and the worn
  Tell of realms where sorrows cease:
  To the outcast and forlorn
    Speak of mercy and of peace.
4 Guard the helpless, seek the strayed,
  Comfort trouble, banish grief;
  With the Spirit's sword arrayed,
    Scatter sin and unbelief.

Home Missions. 349

FEDERAL STREET. L. M.
H. K. OLIVER.

648 *W. C. Bryant.*

Look from thy sphere of endless day,
 O God of mercy and of might;
In pity look on those who stray,
 Benighted, in this land of light.

2 Send forth thy heralds, Lord, to call
 The thoughtless young, the hardened old,
A scattered, homeless flock, till all
 Be gathered to thy peaceful fold.

3 Send them thy mighty word to speak,
 Till faith shall dawn, and doubt depart,
To awe the bold, to stay the weak,
 And bind and heal the broken heart.

4 Then all these wastes, a dreary scene,
 That make us sadden as we gaze,
Shall grow with living waters green,
 And lift to heaven the voice of praise.

STAIR. C. M.
J. P. HOLBROOK.

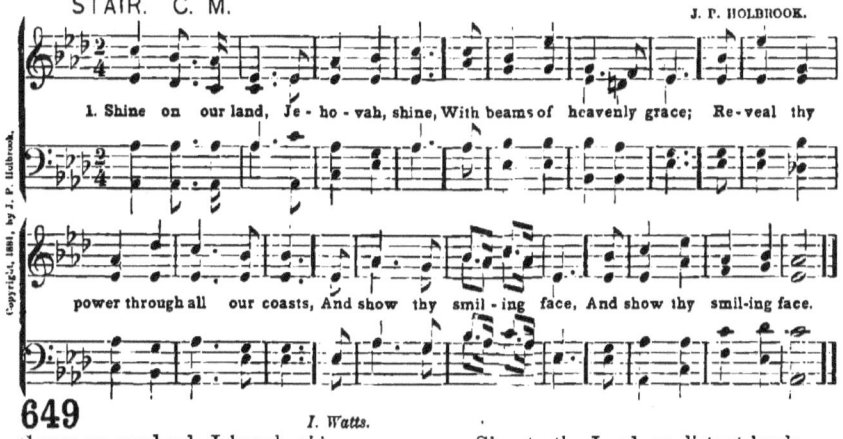

Copyright, 1881, by J. P. Holbrook.

649 *I. Watts.*

Shine on our land, Jehovah, shine,
 With beams of heavenly grace;
Reveal thy power through all our coasts,
 And show thy smiling face.

2 When shall thy name, from shore to shore,
 Sound all the earth abroad,
And distant nations know and love
 Their Saviour and their God?

3 Sing to the Lord, ye distant lands,
 Sing loud with solemn voice;
Let thankful tongues exalt his praise,
 And thankful hearts rejoice.

4 Earth shall confess her Maker's hand,
 And yield a full increase;
Our God will crown his chosen land
 With fruitfulness and peace.

350 CHRISTIAN AND CHURCH.

MISSIONARY HYMN. 7s, 6s.   L. MASON.

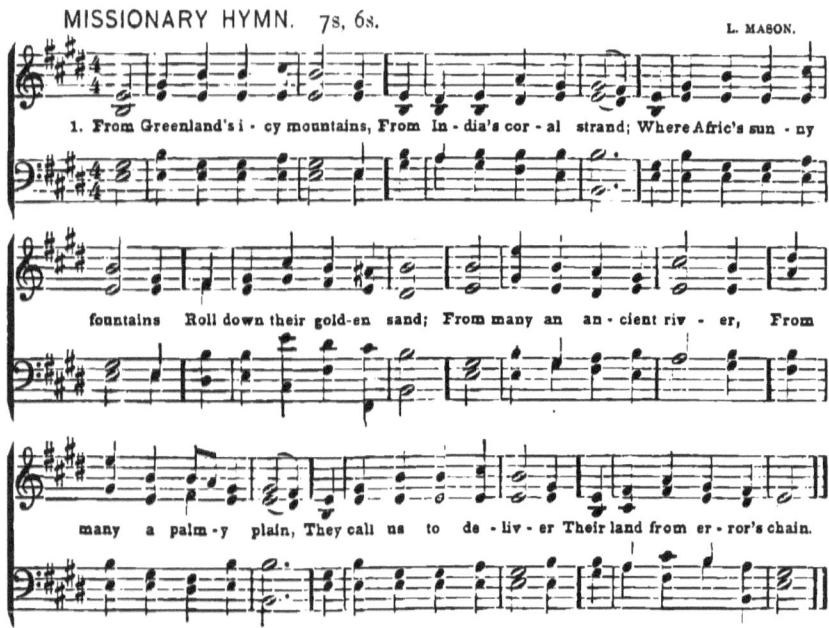

650
R. Heber.

From Greenland's icy mountains,
From India's coral strand;
Where Afric's sunny fountains
Roll down their golden sand;
From many an ancient river,
From many a palmy plain,
They call us to deliver
Their land from error's chain.

2 What though the spicy breezes
Blow soft o'er Ceylon's isle;
Though every prospect pleases,
And only man is vile?
In vain with lavish kindness
The gifts of God are strown;
The heathen in his blindness
Bows down to wood and stone.

3 Shall we whose souls are lighted
With wisdom from on high,
Shall we to men benighted
The lamp of life deny?
Salvation! O salvation!
The joyful sound proclaim,
Till earth's remotest nation
Has learned Messiah's name.

4 Waft, waft, ye winds, his story,
And you, ye waters, roll,
Till, like a sea of glory,
It spreads from pole to pole:
Till o'er our ransomed nature
The Lamb for sinners slain,
Redeemer, King, Creator,
In bliss returns to reign.

651
M. F. Anderson.

Our country's voice is pleading,
Ye men of God, arise!
His providence is leading,
The land before you lies;
Day-gleams are o'er it brightening,
And promise clothes the soil,
Wide fields, for harvest whitening,
Invite the reaper's toil.

2 The love of Christ unfolding,
Speed on from east to west,
Till all, his cross beholding,
In him are fully blest.
Great Author of salvation,
Haste, haste the glorious day,
When we, a ransomed nation,
Thy sceptre shall obey!

Missions. 351

WEBB. 7s, 6s, D.   G. J. WEBB.

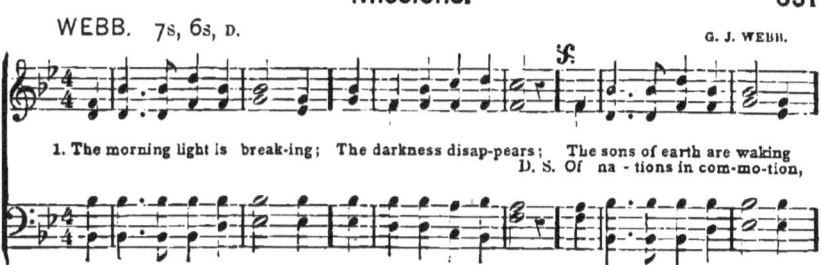

1. The morning light is break-ing; The darkness disap-pears; The sons of earth are waking
D. S. Of na - tions in com-mo-tion,

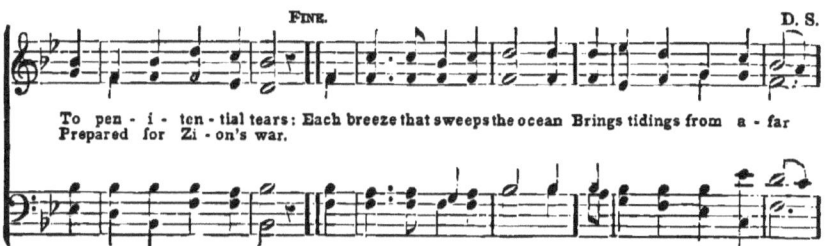

To pen - i - ten - tial tears: Each breeze that sweeps the ocean Brings tidings from a - far
Prepared for Zi - on's war.

652 S. F. Smith.

The morning light is breaking;
    The darkness disappears;
The sons of earth are waking
    To penitential tears:
Each breeze that sweeps the ocean
    Brings tidings from afar
Of nations in commotion,
    Prepared for Zion's war.

2 See heathen nations bending
    Before the God we love,
And thousand hearts ascending,
    In gratitude above;
While sinners, now confessing,
    The gospel call obey,
And seek the Saviour's blessing,
    A nation in a day.

3 Blest river of salvation,
    Pursue thine onward way;
Flow thou to every nation,
    Nor in thy riches stay:
Stay not, till all the lowly
    Triumphant reach their home;
Stay not, till all the holy
    Proclaim, "The Lord is come."

653 J. Montgomery.

Hail to the Lord's Anointed,
    Great David's greater Son!
Hail in the time appointed,
    His reign on earth begun!
He comes to break oppression,
    To set the captive free,
To take away transgression,
    And rule in equity.

2 He shall come down, like showers
    Upon the fruitful earth,
And love, and joy, like flowers,
    Spring in his path to birth:
Before him on the mountains,
    Shall peace, the herald, go;
And righteousness, in fountains,
    From hill to valley flow.

3 For him shall prayer unceasing
    And daily vows ascend;
His kingdom still increasing,—
    A kingdom without end:
The tide of time shall never
    His covenant remove;
His name shall stand forever,—
    That name to us is—Love.

352 CHRISTIAN AND CHURCH.

MISSIONARY CHANT. L. M. — C. ZEUNER.

1. Jesus, we bow before thy throne, We lift our eyes to seek thy face;
To bleeding hearts thy love make known, On contrite souls bestow thy grace.

654 *N. S. S. Deman.*

Jesus, we bow before thy throne,
 We lift our eyes to seek thy face;
To bleeding hearts thy love make known,
 On contrite souls bestow thy grace.

2 See, spread beneath thy gracious eye,
 A world o'erwhelmed in guilt and tears;
Where deathless souls in ruin lie,
 And no kind voice dispels their fears.

3 Lord, arm thy truth with power divine,
 Its conquests spread from shore to shore,
Till suns and stars forget to shine,
 And earth and skies shall be no more.

655 *J. Joyce.*

Lord, visit thy forsaken race,
 Back to thy fold the wanderers bring;
Teach them to seek thy slighted grace,
 And hail in Christ their promised King.

2 The veil of darkness rend in twain,
 Which hides their Shiloh's glorious light;
The severed olive-branch again
 Firm to its parent stock unite.

3 Hail, glorious day, expected long,
 When Jew and Greek one prayer shall pour,
With eager feet one temple throng,
 With grateful praise one God adore.

656

Sovereign of world's, display thy power;
 Be this thy Zion's favored hour;
Bid the bright morning Star arise,
 And point the nations to the skies.

2 Set up thy throne where Satan reigns,
 On Afric's shore, on India's plains,
On wilds and continents unknown,
 And make the nations all thine own.

3 Speak, and the world shall hear thy voice;
 Speak, and the deserts shall rejoice;
Scatter the gloom of heathen night,
 And bid all nations hail the light.

657 *Mrs. Voke.*

Soon may the last glad song arise
 Through all the millions of the skies—
That song of triumph which records
 That all the earth is now the Lord's!

2 Let thrones and powers and kingdoms be
 Obedient, mighty God, to thee!
And, over land and stream and main,
 Wave thou the sceptre of thy reign!

3 O let that glorious anthem swell,
 Let host to host the triumph tell,
That not one rebel heart remains,
 But over all the Saviour reigns!

Missions.

DUKE STREET. L. M. — J. HATTON.

1. Arm of the Lord, a-wake!—a-wake! Put on thy strength—the na-tions shake! Now let the world, a-dor-ing, see Triumphs of mer-cy wrought by thee.

658 W. Shrubsole.

Arm of the Lord, awake!—awake!
Put on thy strength—the nations shake!
Now let the world, adoring, see
Triumphs of mercy wrought by thee.

2 Let Zion's time of favor come!
O bring the tribes of Israel home!
Soon may our wondering eyes behold
Gentiles and Jews in Jesus' fold!

3 Almighty God! thy grace proclaim
Through every clime—of every name!
Let adverse powers before thee fall,
And crown the Saviour Lord of all!

659 J. Montgomery.

O Spirit of the living God,
In all thy plenitude of grace,
Where'er the foot of man hath trod,
Descend on our apostate race.

2 Give tongues of fire, and hearts of love,
To preach the reconciling word;
Give power and unction from above
Where'er the joyful sound is heard.

3 Baptize the nations, far and nigh;
The triumphs of the cross record;
The name of Jesus glorify,
Till every kingdom call him Lord.

660 B. Beddome.

Ascend thy throne, almighty King,
And spread thy glories all abroad;
Let thine own arm salvation bring,
And be thou known the gracious God.

2 O let the kingdoms of the world
Become the kingdoms of the Lord;
Let saints and angels praise thy name,
Be thou through heaven and earth adored.

LONG. L. M. — J. P. HOLBROOK.

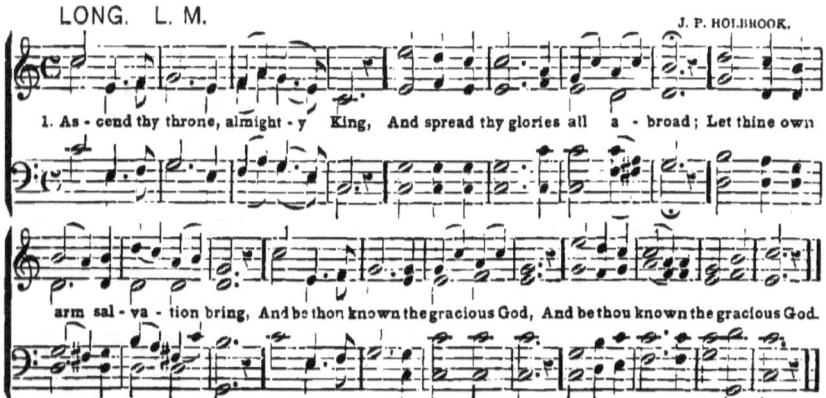

1. As-cend thy throne, almight-y King, And spread thy glories all a-broad; Let thine own arm sal-va-tion bring, And be thou known the gracious God, And be thou known the gracious God.

CHRISTIAN AND CHURCH.

LANCASHIRE. 7s, 6s. — H. SMART.

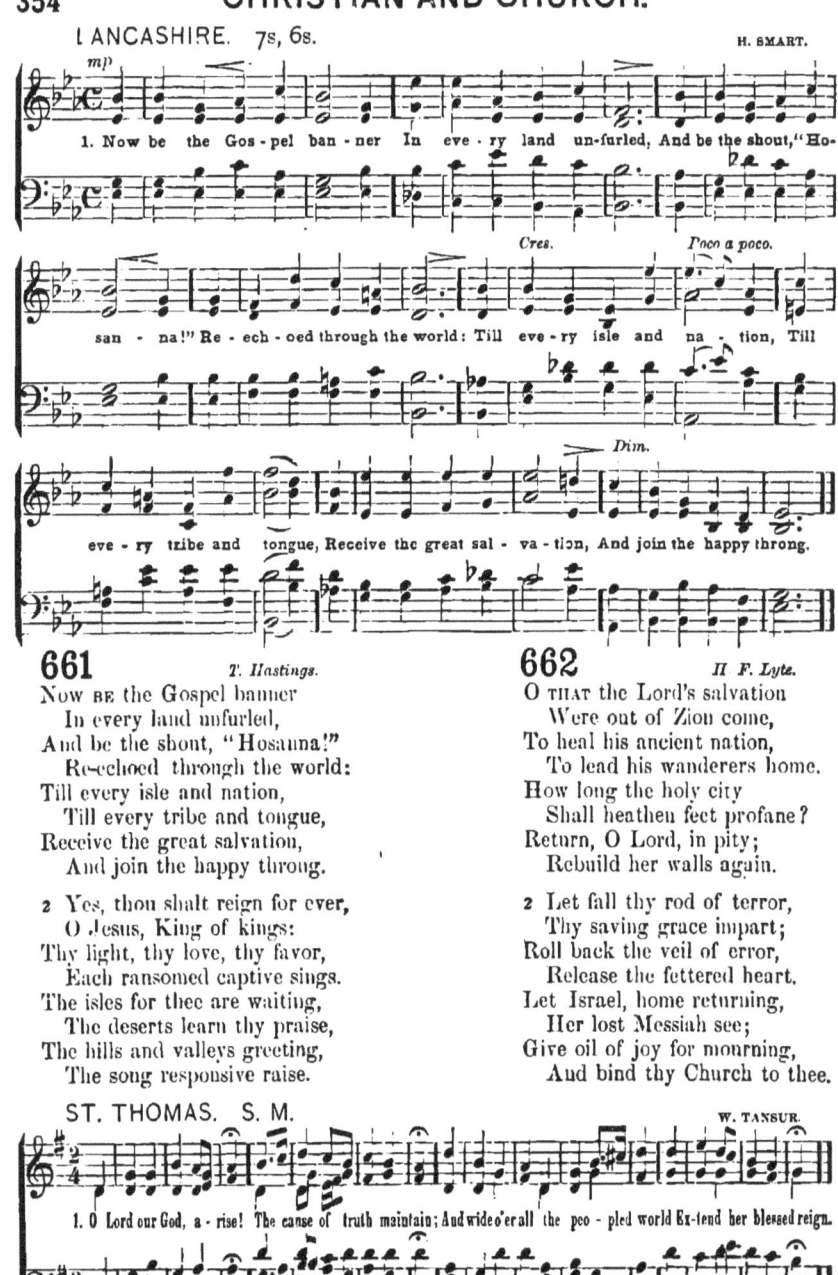

661   *T. Hastings.*

Now be the Gospel banner
  In every land unfurled,
And be the shout, "Hosanna!"
  Re-echoed through the world:
Till every isle and nation,
  Till every tribe and tongue,
Receive the great salvation,
  And join the happy throng.

2 Yes, thou shalt reign for ever,
  O Jesus, King of kings:
Thy light, thy love, thy favor,
  Each ransomed captive sings.
The isles for thee are waiting,
  The deserts learn thy praise,
The hills and valleys greeting,
  The song responsive raise.

662   *H. F. Lyte.*

O THAT the Lord's salvation
  Were out of Zion come,
To heal his ancient nation,
  To lead his wanderers home.
How long the holy city
  Shall heathen feet profane?
Return, O Lord, in pity;
  Rebuild her walls again.

2 Let fall thy rod of terror,
  Thy saving grace impart;
Roll back the veil of error,
  Release the fettered heart.
Let Israel, home returning,
  Her lost Messiah see;
Give oil of joy for mourning,
  And bind thy Church to thee.

ST. THOMAS. S. M. — W. TANSUR.

Missions. 355

EWING. 7s, 6s.   ALEX. EWING.

1. Hasten, the time appointed, By prophets long foretold, When all shall dwell together, One Shepherd and one fold. Let Jew and Gentile, meeting From many a distant shore, Around one altar kneeling, One common Lord adore.

663   *J. Borthwick.*

Hasten the time appointed,
By prophets long foretold,
When all shall dwell together,
One Shepherd and one fold.
Let Jew and Gentile, meeting
From many a distant shore,
Around one altar kneeling,
One common Lord adore.

2 Let all that now divides us
Remove and pass away,
Like shadows of the morning
Before the blaze of day.

Let war be learned no longer,
Let strife and tumult cease,
All earth his blessed kingdom,
The Lord and Prince of Peace.

3 O long-expected dawning,
Come with thy cheering ray;
When shall the morning brighten,
The shadows flee away?
O sweet anticipation,
It cheers the watchers on,
To pray, and hope, and labor,
Till the dark night be gone.

664   s. m.   *R. Wardlaw.*

O Lord our God, arise!
The cause of truth maintain;
And wide o'er all the peopled world
Extend her blessèd reign.

2 Thou Prince of life, arise!
Nor let thy glory cease;
Far spread the conquests of thy grace,
And bless the earth with peace.

3 Thou Holy Ghost, arise!
Extend thy healing wing,
And o'er a dark and ruined world
Let light and order spring.

665   s. m.   *C. Wesley.*

O thou whom we adore!
To bless our earth again,
Assume thine own almighty power,
And o'er the nations reign.

2 The world's Desire and Hope,
All power to thee is given;
Now set the last great empire up,
Eternal Lord of heaven!

3 According to thy word,
Now be thy grace revealed;
And with the knowledge of the Lord,
Let all the earth be filled.

356 CHRISTIAN AND CHURCH.
KENDALL. H. M.
J. P. HOLBROOK.

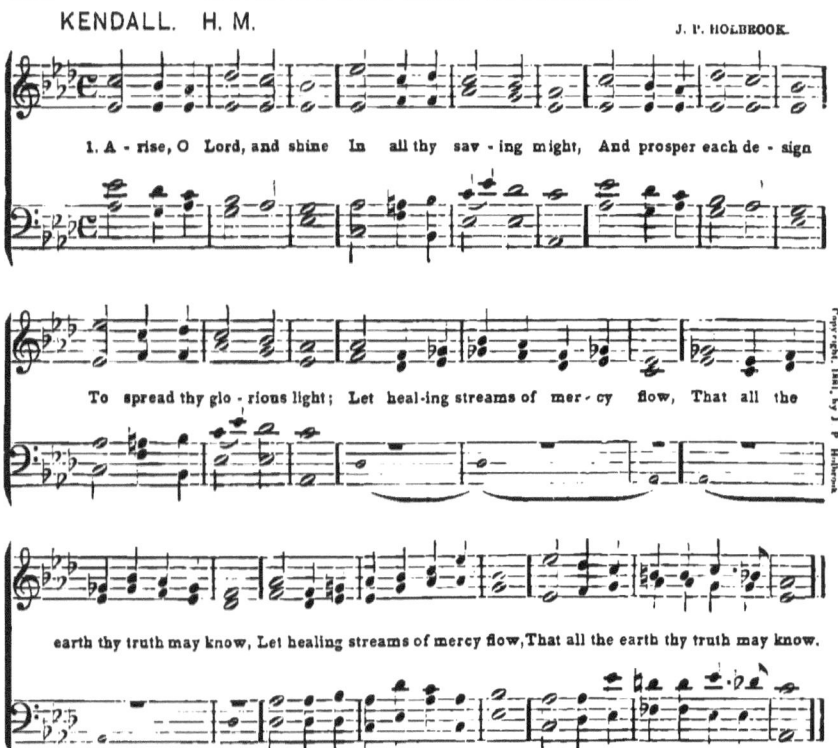

1. A-rise, O Lord, and shine In all thy sav-ing might, And prosper each de-sign To spread thy glo-rious light; Let heal-ing streams of mer-cy flow, That all the earth thy truth may know, Let healing streams of mercy flow, That all the earth thy truth may know.

666
Arise, O Lord, and shine
 In all thy saving might,
And prosper each design
 To spread thy glorious light;
Let healing streams of mercy flow,
That all the earth thy truth may know.

2 Bring distant nations near,
 To sing thy glorious praise;
Let every people hear,
 And learn thy holy ways.
Reign, mighty God! assert thy cause,
And govern by thy righteous laws!

3 Put forth thy glorious power,
 That Gentiles all may see,
And earth present her store
 In converts born to thee:
God, our own God, his church shall bless;
And earth be filled with righteousness!

667 P. Doddridge.
Gird on thy conquering sword,
 Ascend thy shining car,
And march, almighty Lord!
 To wage thy holy war:
Before his wheels, in glad surprise,
Ye valleys! rise; and sink ye hills!

2 Before thy glorious face
 Thy foes submissive fall,
The captives of thy grace,
 That grace which conquers all:
The world shall know, great King of kings,
What wondrous things thine arm can do.

Dox.—To God, the Father, Son,
 And Spirit ever blest,
Eternal Three in One,
 All worship be addressed!
Join all on earth, rejoice and sing;
All glory give to God our King!

Missions.

HUMMEL. C. M. — C. ZEUNER.

1. Come, bless-ed Lord! let ev-ery shore And answering island sing
The prais-es of thy roy-al name, And own thee as their King!

668
E. Denny.

Come, blessed Lord! let every shore
And answering island sing
The praises of thy royal name,
And own thee as their King!

2 Bid the whole earth, responsive now
To the bright world above,
Break forth in sweetest strains of joy
In memory of thy love.

3 Jesus! thy fair creation groans,—
The air, the earth, the sea,—
In unison with loyal hearts,
And calls aloud for thee.

4 Thine was the cross, with all its fruits,
Of grace and peace divine;
Be thine the crown of glory now,
The palm of victory thine!

669
W. Gaskell.

O God, the darkness roll away,
Which clouds the human soul;
And let the bright, the perfect day
Speed onward to its goal.

2 Let every hateful passion die,
Which makes of brethren foes;
And war no longer raise its cry,
To mar the world's repose.

3 Let faith and hope and charity
Go forth through all the earth;
And man in heavenly bearing be
True to his heavenly birth.

4 Yea, let thy glorious kingdom come,
Of holiness and love;
And make this world a portal meet
For thy bright courts above.

670
I. Watts.

Let Zion and her sons rejoice—
Behold the promised hour!
Her God hath heard her mourning voice,
And comes t'exalt his power.

2 Her dust and ruins that remain
Are precious in his eyes;
Those ruins shall be built again,
And all that dust shall rise.

3 The Lord will raise Jerusalem,
And stand in glory there;
Nations shall bow before his name,
And kings attend with fear.

3 This shall be known when we are dead,
And left on long record,
That nations yet unborn may read,
And trust and praise the Lord.

CHRISTIAN AND CHURCH.

RIPLEY. 7s, 5s. J. P. HOLBROOK.

1. Onward speed thy conquering flight, Angel, onward speed! Cast abroad thy radiant light, Bid the shades recede; Tread the idols in the dust, Heathen fanes destroy; Spread the gospel's love and trust, Spread the gospel's joy.

671 S. F. Smith.

ONWARD speed thy conquering flight,
  Angel, onward speed!
Cast abroad thy radiant light,
  Bid the shades recede;
Tread the idols in the dust,
  Heathen fanes destroy;
Spread the gospel's love and trust,
  Spread the gospel's joy.

2 Onward speed thy conquering flight,
  Angel, onward fly!
Long has been the reign of night;
  Bring the morning nigh:
Unto thee earth's sufferers lift
  Their imploring wail;
Bear them heaven's holy gift,
  Ere their courage fail.

3 Onward speed thy conquering flight,
  Angel, onward speed!
Morning bursts upon our sight,
  Lo! the time decreed:
Now the Lord his kingdom takes,
  Thrones and empires fall;
Now the joyous song awakes,
  "God is All in All!"

MOZART. 7s. MOZART.

1. Hark, the song of ju-bi-lee, Loud as might-y thun-ders roar, Or the full-ness of the sea, When it breaks up-on the shore, When it breaks up-on the shore:

Missions. 359

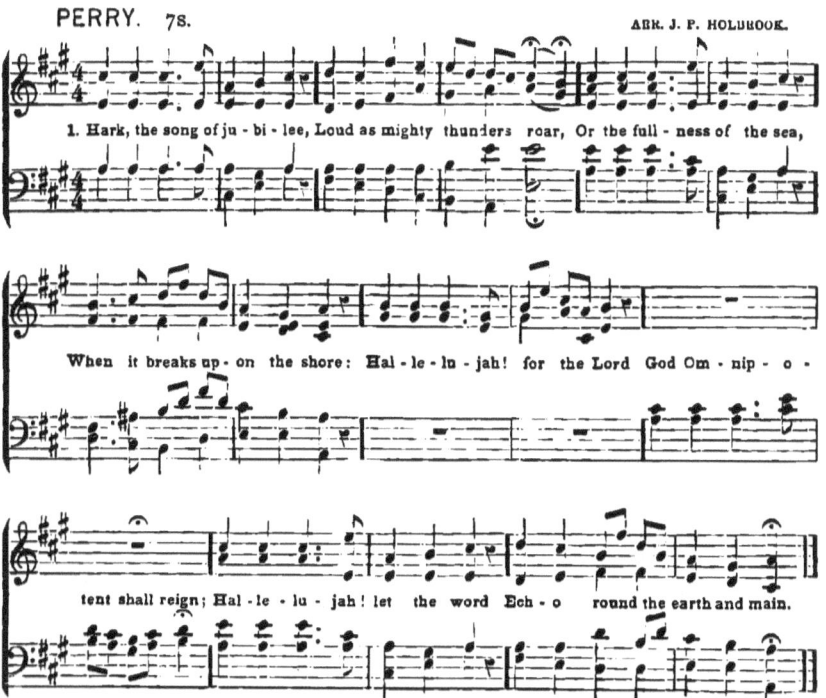

PERRY. 7s. ARR. J. P. HOLBROOK.

1. Hark, the song of ju-bi-lee, Loud as mighty thunders roar, Or the full-ness of the sea, When it breaks up-on the shore: Hal-le-lu-jah! for the Lord God Om-nip-o-tent shall reign; Hal-le-lu-jah! let the word Ech-o round the earth and main.

672 *J. Montgomery.*

HARK, the song of jubilee,
　Loud as mighty thunders roar,
Or the fullness of the sea,
　When it breaks upon the shore:
Hallelujah! for the Lord
　God Omnipotent shall reign;
Hallelujah! let the word
　Echo round the earth and main.

2 Hallelujah! hark, the sound,
　From the depths unto the skies,
Wakes above, beneath, around,
　All creation's harmonies.
See Jehovah's banner furled,
　Sheathed his sword: he speaks; 'tis done,
And the kingdoms of this world
　Are the kingdoms of his Son.

3 He shall reign from pole to pole
　With supreme unbounded sway;
He shall reign, when like a scroll
　Yonder heavens have passed away.
Then the end; beneath his rod
　Man's last enemy shall fall:
Hallelujah! Christ in God,
　God in Christ, is All in all!

673 *H. Auber.*

HASTEN, Lord! the glorious time,
　When, beneath Messiah's sway,
Every nation, every clime,
　Shall the gospel's call obey.
Mightiest kings his power shall own,
　Heathen tribes his name adore;
Satan and his host, o'erthrown,
　Bound in chains, shall hurt no more.

2 Then shall wars and tumults cease;
　Then be banished grief and pain;
Righteousness, and joy, and peace,
　Undisturbed shall ever reign.
Bless we, then, our gracious Lord;
　Ever praise his glorious name;
All his mighty acts record;
　All his wondrous love proclaim.

CHRISTIAN AND CHURCH.

AVISON.

674   W. A. Muhlenberg.

CHOIR.   2 Tell how he cometh; from nation to nation,
           The heart-cheering news let the earth echo round;
           How free to the faithful he offers salvation,
           How his people with joy everlasting are crown'd.

CHOIR.   3 Mortals, your homage be gratefully bringing,
           And sweet let the gladsome hosanna arise;
           Ye angels, the full hallelujah be singing;
           One chorus resound through the earth and the skies.

Missions. 361

MISSIONARY CHANT. L. M.   C. ZEUNER.

1. Je-sus shall reign where'er the sun Does his suc-ces-sive jour-neys run;
His kingdom stretch from shore to shore, Till moons shall wax and wane no more.

675   *I. Watts.*

Jesus shall reign where'er the sun
Does his successive journeys run;
His kingdom stretch from shore to shore,
Till moons shall wax and wane no more.

2 For him shall endless prayers be made,
And endless praises crown his head;
His name like sweet perfume shall rise
With every morning sacrifice.

3 People and realms of every tongue
Dwell on his love with sweetest song;
And infant voices shall proclaim
Their early blessings on his name.

4 Blessings abound where'er he reigns,
The prisoner leaps to loose his chains;
The weary find eternal rest,
And all the sons of want are blest.

5 Let every creature rise, and bring
Peculiar honors to our King:
Angels descend with songs again,
And earth repeat the long amen.

676

O Stone of God, by unseen hands
  Cut from the everlasting hill,
  Accomplish his predestined will,—
Roll in thy greatness through the lands.

2 Grind into dust each adverse power,
Or gold or silver, iron or clay;
Thro' their destruction hold thy way,
And hasten in Christ's promised hour.

3 Break down the dark abodes of sin,
Crush through the prisons of our pain,
The veil of ignorance rend in twain,
And let the light of God shine in.

4 We hail thee, wondrous, glorious Stone!
We see thee rise, and grow, and roll;
We see thee spread from pole to pole,
And fill earth's kingdoms with thine own.

677   *P. Doddridge.*

Triumphant Zion, lift thy head
From dust, and darkness, and the dead:
Though humbled long, awake at length,
And gird thee with thy Saviour's strength.

2 Put all thy beauteous garments on,
And let thy various charms be known:
The world thy glories shall confess,
Decked in the robes of righteousness.

3 God from on high has heard thy prayer,
His hands thy ruins shall repair;
Nor will thy watchful Monarch cease
To guard thee in eternal peace.

CHRISTIAN AND CHURCH.

WATCHMAN. 7s.
J. P. HOLBROOK.

678
J. Bowring.

Watchman! tell us of the night,
 What its signs of promise are.
Traveler! o'er yon mountain's height,
 See that glory-beaming star.
Watchman! does its beauteous ray
 Aught of joy or hope foretell?
Traveler! yes; it brings the day,
 Promised day of Israel.

2 Watchman! tell us of the night;
 Higher yet that star ascends.
Traveler! blessedness and light,
 Peace and truth, its course portends.
Watchman! will its beams alone
 Gild the spot that gave them birth?
Traveler! ages are its own;
 See, it bursts o'er all the earth.

3 Watchman! tell us of the night,
 For the morning seems to dawn.
Traveler! darkness takes its flight;
 Doubt and terror are withdrawn.
Watchman! let thy wanderings cease;
 Hie thee to thy quiet home.
Traveler! lo! the Prince of Peace,
 Lo! the Son of God is come.

ZION. 8s, 7s, 4s.
T. HASTINGS.

Missions.

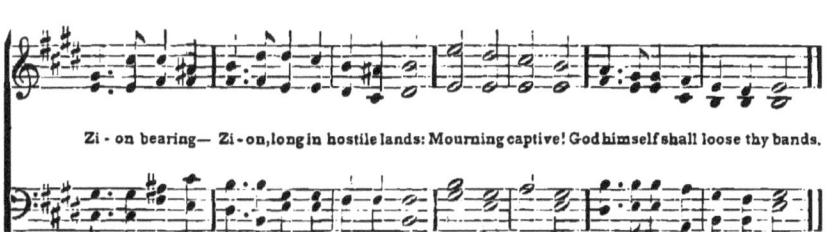

679 *T. Kelly.*

On the mountain's top appearing,
 Lo! the sacred herald stands,
Welcome news to Zion bearing—
 Zion, long in hostile lands:
  Mourning captive!
 God himself shall loose thy bands.

2 Has thy night been long and mournful?
 Have thy friends unfaithful proved?
Have thy foes been proud and scornful,
 By thy sighs and tears unmoved?
  Cease thy mourning;
 Zion still is well beloved.

3 God, thy God, will now restore thee;
 He himself appears thy Friend;
All thy foes shall flee before thee;
 Here their boasts and triumphs end:
  Great deliverance
 Zion's King will surely send.

4 Peace and joy shall now attend thee;
 All thy warfare now is past;
God thy Saviour will defend thee;
 Victory is thine at last:
  All thy conflicts
 End in everlasting rest.

680 *C. F. Alexander.*

Souls in heathen darkness lying,
 Where no light has broken through,
Souls that Jesus bought by dying,
 Whom his soul in travail knew:
  Thousand voices
 Call us, o'er the waters blue.

2 Christians, hearken: none has taught
 Of his love so deep and dear; [them
Of the precious price that bought them;
 Of the nail, the thorn, the spear;
  Ye who know him,
 Guide them from their darkness drear.

3 Haste, O haste, and spread the tidings
 Wide to earth's remotest strand;
Let no brother's bitter chidings
 . Rise against us when we stand
  In the judgment,
 From some far, forgotten land.

4 Lo, the hills for harvest whiten
 All along each distant shore;
Seaward far the islands brighten;
 Light of nations, lead us o'er;
  When we seek them,
 Let thy Spirit go before.

CHRISTIAN AND CHURCH.

CARLTON 8s, 7s.   CONCONE

681

Lord, her watch thy Church is keeping;
  When shall earth thy rule obey?
When shall end the night of weeping?
  When shall break the promised day?
See the whitening harvest languish,
  Waiting still the laborer's toil;
Was it vain—thy Son's deep anguish?
  Shall the strong retain the spoil?

2 Tidings sent to every creature,
  Millions yet have never heard,
Can they hear without a preacher?
  Lord Almighty, give the word!
Give the word!—in every nation
  Let the gospel trumpet sound,
Witnessing a world's salvation,
  To the earth's remotest bound.

3 Then the end! thy Church completed
  All thy chosen gathered in,
With their King in glory seated,
  Satan bound, and banished sin;
Gone forever, parting, weeping,
  Hunger, sorrow, death and pain:—
Lo! her watch thy Church is keeping;
  Come, Lord Jesus, come to reign.

682   A. C. Coxe.

Saviour, sprinkle many nations,
  Fruitful let thy sorrows be;
By thy pains and consolations,
  Draw the nations unto thee.
Of thy cross the wondrous story,
  Be it to the nations told;
Let them see thee in thy glory
  And thy mercy manifold.

2 Far and wide, though all unknowing,
  Pants for thee each mortal breast;
Human tears for thee are flowing,
  Human hearts in thee would rest.
Thirsting, as for dews of even,
  As the new-mown grass for rain,
Thee they seek, as God of heaven,
  Thee, as Man for sinners slain.

3 Saviour, lo! the isles are waiting,
  Stretched the hand and strained the sight
For thy Spirit, new creating,
  Love's pure flame and wisdom's light.
Give the word! and of the preacher
  Speed the foot and touch the tongue;
Till on earth by every creature
  Glory to the Lamb be sung.

Missions.

STOWE. 8s, 7s. J. P. HOLBROOK.

683

Sing ye faithful, sing with gladness;
  Wake your noblest, sweetest strain;
With the praises of your Saviour
  Let his house resound again;
Him let all your voices honor,
  And your songs exalt his reign.

2 For he tasted death for all men,
  He of all mankind the Head,
Sinless One among the sinful,
  Prince of Life among the dead;
So he wrought the full redemption,
  And the captor captive led.

3 Now on high, yet ever with us,
  From his Father's throne the Son
Rules and guides the world he ransomed,
  Till the appointed work be done,
Till he see, renewed and perfect,
  All things gathered into one.

4 Day of promised restitution!
  Fruit of all his sorrows past!
When the crown of his dominions
  He before the Throne shall cast,
And throughout the wide creation
  God be all in all at last.

GREENWOOD. S. M. J. E. SWEETSER.

684
H. D. Johns.

Come, kingdom of our God,
  Sweet reign of light and love,
Shed peace, and hope, and joy abroad,
  And wisdom from above.

2 Come, kingdom of our God,
  And make the broad earth thine;
Stretch o'er her lands and isles the rod
  That flowers with grace divine.

3 Soon may all tribes be blest
  With fruit from life's glad tree;
And in its shade, like brothers, rest,
  Sons of one family.

685
H. Bonar.

Come, Lord, and tarry not!
  Bring the long-looked-for day;
Oh, why these years of waiting here,
  These ages of delay?

2 Come, and make all things new,
  Build up this ruined earth,
Restore our faded paradise,—
  Creation's second birth.

3 Come, and begin thy reign
  Of everlasting peace;
Come, take the kingdom to thyself,
  Great King of Righteousness!

First Lines of Hymns.

CHILDREN'S SONGS.

HYMNS
686 Saviour, blessed Saviour,
687 Brightly gleams our banner,
688 Saviour, like a shepherd lead us,
689 In the vineyard of our Father
690 What a friend we have in Jesus,
691 One there is above all others,
692 Hosanna! loud hosanna!
693 Thou art the King of Israel,

NATIONAL AND THANKSGIVING.

694 My country, 'tis of thee.
695 God bless our native land;
696 Before the Lord we bow,
697 O God, beneath thy guiding hand,
698 We plough the fields
699 Come, ye thankful people, come,

HYMNS
700 Christ, by heavenly hosts adored,
701 Praise to God, immortal praise,
702 Lord God, we worship thee,
703 To thee, O God, we raise

THE YEAR: BEGINNING, CLOSE.

704 Days and moments quickly flying,
705 While with ceaseless course the sun
706 Our Father, through the coming year
707 Great God, we sing that mighty hand,
708 Our helper, God, we bless thy name,

THOSE AT SEA.

709 Eternal Father! strong to save,
710 O God, thou holdest in thy hand,
711 When through the torn sail
712 Star of peace, to wanderers

SAVIOUR, BLESSED SAVIOUR. 6s, 5s.

1. Saviour, blessed Saviour, Listen whilst we sing, Hearts and voices raising Praises to our King. All we have to of-fer, All we hope to be, Bod-y, soul, and spir-it, All we yield to thee, Bod-y, soul, and spir-it, All we yield to thee.

Children's Songs.

FORWARD. 6s, 5s. HAYDN.

1. Saviour, blessed Saviour, Listen whilst we sing, Hearts and voices raising Praises to our King. All we have to of-fer, All we hope to be, Body, soul, and spir-it, All we yield to thee, All we have to of-fer, All we hope to be, Body, soul, and spir-it, All we yield to thee.

686
G. Thring.

SAVIOUR, blessed Saviour,
  Listen whilst we sing,
Hearts and voices raising
  Praises to our King.
All we have we offer,
  All we hope to be,
Body, soul, and spirit,
  All we yield to thee.

2 Nearer, ever nearer,
  Christ, we draw to thee,
Deep in adoration
  Bending low the knee:
Thou for our redemption
  Cam'st on earth to die;
Thou, that we might follow,
  Hast gone up on high.

3 Great and ever greater
  Are thy mercies here,
True and everlasting
  Are the glories there,
Where no pain, or sorrow,
  Toil, or care, is known,
Where the angel-legions
  Circle round thy throne.

687
T. J. Potter.

BRIGHTLY gleams our banner,
  Pointing to the sky,
Waving wanderers onward
  To their home on high.
Journeying o'er the desert,
  Gladly thus we pray,
And with hearts united
  Take our heavenward way.

REF.–Brightly gleams our banner,
  Pointing to the sky,
Waving wanderers onward
  To their home on high.

2 Jesus, Lord and Master,
  At thy sacred feet,
Here with hearts rejoicing
  See thy children meet;
Often have we left thee,
  Often gone astray,
Keep us mighty Saviour,
  In the narrow way.–REF.

3 All our days direct us
  In the way we go;
Lead us on victorious
  Over every foe:
When the toil is over,
  Then comes rest and peace,
Jesus, in his beauty,
  Songs that never cease.–REF.

368 OCCASIONAL.

SAVIOUR, LIKE A SHEPHERD LEAD US. 8s, 7s, 4s.
C STEGGALL.

1. Saviour, like a Shepherd lead us, Much we need thy tender care; In thy pleasant pastures feed us, For our use thy folds prepare. Blessèd Je-sus, Blessed Jesus, Thou hast bought us, thine we are.

688
D A. Thrupp.

Saviour, like a shepherd lead us,
  Much we need thy tender care;
In thy pleasant pastures feed us,
  For our use thy folds prepare.
    Blessèd Jesus,
Thou hast bought us, thine we are.

2 We are weak, do thou befriend us,
  Be the guardian of our way;
Keep thy flock, from sin defend us,
  Seek us when we go astray;
    Blessèd Jesus,
Hear, O hear us when we pray.

3 Thou hast promised to receive us,
  Poor and sinful though we be;
Thou hast mercy to relieve us,
  Grace to cleanse, and power to free;
    Blessèd Jesus,
Let us early turn to thee.

4 Early let us seek thy favor,
  Early let us do thy will;
Holy Lord, our only Saviour,
  With thy grace our bosoms fill;
    Blessèd Jesus,
Thou hast loved us, love us still.

689
T McKellar.

In the vineyard of our Father
  Daily work we find to do;
Scattered gleanings we may gather,
  Though we are but young and few;
    Little clusters
Help to fill the garners too.

2 Toiling early in the morning,
  Catching moments through the day,
Nothing small or lowly scorning,
  While we work, and watch, and pray;
    Gathering gladly
Free-will offerings by the way.

3 Not for selfish praise or glory,
  Not for things of little worth,
But to send the blessèd story
  Of the gospel o'er the earth,
    Telling mortals
Of our Lord and Saviour's birth.

4 Steadfast, then, in our endeavor,
  Heavenly Father, may we be;
And for ever, and for ever,
  We will give the praise to Thee;
    Hallelujah
Singing, all eternity!

Children's Songs. 369

CHAPMAN. 8s, 7s. D. — J. P. HOLBROOK.

690
H. BONAR.

What a Friend we have in Jesus,
All our sins and griefs to bear;
What a privilege to carry
Everything to God in prayer.
O what peace we often forfeit,
O what needless pain we bear—
All because we do not carry
Everything to God in prayer.

2 Have we trials and temptations?
Is there trouble anywhere?
We should never be discouraged,
Take it to the Lord in prayer.
Can we find a Friend so faithful,
Who will all our sorrows share?
Jesus knows our every weakness,
Take it to the Lord in prayer.

691
J. Newton.

One there is, above all others,
Well deserves the name of Friend;
His is love beyond a brother's,
Costly, free, and knows no end.

2 Which of all our friends, to save us,
Could or would have shed his blood?
But our Jesus died to have us,
Reconciled in him to God.

3 When he lived on earth abased,
Friend of sinners was his name;
Now, above all glory raised,
He rejoices in the same.

4 O for grace our hearts to soften!
Teach us, Lord, at length to love;
We, alas! forget too often
What a Friend we have above.

HUNTINGTON. 8s, 7s, 4s. — CH. GOUNOD.

370 OCCASIONAL. (Children.)
BERNARD. 7s, 6s.
J. P. HOLBROOK.

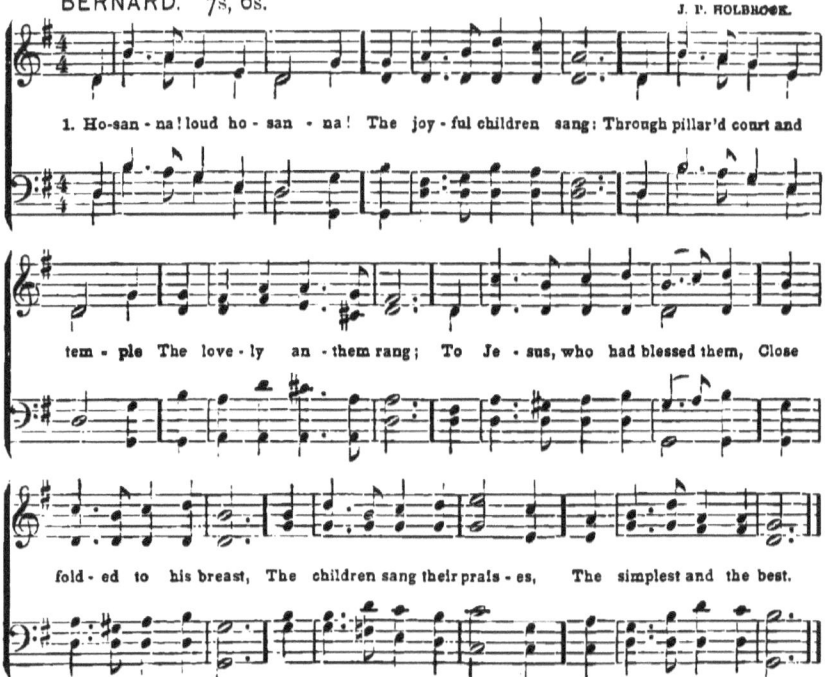

1. Ho-san-na! loud ho-san-na! The joy-ful children sang: Through pillar'd court and temple The love-ly an-them rang; To Je-sus, who had blessed them, Close fold-ed to his breast, The children sang their prais-es, The simplest and the best.

692

Hosanna! loud hosanna!
 The joyful children sang:
Through pillar'd court and temple
 The lovely anthem rang;
To Jesus, who had blessed them,
 Close folded to his breast,
The children sang their praises,
 The simplest and the best.

2 From Olivet they followed,
 'Midst an exultant crowd,
Waving the victor palm branch,
 And shouting clear and loud;
Bright angels joined the chorus,
 Beyond the cloudless sky—
"Hosanna in the highest:
 Glory to God on high!"

3 "Hosanna in the highest!"
 That ancient song we sing,
For Christ is our Redeemer,
 The Lord of heaven our King.
O! may we ever praise him,
 With heart, and life, and voice,
And in his blissful presence
 Eternally rejoice!

693

Thou art the King of Israel,
 Thou David's royal Son,
Who in the Lord's name comest,
 The King and blessèd One.
Ref.—All glory, laud, and honor,
 To thee, Redeemer, King!
To whom the lips of children
 Made sweet hosannas ring.

2 The company of angels
 Are praising thee on high;
And mortal men, and all things
 Created, make reply.
  All glory, etc.

3 Thou dost accept their praises;
 Accept the prayers we bring,
Who in all good delightest,
 Thou good and gracious King.
  All glory, etc.

National and Thanksgiving.

AMERICA. 6s, 4s. H. CAREY.

694 S. F. Smith.

My country 'tis of thee,
Sweet land of liberty,
 Of thee I sing;
Land where my fathers' died,
Land of the pilgrim's pride,
From every mountain side
 Let freedom ring.

2 My native country, thee,
Land of the noble, free,
 Thy name I love;
I love thy rocks and rills,
Thy woods and templed hills;
My heart with rapture thrills
 Like that above.

3 Our fathers' God, to thee,
Author of liberty,
 To thee we sing;
Long may our land be bright
With freedom's holy light;
Protect us by thy might,
 Great, God our King.

BRUNSWICK. 6s, 4s.

Copyright, 1861, by J. P. Holbrook.

695 J. S. Dwight.

God bless our native land;
Firm may she ever stand,
 Through storm and night;
When the wild tempests rave,
Ruler of wind and wave,
Do thou our country save
 By thy great might.

2 For her our prayer shall rise
To God, above the skies;
 On him we wait;
Thou who art ever nigh,
Guarding with watchful eye,
To thee aloud we cry,
 God save the State.

OCCASIONAL.

MALAN. H. M.

696
F. S. Key.

BEFORE the Lord we bow,
  The God who reigns above,
And rules the world below,
  Boundless in power and love:
Our thanks we bring in joy and praise,
Our hearts we raise to heaven's high King.

2 The nation thou hast blessed
    May well thy love declare,
  From foes and fears at rest,
    Protected by thy care;
  For this fair land, for this bright day,
  Our thanks we pay,—gifts of thy hand.

3 May every mountain height,
    Each vale and forest green,
  Shine in thy word's pure light,
    And its rich fruits be seen;
  May every tongue be tuned to praise,
  And join to raise a grateful song.

697
L. Bacon.

O GOD, beneath thy guiding hand,
  Our exiled fathers crossed the sea;
And when they trod the wint'ry strand,
  With prayer and psalm they worshiped thee.

2 Laws, freedom, truth, and faith in God
  Came with those exiles o'er the waves;
  And where their pilgrim feet have trod,
  The God they trusted guards their graves.

3 And here thy name, O God of love,
  Their children's children shall adore,
  Till these eternal hills remove,
  And spring adorns the earth no more.

GILEAD. L. M.

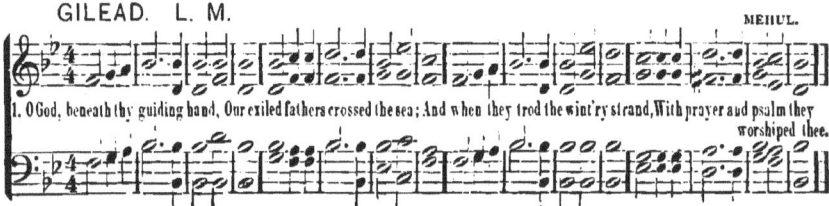

National and Thanksgiving.

698   *J. Campbell*, tr.

WE plough the fields, and scatter
  The good seed on the land,
But it is fed and watered
  By God's almighty hand;
He sends the snow in winter,
  The warmth to swell the grain,
The breezes and the sunshine,
  And soft refreshing rain.

REF.—All good gifts around us
  Are sent from heaven above,
Then thank the Lord, O thank the Lord,
  For all his love.

2 He only is the Maker
  Of all things near and far;
He paints the wayside flower,
  He lights the evening star;
The winds and waves obey him,
  By him the birds are fed;
Much more to us, his children,
  He gives our daily bread.—REF.

3 We thank thee, then, O Father,
  For all things bright and good,
The seed-time and the harvest,
  Our life, our health, our food;
Accept the gifts we offer
  For all thy love imparts,
And, what thou most desirest,
  Our humble, thankful hearts.—REF.

OCCASIONAL.

ST. GEORGE. 7s. D.
S. J. ELVEY.

699
H. Alford.

Come, ye thankful people, come,
Raise the song of Harvest-home;
All is safely gathered in,
Ere the winter storms begin;
God, our Maker, doth provide
For our wants to be supplied;
Come to God's own temple, come,
Raise the song of Harvest-home.

2 All the world is God's own field,
Fruit unto his praise to yield;
Wheat and tares together sown,
Unto joy or sorrow grown;
First the blade, and then the ear,
Then the full corn shall appear:
Lord of Harvest, grant that we
Wholesome grain and pure may be.

3 For the Lord our God shall come,
And shall take his harvest home;
From his field shall in that day,
All offences purge away;
Give his angels charge at last
In the fire the tares to cast;
But the fruitful ears to store
In his garner evermore.

4 Even so, Lord, quickly come
To thy final Harvest-home;
Gather thou thy people in,
Free from sorrow, free from sin;
There, forever purified,
In thy presence to abide:
Come, with all thine angels, come,
Raise the glorious Harvest-home.

HULLAH. 7s. 6l.
HULLAH.

National and Thanksgiving. 375

PERRY. 7s. ARR. J P. HOLBROOK.

1. Christ, by heavenly hosts adored, Gracious, mighty, sovereign Lord, God of nations, King of kings, Head of all cre-a-ted things, By the Church with joy con-fest, God o'er all for-ev-er blest; Pleading at thy throne we stand. Save thy peo-ple, bless our land.

700
H. Harbaugh.

CHRIST, by heavenly hosts adored,
Gracious, mighty, sovereign Lord,
God of nations, King of kings,
Head of all created things,
By the Church with joy confest,
God o'er all forever blest;
Pleading at thy throne we stand,
Save thy people, bless our land.

2 On our fields of grass and grain
Drop, O Lord, the kindly rain;
O'er our wide and goodly land
Crown the labors of each hand;
Let thy kind protection be
O'er our commerce on the sea;
Open, Lord, thy bounteous hand,
Bless thy people, bless our land.

3 Let our rulers ever be
Men that love and honor thee;
Let the powers by thee ordained,
Be in righteousness maintained;
In the people's hearts increase
Love of piety and peace;
Thus, united we shall stand
One wide, free, and happy land.

701
A. L. Barbauld.

PRAISE to God, immortal praise,
For the love that crowns our days;
Bounteous source of every joy,
Let thy praise our tongues employ:
All to thee, our God we owe,
Source whence all our blessings flow.

2 All the blessings of the fields,
All the stores the garden yields,
Flocks that whiten all the plain,
Yellow sheaves of ripen'd grain:
Lord, for these our souls shall raise
Grateful vows and solemn praise.

3 Clouds that drop refreshing dews,
Suns that genial warmth diffuse,
All the plenty summer pours,
Autumn's rich o'erflowing stores,
Lord, for these our souls shall raise
Grateful vows and solemn praise.

4 Peace, prosperity, and health,
Private bliss, and public wealth,
Knowledge, with its gladdening streams,
Pure religion's holier beams;
Lord, for these our souls shall raise
Grateful vows and solemn praise.

376 OCCASIONAL. (Thanksgiving.)

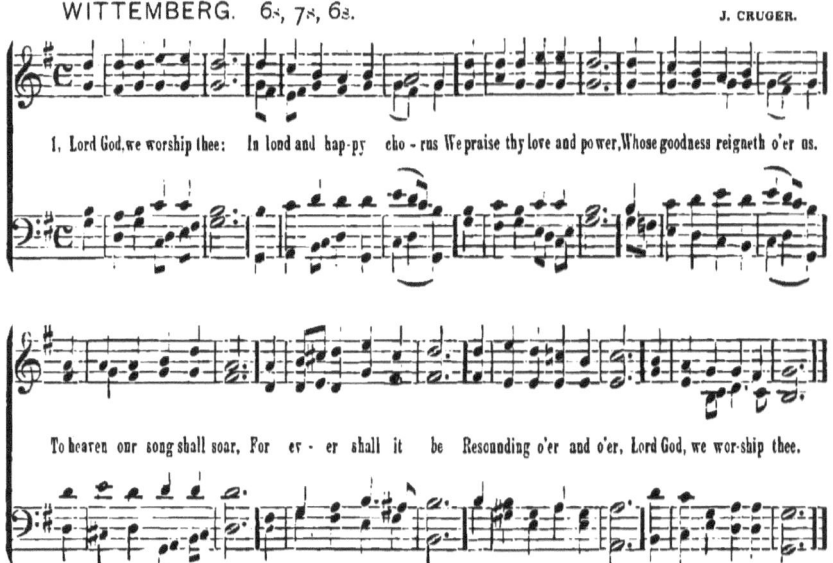

WITTEMBERG. 6s, 7s, 6s. J. CRUGER.

1, Lord God, we worship thee: In loud and hap-py cho-rus We praise thy love and power, Whose goodness reigneth o'er us.

To heaven our song shall soar, For ev - er shall it be Resounding o'er and o'er, Lord God, we wor-ship thee.

702
C. Winkworth, tr.

LORD God, we worship thee:
  In loud and happy chorus
We praise thy love and power,
  Whose goodness reigneth o'er us,
To heaven our song shall soar;
  For ever shall it be
Resounding o'er and o'er,
  Lord God, we worship thee.

2 Lord God, we worship thee:
  For thou our land defendest;
Thou pourest down thy grace,
  And strife and war thou endest.
Since golden peace, O Lord,
  Thou grantest us to see,
Our land with one accord,
  Lord God, gives thanks to thee.

3 Lord God, we worship thee:
  Thou didst indeed chastise us,
Yet still thine anger spares,
  And still thy mercy tries us:
Once more our Father's hand
  Doth bid our sorrows flee,
With plenty fills our land;
  Lord God, we worship thee.

703
A. T. Pierson.

TO THEE, O God, we raise
  Our voice, in choral singing;
We come, with prayer and praise,
  Our hearts' oblations bringing.
Thou art our fathers' God,
  And ever shalt be ours:
Our lips and lives shall laud
  Thy name, with all our powers.

2 Thy goodness, like the dew
  On Hermon's hill descending,
Is every morning new,
  And tells of love unending.
We bless thy tender care
  That led our wayward feet,
Past every fatal snare,
  To streams and pastures sweet.

3 We bless thy Son, who bore
  The cross, for sinners dying;
Thy Spirit we adore,
  The precious blood applying.
Let work and worship send
  Their incense unto thee,
Till song and service blend,
  Beside the crystal sea.

The Year—Opening or Close.

ST. SYLVESTER. P. M.
J. B. DYKES.

For verses 1, 2, 3, 5, 6, 7.

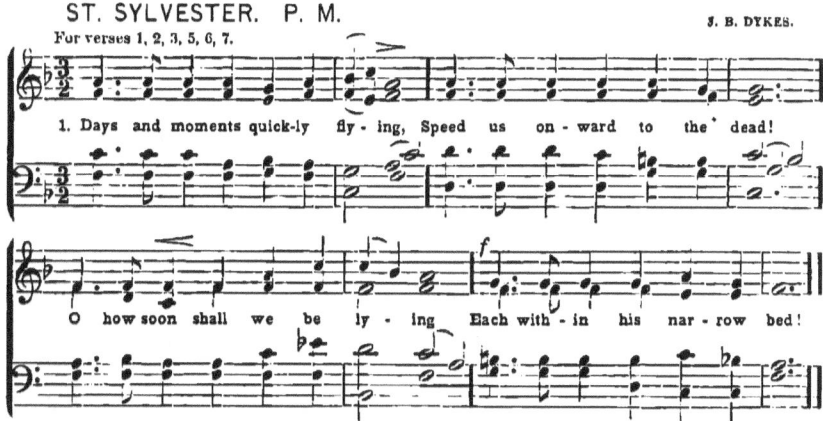

1. Days and moments quick-ly fly-ing, Speed us on-ward to the dead!
O how soon shall we be ly-ing Each with-in his nar-row bed!

704 *E. Caswall.*

Days and moments quickly flying,
   Speed us onward to the dead!
O how soon shall we be lying
   Each within his narrow bed!

2 Jesus, merciful Redeemer,
   Rouse dead souls to hear thy voice;
Wake, O wake each idle dreamer,
   Now to make the eternal choice.

3 Mark we whither we are wending;
   Ponder how we soon must go
To inherit bliss unending,
   Or eternity of woe.

4 Life passeth soon: Death draweth near;
   Keep us, good Lord, till thou appear;
With thee to live, with thee to die,
   With thee to reign through eternity!

5 As a shadow life is fleeting:
   As a vapor so it flies;
For the old year now retreating
   Pardon grant, and make us wise—

6 Wise that we our days may number,
   Strive and wrestle with our sin,
Stay not in our work, nor slumber
   Till thy glorious rest we win.

7 Soon before the Judge all-glorious,
   We with all the dead shall stand;
Saviour, over death victorious,
   Place us then on thy right hand.

8 Life passeth soon: Death draweth near:
   Keep us, good Lord, till thou appear;
With thee to live, with thee to die,
   With thee to reign through eternity.

For verses 4 and 8.

4. Life passeth soon: death draweth near: Keep us, good Lord, till thou appear; With thee to live, with thee to die, With thee to reign through e-ter-ni-ty! A-men.

OCCASIONAL.

BENEVENTO. 7s. D.   S. WEBBE.

705
J. Newton.

While with ceaseless course the sun
Hasted through the former year,
Many souls their race have run,
Never more to meet us here:
Fixed in an eternal state,
They have done with all below;
We a little longer wait,
But how little none can know.

2 As the winged arrow flies
Speedily the mark to find;
As the lightning from the skies
Darts, and leaves no trace behind;
Swiftly thus our fleeting days
Bear us down life's rapid stream:
Upward, Lord, our spirits raise,
All below is but a dream.

3 Thanks for mercies past receive;
Pardon of our sins renew;
Teach us henceforth how to live
With eternity in view:
Bless thy word to young and old;
Fill us with a Saviour's love;
And when life's short tale is told,
May we dwell with thee above.

EVAN. C. M.   W. H. HAVERGAL.

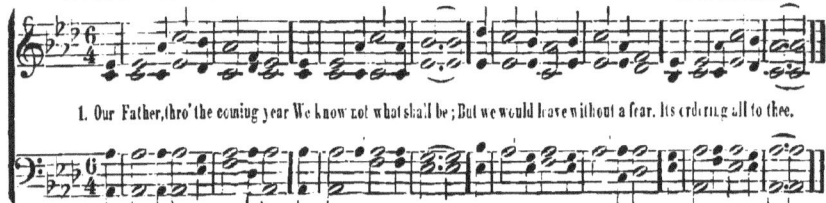

706
W. Gaskell.

Our Father, through the coming year
We know not what shall be;
But we would leave without a fear,
Its ordering all to thee.

2 It may be we shall toil in vain
For what the world holds fair;
And all its good we thought to gain
Deceive, and prove but care.

3 It may be it shall bring us days
And nights of lingering pain,
Or bid us take our farewell gaze
Of these loved haunts of men.

4 But calmly, Lord, on thee we rest:
No fears our trust shall move:
Thou knowest what for each is best;
And thou art perfect love.

The Year—Opening and Close.

DUKE STREET. L. M. — J. HATTON.

1. Great God! we sing that mighty hand, By which supported still we stand: The opening year thy mercy shows; That mercy crowns it till it close.

707
P. Doddridge.

GREAT God! we sing that mighty hand
By which supported still we stand:
The opening year thy mercy shows;
That mercy crowns it till it close.

2 By day, by night, at home, abroad,
Still we are guarded by our God;
By his incessant bounty fed,
By his unerring counsel led.

3 With grateful hearts the past we own;
The future, all to us unknown,
We to thy guardian care commit,
And peaceful leave before thy feet.

4 In scenes exalted or depressed,
Be thou our joy, and thou our rest;
Thy goodness all our hopes shall raise,
Adored through all our changing days.

708
P. Doddridge.

OUR helper, God! we bless thy name,
The same thy power, thy grace the same;
The tokens of thy loving care
Open and crown and close the year.

2 Amid ten thousand snares we stand,
Supported by thy guardian hand;
And see, when we survey our ways,
Ten thousand monuments of praise.

3 Thus far thine arm hath led us on;
Thus far we make thy mercy known;
And, while we tread this desert land,
New mercies shall new songs demand.

4 Our grateful souls on Jordan's shore
Shall raise one sacred pillar more;
Then bear, in thy bright courts above,
Inscriptions of immortal love.

LOUVAN L. M. — V. C. TAYLOR.

1. Our Helper, God! we bless thy name, The same thy power, thy grace the same; The tokens of thy loving care Open and crown and close the year.

380 OCCASIONAL.

MELITA. L. M 6 l. — J. B. DYKES.

1. E-ter-nal Fa-ther! strong to save, Whose arm hath bound the rest-less wave, Who bid'st the might-y o-cean deep Its own ap-point-ed lim-its keep; O hear us when we cry to thee For those in per-il on the sea.

2 O Christ! whose voice the waters heard,
And hushed their raging at thy word,
Who walkedst on the foaming deep,
And calm amidst its rage didst sleep;—REF

3 Most Holy Spirit! who didst brood
Upon the chaos dark and rude,
And bid its angry tumult cease,
And give, for wild confusion, peace;—REF.

709 *W. Whiting.*

ETERNAL Father! strong to save,
Whose arm hath bound the restless wave,
Who bid'st the mighty ocean deep
Its own appointed limits keep;
REF.—O hear us when we cry to thee
For those in peril on the sea.

4 O Trinity of love and power!
Our brethren shield in danger's hour;
From rock and tempest, fire and foe,
Protect them wheresoe'er they go;
Thus evermore shall rise to thee
Glad hymns of praise from land and sea

GILEAD. L. M. — MEHUL.

1. O God, thou holdest in thy hand The waters of the mighty sea, And barrest ocean with the sand By thy perpet-u-al decree.

710 L. M.

O GOD, thou holdest in thy hand
The waters of the mighty sea,
And barrest ocean with the sand
By thy perpetual decree.

2 When they who to the sea go down,
Or in the waters ply their toil,
Are lifted on the surge's crown,
And plunged where seething eddies boil;

3 Rule, then, O Lord, the ocean's wrath,
And bind the tempest at thy will;
Tread, as of old, the waters' path,
And speak thy bidding, "Peace, be still."

4 So with thy mercies ever new,
Thy servants set from peril free,
Shall bless thee, Pilot, wise and true,
Safe in the port where they would be.

For those at Sea. 381

SULLIVAN. 12s.   A. S. SULLIVAN.

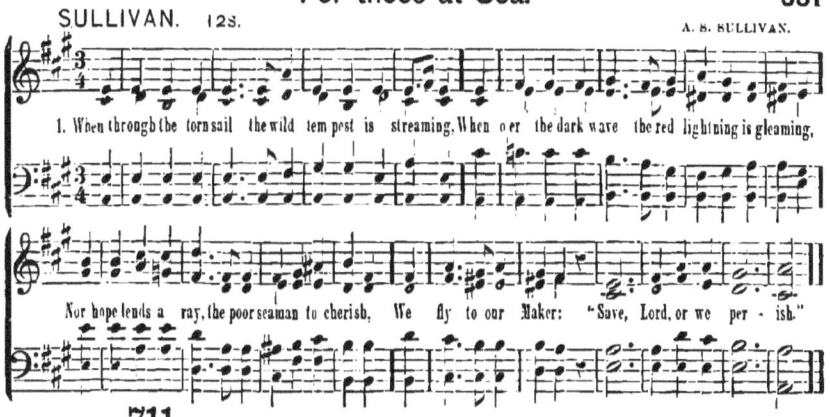

711   *R. Heber.*

When through the torn sail the wild tempest is streaming,
When o'er the dark wave the red lightning is gleaming,
No hope lends a ray, the poor seaman to cherish,
We fly to our Maker,—"Save, Lord, or we perish!"

2 O Jesus, once tossed on the breast of the billow,
Aroused by the shriek of despair from thy pillow,
Now seated in glory, the mariner cherish!
Who cries, in his anguish, "Save, Lord, or we perish!"

HALL. P. M.   J. P. HOLBROOK.

712   *Jane C. B. Simpson.*

Star of peace, to wanderers weary,
  Bright the beams that smile on me;
Cheer the pilot's vision dreary,
  Far, far at sea.

2 Star of hope, gleam on the billow,
  Bless the soul that sighs for thee;
Bless the sailor's lonely pillow,
  Far, far at sea.

3 Star of faith, when winds are mocking
  All his toil, he flies to thee;
Save him on the billows rocking,
  Far, far at sea.

4 Star divine, O safely guide him,
  Bring the wanderer home to thee:
Sore temptations long have tried him,
  Far, far at sea.

SELECTIONS.

First Lines or Headings.

PAGES.
OPENING OR CLOSE OF SERVICE.
382 Sanctus
383 Gloria in Excelsis
384 While we lowly bow
385 How calm and beautiful
388 Dear is the Day
389 Thou who art enthroned
391 Lord, with glowing heart
392 The Lord's Prayer.
393 Peace be to this congregation
393 God is in his holy temple.
394 Return, my roving heart,
395 Evening prayer
396 Father in Heaven
396 Star of Morn and Even

CHRIST.
397 Holy night! peaceful night,
398 He has come! the Christ of God
399 Peace I leave with thee
399 O love that casts out fear,

HOLY SPIRIT.
400 Holy Spirit! gently come
401 Our blest Redeemer, ere he

INVITATION.
402 Come unto me, all ye
403 Rest, weary one, rest

ACCEPTANCE.
406 Just as I am
408 I will arise, and go

PAGES.
410 Thou who didst on Calvary bleed
411 Love me, O Lord, forgivingly
412 Jesus, Lamb of God, for me
412 Jesus, Master, whose I am
413 I heard the voice of Jesus say

PILGRIM SONGS.
414 Sometimes I catch sweet glimpses
415 When streaming from the eastern skies
416 Lead, kindly light,

ANTICIPATION AND LONGING.
418 Let me be with thee
418 This is not my place of resting
419 O loving Lord,
420 Who are these arrayed in white
421 The roseate hues of early dawn
422 Hark! hark, my soul,

DEATH OR BURIAL.
423 Behold the western evening light
423 The good die not
424 Dear is the spot
424 Thy will be done
425 Sleep thy last sleep
425 There is a calm
426 Eternity
427 Responses to commandments.
428 After reading--Gloria Patri.
429 Baptismal chant.
430 Offering.
431 Doxologies.

SANCTUS.

F. CAMIDGE.

Ho - ly, Ho - ly, Ho - ly Lord God of Hosts, Heaven and earth are full of thy glo - ry, Glo - ry be to Thee, O Lord Most High. A - men.

Selections. 383

GLORIA IN EXCELSIS

GLORY be to | God on | high: || and on earth | peace, good | will towards | men.
We praise thee, we bless thee, we | worship | thee: || we glorify thee, we give thanks to thee for | thy great | glory.

O Lord God, | Heavenly | King: || God the | Father | Al . - | mighty!
O Lord, the only-begotten Son | Jesus | Christ: || O Lord God, Lamb of God, | Son, — | of the Father,

That takest away the | sins of the | world: || have mercy | upon | us.
Thou that takest away the | sins of the | world: || have mercy | upon us.
Thou that takest away the | sins of the | world: || re - | ceive our | prayer.
Thou that sittest at the right hand of | God the | Father: || have mercy | upon | us.

A - men.

For thou only | art . — | holy: || Thou | only | art the | Lord.
Thou only, O Christ, with the | Holy | Ghost: || art most high in the | glory of | God the | Father. || A - | men.

Opening or Close of Service.

HOW CALM AND BEAUTIFUL THE MORN.

A. ADAM.

Opening or Close of Service.

HOW CALM AND BEAUTIFUL THE MORN. CONCLUDED.

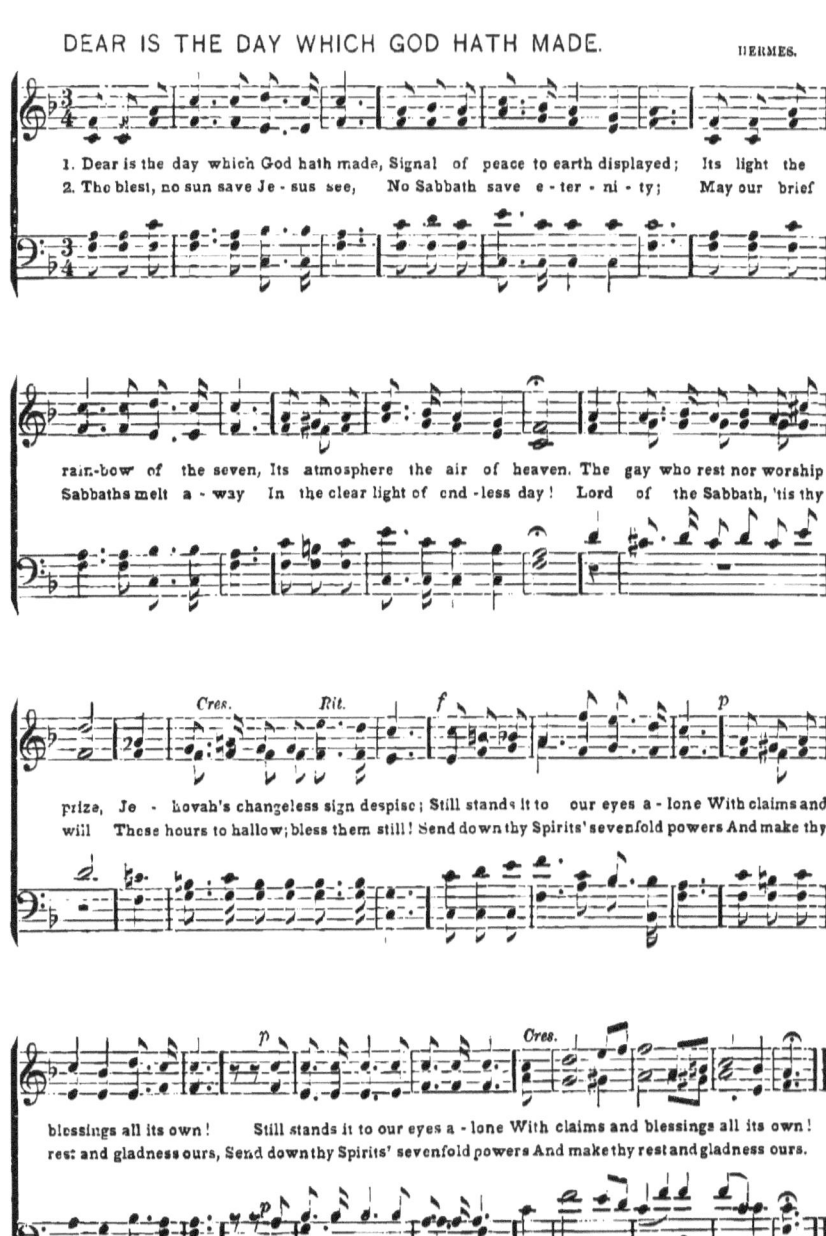

Opening or Closing Service. 389

THOU WHO ART ENTHRONED. 7s. J. P. HOLBROOK.

Opening or Close of Service. 391

THOU WHO ART ENTHRONED. CONCLUDED.

LORD, WITH GLOWING HEART. 8s, 7s.
J. P. HOLBROOK.

1. Lord, with glowing heart I'd praise thee For the bliss thy love bestows; For the pardoning grace that saves me, And the peace that from it flows: Help, O God, my weak endeavor; This dull soul to rapture raise; Thou must light the flame, or never Can my love be warmed to praise.

Lord, with glowing heart I'd praise thee
For the bliss thy love bestows;
For the pardoning grace that saves me,
And the peace that from it flows:
Help, O God, my weak endeavor;
This dull soul to rapture raise;
Thou must light the flame, or never
Can my love be warmed to praise.

2 Praise, my soul, the God that sought thee,
Wretched wanderer, far astray;
Found thee lost, and kindly brought thee
From the paths of death away;
Praise, with love's devoutest feeling
Him who saw thy guilt-born fear,
And, the light of hope revealing,
Bade the blood-stained cross appear.

SELECTIONS.

THE LORD'S PRAYER.

J. P. HOLBROOK.

Opening or Close of Service. 393

PEACE BE TO THIS CONGREGATION. MENDELSSOHN. ARR. E. M. BATTELL.

1. Peace be to this con-gre-ga-tion! Peace to ev-ery heart there-in! Peace, the earn-est of sal-va-tion, Peace, the fruit of conquered sin, Peace, the fruit of conquered sin; Peace that speaks the heavenly Giv-er, Peace, to world-ly minds un-known, Peace that flow-eth as a riv-er, From th'e-ter-nal Source a-lone.

2 O thou God of peace, be near us,
   Fix within our hearts thy home;
With thy bright appearing cheer us,
   Let thy blessed kingdom come:
Come with all thy revelations,
   Truth which we so long have sought;
Come with all thy consolations,
   Peace of God which passeth thought!

1 GOD is in his holy temple;
   In the lowly, reverent mind,
In the heart devout and simple,
   In the soul from sense refined.
Then let every low emotion
   Banished far and silent be,
And our souls in pure devotion,
   Lord, be temples worthy thee!

Opening or Close of Service. 395

RETURN, MY ROVING HEART, RETURN. CONCLUDED.

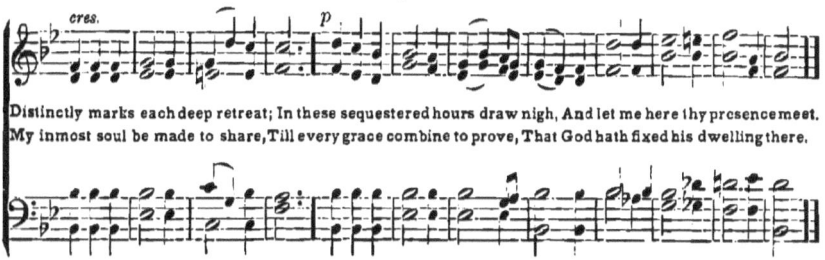

Distinctly marks each deep retreat; In these sequestered hours draw nigh, And let me here thy presence meet.
My inmost soul be made to share, Till every grace combine to prove, That God hath fixed his dwelling there.

EVENING PRAYER. ROSSINI.

1. The day, the day is done! I thank thee, Lord, alone, 'Tis evening, and I cry,
2. The day, the day is done! I bless thee, Mighty One, 'Tis evening, and I cry,

Sav-iour be nigh:
Sav-iour be nigh, Sav-iour be nigh, This night from
Sav-iour be nigh, Sav-iour be nigh; O hear my eve-ning cry: This night, &c.
Sav-iour be nigh:

sin me keep Preserve me when I sleep O hear my evening cry, Dear Saviour be thou nigh.

SELECTIONS. Evening Songs.

FATHER IN HEAVEN.
E. R. SILL.   J. P. HOLBROOK.

1. Fa-ther in heav-en! hum-bly be-fore thee, Kneel-ing in prayer thy children ap-pear,
2. God watching o'er us, sleeps not nor slumbers, Faith-ful night-watches, his an-gels keep,

We in our weak-ness, we in our blindness, Thou in thy wis-dom, hear us, oh, hear.
Through all the dark-ness, un-to the dawn-ing, To his be-lov-ed he giv-eth sleep.

STAR OF MORN AND EVEN.

1. Star of morn and e-ven, Sun of Heaven's heav-en, Sav-iour high and dear,
Toward us turn thine ear; Through whate'er may come, Thou canst lead us home.

2 Though the gloom be grievous,
Those we leant on leave us,
Though the coward heart
Fail its proper part,
Though the tempter come,
Thou wilt lead us home.

3 Star of morn and even,
Shine on us from heaven;
From thy glory-throne
Hear thy very own!
Lord and Saviour, come,
Lead us to our home!

Advent. 397

HOLY NIGHT!

J. BARNBY.

Andante.

1. Ho-ly night! peaceful night! Thro' the darkness beams a light; Ho-ly night! peace-ful night! Thro' the dark-ness beams a light, Thro' the dark-ness beams a light; Yon-der, where they sweet vi-gil keep O'er the Babe, who in si-lent sleep, Rests in heaven-ly peace, Rests in heaven-ly peace.

2 Silent night! holiest night!
Darkness flies and all is light!
Shepherds hear the angels sing—
"Hallelujah! hail the King!
　Christ the Lord is here!"

3 Silent night! holiest night!
Guiding Star, O lend thy light!
See the eastern wise men bring
Gifts and homage to our King!
　Christ the Lord is here!

4 Silent night! holiest night!
Wondrous Star! O lend thy light!
With the angels let us sing
Hallelujah to our King!
　Christ the Lord is here!

Christ—Peace, Love. 399

PEACE I LEAVE WITH YOU.
OTTO.

1. Peace, peace, I leave with you, My peace I give to you, My peace I give to you, Trust to my care! Thus the Redeemer said, And bowed his sacred head, Lone in the garden shade, Wrestling in prayer,.... Wrestling in prayer.
2. Peace, peace, I leave with you, My peace I give to you, My peace I give to you, Perfect and pure; Not as the world doth give, Words that the soul deceive; Ye who in me believe Shall rest secure,...... Shall rest secure.

O LOVE THAT CASTS OUT FEAR.
R. SCHUMANN.

1. O Love that casts out fear, O love that casts out sin, Tarry no more without, But come and dwell within.

2 Great love of God, come in,
  Well-spring of heavenly peace;
Thou living Water, come,
  Spring up, and never cease.

3 Love of the living God.
  The Father and the Son,
Love of the Holy Ghost,
  Fill thou each needy one.

HOLY SPIRIT! GENTLY COME.

The Comforter. 401

OUR BLEST REDEEMER. SCHUBERT.

1. Our blest Redeemer, ere he breathed His tender last farewell,
A Guide, a Comforter bequeathed, With us on earth to dwell.

2. He came in tongues of living flame, To teach, convince, subdue;
All-powerful as the wind he came, And all as viewless, too.

3. He came, sweet influence to impart A gracious, willing Guest,
While he can find one humble heart Wherein to fix his rest.

4. And his that gentle voice we hear, Soft as the breath of even,
That checks each fault, calms every fear, And whispers us of heaven.

"I will give you rest." 403

REST, WEARY ONE, REST.

ROOKE.

404 SELECTIONS.

REST, WEARY ONE, REST. CONTINUED.

"I will give you rest."

REST, WEARY ONE, REST. CONCLUDED.

410 SELECTIONS.

THOU WHO DIDST ON CALVARY BLEED.

MERCADANTE.

1. Thou who didst on Cal - - vary bleed, Thou who dost for sin - - ners plead, Help me in my time of need, Je - - sus, Sav - iour, hear my cry!

4. There on thee I cast my care, There to thee I raise my prayer, Je - sus, save me from de - spair, Save me, save me, or I die!

Penitent Supplication.

THOU WHO DIDST ON CALVARY BLEED. CONCLUDED.

3. Foes with-out and fears with-in, With no plea thy grace to win,
But that thou canst save from sin, Je - sus, to thy cross I fly!

5. When the storms of tri - al lower, When I feel tempt-a - tion's power,
In the last and dark - est hour, Je - sus, Saviour, be thou nigh!

LOVE ME, O LORD, FORGIVINGLY! DORN.

1. Love me, O Lord, for - giv - ing - ly! O! ev - er be my friend;
And still, when thou re - prov - est me, Re - proof with pit - y blend.

2 O pity me, when weak I fall!
And as with saddened eyes
I upward look, O let thy call
Come strengthening me to rise.

3 My sins dispersed by mercy bright,
Like clouds again grow black;
O change the winds that bring such night,
And drive the darkness back.

4 This fearful striving—let it cease!
Then fervent, fruitful days
Shall yield both promise and increase,
And make my growth thy praise.

SELECTIONS.

JESUS, LAMB OF GOD.

2 Never bowed a martyred head,
　Weighed with equal sorrow down;
Never blood so rich was shed,
Never king wore such a crown;
To thy cross and sacrifice
Faith now lifts her tearful eyes.

3 All my soul, by love subdued,
　Melts in deep contrition there;
By thy mighty grace renewed,
　New-born hope forbids despair:
Lord, thou canst my guilt forgive,
Thou hast bid me look and live.

1 Jesus, Master, whose I am,
　Purchased thine alone to be,
By thy blood, O spotless Lamb,

　Shed so willingly for me;
Let my heart be all thine own,
Let me live to thee alone.

2 Other lords have long held sway;
　Now, thy name alone to bear
Thy dear voice alone obey,
　Is my daily, hourly prayer:
Whom have I in heaven but thee?
Nothing else my joy can be.

3 Jesus, Master, I am thine;
　Keep me faithful, keep me near;
Let thy presence in me shine,
　All my homeward way to cheer.
Jesus! at thy feet I fall,
O be thou my All-in-all!

Gladness—Gratitude.

I HEARD THE VOICE OF JESUS SAY.

J. P. HOLBROOK.

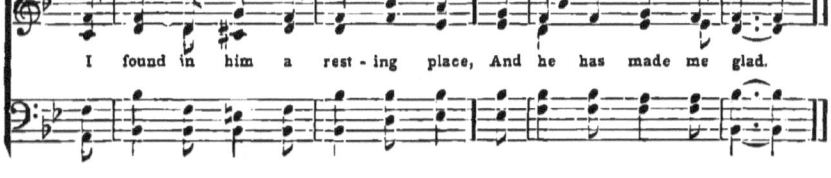

2 I heard the voice of Jesus say,
  " Behold, I freely give
The living water; thirsty one,
  Stoop down and drink, and live."
I came to Jesus, and I drank
  Of that life-giving stream;
My thirst was quenched, my soul revived,
  And now I live in him.

3 I heard the voice of Jesus say,
  " I am this dark world's light;
Look unto me, thy morn shall rise,
  And all thy day be bright."
I looked to Jesus, and I found
  In him my Star, my Sun;
And in that light of life I'll walk
  Till all my journey's done.

Pilgrim Songs.

SOMETIMES I CATCH SWEET GLIMPSES. CONCLUDED.

WHEN STREAMING FROM THE EASTERN SKIES.
J. P. HOLBROOK.

1. When streaming from the eastern skies, The morning light salutes mine eyes, O Sun of righteousness divine, On me with beams of mercy shine! O chase the clouds of guilt away,
2. And when to heaven's all-glorious King My morning sacrifice I bring, And, mourning o'er my guilt and shame, Ask mercy in my Saviour's name; Then, Jesus, cleanse me with thy blood,
3. When each day's scenes and labors close, And wearied nature seeks repose, With pardoning mercy richly blest, Guard me, my Saviour, while I rest; And, as each morning sun shall rise,

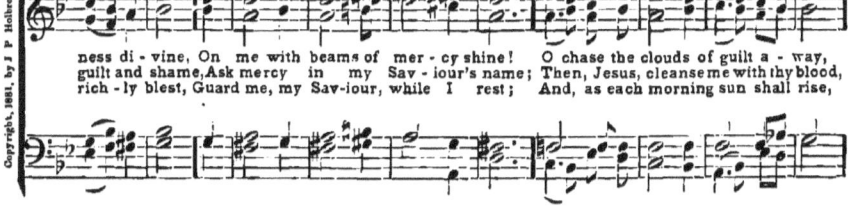

4 And at my life's last setting sun,
My conflicts o'er, my labors done,
Jesus, thy heavenly radiance shed,
To cheer and bless my dying bed;
And, from death's gloom my spirit raise,
To see thy face, and sing thy praise.

Pilgrim Songs. 417

LEAD, KINDLY LIGHT. CONCLUDED.

Anticipation and Longing. 419

O LOVING LORD. R. MOSS.

1. O loving Lord! thy voice hath hope imparted. Through all the weary way thy Church hath passed, And still 'tis music to the broken-hearted. Telling of love, and joy, and peace at last.

2 Of wanderings o'er—of calm and sure abiding
In quiet pastures, far from all earth's strife—
Of streams of living water gently gliding
Beneath the shadow of the Tree of Life.

3 Of God's own home, where "glory that excelleth,"
The temple fills, whose praises never cease;
The heavenly Salem, where Immanuel dwelleth,
And His redeemed ones enter into peace.

4 The peace of God! oh, how our hearts are yearning,
Amid earth's changes, for our Father's home;
To its dear light our eyes are ever turning,
To its dear voice that gently whispers, "Come!"

5 Guide us, O Saviour, guide our footsteps weary,
Show us the comfort of Thy staff and rod,
Till, having travelled through the desert dreary,
We rest forever in the peace of God.

2 Out of great distress they came;
  Washed their robes by faith below,
In thy blood, O reigning Lamb!
  Blood that washes white as snow;
Therefore are they next the throne,
  Serve their Maker day and night;
God resides among his own,
  God doth in his saints delight.

Anticipation and Longing. 421

THE ROSEATE HUES OF EARLY DAWN
ARR. D. R. STANFORD.

1. The roseate hues of early dawn, The brightness of the day, The crimson of the sunset sky, How fast they fade away! O for the pearly gates of heaven! O for the golden floor! O for the Sun of righteousness, That setteth nevermore, That setteth nevermore!

2 The highest hopes we cherish here
How fast they tire and faint!
How many a spot defiles the robe
That wraps an earthly saint!
O for a heart that never sins!
O for a soul washed white!
O for a voice to praise our King,
Nor weary day or night!

3 Here faith is ours, and heavenly hope,
And grace to lead us higher;
But there are perfectness and peace
Beyond our best desire.
Oh, by thy love and anguish, Lord!
Oh, by thy life laid down,
Grant that we fall not from thy grace,
Nor cast away our crown.

SELECTIONS. (Angelic Songs.)

HARK! HARK, MY SOUL.

A. J. N. MACDONALD.

1. Hark, hark, my soul! angelic songs are swelling O'er earth's green fields and ocean's wave-beat shore: How sweet the truth those blessed strains are telling Of that new life when sin shall be no more, **REFRAIN.** Angels of Jesus, angels of light, Singing to welcome the pilgrims of the night.

2 Onward we go, for still we hear them singing,
"Come, weary souls, for Jesus bids you come;"
And through the dark, its echoes sweetly ringing,
The music of the gospel leads us home.—Ref.

3 Rest comes at length, though life be long and dreary;
The day must dawn, and darksome night be past;
All journeys end in welcome to the weary,
And heaven, the heart's true home, will come at last.—Ref.

4 Angels, sing on! your faithful watches keeping;
Sing us sweet fragments of the songs above;
Till morning's joy shall end the night of weeping,
And life's long shadows break in cloudless love.—Ref.

For Burial Service. 423

"BEHOLD THE WESTERN EVENING LIGHT." BEETHOVEN.

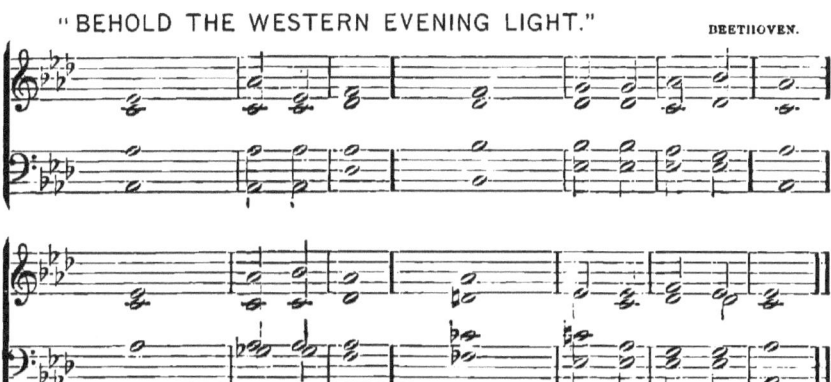

BEHOLD the western evening light!
It melts in | evening | gloom; ||
So calmly Christians sink away,
De- | scending | to the | tomb. ||

2 The winds breathe low, the withering leaf
Scarce whispers | from the | tree: ||
So gently flows the parting breath,
When | good men | cease to | be. ||

3 And now above the dews of night
The rising | star ap- | pears: ||
So faith springs in the heart of those
Whose | eyes are | bathed in | tears. ||

4 But soon the morning's happier light
Its glory | shall re- | store, ||
And eyelids that are sealed in death
Shall | wake to | close no | more. ||

THE GOOD DIE NOT. W. L. REYNOLDS.

1. With silence only as their.... ben - e - diction, God's............an - gels come
Where, in the shadow of a...... great af - fliction, The.............. soul sits dumb.

2 Yet would we say, what every | heart ap-
Our | Father's | will, [proveth,— ||
Calling to him the dear ones | whom he | loveth, ||
Is | mercy | still.

3 Not upon us or ours the | solemn | angel ||
Hath | evil | wrought; ||

The funeral anthem is a | glad e- | van-
The | good die | not! [gel; ||

4 God calls our loved ones, but we | lose not | wholly ||
What | he has | given; ||
They live on earth in thought and | deed, as | truly ||
As | in his | heaven.

SELECTIONS.

DEAR IS THE SPOT.

ARR. J. P. HOLBROOK.

pp Andante.

1. Dear is the spot where Christ-ians sleep, And sweet the strains their spir-its pour; O why should we in an-guish weep?— They are not lost, but gone be-fore, They are not lost, but gone be-fore.

2 Secure from every mortal care,
By sin and sorrow vexed no more,
Eternal happiness they share
Who are not lost, but gone before.

3 To Zion's peaceful courts above
In faith triumphant may we soar,
Embracing, in the arms of love,
The friends not lost, but gone before.

THY WILL BE DONE.

L. MASON.

"Thy will be | done!" || In devious way
The hurrying stream of | life may | run;||
Yet still our grateful hearts shall say,|
 "Thy will be done."

"Thy will be | done!"|| If o'er us shine,
A gladdening and a | prosperous | sun,||

This prayer will make it more divine—|
 "Thy will be done."

"Thy will be done!"|| Though shrouded o'er
Our | path with | gloom,|| one comfort—one
Is ours:—to breathe, while we adore,|
 "Thy will be done."

Close by repeating the first two measures—"Thy will be done."

For Burial Service. 425

"SLEEP THY LAST SLEEP."
J. BARNBY.

1. Sleep thy last sleep, Free from care and sorrow; Rest, where none weep, Till th' eternal morrow; Tho' dark waves roll O'er the silent riv-er, Thine upborne soul Is with Jesus ev-er. A-men.

2 Life's dream is past,
All its sin and sadness;
Brightly at last
Dawns a day of gladness.
Dust unto dust;
Unto God the spirit,
Where, such our trust,
Life it doth inherit.

3 Though we may mourn
Those on earth the dearest,
They shall return,
Christ, when Thou appearest!
Then let Thy voice
Comfort those now weeping;
They shall rejoice,
Now in Jesus sleeping.

THERE IS A CALM.
LACHNER.

1. There is a calm for those who weep, A rest for wea-ry pil-grims found: They soft-ly lie, and sweet-ly sleep, Low in the ground.
2. The storm that racks the win-try sky No more dis-turbs their deep ro-pose Than sum-mer eve-ning's lat-est sigh, That shuts the rose.

SELECTIONS.

ETERNITY. L. M. 7 l.   J. P. HOLBROOK.

1. E-ter-ni-ty! e-ter-ni-ty! How long art thou, e-ter-ni-ty!
And yet to thee time hastes a-way, Like as the war horse to the fray,
Or swift as couriers homeward go, Or ships to port, or......... shaft from bow;
Pon-der, O man, e-ter-ni-ty?

2 Eternity! eternity!
How long art thou, eternity!
As long as God is | God, so | long ||
Endure the pains of | hell and | wrong,||
So long the joys of heaven remain;
O lasting joy; O | lasting | pain! ||
Ponder, O man, eternity!

3 Eternity! eternity!
How long art thou, eternity!
O man, full oft thy | thoughts should | dwell||
Upon the pains of | sin and | hell, ||
And on the glories of the pure,
That shall beyond all | time en- | dure; ||
Ponder, O man, eternity!

SELECTIONS. (Gloria Patri.)

GLORIA PATRI.
DE MONTI.

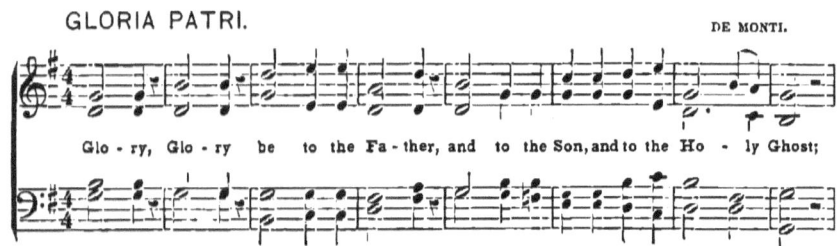

Glo-ry, Glo-ry be to the Fa-ther, and to the Son, and to the Ho-ly Ghost;

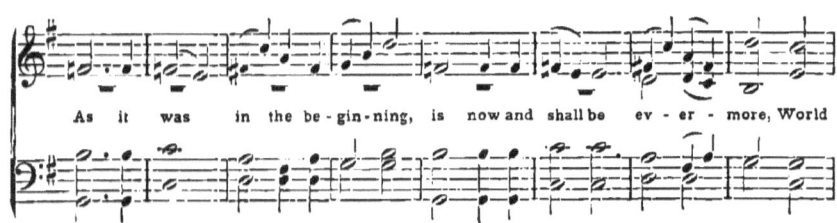

As it was in the be-gin-ning, is now and shall be ev-er-more, World

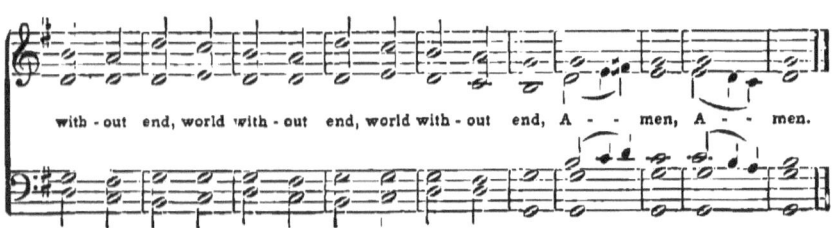

with-out end, world with-out end, world with-out end, A - - men, A - - men.

GLORIA PATRI.
FARRANT.

1 Glory be to the Father, and | to the | Son, || And | to the | Holy Ghost;
2 As it was in the beginning, is now, and | ever | shall be, || World | without | end. A- | men.

430 SELECTIONS. (Offering.)

HOLY OFFERINGS.
R. REDHEAD.

Andante legato.

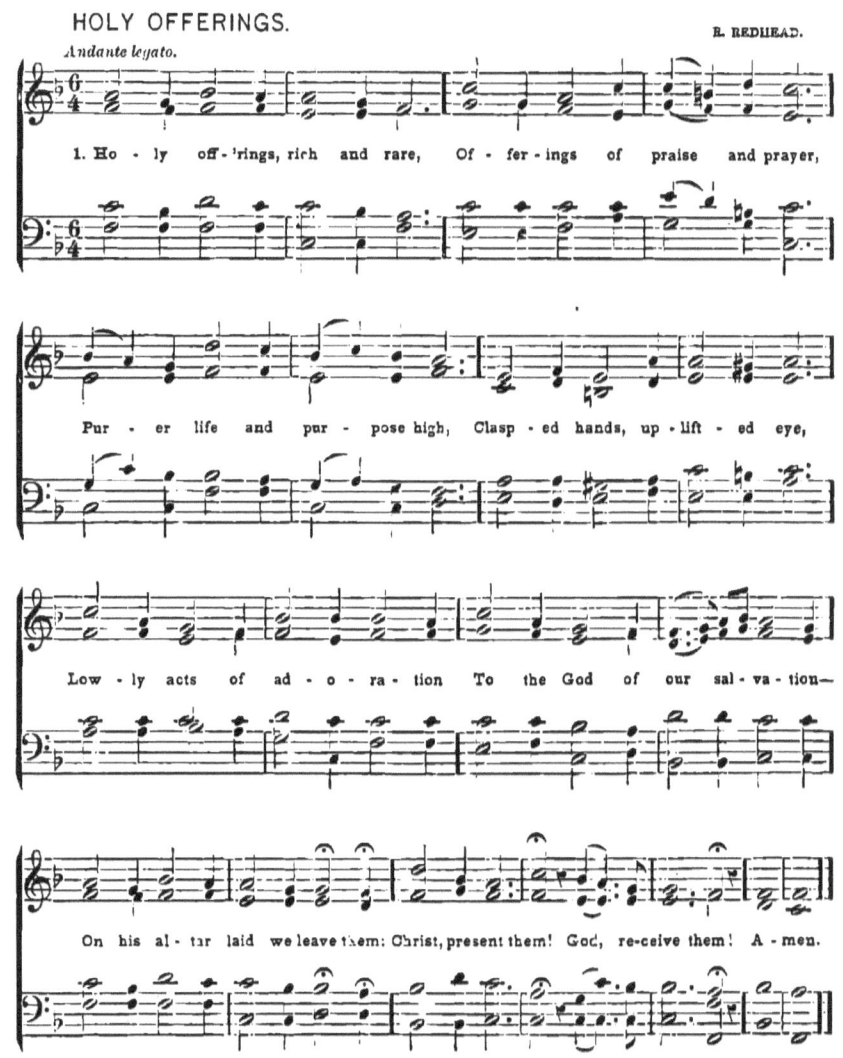

1. Holy off-'rings, rich and rare, Offerings of praise and prayer,
Purer life and purpose high, Clasped hands, uplifted eye,
Lowly acts of adoration To the God of our salvation—
On his altar laid we leave them: Christ, present them! God, receive them! A-men.

2 Promises in sorrow made,
Left, alas! too long unpaid:
Fervent wishes, earnest thought,
Never into action wrought—
Long withheld, we now restore them,
On thy holy altar pour them:
There in trembling faith to leave them,
Christ, present them! God, receive them.

3 To the Father, and the Son,
And the Spirit, Three in One,
Though our mortal weakness raise
Offerings of imperfect praise.
Yet with hearts bowed down most lowly,
Crying, holy! holy! holy!
On thine altar laid we leave them;
Christ, present them! God, receive them!

Doxologies.

1 L. M.

Praise God, from whom all blessings flow!
Praise Him, all creatures here below!
Praise him above, ye heavenly host!
Praise Father, Son, and Holy Ghost!

2 L. M.

To God the Father, God the Son,
And God the Spirit, Three in One,
Be honor, praise, and glory given.
By all on earth, and all in heaven!

3 C. M.

To Father, Son, and Holy Ghost,
One God, whom we adore,
Be glory as it was, is now,
And shall be evermore!

4 C. M.

Let God the Father, and the Son,
And Spirit, be adored,
Where there are works to make him known,
Or saints to love the Lord!

5 S. M.

The Father and the Son
And Spirit we adore;
We praise, we bless, we worship Thee,
Both now and evermore!

6 H. M.

To God, the Father, Son,
And Spirit ever blest,
Eternal Three in One,
All worship be addressed,
As heretofore
It was, is now,
And shall be so
For evermore!

7 7s.

Sing we to our God above
Praise eternal as His love;
Praise Him, all ye heavenly host—
Father, Son, and Holy Ghost!

8 8s & 7s.

Praise the God of our salvation,
Praise the Father's boundless love;
Praise the Lamb, our expiation;
Praise the Spirit from above;
Praise the Fountain of salvation,
Him by whom our spirits live;
Undivided adoration
To the one Jehovah give!

9 8s, 7s & 4.

Great Jehovah, we adore thee,
God the Father, God the Son,
God the Spirit, joined in glory
On the same eternal throne;
Endless praises
To Jehovah, Three in One!

10 7s & 6s. *Iambic.*

To Thee be praise for ever
Thou glorious King of Kings!
Thy wondrous love and favor
Each ransomed spirit sings:
We'll celebrate Thy glory
With all Thy saints above,
And shout the joyful story
Of Thy redeeming love.

11 7s & 6s. *Trochaic.*

Father, Son, and Holy Ghost,
One God, whom we adore,
Join we with the heavenly host
To praise Thee evermore:
Live, by heaven and earth adored,
Three in One, and One in Three,
Holy, holy, holy Lord,
All glory be to Thee!

12 6s & 4s.

To God, the Father, Son,
And Spirit, Three in One,
All praise be given!
Crown Him in every song;
To Him your hearts belong
Let all His praise prolong
On earth, in heaven!

Old or Familiar Tunes

THAT MAY BE USED AS SUBSTITUTES.

L. M.

Tune	Page
All Saints	97
Arnheim	58
Beethoven	48,285
Bera	310
Bishop	249
Blake	258
Brownell	184
Duke St	104,379
Dwight	172,273
Federal St	104,349
Germany	62
Gilead	2,372
Hamburg	175
Hebron	37
Hursley	36,342
Janes	32,155
Louvan	379
Lowry	32
Missionary Chant	178,361
Old Hundredth	1
Rosedale	213
Rose Hill	189
Seasons	207
Tallis Evening Hymn	37
Uxbridge	163
Warner	195

S. M.

Tune	Page
Boylston	190,251
Dennis	244,341
Ferguson	82,341
Greenwood	34,365
Haydn	69
Laban	254
Leighton	13,236
Mornington	13,344
Olmutz	331
Shawmut	198
St. Thomas	179
Thatcher	17

8s, 7s.

Tune	Page
Autumn	242
Bayley	225
Carthage	128
Ellesdie	243
Gaylord	345
Rathbun	90
Sicilian Hymn	45
Westminster	173
Wilmot	132

C. M.

Tune	Page
Antioch	84
Azmon	148,339
Belmont	63,231
Bemerton	39,185
Bradford	230
Bridgman	246
Burlington	116,271
Byefield	343
Chesterfield	66
Christmas	148
Church	216,271
Clinton	327
Coronation	139
Cowper	116
Downs	165
Dundee	52
Elizabethtown	253
Evan	185,378
Maitland	257
Manoah	151,204
Marian	72
Martyrdom (Avon)	122
Merton	156
Naomi	217
Newbold	24,256

7s.

Tune	Page
Benevento (double)	378
Blumenthal (double)	188
Halle (6 lines)	121
Madrid (Spanish Hymn)	121
Mercy	196
Onido (double)	10,227
Perry (double)	375
Pleyel's Hymn	287
Refuge	264
Rosefield	101
Sabbath	20
Seymour	8,191

7s, 6s.

Tune	Page
Amsterdam	280
Bernard	322,337
Ewing	152,355
Miriam	28,278
Missionary Hymn	350
Webb	351

8s, 7s, 4s.

Tune	Page
Zion	181,362

H. M.

Tune	Page
Lenox	180

11s.

Tune	Page
Portuguese Hymn	241

Index of Tunes.

NAMES.	PAGES.	METRES.	NAMES.	PAGES	METRES.
ABBOTT	290	10,4.	Brunswick	16,371	6,4.
Alleluia	336	10.	Burlington	9, 116,164,176,218,271	C. M.
Allen	348	7.	Butler	110	8,7,4.
Alexander	130	C. M. d.	Byefield	343	C. M.
All Saints	65,97	L. M.	CALVARY	105,301	L. M.
America	371	6,4.	Camp	282	7. d.
Amsterdam	280	7,6.	Carlton	14,55,364	8,7.
Angelic Songs	318	P. M.	Carmel	38	10.
Antioch	84	C. M.	Carpenter	5	7.
Ariel	140	C. P. M.	Carthage	54,128	● 8,7.
Arnheim	58	L. M.	Caswall	41	P. M.
Ascension	129	S. M. d.	Chapman	167,369	8,7.
Attlefield	58,145	L. M.	Chant No. 2 ('Troyte')	336	Chant.
Augusta	34,119,245	S. M.	Charity	346	8,7,7.
Aurelia	169	7,6.	Charles Wesley	265	7s, D.
Austen	197,331	L. M.	Chesterfield	66,150	C. M
Autumn	242	8,7.	Childrey	42	P. M.
Avison	360	P. M.	Christmas	85,148,256	C. M.
Azmon	148,179,339	C. M.	Christus Victor	134	P. M.
BAPTISMAL CHANT	429	Chant.	Church	25,216,271	C. M.
Baring-Gould	280	8,7.	Clark	166	6.
Barnby	291	10,4.	Clemens	78	8,7, Pec.
Barnes	118	6,4.	Clinton	71,173,327,339	C. M.
Bartlett	312	L. M.	Cœna Domini	109	10.
Barrows	315	P. M	Colman	96,250	C. M.
Bayley	225	8,7.	Comforter	159	7,5
Bedell	111	9,8.	Come to me	275	L. M.
Bebee (Iambic)	287	8,7.	Come unto me	402	P. M.
Beecher	86	C. M. d.	Come ye disconsolate	269	11,10
Beethoven	48,285	L. M.	Consecration	242	8,7.
Behold the western	423	C. M. d.	Coronation	139	C. M.
Belmont	63,91,231	C. M.	Cowper	116	C. M.
Beman	199,245	S. M.	Crosby	240	11.
Bemerton	5,39,67,149,165,185	C. M.	Cross	300	L. M.
Benediction	46	10.	Culbertson	100	7,6l.
Benevento	378	7,d.	Cummins	177	L. M. 6l.
Bera	301	L. M.	Cutler	101,161	7,6l.
Berlin	30,248,294	10.	DANNER	238	5, 4.
Bernard	322,337,370	7,6.	Dawson	33,64,214,348	L. M.
Bethany	222	6,4.	Dear is the day	388	L. M. d.
Bethlehem	79	P. M	Dear is the spot	424	L. M. d.
Beulah	324	7. d.	Dennis	244,292,341	S. M.
Bishop	81,249	L. M.	Diademata	137	S. M. d.
Blake	258	L. M.	Dijon	274	7.
Blumenthal	188	7. d.	Dix	83	7,6l.
Bonar	205	S. M. d.	Downs	165,234	C. M.
Borthwich	289	10.	Duffield	120.	7.6l.
Bowen	206	L. M.	Duke St.	65,104,141,353,379	L. M.
Boylston	190,251	S. M.	Dulcetta	31,103	8,7.
Bradford	230	C. M.	Dundee	52 60,122,334	C. M.
Brest	316	8,7,4.	Duryea	252	C. M. d.
Bridgman	246	C. M.	Dwight	172,186,273	L. M.
Brownell	184	L. M. 6l.	Dykes	113	7.6l.

Index of Tunes.

NAMES.	PAGES.	METRES.	NAMES.	PAGES	METRES
Edwards	190	S. M.	He has come	398	7.
Eells	22	L. M. d.	Heavenly City	202,321	7, 6l.
Elizabethtown	253,284	C. M.	Hebron	37	L. M.
Ellesdie	243	8,7.	Hollingside	21,264,333	7.d.
Elliott	210	8,4.	Holy Night	397	P. M.
Ely	223	6,4.	Holy Offerings	430	P. M.
Eternity	426	P. M.	Holy Spirit, gently come	400	7.
Evan	43,185,378	C. M.	Home	283	6,4.
Evanston	27,229,338	L. M. 6l.	Hope	73,144,311,345	8,7.
Evening Prayer	395	6,4.	How calm and beautiful	385	C. M. d.
Eventide	294	10.	Hullah	250,374	7,6l.
Ewing	152,304,323,355	7,6.	Hummel	24,209,257,357	C. M.
			Huntington	369	8,7,4.
Faith	268	6,5.	Hurlbut	210	8,6.
Father in heaven	396	10,9.	Hursley	23,36,172,284	L. M.
Federal St.	104,206,349	L. M.			
Ferguson	82,341	S. M.	I heard the voice	413	C. M. d.
Field	87	H. M.	I will arise	408	Sentence.
Finch	198,235,246	C. M.	Ingham	106	L. M.
Fisk	8,160,196	7.	Intercession	211	8,6.
Fiske	57	S. P. M.	Invitation	181	8,7,4.
Forward	261,367	65.	Irenæus	171	P. M.
Franklin	18,69,153	H. M.	Italian Hymn	17	6,4.
Fraser	224	8,7.	Janes	32,155,174	L. M.
Frederick	296	11.	Jesus, Lamb of God	412	7,6l.
			Jewett	247	6.
Galilee	97	8.3.	Jubilate	325,373	P. M.
Gaskell	53,160	7.	Just as I am	406	L. M.
Gaylord	345	8,7.			
Gerhardt	115	7,6.	Keall	107	7,6.
Germany	62,99	L. M.	Kellogg	329	C. M.
Gethsemane	100	7,6l.	Kendall	356	H. M.
Gilead	2,372,380	L. M.	Kimball	197,211	8,6.
Gladness	7,50,74	8,7,4.	Kittredge	220	8,6.
Glentworth	49	P. M.	Laban	254	S. M.
Gloria in Excelsis	383	Chant.	Lancashire	29,82,305,354	7,6.
Gloria Patri	428	Chant.	Langran	108,201,290	10.
Godwin	286	C. M. d.	Langton	230,299,347	S. M.
Goodrich	102	11,5.	Lead, kindly light	416	10,4.
Grace Church	62,186	L. M.	Leavitt	277	7,d.
Greek Hymn	74,259	6,5.	Lebanon	204	S. M. d.
Greenwood	34,199,236,266,365	S. M.	Leighton	13,158,236	S. M.
Guide	159	P. M.	Lenox	180	H. M.
			Leslie	235,308,346	C. M.
Hall	381	P. M.	Let me be with thee	418	L. M.
Halle	121	7,6l.	Llandaff	52	C. M.
Hallett	313	8,7.	Long	127,255,353	L. M.
Hamburg	175	L. M	Lord, with glowing heart	391	8,7.
Hammond	80	L. M. d.	Love divine	224	8,7.
Handy	303	L. M. 6l.	Love me, O Lord	411	C. M.
Hanover	89	11,10	Loving kindness	145	L. M.
Hark, hark, my soul	422	P. M.	Louvan	61,379	L. M.
Hastings	126	7.	Lowell	26	7,d.
Haydn	69	S. M.	Lowry	3,32	L. M.

Index of Tunes. 435

NAMES.	PAGES.	METRES
Luther's	253,317	8,7.
Lux Benigna	291	10,4.
Lyons	12	10,11
Lyte	233	6,4.
MACY	347	6.
Madrid	121	7,6l.
Maitland	257	C. M.
Majesty	51	P. M.
Malan	19,335,372	H. M.
Manning	201	6,10.
Manoah	151,166,204	C. M.
Mansfield	215	6.
Marian	72,146	C. M.
Marth	158	7 5.
Martyrdom (Avon)	122	C. M.
Mayo	218.237,269,360	S. M.
Melcombe	163	L. M.
Melita	380	L. M. 6l.
Mendelsshon	11.88	7.d.
Mercy	196	7.
Merton	156.234	C. M.
Miller	31,117,281	8,7.
Miriam	28,53,162,262,278	7,6.
Mission'y Ch't.	81,143,178,254,352,361	L. M.
Missionary Hymn	350	7,6.
Mornington	13,344	S. M.
Moultrie	306	P. M.
Mozart	89,127,358	7.
Murray	240	11.
NAOMI	217	C. M.
Naumann	328	C. M.
Nearer, my God to thee	222	6,4.
Nelson	45	8,7,4.
Newbold	24,84,138,256	C. M.
Newberry	68	S. M. d.
Newcastle	76	C. M.
Nicæa	4	P. M.
Nightfall	40	11,5.
Noel	147	C. M.
Norwood	213	L. M.
Now the day is over	40	P. M.
Noyes	300	6,4.
Nunda	285	L. M.
O LOVING Lord	419	P. M.
O love that casts out fear	399	6.
Odeon	94,106,175	L. M.
Old Hundredth	1	L. M.
Olivet	119	6,4.
Olmutz	267,331	S. M.
One sweetly solemn thought	293	Chant.
Onido	10,59,227,364	7.d.
Onward	260	6,5.
Our blest Redeemer	401	C. M.

NAMES.	PAGES	METRES
PACKER	209	C. M.
Palestrina	298	C. M.
Palmer	92,117,219,327	C. M.
Paradise	320	P. M.
Park	297	6,10.
Passion chorale	114	7,6.
Passport	238	6,5.
Patterson	314	8,7.
Pax Dei	46	10.
Paxton	228,309	8.
Peace be to this congregation	393	8,7.
Peace I leave with you	399	6,4.
Percy	214,259	L. M.
Perrina	114	7,6.
Perry	359,375	7,d.
Phelps	226	6,5.
Pleyel's Hymn	227,287	7.
Pomeroy	299	P. M.
Portuguese Hymn	241,288	11.
Praise	15,83	6.
RANDOLPH	183	P. M.
Rathbun	75,90,128,144	8,7.
Redhead	56	7.
Refuge	264	7.d.
Regent Square	168	8,7.
Repose	262	7,6l.
Responses to Commandments	427	Chants.
Rest, weary one	403	P. M.
Return, my roving heart	394	L. M.
Rhine	328	C. M.
Rialto	129	S. M.
Richards	194.272	L. M. d.
Ripley	358	7.5.
Rosan	112	7,6l.
Rosedale	213,342	L. M.
Rosefield	101	7.6l.
Rose Hill	23,142,189	L. M.
Roswell	292	S. M.
Russell Place	56	7,6.
SABBATH	20	7.d.
Sacrament	100	8,4.
Salzburg	54,90,132	8,7.
Samson	2	L. M.
Sanctus	382	P. M.
Sanger	311	8,7.
Saul	302	L. M.
Saviour, blessed Saviour	366	6,5.
Saviour, like a shepherd	368	8,7,4.
Schaff	154	L. M. 6l.
Schumann	267,340	S. M.
Scotland	182	12.
Scott	274	7.
Seasons	95,207	L. M.

NAMES.	PAGES.	METRES.	NAMES.	PAGES.	METRES
Segur	44	8,7,4.	The good die not	423	Chant.
Seymour	8,35,191,308	7.	The Lord's Prayer	392	
Shawmut	198	S. M.	The roseate hues	421	C. M. d.
Shining Shore	282	P. M.	There is a calm	425	8,4.
Sicilian Hymn	45	8,7.	This is not my place	418	8.7.
Sidon	60	C. M.	Thou art coming	123	P. M.
Simpson	92,157,208,216	C. M.	Thou who art enthroned	389	7.
Sleep thy last sleep	425	P. M.	Thou who didst on Calvary	410	7.
Smith	326	8,7.	Thy will be done	424	Chant.
Solitude	99	L. M.	Time, thou speedest	310	8,7.
Sometimes I catch sweet glimpses	414	P. M.	Toplady	113	7,61.
St. Alban	94	L. M.	Toulon	96	10.
St. Albinus	303	P. M.	Triumph	125	10.11,12.
St. Ambrose	118	6,4.	Troyte's Chant	277	Chant.
St. Anatolius	41	7,6,8.	Truman	71,203	C. M. d.
St. Anns	335	C. M.	Trust	268	6,5.
St. Bernard	63,156	C M.	Tucker	215	6.
St. Chad	14	8,7.	UXBRIDGE	163	L. M.
St. Clement	183	P. M.	VALENTIA	212	C. M.
St. Ebbe	332	H. M.	Valete	47	L. M. 61.
St. Edmunds	98	L. M.	Venetia	141	C. P. M.
St. George	374	7,d.	Vincent	221,239	P. M.
St Hilda	200	7,6.	Vox Jesu	107,187,232,295.	7,6.
St. Leonard	70	C. M.			
St. Paul	28,279	7,6.	WALDRON	316,363	8,7,4.
St. Sylvester	377	P. M.	Walsham	9	7.
St. Thomas	179,354	S. M.	Warner	195	L. M.
Stainer	30	11,10	Watchman	362	7.d.
Stair	349	C. M.	Webb	263,351	7,6.
Star of morn	396	6,5.	Welcome, happy morning	124	11.
Stone	79	C. M.	Westminster	73,173,312	8,7.
Stoneleigh	42	P. M.	When streaming from	415	L. M. 61.
Storrs	319	9,8.	While we lowly bow	384	8,7,4.
Stoughton	133,170	8,7.	Whipple	343	L. M.
Stowe	6,136,365	8,7.	Who are these arrayed	420	7,d.
Strickland	330	S. M. d.	Wilkes	191	S. M.
Submission	276	8,4.	Wilmot	132	8,7.
Sullivan	381	12.	Wittemberg	376	6,7,6.
Sumner	223	6,4.	Wood	188	6,4.
TALLIS' Evening Hymn	37	L. M.	Woolsey	307	8,7.
Thallon	270	C. M.			
Thatcher	17	S. M.	ZION	111,181,362	8,7,4.

Index of First Lines of Hymns.

HYMNS.	HYMNS.
A broken heart, my God, my King....,..365	Behold the Bridegroom cometh..........576
A charge to keep I have................477	Behold the Lamb of God, who bears.....347
A debtor to mercy alone...............433	Behold the western (*Selections*, p. 423)...
A few more years shall roll..............555	Beneath our feet and o'er our head......562
A glory gilds the sacred page...........306	Bless, O my soul, the living God........ 8
A pilgrim and a stranger................533	Blessed be God! forever blest..........385
A pilgrim through this lonely world......176	Blessed Saviour, thee I love.............224
A stranger in the world below..........545	Blest be the tie that binds..............630
Abide with me, fast falls..... 557	Blest be thou, O God of Israel..........104
Again as evening's shadow falls..... 66	Blest be thy love, dear Lord....... 465
Ah, how shall fallen man...............360	Blest Trinity, from mortal sight 328
Alas, and did my Saviour bleed.........227	Blow ye the trumpet, blow.............312
All as God wills, who wisely heeds......542	Bread of the world, in mercy broken....211
All hail the power of Jesus name........250	Brief life is here our portion............600
All people that on earth do dwell........ 4	Brighter still and brighter.............430
All praise to thee, eternal Lord..........154	Brightest and best of the sons.........168
Almighty God, I call to thee............482	Brightly gleams our banner............687
Am I a soldier of the cross..............490	By Christ redeemed, in Christ restored..208
And dost thou say "Ask what"..........633	By faith in Christ I walk with God......544
And will the Judge descend............359	
And wilt thou now forsake me, Lord....441	CALL Jehovah thy salvation............142
Another six days work is done.......... 44	Can aught beneath a power divine......293
Arise, O Lord, and shine................666	Cast thy burden on the Lord...........525
Arm of the Lord, awake................658	Chief of sinner though I be............225
Around the Saviour's lofty throne......265	Children of God, who, faint and slow,...481
Art thou not mine, my living Lord......391	Christ above all glory seated.......... 235
Art thou weary, art thou languid........345	Christ by heavenly hosts adored........700
As Christ upon the cross................ 84	Christ is made the sure foundation.....317
As pants the heart for cooling..........412	Christ is my prophet, priest, and king...278
As with gladness men of old............158	Christ is his own best evidence.........178
Ascend thy throne, almighty King......660	Christ, of all my hopes the ground......432
Asleep in Jesus! blessed sleep..........568	Christ the Lord is risen again..........233
At evening time let there be light......571	Christ the Lord is risen to-day.........232
At thy command, our dearest Lord......204	Christ will gather in his own..........579
Awake, and sing the song............. 28	Christ with eternal glory crowned......249
Awake, my soul, lift up thine eyes......483	Christian, the morn breaks.............597
Awake my soul, stretch every nerve....480	City of God, how broad and far.........619
Awake, my soul, to joyful lays..........264	Come, blessed Lord, let every shore....668
Awake, our souls, away our fears........487	Come, ever blessed Spirit, come........329
Awake ye saints, awake................ 36	Come, gracious Spirit, heavenly Dove... 288
Away from earth my spirit turns........409	Come, holy Spirit, come, Let...........295
Awhile in Spirit, Lord, to thee..........182	Come, holy Spirit, heavenly Dove......292
	Come, humble sinner, in whose breast...350
BE still, my heart, these anxious cares...520	Come, kingdom of our God............684
Before Jehovah's awful throne. 3	Come let us join in songs of praise......267
Before the Lord we bow................696	Come let us join our cheerful songs....247
Before the throne.....................590	Come let us sing the song of songs 198
Before thy cross, my dying Lord........203	Come, Lord, and tarry not.............685
Begin, my tongue, some heavenly theme.312	Come, my soul, thy suit prepare........ 17
Behold a stranger at the door..........352	Come, thou almighty King............. 33
Behold the blind their sight receive.....187	

Index of First Lines of Hymns.

HYMNS	
Come, thou desire of all thy saints...... 12	From all that dwell below the skies..... 2
Come, thou fount of every blessing......263	From all thy saints in warfare..........624
Come, thou long-expected Jesus.........170	From deep distress and troubled thoughts.363
Come unto me, all ye (Selections, p. 40-)..	From every stormy wind that blows.....632
Come unto me, ye weary................353	From Greenland's icy mountains........650
Come we that love the Lord............. 27	From lips divine, like healing balm......514
Come, weary souls, with sin distressed...351	Full of glory, full of wonders........... 93
Come ye disconsolate...................513	GENTLY, Lord, O gently lead us......... 62
Come, ye sinners, poor and wretched....343	Gird on thy conquering sword..........667
Come, ye thankful people, come.........609	Give to the winds thy fears.............509
Commit thou all thy griefs..............508	Gloria in Excelsis (Selections, p. 383)......
Compared with Christ, in all beside.....448	Gloria Patri (Selec'ions. p. 428)..........
Complete in thee! no work of mine......256	Glorious things of thee are spoken......319
Creator Spirit, by whose aid............285	Glory be to God the Father............. 15
Crown him, with many crowns.... 246	Glory to God on high................... 32
Crown his head with endless blessing ...240	Glory to thee, my God, this night....... 76
	Go forward, Christian soldier...........502
DAY of judgment, day of wonders!......592	Go, labor on, spend and be spent.......472
Days and moments quickly flying.......704	"Go, preach my Gospel," saith the Lord.337
Dear is the day (Selections, p. 388).......	Go to dark Gethsemane.................193
Dear is the spot (Selections, p. 424).......	Go worship at Immanuel's feet..........152
Dear Refuge of my weary soul..........518	God bless our native land..............695
Dear Saviour, we are thine..............631	God calling yet! shall I not hear........366
Depth of mercy! can there be...........368	God from on high hath heard...........157
Did Christ o'er sinners weep............373	God, in the gospel of his son............305
Draw near, O holy Dove, draw near.....199	God is in his holy (Select'ons, p. 393)....
	God is love, his mercy brightens........146
ERE another sabbath's close............. 71	God is love, that anthem olden..........143
Ere the blue heavens were stretched abroad 151	God is the name my soul adores........114
Eternal Father, strong to save..........709	God is the refuge of his saints..........125
Eternal King! in power and love excelling.196	God moves in a mysterious way........127
Eternal Light! Eternal Light!..........147	God, my King, thy might confessing....145
Eternal Spirit, we confess...............287	God, my supporter and my hope........139
Eternity (S lections, p. 426)............ ...	God of mercy, God of grace............. 41
Ever would I fain be reading...........315	God of my life, to thee I call...........519
	God's free mercy streameth............144
FAITH is a living power from heaven.....393	God, the Lord, a king remaineth........ 95
Far beyond our skies of gladness........588	God that madest earth and heaven...... 85
Far down the ages now.................629	Grace 'tis a charming sound............452
Father, adored in worlds above........... 75	Gracious Spirit, dwell with me..........301
Father, how wide thy glory shines.......270	Gracious Spirit, Love divine.... 300
Father, I know that all my life..........423	Granted is the Saviour's prayer.........299
Father in heaven (Selections, p. 396).....	Great God, attend while Zion sings...... 46
Father of heaven, whose love profound.. 5	Great God, how infinite art thou..... 98
Father of love, our Guide and Friend...417	Great God, this sacred day of thine...... 56
Father of mercies, in thy word..........311	Great God, we sing that mighty hand... 707
Father, replenish with thy grace........424	Great God, what do I see and hear......593
Father, whate'er of earthly bliss.........414	Great is the Lord, what tongue can frame.115
Fierce raged the tempest o'er the deep...186	Guide me, O thou great Jehovah........ 88
For all the saints who from their labors rest.623	HAIL, Israel's King! hail, David's Son....189
For ever here my rest shall be..........394	Hail, thou God of grace and glory.......641
For ever with the Lord.................615	Hail to the Lord's anointed............653
For the beauty of the earth............. 22	Hail, tranquil hour of closing day....... 70
For thee, O dear, dear country..........601	Hallelujah! Christ is mine!.............381
Forward! be our watchword........... 499	Hallelujah! Hallelujah!........ 236
Fountain of grace, rich, full and free....258	

Index of First Lines of Hymns.

HYMNS	
Happy the souls to Jesus joined	627
Hark! hark, my soul, angelic songs	596
Hark! hark, my soul (*Selections*, p. 422)	
Hark, hark, the notes of joy	165
Hark, ten thousand harps and voices	245
Hark, the church proclaims her honor	320
Hark, the glad sound, the Saviour comes	160
Hark, the herald angels sing	167
Hark! the song of Jubilee	672
Hark, the sound of holy voices	606
Hark, the voice of love and mercy	210
Hark, through the courts of heaven——	639
Hark, what mean those holy voices	169
Hasten, Lord, the glorious time	673
Hasten, sinner, to be wise	362
Hasten the time appointed	663
He has come! the Christ (*Selections*, p. 398).	
He is gone, and we remain	617
He lives! the great Redeemer lives	259
He reigns! the Lord the Saviour reigns	594
He who, a little child, began	323
He who on the accursed tree	548
Heavenly Father, to whose eye	20
Here behold me, as I cast me	427
Here I can firmly rest	454
Here, O my Lord, I see thee	207
High in the heavens, eternal God	124
Holy Ghost, the Infinite	298
Holy, holy, holy Lord, Be thy	11
Holy, holy, holy, Lord God Almighty	10
Holy, holy, holy, Lord God of hosts	111
Holy night! (*Selections*, p. 397)	
Holy offerings, rich (*Selections*, p. 430)	
Holy Spirit, gently come (*Selections*, p. 400)	
Hosanna, loud hosanna	692
Hosanna! raise the pealing hymn	161
How beauteous are their feet	340
How blest the righteous when he dies	569
How calm and beautiful (*Selections*, p. 385)	
How firm a foundation, ye saints	459
How gentle God's commands!	463
How large the promise, how divine!	325
How pleasant, how divinely fair	47
How precious is the book divine	307
How sweet and awful is the place	228
How sweet the name of Jesus sounds	273
How sweetly flowed the gospel's sound	183
How vain is all beneath the skies	543
How wondrous was the burning zeal	177
I BLESS the Christ of God	438
I cannot always trace the way	400
I cannot walk in darkness long	128
I close my weary eye	510
I come, O Lord, to thee	380

HYMNS	
I do not ask, O Lord, that life may be	553
I hear the words of love	223
I heard the voice of Jesus say	383
I heard the voice (*Selections*, p. 413)	
I journey through a desert	552
I know no life divided	574
I know that my Redeemer lives	442
I lay my sins on Jesus	443
I love thee, Saviour mine	440
I love thy kingdom, Lord	628
I once was a stranger to grace	458
I send the joys of earth away	486
I was a wandering sheep	387
I will arise (*Selections*, p. 408)	
I worship thee, sweet Will of God	467
I would not live alway	560
I would not walk alone	439
If Jesus be my Friend	453
If on our daily course our mind	541
If through unruffled seas	507
I'm but a stranger here	540
I'm not ashamed to own my Lord	398
In all my vast concerns with thee	119
In heavenly love abiding	530
In the cross of Christ I glory	262
In the vineyard of our Father	689
In vain we seek for peace	277
Is it not strange, the darkest hour	523
It came upon the midnight clear	164
It is not death to die	565
It is thy hand, my God	512
I've wrestled on toward heaven	558
JEHOVAH God, thy gracious power	120
Jehovah reigns! he dwells in light	110
Jehovah reigns! his throne is high	109
Jerusalem, my happy home	613
Jerusalem, the glorious	603
Jerusalem, the golden	602
Jesus, and shall it ever be	390
Jesus, blessed Mediator	597
Jesus, engrave it on my heart	257
Jesus, hail enthroned in glory	239
Jesus, I come to thee	374
Jesus, I live to thee	464
Jesus, I my cross have taken	460
Jesus is God! the glorious bands	149
Jesus, Lamb of God, for me	194
Jesus, Lamb of God (*Selections*, p 412)	
Jesus lives! no longer now	572
Jesus, lover of my soul	504
Jesus, Master, whom I serve	475
Jesus, Master, whose (*Selections*, p. 412)	
Jesus, my boast, my light, my joy	436
Jesus, my Saviour, look on me	528

Index of First Lines of Hymns

	HYMNS.		HYMNS.
Jesus, my Saviour, who could dare	336	Lord of all being, throned afar	116
Jesus, name of wondrous love	19	Lord of earth, thy forming hand	112
Jesus, our best beloved Friend	635	Lord of the worlds above	37
Jesus shall reign where'er the sun	675	Lord, thou hast joined my soul	578
Jesus, the Christ of God	156	Lord, thou hast searched and seen me	118
Jesus, the name high over all	341	Lord, thy glory fills the heaven	103
Jesus, the very thought of thee	449	Lord, thy Word abideth	314
Jesus, these eyes have never seen	450	Lord, visit thy forsaken race	655
Jesus, thou joy of loving hearts	408	Lord, we come before thee now	18
Jesus, thy blood and righteousness	260	Lord, when I quit this earthly stage	407
Jesus, thy name I love	444	Lord, when this holy morning broke	74
Jesus, too late I thee have sought	389	Lord, when we bend before thy throne	13
Jesus, we bow before thy throne	654	Lord, with glowing heart I'd praise thee	29
Join all the glorious names	283	Lord, with glowing heart (*Selections*, p. 391)	
Joyful be the hours to-day	21	Love divine, all love excelling	428
Joy to the world! the Lord is come	159	Love me, O Lord (*Selections*, p. 411)	
Just as I am, without one plea	370	Lowly and solemn be	566
Just as I am (*Selections*, p. 406)		MAJESTIC sweetness sits enthroned	269
KEEP silence, all created things	126	May the grace of Christ the Saviour	90
King of saints, to whom the number	607	Meet and right it is to sing	106
LADEN with guilt and full of fears	309	'Mid the homes of want and woe	647
Lamb of God, whose bleeding love	215	Mighty God, the First, the Last	99
Lamp of our feet, whereby we trace	308	Mighty God, while angels bless thee	242
Lead, kindly light, amid th' encircling	554	More love to thee, O Christ	426
Lead, kindly light (*Selections*, p. 416)		Must Jesus bear the cross alone	491
Let me be with thee where thou art	586	My country, 'tis of thee	694
Let me be with thee (*Selections*, p. 418)		My days are gliding swiftly by	539
Let saints below in concert sing	626	My dear Redeemer, and my Lord	180
Let songs of praises fill the sky	290	My faith looks up to thee	221
Let us, with a joyful mind	43	My God, accept my heart this day	332
Let Zion and her sons rejoice	670	My God, fill thou my life with praise	386
Life can bring with it nothing	532	My God, how wonderful thou art	140
Life is the time to serve the Lord	357	My God, my Father, blissful name!	130
Lift your glad voices in triumph	231	My God, my Father, while I stray	527
Light of life, seraphic fire	431	My God, my King, thy various praise	64
Like Noah's weary dove	376	My God, my reconciled God	294
Lo! God, our God, has come	166	My God, the covenant of thy love	405
Lo, he comes with clouds	591	My God, the spring of all my joys	446
Lo, the day of Life approacheth	584	My God, 'tis to thy mercy-seat	404
Lo, the seal of death is breaking	589	My gracious Lord, I own thy right	473
Look from thy sphere of endless day	648	My heart and voice I raise	108
Look, ye saints, the sight is glorious	244	My hope is built on nothing less	435
Lord, as to thy dear cross we flee	174	My Jesus, as thou wilt	468
Lord, dismiss us with thy blessing	80	My Saviour, my almighty Friend	251
Lord God of hosts, by all adored	7	My Saviour, whom absent I love	582
Lord God, the Holy Ghost	296	My Saviour, what thou didst of old	384
Lord God, we worship thee	702	My soul, be on thy guard	483
Lord, her watch thy church is keeping	681	My soul, how lovely is the place	51
Lord, I am thine, entirely thine	330	My soul, repent his praise	133
Lord, I approach the mercy seat	371	My spirit longs for thee	410
Lord, I have made thy word my choice	310	My spirit on thy care	461
Lord, it belongs not to my care	608	NEARER, my God, to thee	425
Lord Jesus, are we one with thee	280	No change of time shall ever shock	141
Lord Jesus, when we stand afar	202	No more, my God, I boast no more	392

Index of First Lines of Hymns. 441

	HYMNS
None loves me, Saviour, with thy love	406
No, no, it is not dying	564
Not all the blood of beasts	222
Not only doth the voiceful day	67
Not what I am, O Lord	470
Now be the gospel banner	661
Now for a song of lofty praise	255
Now God be with us, for the night is	81
Now I have found a friend	445
Now I have found the ground	437
Now the day is over	82
Now to the Lord a noble song	254
Now to thy sacred house	39
Now when the dusky shades of night	59
O BLESS the Lord, my soul, His	132
O bless the Lord, my soul, Let	134
O could I find from day to day	415
O could I speak the matchless worth	252
O day of rest and gladness	57
O Everlasting strength	418
O Father, compass me about	396
O Father, humbly we repose	123
O for a closer walk with God	416
O for a faith that will not shrink	395
O for a heart to praise my God	413
O for a thousand tongues to sing	272
O for the happy hour	637
O Fount of good, to own thy love	643
O Gift of gifts! O grace of faith	403
O God, beneath thy guiding hand	697
O God of mercy, hear my call	372
O God, the darkness roll away	669
O God, the Rock of ages	100
O God, thou holdest in thy hand	710
O happy band of pilgrims	534
O happy day that fixed my choice	331
O Holy, holy, holy Lord, Bright	6
O Holy Saviour, Friend unseen	309
O Jesus, I have promised	378
O Jesus, Light of all below	421
O Jesus, sweet the tears I shed	219
O Jesus, thou art standing	377
O Jesus, when I think of thee	274
O Lamb of God, still keep me	500
O Lord impart thyself to me	420
O Lord, I would delight in thee	422
O Lord, my best desires fulfil	515
O Lord of heaven and earth and sea	646
O Lord of health and life	184
O Lord, our God arise	664
O Lord, thy work revive	638
O Lord, we would the path retrace	171
O Love divine, how sweet thou art	253
O Love divine, that stooped to share	521

	HYMNS
O Love that casts out (Selections, p. 399)	
O loving Lord (Selections, p. 419)	
O Mother dear, Jerusalem	611
O One with God the Father	281
O Paradise, O Paradise	598
O Sacred Head, now wounded	216
O Source Divine, and Life of all	94
O Spirit of the living God	659
O Stone of God, by unseen hands	656
O that the Lord's salvation	662
O that the Lord would guide	419
O the sweet wonders of that cross	201
O thou great Friend to all	471
O thou, in all thy might so far	129
O thou, the contrite sinner's friend	402
O thou, to whose all-searching sight	494
O thou, whom we adore	665
O where are kings and empires now	620
O where shall rest be found	361
O who like thee, so calm, so bright	179
O wondrous type, O vision fair	188
O word of God Incarnate	303
O worship the king, all-glorious	25
Of the Father's love begotten	148
On the mountain's top appearing	679
Once blind with sin and self	388
One holy church of God appears	621
One sole baptismal sign	618
One sweetly solemn thought	556
One there is above all others	691
Onward, christian soldiers	498
Onward speed thy conquering flight	671
Our blest Redeemer, ere he breathed	297
Our blest Redeemer (Selections, p. 401)	
Our country's voice is pleading	651
Our day of praise is done	68
Our Father, through the coming year	706
Our God, our help in ages past	97
Our Helper God! we bless thy name	708
Our Lord is risen from the dead	234
Our yet unfinished story	531
Out of the deep I call	375
PEACE be to this (Selections, p. 393)	
Peace I leave with you (Selections, p. 399)	
Peace, troubled soul, whose plaintive	348
Pleasant are thy courts above	42
Plunged in a gulf of dark despair	276
Pour out thy Spirit from on high	339
Praise God from whom all blessings flow	1
Praise Him! praise the conquering King!	243
Praise, my soul, the King of heaven	14
Praise Him, his glories show	23
Praise the Lord, who reigns above	105
Praise the Lord, ye heavens adore him!	102
Praise to God, immortal praise	701

Index of First Lines of Hymns.

HYMNS	
Praise to thee, thou great Creator	101
Praises to Him, whose love has given	63
Prayer is the soul's sincere desire	636
Purer yet, and purer	429
QUIET, Lord, my froward heart	501
REJOICE, rejoice, believers	575
Rejoice, the Lord is King	284
Rest for my soul I long to find	495
Rest of the weary	455
Rest, weary one (*Selections*, p. 403)	
Return, my roving heart (*Selections*, p. 394)	
Return, O wanderer, now return	349
Ride on, ride on in majesty	190
Rise, my soul, and stretch thy wings	536
Rock of ages, cleft for me	212
Rock of ages, cleft for me	213
SAFELY through another week	40
Salvation, O the joyful sound	275
Salvation's giver, Christ, God's only Son	209
Saviour, again to thy dear name	91
Saviour, blessed Saviour	686
Saviour, breathe an evening blessing	61
Saviour, like a shepherd lead us	688
Saviour, sprinkle many nations	682
Saviour, visit thy plantation	640
Saviour, whom I fain would love	54
Saviour, who thy flock art feeding	324
See, Israel's gentle Shepherd stand	326
See the Conqueror mounts in triumph	241
Servant, at once, and Lord of all	172
Serve we our God in faith	479
Shine on our land, Jehovah, shine	619
Shout the glad tidings	674
Show pity Lord, O Lord, forgive	364
Sing to the Lord a joyful song	9
Sing to the Lord, and loud proclaim	634
Sing, ye faithful, sing with gladness	683
Sinners, turn, why will ye die	354
Sleep thy last sleep (*Selections*, p. 425)	
So heaven is gathering one by one	580
So let our lips and lives express	474
Softly fades the twilight ray	72
Softly now the light of day	70
Soldiers of Christ, arise	484
Sometimes I catch sweet (*Selections*, p. 414)	
Son of God, to thee I cry	214
Songs anew of honor framing	16
Songs of praise the angels sang	24
Soon may the last glad song arise	657
Souls in heathen darkness lying	680
Sound aloud Jehovah's praises	321
Sounding loud or low	456
Source divine, of strength and power	302
Sovereign of worlds, display thy power	656

HYMNS	
Sow in the morn thy seed	478
Spirit of life and light and love	291
Spirit of power and truth and love	286
Stand up and bless the Lord	30
Stand up, my soul, shake off thy fears	485
Stand up, stand up for Jesus	503
Stand we prepared to see and hear	577
Star of morn and even (*Selections*, p. 396).	
Star of peace, to wanderers weary	712
Still, still with thee	60
Sun of my soul, thou Saviour dear	73
Sweet is the work, my God, my King	45
Sweet is the work, O Lord	69
Sweet Saviour, bless us ere we go	92
Sweet the moments, rich in blessing	220
Sweet the time, exceeding sweet	53
TEMPTATION cannot come to me	497
Ten thousand times ten thousand	605
That day of wrath, that dreadful day	595
That holy One	346
The atoning work is done	282
The church's one foundation	318
The city paved with gold	622
The day is gently sinking to a close	78
The day is past and over	83
The day of resurrection	58
The day, the day is (*Selections*, p. 395)	
The eternal gates lift up their heads	238
The head that once was crowned	248
The heavens declare thy glory	304
The king of love my Shepherd is	547
The Lord be with us, as we bend	87
The Lord has promised good to me	447
The Lord is just; this is his throne	122
The Lord is my Shepherd, no want	549
The Lord Jehovah reigns	107
The Lord my Shepherd is	451
The Lord of glory is my light	49
The Lord our God is clothed with might	113
The Lord's my Shepherd, I'll not want	546
The Lord's prayer (*Selections*, p. 392)	
The loving Friend to all	173
The mercies of my God and King	313
The moment comes when strength	567
The morning light is breaking	652
The promise of my Father's love	333
The roseate hues (*Selections*, p. 421)	
The saints of God, their conflicts past	625
The Son of God goes forth to war	492
The Spirit came! that mighty Breath	289
The voice of free grace cries "Escape"	344
The Word is made incarnate	155
Thee we adore, eternal Name	561
There is a blessed home	411

Index of First Lines of Hymns.

HYMNS.
There is a calm for (*Selections*, p. 425)....
There is a fountain filled with blood....217
There is a land immortal..............573
There is a land of pure delight..........612
There is a safe and secret place......... 131
There is an hour of peaceful rest........610
There is no night in heaven............614
There is none other name than thine....261
There's a wideness in God's mercy......197
There's not a hope with comfort fraught.181
Thine arm, O Lord, in days of old......185
Thine earthly Sabbaths, Lord, we love... 65
This day, at thy creating word.......... 55
This God is the God we adore...........434
This is not my place of resting..........537
This is not my place (*Selections*, p. 418)..
This is the day of light................. 35
This is the day the Lord hath made..... 50
This is the sweetness of my life.........466
Those eternal bowers...................496
Thou art coming; at thy table..........229
Thou art gone up on high..............237
Thou art my hiding place, O Lord.......397
Thou art the King of Israel.............693
Thou art the Way, to thee alone........279
Thou hadst no youth, great God......... 96
Thou knowest, Lord, the weariness......551
Thou Lord, who daily feedest thy sheep. 52
Thou Lord of life, whose tender care.... 80
Thou only Sovereign of my heart........493
Thou, to whom the sick and dying......612
Thou very present aid..................506
Thou who art enthroned (*Selections*, p. 389)
Thou who didst on Calvary bleed........369
Thou who didst (*Selections*, p. 410).......
Thou who didst stoop below............559
Though faint yet pursuing we go........550
Though in a foreign land..............505
Through all the changing scenes of life..138
Through every age, eternal God........117
Through the day thy love has spared us. 86
Through the night of doubt and sorrow..535
Thus far the Lord has led me on........ 77
Thy life was given for me..............645
Thy servants now, O Triune Lord......327
Thy way is on the deep, O Lord........516
Thy way, not mine, O Lord............469
Thy Will be done (*Selections*, p. 424)....
"Till He come"—O let the words 226
Time, thou speedest on but slowly......583
"'Tis finished"—so the Saviour cried....192
'Tis midnight—and on Olive's brow.....191
To Calvary, Lord, in spirit now.........218
To-day the Saviour calls... 355

HYMNS.
To him who hears I whisper all..........401
To our Redeemer's glorious name........271
To thee, my Shepherd, and my Lord....266
To thee, O God, we raise...............703
To us a child of hope is born...........162
Triumphant Zion, lift thy head..........677
Unveil thy bosom, faithful tomb........570
Upon thy grace we banquet here........205
Upward I lift mine eyes................135
Wait, O my soul, thy Maker's will.. ...121
Watchman, tell us of the night..........678
We come, O only Saviour...............206
We give thee but thine own...... 644
We love the place, O God.............. 31
We plough the fields, and scatter........698
We praise thee, Saviour, for the grace ...322
We pray for childlike hearts............462
We saw thee not when thou............335
"We shall see him" in our nature.......585
We speak of the realms of the blest... ..581
Weary of earth and laden with my sin...379
Welcome! delightful morn.............. 38
Welcome, happy morning..............230
Welcome, sweet day of rest............. 34
What a Friend we have in Jesus.........690
What a strange and wondrous story......316
Whate'er my God ordains is right.......457
What grace, O Lord, and beauty shone..175
What laws, my blessed Saviour.........195
What shall I render to my God..........334
What sinners value I resign.............616
When all thy mercies, O my God........137
When along life's thorny road..........538
When day's shadows lengthen..........511
When from far thy towers shall shine....599
When I can read my title clear..........609
When I survey the wondrous cross... ..200
When languor and disease invade........517
When marshalled on the nightly plain...153
When our heads are bowed with woe....529
When streaming from (*Selections*, p. 415).
When the dark waves round us roll......524
When this passing world is done....... 382
When through the torn sail the wild....711
When time seems short, and death is near.522
While life prolongs its precious light.....356
While shepherds watched their flocks....163
While thee I seek, protecting Power.....136
While we lowly bow (*Selections*, p. 384)...
While with censeless course the sun.....705
Whither goest thou, O Saviour.........150
Who are these arrayed (*Selections*, p. 420).
Who are these in bright array...........604
Why do we mourn departing friends.....563

Index cf First Lines of Hymns.

HYMNS	HYMNS
Why will ye waste on trifling cares......358	With tearful eyes I look around.........526
With broken heart and contrite sigh.....367	Workman of God, O lose not heart.......476
With joy we hail the sacred day......... 48	Ye Christian heralds, go, proclaim.......338
With joy we meditate the grace..........268	Ye servants of God, your master proclaim 26
With silence, as their (*Selections*, p. 423)..	Ye servants of the Lord.................480

SUMMARY OF CONTENTS.

Classified Subjects and Explanatory Note... .... ⎫
Title... ⎬ First four pages.
First Lines of Part I.—WORSHIP.................................... ⎭

First Lines of Part II.—GOD..Page 48.

First Lines of Part III.—CHRIST...Pages 76,77.

First Lines of Part IV.—HOLY SPIRIT..Page 154.

First Lines of Part V.—SCRIPTURES..Page 162.

First Lines of Part VI.—CHURCH..Page 168.

First Lines of Part VII.—SPIRIT AND BRIDE SAY, COME..........................Page 180.

First Lines of Part VIII.—THE CHRISTIAN.................................Pages 192,193.

First Lines of Part IX.—LAST THINGS...Page 296.

First Lines of Part X.—THE CHRISTIAN AND CHURCH.............................Page 332.

First Lines of Part XI.—OCCASIONAL..Page 366.

First Lines of Part XII.—SELECTIONS...Page 382.

Indexes—Old or Familiar Tunes (Special)... ....Page 432.

  Alphabetical Order of Tunes (General).............................Page 433.

  Alphabetical First Lines of Hymns.................................Page 437.

www.ingramcontent.com/pod-product-compliance
Lightning Source LLC
Chambersburg PA
CBHW021233300426
44111CB00007B/530